Healthcare Financing and Insurance

Shankar Prinja
Editor

Healthcare Financing and Insurance

A Guide for Practitioners, Professionals, and Policymakers

Springer

Editor
Shankar Prinja
Department of Community Medicine and School of Public Health
Post Graduate Institute of Medical Education and Research (PGIMER)
Chandigarh, India

ISBN 978-981-95-3512-5 ISBN 978-981-95-3513-2 (eBook)
https://doi.org/10.1007/978-981-95-3513-2

This Springer imprint is published by the registered company Springer Nature Singapore Pte Ltd.
The registered company address is: 152 Beach Road, #21-01/04 Gateway East, Singapore 189721, Singapore

This book is dedicated to my father—Late ***Dr. Bimal Kumar Prinja****, who always encouraged and supported me to pursue academic excellence*

Foreword 1

It gives me great pleasure to write the foreword for this very timely and relevant textbook on health financing and insurance, a subject that is truly the need of the hour. Today, as India and many other countries strive to achieve Universal Health Coverage (UHC), they must also deal with the complex realities of financing healthcare needs within the context of increasing demands due to demographic transition, and the evolving dual burden of disease. In this context, health financing is a key pillar for building strong, resilient health systems.

This book is an excellent guide to understanding the core concepts of health financing and the reforms underway in India. Part I of the book explains with clarity the essential components of financing, such as revenue collection, risk pooling, and strategic purchasing. These are not merely technical or academic discourses but also serve as the building blocks of equity, efficiency, and responsiveness in health care. Part II shifts the lens to the Indian context, which is especially valuable. India's health financing landscape is dynamic, marked by ambitious reforms including Ayushman Bharat, and an increasing emphasis on value-based care. This part offers a critical analysis of these initiatives and explores viable pathways to finance UHC in a manner that is sustainable and inclusive. Part III rightly moves from policy to practice. By addressing operational themes like fraud management, governance, monitoring and evaluation, and the strategic use of digital technologies, the book equips insurers and policymakers with the tools needed for effective implementation. These are real-world challenges that must be addressed for reforms to make a meaningful difference.

This timely and well-crafted textbook, edited by Professor Shankar Prinja, a distinguished health economist and public health expert whose contributions have significantly shaped health policy and systems research, will be a valuable resource for students, researchers, practitioners, and policymakers working to strengthen health systems in India and beyond. The team of authors that have been put together for drafting different chapters comprises not only of academicians and researchers but also policymakers and practitioners, who have put in their practical experience to enrich the book content. I congratulate Dr. Prinja and the contributing authors for this scholarly and policy-relevant contribution.

Government of India, National Institution
for Transforming India
NITI Aayog
New Delhi, India

Vinod K. Paul

Foreword 2

The effectiveness of any health system is closely tied to how it is financed. Financing determines not just who receives care but also the quality, timeliness, and dignity with which that care is delivered. It shapes provider behavior, influences service delivery, and underpins the sustainability of health gains across populations. Yet, despite its critical role, health financing has often remained underexplored in professional education—particularly in the Indian context.

That is why this book—*Healthcare Financing and Insurance: A Guide for Practitioners, Professionals, and Policymakers*—is so timely, relevant, and necessary.

Having worked at the intersection of public health, economic policy, and development finance, I see three reasons why this book is especially valuable. First, it demystifies the complex field of health financing and insurance for a wide range of readers—students, program managers, public health professionals, and private insurers alike. Second, it situates India's journey within a global comparative framework, drawing out both lessons and cautionary tales. Third, it reminds us that strengthening health systems is not just a technical task—it is a political and institutional endeavor, requiring strategy, capable institutions, and continuous learning.

The book is both comprehensive in scope and practical in orientation. It starts with foundational principles, helping readers grasp why terms like revenue collection, risk pooling, and strategic purchasing are not abstract jargon, but essential levers for delivering timely, equitable, and high-quality care. In my own experience designing and implementing the Ayushman Bharat Pradhan Mantri Jan Arogya Yojana (PM-JAY), these concepts were not theoretical—they guided real-world decisions. From setting provider payment rates and verifying claims to designing fraud prevention protocols, the principles of health financing were central to achieving both scale and impact.

What makes this book particularly valuable is its grounding in the Indian context. It goes beyond frameworks and theories to address the realities of India's institutional landscape—the interplay between central and state schemes, the promise and complexity of digital health integration, the challenges of governance, and the pursuit of value-based care. These are not just academic debates. They are the daily dilemmas faced by policymakers, insurance administrators, health officials, hospital managers, and development partners in India and across the Global South.

My work across countries such as Thailand, Viet Nam, Cambodia, China, Mongolia, Ghana, Nigeria, and Egypt has reaffirmed a crucial truth: while each nation's path to universal health coverage is different, the core questions are remarkably similar. How can we raise adequate resources without deepening poverty? How do we align provider incentives with quality? How do we protect public funds from fraud and misuse? How do we build resilient institutions that can adapt to demographic and epidemiological transitions?

This book addresses these questions with clarity and insight. Its final part, focused on strategic applications for insurers and policymakers, is especially relevant. Topics such as fraud management, governance, benefit incidence analysis, and the use of digital technologies are often underrepresented in academic literature—but they are vital for implementation. The authors do not simplify the complexity, but they provide usable frameworks and real-world case studies that will resonate with practitioners.

For students of public health and hospital administration, this book serves as a bridge between theory and practice. For government officials and program managers, it offers practical tools. For development partners and donors, it provides essential context. And for private insurers and providers, it offers a lens through which to align business objectives with public interest.

More importantly, this book helps address a deep gap in professional training. We teach medicine and management, but often neglect financing. Yet, as I have often said, a public health professional without a grounding in health economics is like a doctor without diagnostic skills. Good intentions are not enough—one must also have the tools to build systems that work.

The book's language is lucid but rigorous. Its insights are grounded in real experience. And its contributors bring both academic depth and field-level understanding. I congratulate the authors and editors for this important contribution to the growing body of work on health system strengthening in India and beyond.

India today stands at a pivotal moment. The COVID-19 pandemic exposed longstanding weaknesses but also created an opportunity for reform. Recent developments—such as the expansion of PM-JAY, the Ayushman Bharat Digital Mission, and greater convergence across state and central schemes—point to a future where India can lead in designing inclusive, efficient, and scalable health financing models.

But this future will not unfold automatically. It will require professionals who understand the architecture of health financing, who can bridge the gaps between public health, actuarial science, and digital innovation, and who are committed to institution-building. This book is a valuable resource for shaping that next generation of health leaders.

I commend it to all readers who care about making healthcare systems work—not just for the few, but for the many.

Indu Bhushan

President, India Lead Elimination
Action Partnership (i-LEAP)
Founding (ex-)CEO, Ayushman Bharat – PMJAY
and National Health Authority
Former Director General
Asian Development Bank
New Delhi, India

Preface

The genesis of this book is divided into two parts. The first inspiration to write a book on this subject came when I developed the online course in health economics in 2012. The learning materials and lecture notes were developed for the course with the long-term vision of using those to publish a book. However, competing priorities, and the vastness of topics to be covered to encompass all the relevant concepts in health economics, led the idea being put in abeyance.

The second and successful motivation to write the textbook came in 2023, when I returned back to the academia after my stint at the National Health Authority (NHA), where I served as its Executive Director, tasked with several key jobs for Ayushman Bharat Pradhan Mantri Jan Arogya Yojana, such as developing its Health Benefits Package, pricing, standard treatment guidelines, as well as quality benchmarking and its related incentives. My tenure at the NHA made me realize the imminent need to build capacity for all relevant stakeholders in the field of public health, healthcare financing, and insurance sector on several important aspects, which re-ignited the old desire. It also helped me understand the precise learning needs for successful implementation of such schemes.

The writing of this book also involved two key aspects—identifying the right concepts that can be weaved in different chapters and organizing them in a logical way, and, secondly identifying the set of authors who not only bring in academic rigor but also instill the learning from their experience of working in the field. Due care has been taken to incorporate both these points. Several of the authors who have contributed to different chapters are my current or former colleagues from either the academia, the NHA, and the Insurance Information Bureau of India.

The book has been written keeping the specific needs of students, academics, and researchers in the field of healthcare financing, insurance, health administration, and public health, as well as those developing policies and managing the healthcare funds in organizations running large public health and insurance schemes—especially the Government-funded health insurance schemes. Care has been taken to have a writing style which facilitates learning and builds knowledge and skills. The book is grounded in Indian healthcare delivery system and uses real-world examples and case studies to illustrate important concepts. I personally consider the recap questions and Q&A section in each chapter as vital for readers to test their understanding.

I must acknowledge my deep appreciation to all the chapter authors who have put together wonderful drafts, and diligently addressed all the editorial suggestions during the revision process, while managing the tight timelines. I would also like to thank the publisher team who have been extremely flexible with the book outline. In fact, the table of content, the length and breadth of each chapter, as well as the timelines also underwent significant changes since the inception of the idea to publish this book till the time the final book was published. This also reflects their deep sense of understanding and ability to engage with the editors and authors.

I would be failing in my duty if I do not thank my wife—Dr. Nidhi Gupta, and my children—Raghav and Sadhika, whose precious time over these years I took away—sitting late in office or away from home in conferences or meetings, to be able to gain my knowledge and understanding in the subject of healthcare financing and economics, which made me capable of writing and editing this textbook.

I sincerely hope that the readers find this book not only useful, but also enjoy the learning as they sift through the pages.

Chandigarh, India
December 2025

Shankar Prinja

Introduction

To achieve the overarching goal of good health, a robust health system is indispensable [1]. World Health Report (2010) states that "*a health system can be broadly defined as all the activities whose primary purpose is to promote, restore, and maintain health*" [2]. It encompasses a complex web of actors, institutions, and resources that work together to improve the health of a population [2, 3]. While the specific structures and operations of health systems vary greatly from country to country, their fundamental objectives remain consistent: improving the health of the population they serve, responding to people's expectations, and providing financial protection against the costs of ill-health. A well-functioning health system is much more than just the providers of direct health services; it includes the entire apparatus that ensures these providers are adequately trained, informed, financed, supplied, inspired, and led [3].

Among the critical components and functions of a health system, financing stands out as a cornerstone [1]. Healthcare financing is concerned with the mobilization, accumulation, and allocation of money to cover the health needs of the people, both individually and collectively [4–6]. The purpose of health financing is to make funding available and to set the right financial incentives for providers to ensure that all individuals have access to effective public health and personal healthcare [3, 6]. The World Health Organization (WHO) further elaborates that a good health financing system raises adequate funds for health, ensuring that people can use needed services while being protected from financial catastrophe or impoverishment associated with paying for them, and provides incentives for providers [7].

Understanding the intricacies of healthcare financing is integral in terms of knowledge and expertise for a wide range of stakeholders engaged in the health system. Public health professionals need to grasp financing mechanisms to design and implement effective health programs and interventions. Policymakers rely on this knowledge to formulate and reform health policies that promote equity, efficiency, and sustainability. Academicians and researchers contribute to the evidence base by evaluating the impact of different financing models on health outcomes and system performance. Furthermore, healthcare administrators, providers, and even informed citizens benefit from a deeper understanding of how health systems are financed and the implications for access and quality of care.

This book is conceived with the understanding that strengthening healthcare financing is paramount for achieving UHC and improving population health outcomes. It aims to build the capacity of various stakeholders engaged in the health system, including public health professionals, policymakers, healthcare administrators, and researchers. The main objective of this book is to provide comprehensive knowledge and practical guidance to these stakeholders who are actively working to strengthen the health financing function, particularly within the context of the Indian health system. By elucidating the core concepts, principles, and practical applications of healthcare financing, this book endeavors to empower stakeholders with the necessary tools and insights to navigate the complexities of health financing reforms and contribute effectively to the journey toward universal health coverage in India. Recognizing that India, like many other nations, is striving to expand health insurance coverage and ensure sustainable public health funding as key steps toward achieving UHC, this book seeks to provide timely and relevant knowledge to support these critical efforts.

This book is specifically designed to contextualize the principles of healthcare financing within the Indian framework, with a particular focus on Government-Funded Health Insurance Schemes (GFHIs). To enhance learning, each chapter includes recap questions, allowing readers to self-assess their understanding of key concepts. The authors have drawn upon the latest available literature on the subject, while also incorporating insights from their own extensive experience in healthcare financing. This comprehensive textbook on health financing is divided into three distinct parts, offering a step-by-step exploration of foundational concepts, the Indian perspective in healthcare financing, and strategic applications of health financing:

Part I: Foundational Concepts in Health Financing comprising Chaps. 1, 2, 3, 4, 5, and 6 lays the groundwork by introducing core principles and frameworks of health financing:

Chapter 1, "Health Systems and Health Financing: An Overview," will introduce you to the fundamental definition of a health system, its overarching goals and core functions, and the indispensable role that financing plays in achieving these objectives. You will gain insights into various health system models that have evolved historically and their relevance to the specific context of the Indian healthcare landscape. Understanding these foundational concepts is crucial for grasping the subsequent discussions on revenue collection, risk pooling, and purchasing.

Chapter 2, "Revenue Collection," delves into the diverse sources and methods of revenue collection for healthcare in India, including taxation, social health insurance contributions, and out-of-pocket payments. You will gain a clear understanding of the advantages and disadvantages of these different mechanisms, as well as their implications for the sustainability and equity of healthcare financing.

Chapter 3, "Risk Pooling," will elucidate the critical concept of risk pooling in health financing, demonstrating how it effectively spreads the financial risk associated with healthcare costs across a group. You will understand its vital role in providing financial protection to individuals and improving their access to healthcare services. The chapter further explores the mechanisms of risk pooling in the Indian context, particularly within voluntary private health insurance, and examines the factors that can contribute to its success or failure.

Chapter 4, "Strategic Purchasing," explores the principles and objectives of strategic purchasing in healthcare, highlighting its significance in optimizing resource use, enhancing service quality, and promoting equity within health systems. You will learn about the core components of strategic purchasing, such as benefit package design, provider selection, and payment mechanisms. The chapter also emphasizes the crucial role of cost data and various payment methods like capitation and bundled payments in driving cost-effectiveness and supporting financial sustainability for health insurers.

Chapter 5, "Provider Payment Methods (PPMs)," offers a comprehensive overview of various PPMs, detailing their key characteristics, potential benefits, and inherent risks. The chapter contextualizes these payment systems within the complexities of the healthcare market, with specific attention paid to the methods employed in India and relevant global examples. Understanding these methods is crucial for effective strategic purchasing and ensuring efficient healthcare delivery.

Chapter 6, "Use of Health Technology Assessment (HTA) for Strategic Purchasing of Healthcare Services," underscores the pivotal role of HTA in informing strategic purchasing decisions, particularly within the context of India's *Ayushman Bharat—Pradhan Mantri Jan Arogya Yojana* (AB PM-JAY). Readers will understand how HTA systematically evaluates the clinical, economic, social, and ethical dimensions of health technologies to ensure the efficient allocation of limited healthcare resources. The chapter also highlights the institutionalization of HTA in India through HTAIn and its coordination with the National Health Authority to generate evidence for HTA in India.

Part II: Health Financing: Indian Perspective comprising Chaps. 7, 8, 9, 10, and 11 delves into the specific context of the status of health financing in India:

Chapter 7, "Healthcare Financing in India," provides a comprehensive overview of India's health financing landscape, drawing on insights from the National Health Account estimates. You will gain an understanding of the structure, composition, and trends in healthcare expenditures across public and private sectors, as well as key indicators like Total Health Expenditure (THE), Out-of-Pocket Expenditure (OOPE), etc. The chapter also compares India's health financing situation with other countries in the Southeast Asia region.

Chapter 8, "Universal Health Coverage: How to Finance It?", explores the concept of Universal Health Coverage (UHC) and the various strategies for financing it in the Indian context. You will understand the three key dimensions of UHC: population coverage, service coverage, and financial risk protection. The chapter discusses the evolution of UHC at global and Indian level, the role of publicly financed health insurance schemes like AB PM-JAY, and strategies for expanding coverage to the "missing middle" population of India.

Chapter 9, "Government-Funded Health Insurance Schemes in India," examines the evolution and implementation of Government-Funded Health Insurance Schemes (GFHIS) in India, with a specific focus on the AB PM-JAY. You will learn about the historical shift from supply-side to demand-side financing and the key features, design, financing, and implementation of these schemes, including the world's largest publicly financed health assurance scheme, i.e., AB PM-JAY.

Chapter 10, "Demand-Side Financing for Healthcare in India," provides an overview of demand-side financing mechanisms and explores the challenges faced in their implementation in India. Despite the potential of demand-side financing to improve healthcare utilization, the chapter highlights various obstacles such as delays in accessing care, high out-of-pocket expenses, and lack of awareness. You will understand the core features and different mechanisms of demand-side financing, including vouchers and direct benefit transfers, as well as strategies to overcome these challenges.

Chapter 11, "Value-Based Care," introduces the crucial concept of Value-Based Care in health insurance programs. You will understand the concepts, need, and potential applications of Value-Based Care within the Indian context, where achieving universal health coverage is a priority. The chapter also highlights the role of the National Health Authority (NHA) in formulating and transmitting the concept of value within the health system.

Part III: Strategic Application for Health Insurers and Policymakers comprising Chaps. 12, 13, 14, and 15 focuses on niche areas that demand specialized knowledge and expertise for the effective implementation of insurance programs:

Chapter 12, "Fraud Management," addresses the significant problem of health insurance fraud, its multidimensional impact on patients, businesses, taxpayers, and insurance providers. You will gain an understanding of the different types of fraud, their impact on financial resources and insurance costs, and the mitigation strategies that can be employed. The chapter also explores emerging trends, prevention and detection techniques using advanced tools, and global practices in managing health insurance fraud.

Chapter 13, "Governance, Monitoring and Evaluation, and Capacity Building," explores the essential structural determinants for successful health financing strategies. You will understand the critical roles of strong governance, including oversight, regulation, and accountability, as well as capacity building for human resources and effective monitoring and evaluation to assess the impact of health financing policies. The chapter emphasizes the interdependencies of these elements for achieving efficient and equitable health financing systems.

Chapter 14, "Applications of Digital Technologies for Healthcare Financing," examines the transformative power of digital technologies in revolutionizing healthcare financing processes in India. You will explore how technologies like data analytics, advanced risk scoring algorithms, blockchain, and telemedicine are optimizing insurance processes, strengthening fraud detection, and enhancing patient engagement. The chapter also addresses the importance of regulatory frameworks, such as India's Digital Personal Data Protection (DPDP) Act, and robust data governance to safeguard sensitive health information.

Chapter 15, "Evaluating Equity in Healthcare Financing: The Benefit Incidence Analysis," introduces Benefit Incidence Analysis (BIA) as a vital method for assessing how the benefits of government spending and subsidies in healthcare are distributed across different socioeconomic groups. You will understand the rationale and development of BIA, various approaches to conducting the analysis, and its implications for developing equitable health financing policies. The chapter also presents case studies illustrating the application of BIA in evaluating the equity implications of health insurance schemes.

We hope this book serves as a valuable resource for students, academicians, healthcare practitioners, and policymakers involved in health systems, healthcare finance, and public health.

References

1. Wang H. Comparative health systems. International Encyclopedia of Public Health; 2008. p. 799–806.
2. The world health report (2010): health systems financing: the path to universal coverage. https://iris.who.int/handle/10665/44371. Accessed 3 Apr 2025.
3. The world health report 2000. https://www.who.int/publications/i/item/924156198X. Accessed 29 Oct 2024.
4. Sodani PR, Nair KS, Agarwal K. Health system financing: a comparative analysis of India and Saudi Arabia. J Health Manag. 2023;25:40–52.
5. Feyisa D. Toward universal health coverage: the role of health insurance system. In: Health insurance. IntechOpen; 2022. Epub ahead of print 19 October 2022. https://doi.org/10.5772/intechopen.106431.
6. Liaropoulos L, Goranitis I. Health care financing and the sustainability of health systems. Int J Equity Health. 2015;14:80.
7. The world health report 2007: a safer future: global public health security in the 21st century. https://www.who.int/publications/i/item/9789241563444. Accessed 3 Apr 2025.

Contents

About the Editor

Shankar Prinja is a health economist, a public health professional, and formerly a senior administrator within the Government of India. He has published over 300 articles in peer-reviewed national and international journals. His research on costing of healthcare services has led to revision of prices under the national flagship health insurance scheme—*Ayushman Bharat Pradhan Mantri Jan Arogya Yojana*. His research on health technology assessment has led to several policy and program developments and reforms at both state and national levels. He was the executive director of the National Health Authority, Government of India, in 2022–23, where he led the design of several important policies for *Ayushman Bharat Pradhan Mantri Jan Arogya Yojana*, including the major revision of its health benefit package and pricing, and introducing several important policy reforms for provider payments and value-based care. He was also a member of several high-level international and national expert groups, which have contributed significantly to both development of research methods, policy, and programs. He has also developed several online courses in basic and advanced health economics, and health systems, which have been running since past more than 12 years, and contributed to the design of master's course in health economics and technology assessment, which has been approved by the Indian Council of Medical Research (ICMR) and University Grants Commission (UGC).

Abbreviations

AAMs	*Ayushman Arogya Mandirs*
ABDM	*Ayushman Bharat Digital Mission*
ABHA	Ayushman Bharat Health Account
ABHIM	*Ayushman Bharat Health and Infrastructure Mission*
ACA	Affordable Care Act
ACCORD	Action for Community Organisation, Rehabilitation and Development
ACEO	Additional Chief Executive Officer
ACS	Amount Paid per Claim
AHPRA	Australian Health Practitioner Regulation Agency
AI	Artificial Intelligence
AIDS	Acquired Immunodeficiency Syndrome
AML	Anti-Money Laundering
ANC	Antenatal Care
ANM	Auxiliary Nurse Midwife
API	Application Programming Interface
ASHA	Accredited Social Health Activist
AWW	*Anganwadi* Worker
AYUSH	*Ayurveda, Yoga, Naturopathy, Unani, Siddha, and Homeopathy*
BI	Business Intelligence
BIA	Benefit Incidence Analysis
BIS	Bureau of Indian Standards
BMGF	Bill & Melinda Gates Foundation
BNS	*Bharatiya Nyaya Sanhita*
BoCW	Building and Other Construction Workers
BoCWB	Building and Other Construction Workers Welfare Board
BPL	Below Poverty Line
BSBY	*Bhamashah Swasthya Bima Yojana*
CAG	Comptroller and Auditor General of India
CAPF	Central Armed Police Forces
CBA	Cost-Benefit Analysis
CBC	Capacity Building Commission
CBHI	Community-Based Health Insurance
CBPR	Community-Based Participatory Research

CCs	Concentration Curves
CCT	Conditional Cash Transfer
CDK4/6i	Cyclin-Dependent Kinase 4/6 Inhibitors
CDSCO	Central Drugs Standard Control Organization
CEA	Cost-Effectiveness Analysis
CEO	Chief Executive Officer
CGHS	Central Government Health Scheme
CHAI	Clinton Health Access Initiative
CHC	Community Health Centre
CHE	Catastrophic Health Expenditure
CHE	Current Health Expenditure
CHSI	Costing of Health Services in India
CI	Concentration Index
CINI ASHA	Child in Need Institute-Accredited Social Health Activist
CMCHIS	Chief Minister's Comprehensive Health Insurance Scheme
CMS	Centers for Medicare and Medicaid Services
CoC	Continuum-of-Care
COTS	Commercial Off the Shelf
CPDs	Claims Processing Doctors
CPHC	Comprehensive Primary Health Care
CSB	Care-Seeking Behavior
CSMA	Central Services Medical Attendance
CSMBS	Civil Servant Medical Benefit Scheme
CSR	Corporate Social Responsibility
CUA	Cost-Utility Analysis
CVD	Cardiovascular Disease
CY	*Chiranjivi Yojana*
DALYs	Disability-Adjusted Life Years
DBT	Direct Benefit Transfer
DFU	Digital Forensics Unit
DHR	Department of Health Research
DHS	Demographic and Health Survey
DIU	District Implementation Unit
DPDP	Digital Personal Data Protection Act
DPT	Diphtheria, Pertussis, Tetanus
DRG	Diagnosis Related Group
DSF	Demand-Side Financing
DTx	Digital Therapeutics
e-RUPI	Electronic Rupee
EAG	Empowered Action Group
ECHS	Ex-Servicemen Contributory Health Scheme
EHCP	Empanelled Health Care Provider
EHFCN	European Health Insurance Fraud and Corruption Network
EHIF	Estonian Health Insurance Fund
EHR	Electronic Health Records

ENCR	European Network of Cancer Registries
EPS	Electronic Prescription Service
ESI	Employees' State Insurance
ESIC	Employees' State Insurance Corporation
ESIS	Employees' State Insurance Corporation
FACTS	Fraud Analytics Control Tracking System
FFS	Fee-for-Service
FHIR	Fast Healthcare Interoperability Resources
FHW	Female Health Worker
FICCI	Federation of Indian Chambers of Commerce & Industry
FPG	Fasting Plasma Glucose
FSSHIP	Formal Sector Social Health Insurance Programme
FWA	Fraud, Waste, and Abuse
GAVI	Global Alliance for Vaccines and Immunization
GB	Governing Board
GBD	Global Burden of Disease
GDP	Gross Domestic Product
GDPA	General Data Protection Regulations
GDPR	General Data Protection Regulation
GFATM	Global Fund to Fight AIDS, Tuberculosis, and Malaria
GFHI	Government-Funded Health Insurance
GFHIS	Government-Funded Health Insurance Schemes
GGE	General Government Expenditure
GGE-D	Direct General Government Expenditure
GHE	Government Health Expenditure
GIZ	Deutsche Gesellschaft für Internationale Zusammenarbeit (German Development Agency)
GLC4HSR	Global Learning Collaborative for Health Systems Resilience
GLSS	Ghana Living Standard Survey
GOI	Government of India
GP	General Practitioner
GST	Goods and Services Tax
HBP	Health Benefit Package
HCFA	Health Care Financing Administration
HCPs	Healthcare Providers
HDU	High-Definition Unit
HeFTA	Health Financing and Technology Assessment
HEM	Hospital Empanelment Module
HES	Hospital Episode Statistics
HI	Health Insurance
HIE	Health Information Exchange
HIE-CM	Health Information Exchange and Consent Manager
HIPAA	Health Insurance Portability and Accountability Act
HIPs	Health Information Providers
HIUs	Health Information Users

HIV	Human Immunodeficiency Virus
HLEG	High-Level Expert Group
HNIs	High-Net-Worth Individuals
HOPE	Healthcare Organization for Platform for Entry level Certification
HRA	Health Risk Assessment
HRQoL	Health-Related Quality of Life
HTA	Health Technology Assessment
HTAIn	Health Technology Assessment in India
HWC	Health and Wellness Centre
ICD	International Classification of Diseases
ICDS	Integrated Child Development Services
ICER	Incremental Cost-Effectiveness Ratio
ICHI	International Classification of Health Interventions
ICR	Incurred Claims Ratio
ICU	Intensive Care Unit
ID	Identification
IEC	Information, Education, and Communication
IGMSY	*Indira Gandhi Matritva Sahyog Yojana*
iGOT	Integrated Government Online Training *Karmayogi*
IHR	International Health Regulations
IIB	Insurance Information Bureau
IIHMR	Indian Institute of Health Management Research
IIM	Indian Institute of Management
IIT	Indian Institute of Technology
IMF	International Monetary Fund
INGAF	Institute of Government Accounts and Finance
IP	Inpatient
IPC	Indian Penal Code
IRDAI	Insurance Regulatory and Development Authority of India
ISAs	Implementation Support Agencies
ISB	Indian School of Business
ISMS	Information security management system
ISTM	Institute of Secretariat Training and Management
IT	Information Technology
ITN	Insecticide-Treated Nets
JAM	*Jan Dhan, Aadhaar, Mobile*
JAMIA	Journal of the American Medical Informatics Association
JCI	Joint Commission International
JLI	Joint Learning Initiative
JSY	*Janani Suraksha Yojana*
KPIs	Key Performance Indicators
KTA	Knowledge-to-Action
KYC	Know Your Costumer
LCFS	Local Counter Fraud Specialists

LMIC	Low- and Middle-Income Countries
LMS	Learning Management System
LoS	Length of Stay
LSMS	Living Standards Measurement Survey
MBIA	Marginal Benefit Incidence Analysis
MCH	Maternal and Child Health
MDGs	Millennium Development Goals
MFA	Multi-Factor Authentication
MGNREGS	Mahatma Gandhi National Rural Employment Guarantee Scheme
MHMS	Ministry of Health and Medical Services
ML	Machine Learning
MMSY	*Mukhya Mantri Maiya Samman Yojana*
MoF	Ministry of Finance
MoH	Ministry of Health
MoHFW	Ministry of Health and Family Welfare
MoU	Memorandum of Understanding
MPCE	Monthly Per Capita Expenditure
MSAs	Medical Savings Accounts
NABH	National Accreditation Board for Hospitals & Healthcare Providers
NAFU	National Anti-Fraud Unit
NCDs	Non-Communicable Diseases
NDHM	National Digital Health Mission
NEDL	National Essential Diagnostic Lists
NFHS	National Family Health Survey
NGO	Non-Governmental Organization
NHA	National Health Accounts
NHA	National Health Authority
NHCAA	National Health Care Antifraud Association
NHCX	National Health Claims Exchange
NHI	National Health Insurance
NHIS	National Health Insurance Scheme
NHM	National Health Mission
NHS	National Health Services
NHSCFA	National Health Service Counter Fraud Authority
NHSRC	National Health Systems and Resource Centre
NIHFW	National Institute of Health and Family Welfare
NIMHANS	National Institute of Mental Health and Neurosciences
NITI	National Institution for Transforming India
NLEM	National List of Essential Medicines
NLP	Natural Language Processing
NMC	National Medical Commission
NPCI	National Payments Corporation of India
NPI	National Provider Identifier

NPISH	Non-Profit Institutions Serving Households
NPPA	National Pharmaceutical Pricing Authority
NQAS	National Quality Assurance Standards
NRC	National Release Centre
NRCMS	New Rural Cooperative Medical Scheme
NRHM	National Rural Health Mission
NSSO	National Sample Survey Office
OECD	Organization for Economic Co-operation and Development
OOP	Out-of-Pocket
OOPE	Out-of-Pocket Expenditure
OP	Outpatient
OSS	Open-Source Software
OTC	Over-the-Counter
PAC	Public Accounts Committee
PED	Pre-existing Diseases
PHC	Primary Health Centre
PHE-D	Private Health Expenditure – Direct
PHI	Private Health Insurance
PHR	Personal Health Records
PICO	Population, Intervention, Comparator, Outcome
PM-JAY	*Pradhan Mantri Jan Arogya Yojana*
PM-KISAN	*Pradhan Mantri Kisan Samman Nidhi*
PMAM	*Pradhan Mantri Arogya Mitra*
PMMVY	*Pradhan Mantri Matru Vandana Yojana*
PMRT	Post-mastectomy Radiation Therapy
PNC	Postnatal Care
PPDs	Pre-authorization Processing Doctors
PPMs	Provider Payment Methods
PPP	Public Private Partnerships
PRI	*Panchayati Raj Institutions*
PROM	Patient-Reported Outcome Measure
PTCA	Percutaneous Transluminal Coronary Angioplasty
QALYs	Quality-Adjusted Life Years
QBS	Quality Bonus Scheme
QCI	Quality Council of India
RADAR	Risk Assessment Detection and Analytical Reporting
RCT	Randomized Control Trial
RDHS	Rwanda Demographic and Health Survey
RGJAY	*Rajiv Gandhi Jeevandayee Arogya Yojana*
ROHINI	Registry of Hospitals In the Network of Insurance
RPM	Remote Patient Monitoring
RRCs	Regional Resource Centers
RSBY	*Rashtriya Swasthya Bima Yojana*
RT	Radiation Therapy
RTI	Reproductive Tract Infection

RWE	Real-World Evidence
RWs	Relative Weights
SAFU	State Anti-Fraud Unit
SDGs	Sustainable Development Goals
SECC	Socio-Economic and Caste Census
SEER	The Surveillance, Epidemiology, and End Results
SES	Socio-Economic Status
SEWA	Self Employed Women's Association
SHAs	State Health Agencies
SHA	System of Health Accounts
SHG	Self-Help Group
SHI	Social Health Insurance
SLA	Service Level Agreements
SMR	Standardized Mortality Rates
SNA	Social Network Analysis
SNOWMED-CT	Systematized Nomenclature of Medicine - Clinical Terms
SOP	Standard Operating Protocol
SQL	Structured Query Language
SSE	Social Security Expenditure
SSF	Supply-Side Financing
SSS	Social Security Scheme
STG	Standard Treatment Guidelines
STI	Sexually Transmitted Infection
TAC	Technical Advisory Committee
TAT	Turnaround Time
TB	Tuberculosis
TCAM	Traditional, Complementary, and Alternative Medicine
THE	Total Health Expenditure
TMS	Transaction Management System
TPAs	Third-Party Administrators
TPE	Total Pharmaceutical Expenditure
TPs	Technical Partners
UCS	Universal Coverage Scheme
UEMBI	Urban Employment-Based Medical Insurance
UHC	Universal Health Coverage
UHI	Unified Health Interface
UHIS	Universal Health Insurance Scheme
UI	User Interface
UK	United Kingdom
UN	United Nations
UPI	Unified Payments Interface
URBMI	Urban Resident Basic Medical Insurance
URRBMI	Urban and Rural Resident Basic Medical Insurance
US	United States
USA	United States of America

USAID	United States Agency for International Development
USD	United States Dollar
UTs	Union Territories
UX	User Experience
VBC	Value-Based Care
VBP	Value-Based Purchasing
VGF	Viability Gap Funding
VHI	Voluntary Health Insurance
VPHI	Voluntary Private Health Insurance
WHO	World Health Organization

Part I

Foundational Concepts in Health Financing

Health Systems and Health Financing: An Overview

1

Yashika Chugh, Prakash Singh, and Shankar Prinja

Abstract

This introductory chapter of the book *Healthcare Financing and Insurance: A Guide for Practitioner, Professionals, and Policymakers* provides a foundational framework for understanding health systems and their financing mechanisms. It begins by defining the concept of a health system, outlining its goals and core functions. The chapter then explores the critical role of financing function of health system in achieving these goals, emphasizing the key functions of health financing—revenue collection, fund pooling, strategic purchasing of services, and service provision. Further, the chapter introduces various health financing models that have evolved historically and examines their relevance to the Indian healthcare landscape. The discussion also extends to the role of health financing in strengthening health systems, aligning with the Sustainable Development Goals (SDG), and advancing the agenda of Universal Health Coverage (UHC).

By providing a comprehensive overview of health systems and role of health financing in health systems, this chapter lays the groundwork for the readers of the book, equipping them with the essential knowledge required to navigate and contribute to India's evolving health financing landscape.

Keywords

Health systems · Health system functions · Health financing · Universal Health Coverage · Sustainable Development Goals

Y. Chugh · P. Singh · S. Prinja (✉)
Department of Community Medicine and School of Public Health, Post Graduate Institute of Medical Education & Research, Chandigarh, India

S. Prinja (ed.), *Healthcare Financing and Insurance*,
https://doi.org/10.1007/978-981-95-3513-2_1

Learning Objectives

After going through the chapter, you will be able to understand the:

- Concept of health system
- Functions and goals of the health system
- Importance of financing in health system
- Models of health system
- Role of health financing in achieving Universal Health Coverage (UHC)

Key Terms

- *Health System*: A health system comprises all organizations, people, and actions whose primary intent is to promote, restore, or maintain health. It includes both public and private actors involved in health service delivery, health promotion, disease prevention, and governance, provided their primary objective is to improve health outcomes.
- *Health Financing*: Health financing refers to the mechanisms through which a health system mobilizes, pools, and allocates financial resources to ensure that individuals can access needed health services without facing financial hardship.
- *Revenue Collection*: Revenue collection is the process through which funds are generated to finance the health system, either through taxation, social health insurance, voluntary private insurance, external donor funding, or out-of-pocket payments.
- *Pooling*: Pooling refers to the accumulation of funds to distribute the financial risk of illness across a population.
- *Purchasing*: Purchasing is the process through which pooled funds are allocated to healthcare providers on behalf of the population.
- *Universal Health Coverage*: Universal Health Coverage means that all individuals receive the health services they need—of sufficient quality—without suffering financial hardship.

1.1 What Is a Health System?

Health systems are inherently complex, and their definition has evolved as scholars and institutions have attempted to conceptualize them in different ways. One of the earlier definitions, provided by Roemer (1991), describes a health system as "the combination of resources, organization, financing, and management that culminate in the delivery of health services to the population" [1]. This definition primarily emphasizes the inputs necessary for a functioning health system, focusing on the structural components that enable healthcare delivery. A more widely recognized definition, presented in the World Health Report 2000, takes a broader approach. It defines a health system as "all organizations, people, and actions whose primary intent is to promote, restore, or maintain health" [2]. Unlike Roemer's input-focused perspective, this definition shifts attention towards the outcomes and objectives of a health system. The report categorizes all activities—whether undertaken by individuals, organizations, or institutions—as part of the health system, if their primary purpose is to enhance health outcomes.

Under this broad definition, a wide range of activities and entities are encompassed within a health system. In the context of India's public healthcare infrastructure, this includes all levels of health facilities—from subcenters and health and wellness centers to tertiary care medical colleges. Medications, whether distributed through formal health facilities, purchased over the counter, or even self-prescribed, are also considered part of the health system. Furthermore, activities related to health promotion and disease prevention, even if they extend beyond conventional healthcare services, contribute to the health system. For example, road safety measures aimed at reducing accidents align with public health objectives and, therefore, fall within the system's broader scope.

Despite the expansive nature of the World Health Organization's (WHO) definition, it is equally important to delineate what falls outside the health system [2]. Many activities influenced by social determinants of health—such as education, employment, and access to clean water—significantly impact population health but are not primarily designed to restore, maintain, or improve health. For instance, education plays a crucial role in shaping health outcomes by increasing awareness, literacy, and economic opportunities. However, since its primary purpose is to enhance human capital and workforce productivity, education policies and programs fall outside the formal boundaries of the health system. Similarly, employment programs that generate job opportunities and ensure financial security contribute to well-being but do not have health improvement as their primary objective, placing them beyond the direct scope of the health system. The same distinction applies to certain social insurance programs—while health insurance covering medical treatment is an integral part of the health system, wage replacement schemes for sickness benefits primarily serve economic security rather than health restoration, placing them outside the health system's core definition.

1.2 Health Systems: Goals and Functions

Health systems are designed to achieve multiple objectives. According to the World Health Report 2000, the fundamental goals of a health system include

1. Enhancing health and reducing health disparities by preventing diseases and improving health outcomes, particularly for vulnerable groups
2. Ensuring that health systems are responsive to population needs by providing accessible, high-quality care and addressing broader social determinants of health

3. Protecting individuals from financial hardship due to healthcare costs, thereby ensuring access to essential services without undue financial burden
4. Optimizing resource use to maximize efficiency and effectiveness in service delivery [2, 3]

Fair financing is a common principle across all societal systems, regardless of whether services are publicly funded or individually purchased. The perception of fairness, however, differs by context—while "paying for what one gets" may seem reasonable in market-based transactions, healthcare is often seen as requiring a more equitable approach. In healthcare, fair financing implies that the healthcare payments made by individuals are in accordance with their ability to pay, that is, the rich pay a higher proportion of their income compared to poor people. In all systems, people hold expectations regarding how they should be treated, both in terms of service provision and interpersonal interactions. Responsiveness, therefore, is a fundamental social objective and refers to how well the health system meets the legitimate expectations of the population for the non-health-enhancing aspects of the health system [4].

To meet these overarching goals, health systems must effectively carry out certain core functions. The World Health Report identifies four essential functions: delivering healthcare services, ensuring the availability of human and physical resources necessary for service provision, mobilizing and pooling financial resources to fund healthcare, and most importantly, stewardship that involves setting policies, regulating healthcare systems, and providing strategic direction to coordinate the various actors involved in healthcare (Fig. 1.1) [2, 3].

Service Provision The most essential function that a health system must fulfill is delivering healthcare services. Other functions—such as financing, training, and resource allocation—are important mainly because they support effective service delivery. When essential and affordable healthcare interventions fail to reach those who need them, it signals a fundamental weakness in the system.

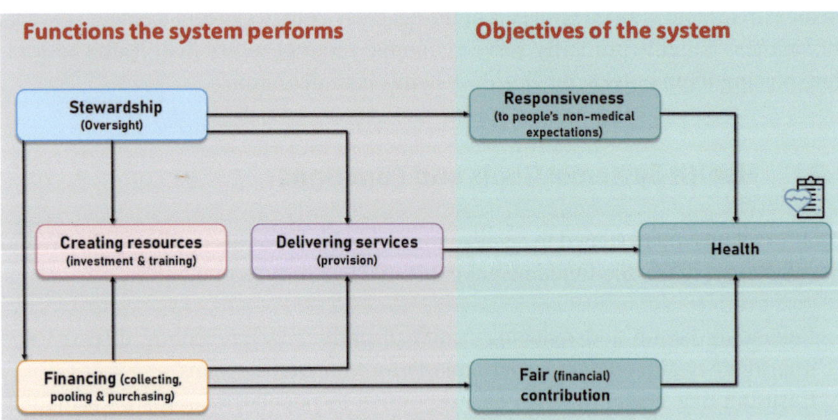

Fig. 1.1 Health systems performance framework. (Source: Health Systems: Improving Performance [2])

At its core, service provision involves determining which healthcare services should be prioritized, how they should be delivered, and how to manage resource constraints to ensure that those priorities translate into meaningful access to care. It also involves designing an efficient organizational structure that ensures services reach the right people at the right time.

Resource Generation Delivering healthcare requires bringing together a wide range of resources to produce an equally diverse set of services. The three key inputs in any health system are human resources, physical infrastructure, and supplies in the form of medicines and consumables. Making investment decisions in healthcare is particularly challenging because such decisions are often irreversible—once money is allocated to building hospitals, training professionals, or purchasing equipment, it is difficult to reverse or scale down those commitments. The challenge becomes even greater when some of these decisions fall outside the direct control of health authorities.

Healthcare capital refers to the existing stock of assets that support service delivery, including trained health professionals, hospitals, and mobile clinics. Any effort to expand these resources—such as hiring additional staff, building new facilities, or acquiring more equipment—is considered an investment. Human capital, like physical capital, requires continuous investment in the form of education and training to keep up with evolving medical knowledge and technological advancements. While knowledge itself does not wear out, outdated skills can become ineffective, making ongoing training essential. Investment also extends beyond infrastructure and workforce development to include research and innovation, which drive improvements in medical technology, diagnostics, and pharmaceuticals.

Striking the right balance between investment in new assets and the ongoing costs of maintaining existing resources is crucial, especially in low-income countries where financial flexibility is limited.

Financing Healthcare costs have risen significantly worldwide, pushing societies to find financing systems that ensure no one is denied care due to an inability to pay. Many countries have long considered universal access to healthcare a fundamental goal, making health financing a crucial component of the system. Effective financing ensures that resources are available, pooled appropriately, allocated for the right mix of services, sets appropriate incentives for healthcare providers, and protects individuals from financial hardship when seeking care. Without a well-structured financing system, people may either forego necessary treatment or face financial ruin trying to afford it.

Stewardship Stewardship is the cornerstone of a well-functioning health system as it defines the government's ultimate responsibility for ensuring its overall performance. Unlike other health system functions—service delivery, resource generation, and financing—stewardship is overarching, influencing and shaping all aspects of the system. Its role is to ensure that healthcare services improve population health, meet public expectations, and distribute financial burden fairly. Without effective stewardship, even the best-designed healthcare structures may fail to deliver equitable and efficient care.

At its core, stewardship involves strategic oversight, requiring vision, intelligence, and influence. The health ministry plays a central role in directing and coordinating national health initiatives, ensuring that policies align with broader governmental priorities. However, some responsibilities extend beyond the ministry's control. For example, drug pricing and regulation fall under the Ministry of Chemicals and Fertilizers, specifically the Department of Pharmaceuticals and the National Pharmaceutical Pricing Authority (NPPA). These entities set ceiling price for essential medicines and regulate pharmaceutical markets, impacting healthcare affordability and access. Ensuring coherence across departments is essential, sometimes necessitating broader public sector reforms to create a unified approach to health governance.

Beyond government, stewardship is also the responsibility of health service purchasers and providers, who must ensure that resources are used effectively to maximize health outcomes. At the international level, stewardship includes managing external assistance and aligning donor contributions with national health priorities. However, the government remains the primary actor in steering the system.

1.2.1 Framework of Healthcare Financing

Financing is a fundamental pillar of any health system, shaping the way resources are mobilized, allocated, and utilized to achieve health system goals. Governments face intense competition for resources, balancing multiple priorities while striving to improve equity, efficiency, and quality of care. The financing function is at the heart of this balancing act, influencing the ability of the health system to deliver services, train and retain healthcare professionals, and ensure financial protection for populations.

Kutzin (2001) explains the underlying subfunctions of health financing system as which serve as a framework for analyzing a country's healthcare financing system, offering a structured way to describe existing resource allocation mechanisms and their impact (Fig. 1.2) [5]. The central part of the figure illustrates how the funds, which are collected and pooled, move through the health system, from their sources to service providers. In this context, pooled funds refer to financial resources that are managed collectively for groups of people or the entire population, excluding direct out-of-pocket (OOP) payments made by individuals to providers. The arrows in the figure indicate the connections between different health system functions and the population or individual service users.

To achieve equitable access to healthcare, financing systems rely on three interconnected functions: revenue collection, resource pooling, and purchasing of health services:

- Revenue collection refers to how the health system obtains funds, whether through general taxation, mandatory social health insurance, voluntary private insurance, OOP payments, or donor contributions.

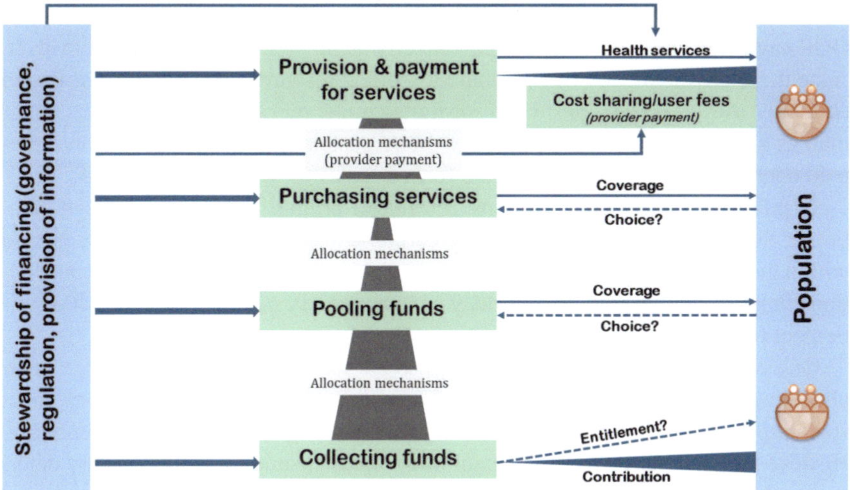

Fig. 1.2 Kutzin's framework: health system financing functions and population links

- Pooling then ensures that financial risk is shared across a group of people rather than being borne individually. This is the essence of health insurance, whether explicitly through enrolment in an insurance scheme or implicitly through tax-funded healthcare. The purpose of pooling is to spread the financial burden of healthcare needs, which are often unpredictable so that no single individual has to shoulder the full cost of an expensive medical intervention.
- Once funds are collected and pooled, they must be used efficiently to purchase healthcare services. Purchasing can be done in two ways: passively or strategically. Passive purchasing simply follows a fixed budget or pays providers based on services rendered, without assessing value or efficiency. In contrast, strategic purchasing actively seeks to optimize health system performance by deciding which services to fund, which providers to contract, and how to structure incentives to improve quality and efficiency.

1.2.1.1 Revenue Collection

Revenue collection or raising is the process through which funds are generated to finance the health system. With the exception of external donor funding, all health system financing ultimately comes from the population, including individuals and businesses, as shown by the "Contributions" arrow in Fig. 1.2. These sources of revenue collection are typically categorized into general government revenues, social health insurance (SHI), and other classifications based on the National Health Accounts (NHA) framework [6]. The way revenue is raised influences who has access to healthcare, how financial risks are distributed, and the overall sustainability of the system.

Health systems rely on different mechanisms to collect revenue. One approach is OOP payments, where individuals pay directly at the point of service use. However, since these payments do not contribute to pooled resources that can be distributed equitably, they are often considered separately under purchasing mechanisms rather than as a core revenue-raising strategy. More sustainable approaches involve prepaid contributions, which can take the form of taxes or insurance premiums.

In public or quasi-public systems, revenue is primarily collected through taxation or SHI contributions. Taxes may be earmarked specifically for health or pooled within general government revenues and then allocated to healthcare. SHI contributions function similarly to taxes as they are compulsory payments that provide entitlement to care.

One of the most direct ways to increase pooled resources for healthcare is by allocating more public funds. This can be achieved either by shifting government spending from other sectors to health or by increasing overall public expenditure. However, significant budget reallocations are rare, meaning that the primary determinant of healthcare funding remains the total amount of public revenue collected through taxation. This poses a greater challenge for low-income countries as their ability to generate public revenue is much lower than that of high-income countries [7]. As a result, policymakers in these settings must recognize that the availability of health funds largely depends on broader economic conditions and the effectiveness of tax collection, both of which are beyond their direct control.

Expanding health financing through compulsory insurance contributions—such as payroll taxes for SHI—is another option. The state of the labor market is an important determinant for its success [8]. If the economy is strong, there may be opportunities to introduce new financing mechanisms. However, during economic downturns or when formal employment levels are low, increasing health insurance contributions can be difficult and may even negatively impact employment and economic growth.

Another approach to revenue collection is through voluntary health insurance (VHI) that includes voluntary private health insurance as well as community-based health insurance (CBHI), that is, usually not for profit. Whether structured for profit or not, VHI raises revenue through insurance premiums paid by individuals or employers. These premiums may be set at a uniform rate for all members within a defined area (community-rated) or determined based on an individual's anticipated health risks (risk-rated).

Unlike taxation or social health insurance, which mandate contributions according to income or salary levels, voluntary private insurance ties premium payments to an individual's likelihood of requiring healthcare rather than their financial capacity. In the case of CBHI, contributions are not structured proportionally to income or in relation to individual health risks. Instead, a collective of individuals or households agrees on a standardized contribution rate, pooling their resources to cover healthcare expenses for all members. Additionally, private insurance revenues can be indirectly influenced by tax policies, particularly when premiums are paid using pre-tax income, effectively providing a form of subsidy for private insurance coverage.

An important issue is the entitlement associated with insurance contributions. People who pay specifically for "health insurance" expect a guaranteed set of benefits in return. This can increase inequities, especially in low-income countries, where formal sector workers—who tend to be better off—receive more comprehensive healthcare benefits than the rest of the population. While all these mechanisms contribute to revenue generation, their design has significant implications for equity, financial protection, and system sustainability. A well-structured revenue-raising strategy ensures that healthcare financing is predictable, sufficient, and fair, allowing the health system to function efficiently while minimizing financial barriers to care. A more detailed discussion of the revenue collection has been provided in the subsequent chapter on revenue collection (Chap. 3).

1.2.1.2 Pooling

Pooling refers to the process of accumulating prepaid healthcare funds on behalf of the population. It is essential to distinguish between pooling and revenue collection as they represent separate functions within health financing. Revenue raising pertains to the sources of funding, essentially identifying who contributes financially to the system, which in turn provides insight into whether the financial burden is distributed equitably. In contrast, pooling determines who benefits from healthcare expenditures as it establishes how prepaid funds are redistributed across a given population. In Fig. 1.2, the arrow from "pooling of funds" to "individuals" represents the coverage of healthcare costs for the population for whom these funds are pooled, whether by a single entity or multiple pooling organizations. The dotted line in the opposite direction indicates that, in certain cases, individuals have the option to choose their pooling organization.

To ensure an equitable distribution of resources, health financing systems often implement allocation or equalization mechanisms. These may involve transferring funds from a central revenue-collecting entity, such as a Ministry of Finance, to a pooling agency like a Ministry of Health. Alternatively, funds may flow directly from their original source to pooling organizations, as is the case when private insurers manage both collection and pooling. Additionally, financial transfers can occur between pools, such as from a central fund to regional or competing pools, often using risk adjustment measures. These mechanisms account for variations in population characteristics that influence healthcare costs, including age, health status, and socioeconomic factors.

The nature of pooling also varies based on the level of choice, and obligation associated with participation. In some systems, individuals have the option to select which pool they join, while in others, participation is determined by legal or administrative criteria. Compulsory participation requires specific groups or the entire population to be covered by a designated pool, with mandatory contributions made directly or on their behalf. In contrast, automatic participation is often based on legal entitlements linked to citizenship, residency, or income level, with funding drawn primarily from general government revenues rather than direct contributions. In such cases, while individuals may contribute indirectly through taxation, there is no explicit link between payment and entitlement. Voluntary enrolment, by contrast, involves individuals choosing to make prepayments into a scheme, without a legal requirement to do so.

The way in which individuals are included in, or assigned to, pools have significant implications for efficiency, financial sustainability, and the extent to which risks and resources are shared.

Without strong government intervention, voluntary insurance markets tend to become segmented, dividing people into different risk groups. Those in poorer health often end up in high-cost insurance pools, making it difficult to sustain their coverage on a private basis. Over time, this can lead to declining insurance coverage in the population.

However, in countries with limited public healthcare funding, voluntary insurance may still be preferable to OOP payments. Policies that encourage the expansion of voluntary prepayment models can help improve access to healthcare [9–11]. That said, the goal should not simply be to create insurance schemes but to ensure they contribute effectively to the healthcare system's overall objectives.

1.2.1.3 Purchasing Goods and Services

Purchasing refers to the allocation of pooled healthcare funds to service providers on behalf of the population for which these funds were collected. As illustrated in Fig. 1.2, pooling and purchasing together ensure healthcare coverage for a defined population. Various entities can act as purchasers of healthcare services, including ministries of health (at central or decentralized levels), local government health authorities, social and private health insurance funds, employer-based health plans, member-owned mutual insurers, and fundholding providers. In many cases, the same organization is responsible for both pooling and purchasing, leading to overlaps in their roles and functions.

When designing purchasing arrangements, two key policy considerations arise. First, what role do purchasers play in relation to healthcare providers—are they merely financial intermediaries, or do they leverage their financial influence to drive improvements in quality and efficiency? Second, what is the market structure of purchasing organizations? The latter includes determining whether a single-payer operates within a specific geographic region, whether multiple insurers exist, and if so, whether they compete for enrollees or operate in a noncompetitive framework. Additionally, in public healthcare systems, it is important to identify whether a designated organizational unit is explicitly responsible for purchasing healthcare services.

Therefore, there are three primary approaches to carrying out this function. First, governments can allocate budgets directly to their own healthcare providers, integrating both the purchasing and provision of services, using general government revenues. Second, an independent institution, separate from service providers, can purchase healthcare services on behalf of the population, creating a purchaser–provider split. Purchasing is often seen as a more strategic function than simply paying for services, as it implies an active approach to resource allocation. Active, or strategic, purchasing involves mechanisms such as selecting accredited providers, prioritizing cost-effective services, and designing payment methods that incentivize quality and efficiency in service delivery. In contrast, passive purchasing occurs when funds are allocated without consideration of provider performance or service quality—such as when historical budgets dictate spending, or when a third-party payer reimburses providers indiscriminately.

Shifting from passive to strategic purchasing means linking provider payments, at least partially, to performance indicators or the health needs of the population served. Thus, provider payment mechanisms are an essential component of the purchaser–provider interaction as the method of payment affects who bears the risk of patient costs, thus influencing the provider response to the type of care a patient receives, the quality of this care, and the cost of healthcare provision. These have been discussed in detail in later chapters on strategic purchasing and provider payment methods.

Third, individuals may directly pay healthcare providers OOP for the services they receive. OOP payments, which are direct payments made by individuals at the point of service, can also be considered part of purchasing. These payments may be formal or informal and can cover the full cost of care where no insurance exists or a partial cost where some financial protection is available. While OOP payments serve as a financing mechanism, they are also a key component of benefit package design. Policymakers may use them to limit coverage for low-value services or target benefits to specific population groups that are most likely to benefit.

The role of OOP payments in purchasing is debated. Some policymakers view them as a tool to regulate demand by discouraging unnecessary healthcare use through financial deterrents, though evidence suggests this approach may be ineffective in rationalizing service use. In certain contexts, OOP payments also function as a revenue-generating mechanism. However, because these payments are not pooled, they are best understood as a purchasing subfunction rather than a revenue-raising strategy. The inclusion of OOP payments in purchasing highlights the broader policy decisions that influence healthcare financing, benefit package design, and the distribution of financial risk within health systems. In this book, we have described the OOP payments both as a mechanism of raising resources in the chapter on revenue collection and a form of provider payment in the chapter on provider payment mechanisms.

Check Your Learning by Answering These Questions

1. What are the four fundamental goals of a health system as outlined in the World Health Report 2000?
2. Explain the three interconnected functions of health financing identified by Kutzin (2001) that are crucial for achieving equitable access to healthcare?
3. Use the framework of healthcare financing to describe any health financing scheme?

decentralized management, depending on the country. One challenge of the Beveridge model is that public financing competes with other government priorities, which can impact healthcare quality and outcomes. However, as the sole payer, the government retains full control over healthcare costs, ensuring affordability and access for all citizens [18, 19].

1.3.2 The Semashko Model

The Semashko model closely resembles the Beveridge model in that the state plays a central role in ensuring social and healthcare services. Rooted in socialist ideology, this model was widely implemented in the former Soviet Union and other socialist countries, evolving alongside the Beveridge model [20]. Introduced by the Bolsheviks after coming to power in 1917, the model was named after Nikolai Semashko, the Soviet People's Commissar for Healthcare. Over time, many former Soviet countries have restructured or moved away from this system, though variations of it still exist in Russia and several post-Soviet states. It is a state-funded, single-payer healthcare system that provides free healthcare to all citizens, financed through the national budget [21].

Under this model, the Soviet Union divided its territory into districts, each assigned outpatient hospitals and local physicians responsible for treating common illnesses. More complex cases were referred to regional hospitals. A distinctive feature of the Semashko model is the "dynamic dispensary surveillance" approach, introduced in the late 1960s, which established structured guidelines for managing serious diseases. This approach included treatment planning, documentation, specialist consultations, monitoring processes, and outcome evaluations [21].

1.3.3 The Bismarck Model

The Bismarck model, named after Prussian Chancellor Otto von Bismarck, was introduced during Germany's unification as part of state welfare reforms [13]. Over time, several countries, including Germany, France, the Netherlands, Belgium, Switzerland, Japan, and parts of Latin America, have adopted variations of this model, often referred to as the Social Health Insurance Model [22]. This system mandates compulsory contributions to a social insurance fund, historically known as "sickness funds," which is financed through payroll deductions from both employees and employers [13, 23]. Government regulations ensure that these funds operate on a nonprofit basis, keeping healthcare services affordable and accessible to the majority of the population. One of the defining features of the Bismarck model is its reliance on both public and private healthcare providers. However, its implementation varies across countries—some, like France and Namibia, have centralized systems, whereas others, such as the Netherlands and Germany, operate decentralized models.

1.3.4 The National Health Insurance Model (NHI)

The National Health Insurance (NHI) model is often considered a variation of the Bismarck model, but with a key distinction—it operates as a single-payer system rather than relying on multiple insurance funds. In this model, a central fund collects mandatory contributions and directly reimburses healthcare providers. While contributions are compulsory, the system ensures coverage for all individuals, including those who do not contribute. Funding for the NHI model primarily comes from payroll contributions, supplemented by government subsidies. Healthcare services are delivered by both public and private providers, though private facilities and practitioners tend to dominate in many countries using this system. Nations such as South Korea and Taiwan have implemented NHI successfully [24]. The fundamental difference between the NHI model and Social Health Insurance (SHI) models like the Bismarck model lies in their approach to coverage. The NHI system is designed to provide Universal Health Coverage (UHC) from the outset, ensuring healthcare access for all citizens. In contrast, SHI models typically limit benefits to specific groups, such as employees who contribute to the system, excluding those who are unemployed or unable to pay. Also known as single-payer national health insurance, the NHI model blends aspects of both the Bismarck and Beveridge models [17]. Like the Beveridge model, the government serves as the sole payer for healthcare services, ensuring cost control and equity. However, similar to the Bismarck model, providers operate mostly within the private sector. This system is currently in place in countries such as Canada, Taiwan, and South Korea [25].

1.3.5 The Commercial Model: Private Health Insurance (PHI)

Commercial healthcare systems operate with multiple private insurers offering a variety of coverage plans. Unlike the traditional Bismarck model, these insurance providers can function as for-profit entities. The system is market-driven, allowing individuals to choose from different insurance options, with premiums determined through risk assessments. Insurers also have the discretion to deny coverage. Government involvement is minimal, primarily limited to regulatory oversight. A notable example of this model existed in the United States before the implementation of the Patient Protection and Affordable Care Act (ACA) in 2010 under President Barack Obama [26, 27].

1.3.6 The Out-of-Pocket (OOP) Model

The OOPt model operates on direct payments made by patients to healthcare providers at the point of service. This approach lacks a structured system to guarantee healthcare access for all individuals, often leading to disparities based on financial capacity. Despite expectations, this model is prevalent in many countries, as only a minority have fully established and organized healthcare systems following one of the previously discussed models [13]. This model is prevalent in many developing countries and for several type of curative services. In nations with limited resources to establish universal healthcare, individuals must cover their medical expenses directly. As a result, those with insufficient financial means often struggle to access necessary healthcare services.

1.3.7 The Indian Healthcare System

India's healthcare system is a complex hybrid that integrates elements from multiple global healthcare models, reflecting the country's diverse population, economic disparities, and evolving policy landscape. Rather than adhering to a single framework, India employs a combination of health systems (Fig. 1.2).

Elements of Different Healthcare Models in India:

1. *Beveridge model*: This model is characterized by government-funded and government-provided healthcare services. In India, the public healthcare system, which includes subcenters, primary health centers (PHCs), community health centers (CHCs), district hospitals, and tertiary medical colleges, is primarily funded through taxation. Services offered at these public facilities are either free or heavily subsidized.
2. *Bismarck model*: India has several social health insurance schemes that operate on the employer–employee contribution model, similar to the Bismarck system found in Germany. Examples include.

    (i) *Employees' State Insurance (ESI)*: provides healthcare benefits to employees in the organized sector and their families, funded through payroll contributions.
    (ii) *Central Government Health Scheme (CGHS)*: covers central government employees and pensioners, offering medical services at government-run dispensaries and empaneled private hospitals.
    (iii) *Ex-Servicemen Contributory Health Scheme (ECHS)*: ensures healthcare access for retired armed forces personnel and their dependents through a mix of government and private hospitals.
3. *National Health Insurance (NHI) Model*: This model combines tax-based financing with service provision from both public and private sectors. A key example in India is *Ayushman Bharat Pradhan Mantri Jan Arogya Yojana* (AB PM-JAY): The world's largest government-funded health insurance scheme, providing financial protection to over 500 million low-income individuals. AB PM-JAY covers secondary and tertiary care services in both public and private hospitals, ensuring broader healthcare access for economically disadvantaged populations.
4. *Out-of-Pocket (OOP) Model*: Despite the existence of public health services and insurance schemes, a large proportion of healthcare expenses in India continue to be borne directly by individuals. Out-of-pocket expenditure (OOPE) spending remains high, accounting for around 45.1% of current health expenditure (CHE) [28].

Most modern healthcare systems incorporate aspects of multiple models rather than strictly following one framework, and India is a prime example of this approach. The public health infrastructure follows the Beveridge model, employer-based schemes resemble the Bismarck model, government-funded insurance aligns with the National Health Insurance model, and high OOPE reflect gaps in coverage.

1.4 Strengthening Financing for Health System Goals: Linking to Sustainable Development Goals

The primary aim of any health system is to maximize the achievement of its objectives, considering the relative importance each country assigns to them. The United Nations (UN) Sustainable Development Goals (SDGs), endorsed by all member states in 2015 and reaffirmed in the 2023 UN General Assembly High-Level meetings, prioritize global peace and prosperity, with a fundamental commitment to eradicating poverty, hunger, and disease [29]. Among the 17 SDGs and 169 specific targets, SDG 3 focuses on ensuring health and well-being for all, emphasizing support for vulnerable populations and regions facing the highest disease burden [30]. This goal includes 13 specific targets, such as reducing maternal, neonatal, and under-five mortality rates, eliminating epidemics of infectious diseases like acquired immunodeficiency syndrome, tuberculosis, and malaria, and decreasing premature mortality from noncommunicable diseases (NCDs) [31].

However, progress toward these goals is shaped by various external factors, including a country's economic status, educational levels, and political environment. In terms of healthcare financing, many countries face challenges such as limited access to innovative medicines in public health facilities, insufficient financial resources, and a high OOP expenditure burden on individuals. Additionally, implementation challenges include political instability, inconsistent use of information technology and patient data systems, disparities in healthcare infrastructure and workforce distribution between urban and rural areas, and difficulties in training and retaining skilled healthcare professionals [32]. Therefore, to address these and as depicted by the central arrow in Fig. 1.1, it is crucial to understand how different health system functions interact and contribute to achieving broader health system goals.

While these goals are also shaped by external social determinants beyond the health sector, the focus here is on health financing policies and interventions. More specifically, the question is how the design and functioning of the health system impact the achievement of these goals, considering the influence of broader socioeconomic factors in a given country, and, conversely, how targeted reforms in health system operations can enhance goal achievement.

The Kutzin's framework offers a structured way to understand how health financing functions translate into broader health system goals, supporting the achievement of SDG 3. A key aspect of SDG 3, particularly Target 3.8, is the commitment to achieving UHC, ensuring that everyone can access the healthcare services they require, whenever and wherever necessary, without facing financial strain. Figure 1.3

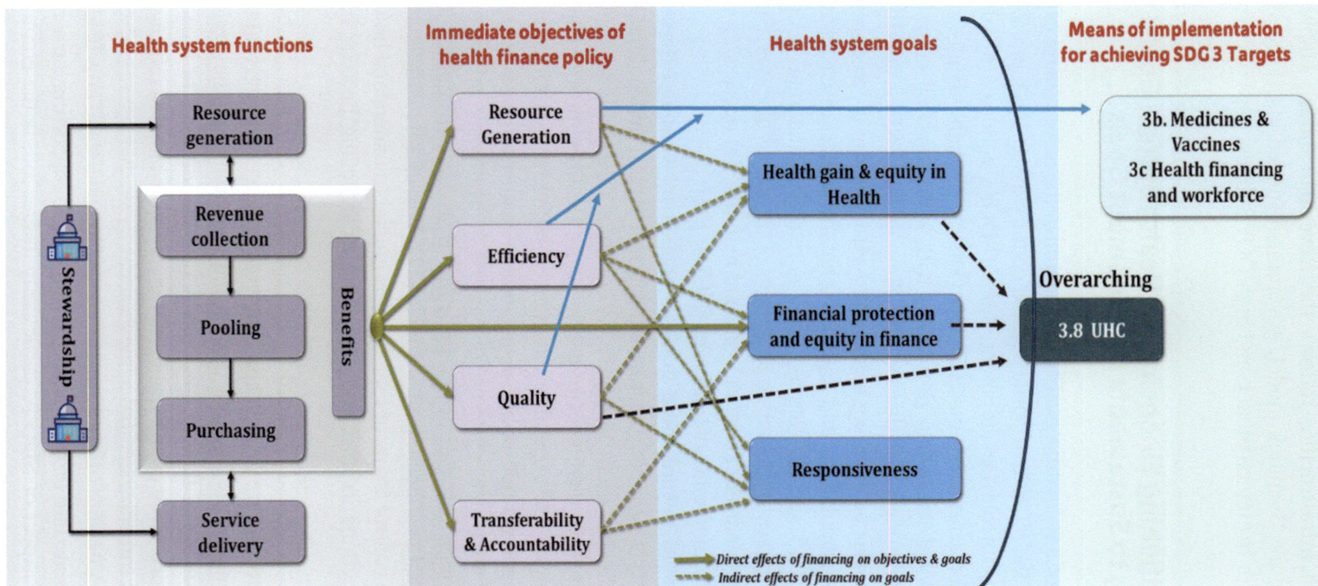

Fig. 1.3 Kutzin's framework for UHC: health system goals and health financing policy objectives. UHC Universal Health Coverage, SDG Sustainable Development Goals. (Author's adaptation based on Kutzin [34])

demonstrates that financing mechanisms—resource mobilization, pooling, and strategic purchasing—are not just technical processes; they fundamentally shape the efficiency, equity, and responsiveness of healthcare systems.

A well-functioning health financing system directly influences intermediate objectives, and these, in turn, determine whether the broader health system goals—health equity, financial protection, and responsiveness—can be realized. However, the impact of financing extends beyond direct linkages. The way funds are mobilized and allocated determines whether essential medicines and vaccines (SDG means of implementation 3b) are affordable and accessible, and whether health workforce investments (SDG means of implementation 3c) are sufficient to sustain quality care delivery.

This interplay underscores that financing is not an isolated function but a cross-cutting determinant of health system performance. Thus, strengthening health financing governance—through transparency, accountability, and efficiency—becomes central to achieving SDG 3.8 of UHC, which can be seen as an overarching one that supports the achievement of the other targets.

1.5 Where Does UHC Fit In?

The concept of UHC can be visualized using the "coverage cube," as depicted in the World Health Report 2010. This cube represents three critical dimensions of health coverage: population, service, and cost. The WHO cube (Fig. 1.4) highlights the

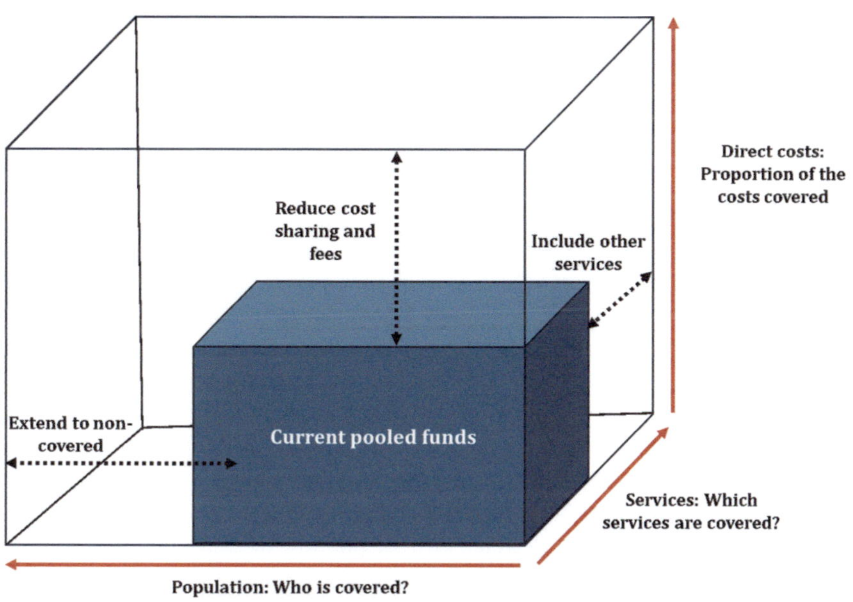

Fig. 1.4 The Universal Health Coverage (UHC) cube

difference between a country's current coverage position (represented by the blue cube) and the policy aim of UHC—the larger transparent cube. To effectively achieve UHC, all three factors—services, costs, and coverage—need to be effectively addressed by countries. In this figure, the population axis reflects the goal of ensuring that all individuals have access to both healthcare services and financial protection. The services axis focuses on ensuring that people receive the healthcare services they need and that these services are of high quality. Lastly, the cost axis relates to the financial burden on individuals and must be understood in the context of their ability to pay. These dimensions are directly linked to health financing policies and serve as key indicators for monitoring UHC progress.

The coverage cube serves both as a policy framework and a monitoring tool for UHC. Ex ante, it provides a basis for designing benefits packages, determining eligibility criteria, defining service entitlements, and establishing financial contributions required from individuals at the point of care. However, benefit package design alone is insufficient; it must be aligned with policies on revenue collection, risk pooling, and provider payment mechanisms to ensure that entitlements translate into real access to care [5].

Ex post, the cube serves as a monitoring framework, capturing data on service utilization, financial protection, and quality of care. This can be represented by the proportion of the cube that is filled with pooled funds. Refinements to this approach can incorporate additional metrics, such as OOP payments relative to individuals' ability to pay or service utilization in relation to healthcare needs [33]. However, UHC is not merely about expanding coverage to "fill the cube"; rather, it involves continuous improvements in health financing mechanisms to achieve better outcomes.

The 2010 World Health Report outlined three broad financing strategies for advancing UHC:

- Raise "more money for health."
- Get "strength in numbers," that is, increase the share of prepaid, pooled funding in the system while reducing barriers to redistribution of those funds.
- Get "more health for the money," that is, improve efficiency and equity in the use of health system resources.

To achieve UHC, several key health financing strategies can be implemented [34]. One key approach is increasing public health revenues by expanding compulsory prepaid funding through new revenue-raising mechanisms or allocating a greater share of government spending to health, ensuring broader access to healthcare services. Secondly, equitable resource distribution plays a vital role in reducing disparities by adjusting budget allocations based on population health needs rather than uniform distribution, thereby directing resources toward vulnerable groups. Thirdly, strengthening financial risk pooling by consolidating multiple risk pools enhances financial protection and promotes a fairer distribution of healthcare resources. Additionally, improving awareness of health benefits through the simplification and promotion of benefit packages helps individuals understand their entitlements, leading to better utilization of services and reduced financial uncertainty. Lastly, transitioning to performance-based provider payments, rather than volume-driven models, fosters efficiency, cost-effectiveness, and improved service quality by aligning provider incentives with desired health outcomes. Together, these strategies create a robust financing framework that supports the goals of UHC.

While these are just a few ways, they underscore how financing mechanisms—covering revenue collection, risk pooling, purchasing, and benefit design—play a fundamental role in advancing UHC. Furthermore, health financing systems, regardless of their labels (e.g., insurance-based or tax-funded), share these common functions. Moving toward UHC is a goal for all countries, and financing decisions must be guided by the broader objectives of financial protection, equitable access, and efficient service delivery rather than rigid adherence to specific system classifications.

This book explores the theoretical foundations and practical applications of health financing functions, equipping health insurance stakeholders with the knowledge needed to make informed decisions in their respective health system contexts.

Activity Box 1.1

1. Compare and Contrast Health System Models: Based on Table 1.1, create a table or a Venn diagram comparing and contrasting the Beveridge, Bismarck, and National Health Insurance (NHI) models across the features of "Source of Funding," "Mandatory/Voluntary," and "Healthcare Provider." Discuss which model you think best aligns with the goal of Universal Health Coverage (UHC) based on the chapter.
2. Analyze the Role of Health Financing Functions in Achieving UHC: Choose one of the three core health financing functions (revenue collection, pooling, or purchasing) and explain in detail how its effective implementation can contribute to achieving the three dimensions of Universal Health Coverage as represented by the "coverage cube": population, service, and cost. Cite specific examples or strategies mentioned in the chapter.
3. Evaluate India's Hybrid Healthcare System: The chapter describes India's healthcare system as a hybrid incorporating elements of various models. Identify at least two examples of how different models are manifested in India's healthcare financing and service delivery (e.g., AB PM-JAY, ESIS, public health facilities). Discuss the advantages and challenges of such a hybrid approach in the context of achieving Universal Health Coverage in India, drawing on information from the chapter.

References

1. Roemer M. National health systems of the world. Vol. 1: the countries. Oxford: Oxford University Press; 1991.
2. The World Health Report 2000. https://www.who.int/publications/i/item/924156198X. Accessed 29 Oct 2024.
3. Murray CJL, Frenk J. A framework for assessing the performance of health systems. Bull World Health Organ. 2000;78:717.
4. Darby C, et al. World Health Organization (WHO): strategy on measuring responsiveness. https://iris.who.int/handle/10665/68703. Accessed 2 Apr 2025.
5. Kutzin J. A descriptive framework for country-level analysis of health care financing arrangements. Health Policy (New York). 2001;56:171–204.
6. Berman PA. National health accounts in developing countries: appropriate methods and recent applications. Health Econ – Wiley Online Library. 1997. https://onlinelibrary.wiley.com/doi/10.1002/(SICI)1099-1050(199701)6:1%3C11::AID-HEC238%3E3.0.CO;2-7. Accessed 2 Apr 2025.
7. Schieber GJ. Innovations in health care financing. In: Proceedings of a World Bank conference, March 10–11, 1997. World Bank – discussion papers. https://ideas.repec.org/p/fth/wobadi/365.html. Accessed 2 Apr 2025.
8. Ensor T. Developing health insurance in transitional Asia. Soc Sci Med. 1999;48:871–9.
9. Contribution of mutual health organisations to financing, delivery and access to health care | International Labour Organization. https://www.ilo.org/publications/contribution-mutual-health-organisations-financing-delivery-and-access. Accessed 2 Apr 2025.
10. Bloom G, Shenglan T. Rural health prepayment schemes in China: Towards a more active role for government. Soc Sci Med. 1999;48:951–60.
11. Kaddar M, Galland B, editors. Prepayment of health care. Paris: International Children's Centre; 1997.
12. Haring R, Kickbusch I, Ganten D, et al. Handbook of global health: with 362 figures and 152 tables. Cham: Springer; 2021. p. 1–2917.
13. Kos M. Introduction to healthcare systems. In: The pharmacist guide to implementing pharmaceutical care. Cham: Springer International Publishing; 2019. p. 437–41.
14. Vienonen MA, Wlodarczyk WC. Health care reforms on the European scene: evolution, revolution or seesaw? World Health Stat Q. 1993;46:166–9.
15. Or Z, Cases C, Lisac M, et al. Are health problems systemic? Politics of access and choice under Beveridge and Bismarck systems. Health Econ Policy Law. 2010;5:269–93.
16. Gaeta M, Campanella F, Capasso L, et al. An overview of different health indicators used in the European Health Systems. J Prev Med Hyg. 2017;58:E114.
17. Health care reform: learning from other major health care systems | Princeton Public Health Review. https://pphr.princeton.edu/2017/12/02/unhealthy-health-care-a-cursory-overview-of-major-health-care-systems/. Accessed 27 Mar 2025.
18. Van Der Zee J, Kroneman MW. Bismarck or Beveridge: a beauty contest between dinosaurs. BMC Health Serv Res. 2007;7:1–11.
19. Grosios K, Gahan PB, Burbidge J. Overview of healthcare in the UK. EPMA J. 2010;1:529–34.
20. Antoun J, Phillips F, Johnson T. Post-Soviet transition: improving health services delivery and management. Mt Sinai J Med. 2011;78:436–48.
21. Sheiman I, Shishkin S, Shevsky V. The evolving Semashko model of primary health care: the case of the Russian Federation. Risk Manag Healthc Policy. 2018;11:209–20.
22. Sawicki P, Bastian H. German health care: a bit of Bismarck plus more science. BMJ. 2008;337:1142–5.
23. Braveman PA, Cubbin C, Egerter S, et al. Socioeconomic disparities in health in the United States: what the patterns tell us. Am J Public Health. 100:S186–96. Epub ahead of print 1 April 2010. https://doi.org/10.2105/AJPH.2009.166082.

24. National health systems: public service vs. insurance-based models | Hospital Association of South Africa. https://hasa.co.za/2011/09/17/health-reform-note-15-national-health-systems-public-service-vs-insurance-based-models/. Accessed 27 Mar 2025.
25. Grumbach K. National health insurance in America–can we practice with it? Can we continue to practice without it? West J Med. 1989;151:210–6.
26. Cheromcha K. The health care hand-book: a clear and concise guide to the United States health care system. J Med Libr Assoc. 2015;103:159.
27. Rosenbaum S. The Patient Protection and Affordable Care Act: implications for public health policy and practice. Public Health Rep. 2011;126:130.
28. National health accounts | National Health Systems Resource Centre. https://nhsrcindia.org/national-health-accounts-records. Accessed 25 Mar 2025.
29. The 17 Goals | Sustainable Development. https://sdgs.un.org/goals. Accessed 2 Apr 2025.
30. Goal 3 | Department of Economic and Social Affairs. https://sdgs.un.org/goals/goal3. Accessed 2 Apr 2025.
31. SDG Goal 3: good health and well-being – UNICEF DATA. https://data.unicef.org/sdgs/goal-3-good-health-wellbeing/. Accessed 2 Apr 2025.
32. Sustainable healthcare financing for SDG3 in ASEAN-6. https://www.lse.ac.uk/business/consulting/reports/sustainable-healthcare-financing-for-sdg3-in-asean-6. Accessed 2 Apr 2025.
33. Evans D, Saksena P, Elovainio R, et al. Measuring progress towards universal coverage. Geneva: World Health Organization; 2012.
34. Kutzin J. Health financing for universal coverage and health system performance: concepts and implications for policy. Bull World Health Organ. 2013;91:602.

Revenue Collection

2

Neha Purohit and V. R. Muraleedharan

Abstract

The health financing system encompasses three major functions: revenue collection, fund pooling, and healthcare purchasing. This chapter focuses specifically on the first function, "revenue collection," and examines the various options available to policymakers for raising funds and the implications of different revenue collection mechanisms. It provides a detailed examination of the sources and methods of revenue collection for healthcare in India, analyzing their relative advantages and disadvantages, and critically evaluating these methods in terms of sustainability and equity.

In India, healthcare financing is achieved through a combination of revenue collection methods, including taxation, social health insurance contributions, community-based health insurance, voluntary private health insurance, out-of-pocket payments, and external aid such as loans, grants, and donations. Each of these mechanisms differs in terms of timing, source, nature, and amount of contributions, and thus has distinct implications for equity, access to healthcare, cost containment, and fiscal sustainability.

Decisions regarding the optimal approach to healthcare financing should be made with careful consideration of how to raise resources in an equitable and efficient manner, taking into account the political, social, and economic context of the country. The chapter brings out the importance of a balanced revenue collection to ensure sustainable and equitable healthcare financing.

N. Purohit (✉)
Department of Community Medicine and School of Public Health, PGIMER, Chandigarh, India

V. R. Muraleedharan
Department of Humanities and Social Sciences, Indian Institute of Technology, Madras, Chennai, India

S. Prinja (ed.), *Healthcare Financing and Insurance*,
https://doi.org/10.1007/978-981-95-3513-2_2

Keywords

Healthcare revenue · Taxation · Social health insurance · Community-based health insurance · Out-of-pocket payments

Learning Objectives

After going through the chapter, you will be able to:

- Understand the sources of revenue for healthcare.
- Describe and distinguish between different means of revenue collection in India.
- Discuss the relative advantages and disadvantages, and implications of use of different revenue collection mechanisms.

Key Terms

- *Adverse selection*: A phenomenon where higher proportion of individuals, whose actual risk of falling ill is higher than the pooled population risk of illness known to the insurance company, get enrolled in a voluntary risk-pooling scheme.
- *Balance billing*: Additional fee levied by the provider to the consumer over and above the payment received from third-party payer.
- *Co-insurance*: Percentage of the total charge per service paid by the insured consumer upon utilization of care.
- *Compulsory payment*: People are mandated to pay irrespective of their utilization of health services.
- *Co-payment*: Flat fee per service paid by the insured consumer upon utilization of care.
- *Cream-skimming*: Enrolment of people with low risk of falling ill by the insurance company/managers to improve profitability.
- *Direct tax*: Any tax that is levied on the income or revenue of an individual or organization.
- *Deductible*: Predefined payment made by the insured individual before the insurance coverage starts to provide benefits of financial protection.
- *Economies of scale*: Economic advantages gained by increasing the coverage of population.
- *Efficiency*: Ability to maximize the output within the given resources, or minimize the resource use for the same level of output.
- *Equity*: Absence of unfair, avoidable or remediable differences among groups of people.
- *General tax*: Taxes collected without pre-decided allocation.
- *Horizontal equity*: Equal treatment of those with equal need. In the context of healthcare financing, it refers to the idea that people on same income take on same share of the responsibility for paying for healthcare.

- *Hypothecated/earmarked tax*: Taxes collected specifically to be used for a purpose, such as healthcare.
- *Income*: Sum of all forms of earnings, such as wages, pension, profits, interest payments, shares, rents, etc.
- *Indirect tax*: Any tax that is imposed on the consumption/ purchase of goods and services.
- *Informal payments*: Payments to providers, which fall outside the official payment. Channels or made for purchases that are mandated to be provided free by the healthcare system.
- *Monopsony purchasing power*: When one buyer faces little competition from other buyers for purchase of goods.
- *Moral hazard*: A situation wherein when one is protected from financial risk arising from utilisation of healthcare, there is likelihood of a higher consumption of healthcare than necessary or than one would have otherwise consumed.
- *Out-of-pocket payments*: Payments made by individuals/ households for provision of care after the occurrence of an illness.
- *Post-payment*: A healthcare payment made for seeking care once illness has occurred, usually in the form of out-of-pocket payment.
- *Pre-payment*: A healthcare payment made before falling ill, usually in the form of some insurance/risk pooling arrangement.
- *Progressive revenue collection method*: A fund-raising mechanism whereby higher-income groups contribute a higher percentage of their income to health payments than do lower-income groups.
- *Proportional revenue collection method*: A fund-raising mechanism, whereby everyone contributes the same percentage of income to funding the health system, irrespective of income level.
- *Regressive revenue collection method*: A fund-raising mechanism whereby lower-income groups contribute a higher percentage of their income to health payments than higher-income groups.
- *Revenue collection*: Consists of sources of funds for healthcare or from whom healthcare funding contributions are collected, how these funding contributions are structured, and who collects these funds.
- *Risk-rated premium*: Premium based on risk of falling ill/seeking care. This is also called actuarial-based premium.
- *User fee*: A sum of money (compulsory payment) that the consumer or user pays in lieu of provision of services.
- *Vertical equity*: Unequal treatment for those with unequal needs. In the context of healthcare financing, it refers to the idea that people with higher income contribute a greater share of healthcare payments.
- *Voluntary payment*: Payments made when choice to spend on healthcare is made by individuals themselves This is inclusive of voluntary private/ CBHI premium as well as OOPE.
- *Wage*: Monetary compensation of work paid on regular basis.

2.1 Introduction

The sustainability of healthcare systems is contingent on reliable access to financial resources to pay for securing human, capital, and consumable resources. Ensuring a stable flow of funds to the health sector is important to avoid disruptions in service delivery. As we are witnessing a rise in the elderly population and growing demands for chronic and long-term care, along with an increase in healthcare costs, there are constant discussions on how to raise funds for healthcare on a sustainable basis. Additionally, ensuring that the funds are collected in an equitable and efficient way is also an important consideration. Apparently, the questions that come to mind here are who actually pays for healthcare, what are the means of fund collection, who collects these funds, and ultimately what should be the "ideal" way to raise funds for healthcare.

Revenue collection has three specific aspects:

(a) Sources of funds for healthcare
(b) Mechanisms of funding contributions
(c) Collection of funds

Figure 2.1 illustrates the diversity in these three aspects of revenue collection. The source of funds is primarily the population, comprising households and firms/employers. The domestic funds are supplemented with external or donor funding. The funding mechanisms comprise taxation, social health insurance (SHI) contributions, prepaid insurance premiums, out-of-pocket (OOP) payments, and external aid in the form of loans, grants, and donations. The collection of funds may be facilitated by government, for-profit or not-for-profit entities, or may be used for direct payments to the providers.

The System of Health Accounts [2] differentiates revenue sources in the following terms:

(a) Compulsory versus voluntary
(b) Prepaid versus payment at the time-of-service use (post-payment)
(c) Domestic versus foreign

The category of "compulsory" implies that the people are required to pay irrespective of whether or not and the level of utilization of healthcare. Thus, compulsory sources are prepaid and include taxation or social insurance contributions (Fig. 2.2). On the other hand, the "voluntary" sources imply that the choice to spend on healthcare is made by individuals themselves. Such payments may be either prepaid (premium payment for commercial or community-based health insurance schemes) or paid at the time-of-service use as out-of-pocket expenditure (OOPE). The latter includes payments for direct purchase of services, spending as a part of formal cost-sharing required under specific health financing mechanisms, informal

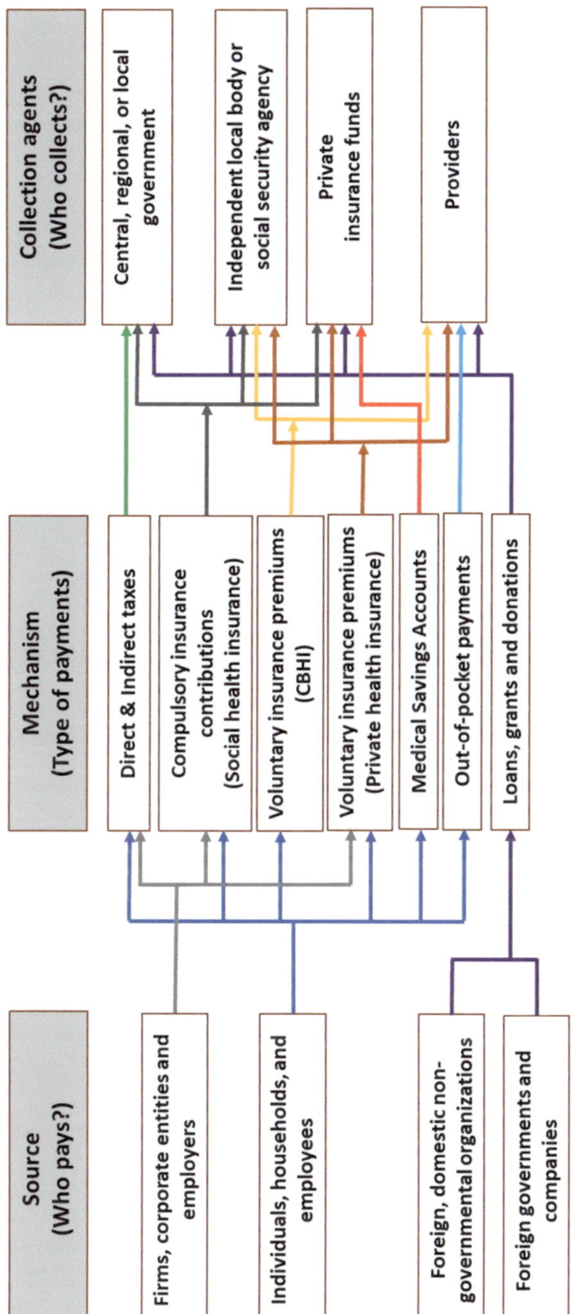

Fig. 2.1 Sources, contribution mechanisms, and revenue collection agents for healthcare in the Indian context. CBHI community-based health insurance. (Adapted from Mossialos et al. [1]). Illustration of payment methods for healthcare in India: sources, contribution mechanisms, and revenue collection agents

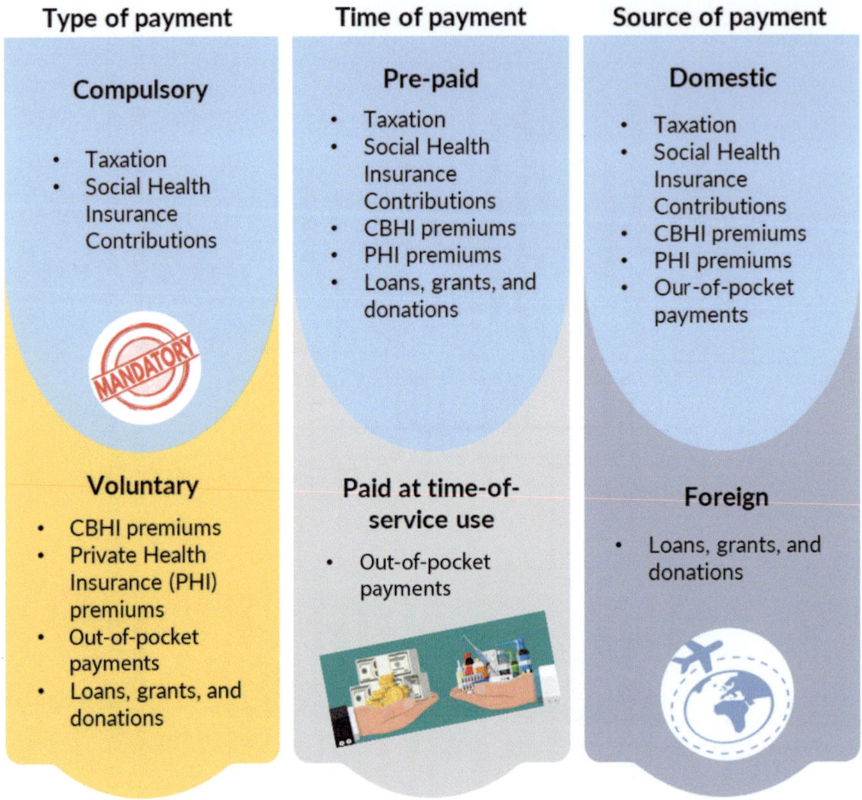

Fig. 2.2 Classification of means of revenue collection (System of Health Accounts). CBHI community-based health insurance, PHI private health insurance. Illustration depicting categorization of revenue collection methods for healthcare based on type, time, and payment source

payments to health workers, or for services as diagnostics or medicines that are either not covered under the benefit packages and/or were not available at the time-of-service use [3, 4].

2.2 Means of Revenue Collection

The mobilization of funds for healthcare in India is done through a mix of the following revenue collection methods. These include

(a) Taxation
(b) Social health insurance contributions
(c) Community-based health insurance premiums
(d) Voluntary private health insurance premium
(e) Medical saving accounts

(f) Out-of-pocket payments
(g) External aid: loans, grants, and donations

Now this chapter will take you through each revenue collection mechanism in detail.

2.3 Taxation

Taxation is a major source of revenue collection and fund generation to finance public health facilities and programs in India, or for the purchase of healthcare services from the private sector by the government. It is important to understand that taxation is diverse in nature and can manifest in various forms, each of which can influence the overall efficiency and equity differently. Taxes can be classified on basis of sources (direct or indirect), levels of tax collection (national or subnational), and allocation of the collected revenue (general or earmarked to health) [1, 4].

2.3.1 What Are Direct and Indirect Taxes?

Any tax that is levied on the income or revenue of an individual or organization is a direct tax, whereas tax that is imposed on the purchase of goods and services is called an indirect tax. Typically, in an Indian context, income tax, property tax, and corporate tax are direct taxes, whereas the goods and services tax (GST), custom duty, and service tax are classified as indirect taxes [5].

Consequently, direct taxes are progressive in nature since they are proportional to the income, that is, tax rates are higher for populations with higher incomes, and lower/exempted for those with lower incomes. It is therefore considered an equitable mechanism of revenue collection with a comprehensive population coverage. On the contrary, indirect taxes on transactions and commodities including GST, and import and export taxes, are regressive since these are fixed amounts, regardless of income level. For example, if there is 5% GST on essential items, all individuals are required to pay the same for a similar quantity of consumption, irrespective of their paying capacity. Therefore, this form of taxation is relatively regressive compared to direct taxation.

However, indirect taxation is a highly visible and easily identifiable source with a low scope of evasion. It forms an important source of taxes, especially in a large informal economy as India (with 88% of workforce in informal sector). Moreover, higher rates of taxation on harmful goods, as tobacco and alcohol, may discourage consumption and promote health. As per the World Bank, a 50% rise in prices of such goods through excise taxation could increase the tax–GDP ratio by 0.7% points in countries as India. An appropriate mix of direct (income based) and indirect (consumption based) taxes should be determined to balance the trade-offs between administrative complexity for ensuring compliance and equity [6] (Box 2.1).

Box 2.1 You May Have Understood that Direct Taxes Are Progressive; However, Indirect Taxes in General Are Regressive

But what if higher GST is levied on luxury goods that are likely to be consumed by rich and very low or no charge on the essential goods that would be consumed by the rich and poor alike? What will happen to its progressivity if rich pay more, while poor contribute less to indirect taxes?

Yes! The degree of progressivity of indirect taxes is likely to increase this way. This is how countries that use the indirect taxes as a major mechanism of financing healthcare services can potentially make an indirect tax-driven health system appear equally to a direct tax.

2.3.2 What Are National and Local Taxes?

The second classification of taxes is according to level of collection (national or local level). There are several arguments in favor of both national- and local-level tax collection. Collection of taxes at the national level has the advantage of economies of scale and hence relatively lower administrative costs. This means that when the government collects taxes for the entire country, it can spread the associated fixed costs over a larger tax base, making the process more efficient and less expensive per unit of tax collected. However, national taxation involves the division of revenues between health and other public departments and therefore there are trade-offs with other programs or debt reduction. In this regard, taxation at the local level is likely to improve accountability, responsiveness to local needs, and separates health from competing national priorities.

An aspect of the federal structure of India presents an important contextual factor that is relevant in this discussion. Different states differ in their level of wealth, and this has an impact on the level of tax revenue that they can generate. The absolute and per-capita amount of tax that a state like Bihar, Orissa, or Jharkhand can raise is perhaps less than the tax that a wealthier state like Haryana or some of the southern states may be able to raise [7]. On the other hand, the fiscal needs may follow the opposite pattern, with higher requirements in poor states that have a higher, illness rate, morbidity rate, or low availability of healthcare services.

Here, one should understand that there is a difference between "tax collection and utilization of funds at the local level," and "tax collection at the local level followed by revenue pooling at the national level and local re-distribution of tax revenues." The first case is likely to increase inequities across different regions due to differential capacity to generate revenue. However, the latter case though also starts with a regional revenue collection but is followed by pooling of funds at the national level, and redistribution of funds across the states/regions in an equitable manner. A clear example of this is the higher per-capita allocation formula for National Health Mission grants for the Empowered Action Group (EAG) and northeastern states. Hence, having a local tax collection (and subsequent local pooling) may score poorly on an equity scale compared to the national-level revenue generation and pooling. Therefore, pooling is an enabling function to allocate the accumulated funds fairly. You will learn in detail about the concept of pooling in the next chapter.

2.3.3 What Are General and Hypothecated Taxes?

The third classification is on the basis of the allocation of the collected tax. General tax refers to a contribution that is levied without any specified earmarked purpose at the time of revenue collection. The fund collected is pooled collectively and then allocated to different sectors depending on the need and other factors. However, the actual allocation to healthcare is subject to negotiations among and persuasive power of relative financial positions and importance accorded to healthcare by different ministries. This may politicize the process and lead to trade-offs between healthcare and other sectors, reliant on public expenditure. Hypothecated or earmarked taxes are reserved to be specifically used for a particular purpose, such as education, healthcare, or any other functions. These can be either direct or indirect taxes. The classical examples of hypothecated taxes in India are the *Swachh Bharat* tax and education cess. The education cess on taxable income is used to fund the *Sarva Shiksha* campaign, whereas the *Swachh Bharat* tax on taxable services provides revenues for the *Swachh Bharat Abhiyan* implemented by the Ministry of *Jal Shakti* (erstwhile known as the Ministry of Drinking Water and Sanitation).

The advantages of earmarked tax are that there is a greater acceptance among people to pay earmarked taxes because they see a direct utilization of money for a particular purpose, and such taxes are less susceptible to political manipulation [8]. This type of tax also makes funding for healthcare more responsive and transparent. Earmarked taxes are generally a supplementary source of revenue collection. However, if they are the single largest source of revenue, the revenue collection for healthcare would be impacted by fluctuations in the overall economic growth. Other disadvantage of earmarked taxes is that they impose rigidity on the budgetary process. Specifically, expenditure becomes constrained by the revenue generated rather than being guided by policy decisions, which can limit flexibility and responsiveness in addressing evolving needs. Additionally, it is anticipated that splitting healthcare from other sectors of public expenditure may lead to demands by other departments to have earmarked budgets, thus leading to fragmented financing. Figure 2.3 lists the different types of taxes and their relative advantages and disadvantages.

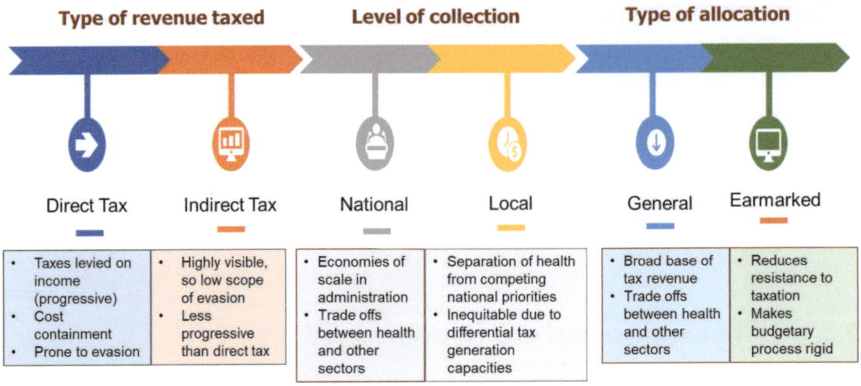

Fig. 2.3 Advantages and disadvantages of different types of taxes. Illustration depicting the pros and cons of different types of tax collection methods

2.3.4 Assessing Revenue Generation Capacity by Taxation in India

The tax-to-GDP ratio provides an account of country's tax revenue relative to the size of its economy and has been used to measure the tax-generating capacity of a nation. It has remained steady at 10–11% in the last 10 years in India and hovers below the minimum threshold of 15% set by the International Monetary Fund (IMF) and Organization for Economic Co-operation and Development's (OECD) average of 34% [9]. This is suggestive of low tax collection capacity, which has implications for the allocation of planned expenditure. Other indicators used to assess the government's capacity to raise and spend adequate revenue to fund healthcare are presented in Box 2.2.

The proportion of direct taxes in India has increased steadily; however, there are challenges in the accumulation of direct taxes. According to government's data, in 2018–19, approximately 40% of individuals who filed for tax had zero tax liability, and some amount of tax was paid by 6% of labor workforce. Additionally, the corporate tax has been lowered over the years to keep it competitive internationally, thus impacting the overall revenue collected [10]. But this policy has likely increased the compliance rate to taxation. The constraints to expand tax collection in India include the size of informal economy, levels of income inequality that restrict the number of people who can afford to pay taxes, resource constraints at tax agencies, and administrative challenges to ensure compliance [11, 12]. However, the share of indirect taxes to total tax collection has varied with time and constituted 53% of the total taxes collected in 2022–23 [9].

Box 2.2 Key Fiscal Indicators (Does the Government Have Revenues for Adequate Health Spending?)

1. Government expenditure to GDP ratio: Government spending (current and capital expenses) relative to GDP. This is also called as fiscal capacity/fiscal envelope.
2. Tax to GDP ratio: Capacity to generate taxes relative to GDP. If tax to GDP ratio is high, it would indicate higher availability of tax funds for allocation to healthcare.
3. Budget deficit: Condition when spending exceeds the revenue generation within a specific timeframe. In such a case of reduced economic growth, the revenue for health is likely to be lower.
4. Debt to GDP ratio: Total public debt under which government is functioning relative to GDP. It indicates the size of country's debt relative to its economic output. A higher debt to GDP ratio could lead to low allocation of funds to healthcare.

GDP gross domestic product

Activity Box 2.1

Consider:

Case A: Government raises ₹20 million from direct taxes and ₹15 million from indirect taxes. Government allocates 3% of direct taxes and 6% of indirect taxes for healthcare.

Case B: Government raises ₹15 million from direct taxes and ₹20 million from indirect taxes. Government allocates 6% of direct taxes and 3% of indirect taxes for healthcare.

1. In which case, the means of overall revenue generation is more progressive?
2. In which case, the means of revenue generation for healthcare is more progressive?
3. Name the direct and indirect taxes that may have been levied on the population.
4. Consider that there are certain exemptions on direct taxes (on mortgage interest payments, insurance premiums). Will progressivity differ?
5. Consider that everyone above 60 years is exempted from direct taxes. To what extent the revenue generation be impacted? Will the equity be affected in such a case?

Cues to Answers

1 & 2. Remember in general, direct tax is more progressive than indirect tax.

4. Think that who are likely to pay mortgage interest payments, insurance premiums—rich or poor. What is likely to happen if proportion of their income is exempted from tax?

5. Think about the relative income and contribution of elderly to the direct tax.

2.4 Social Health Insurance Contributions

The second type of source of revenue for healthcare is the social health insurance contribution. Social health insurance (SHI) schemes traditionally include the following characteristics:

1. Compulsory membership, limited to those employed in the formal sector
2. Earmarked deduction as prepayment contribution, usually as a fixed proportion of their "wages"
3. Cross-subsidization through other additional government financing
4. Contributions managed by quasi-independent public body that acts as a third-party payer for healthcare

To fully understand the difference in revenue collection mechanisms, it is crucial to understand the difference between "income" and "wage":

- *Wage* refers to monetary compensation received regularly for work performed. SHI contributions are wage-based in nature.
- *Income* offers a more comprehensive view of an individual's financial situation. It encompasses all forms of earnings, including wages, pensions, profits, interest payments, dividends, and rental income. Taxation is based on income/wealth.

SHI contributions are also called payroll taxes and are earmarked in nature. The SHI schemes in the Indian context are Employees' State Insurance Scheme (ESIS) and Central Government Health Scheme (CGHS). ESIS and CGHS provide insurance cover to 133 million and 3.4 million individuals, respectively, across India. Under the ESIS, all employees in establishments with more than 10 employees, earning up to ₹21,000 per month, are enrolled in the scheme, along with their dependents. Employee contributions to the scheme amount to 0.75% of their wages, while employers contribute an additional 3.25% [13]. In a similar vein, the CGHS extends coverage to central government employees, pensioners, members of parliament, governors, and accredited journalists (individuals who have been registered by the

Press Information Bureau as professional journalists as professional journalists or authorized government agencies) and their dependents. Under this scheme, the family is the unit of enrolment, and employees' contribution ranges from ₹50 to ₹500 per month based on salary, while the remaining bulk of spending is contributed by the government [14].

The financial flows in case of SHIs are transparent, thus the contributions under this mechanism of revenue collection are more acceptable to the public. Secondly, the revenue depends on mandatory contributions at predetermined rates, and therefore, the collection mechanism is protected from any manipulation or diversion of funds. Thirdly, greater transparency is built in through separate structures for collecting and managing funds [1, 15].

There are certain limitations of the SHI contributions (Fig. 2.4). It is important to recognize that SHI depends on a relatively narrow revenue base, primarily derived from the contributions of formally employed individuals. As a result, it may not generate adequate revenue in countries with low formal labor force participation, such as India.

Additionally, despite the wage slab system used to determine contributions, SHI contributions generally exhibit less equity compared to taxation. Unlike income-based taxation, wage-related contributions under SHI do not account for an individual's or household's wealth accumulated through savings or investments. Consequently, as the ratio of income from capital to earned income increases, wage-related contributions under SHI become progressively less equitable. Moreover, the extent of the ability of pooling the funds is limited due to the narrow revenue base and hence limits the extent of equity that can be achieved relative to taxation. This will be elaborated in the next chapter.

Fig. 2.4 Strengths and weaknesses of social health insurance contributions. SHI social health insurance. Illustration of the evaluation of strengths and weaknesses in the SHI funding model

Activity Box 2.2

Now please try out this activity to check if you can write the implications of each feature of SHI contributions. The boxes on the left side list the features of SHI contributions, and the boxes on the right side should be completed to fill in what you feel may be the impact of the features.

Features of SHI contributions		Implications
Compulsory payment	→	1.
Limited to formal sector employees	→	2.
Earmarked deduction as prepayment	→	3.
Wage based contributions	→	4.
Cross-subsidization	→	5.
Separate stuctures for collecting and managing funds	→	6.

Cues to Answers

1. Think of the resource pool.
2. Think in terms of implications for the Indian settings.
3. Think in terms of hesitancy of eligible population to contribute to the scheme, and if the resource mechanism can be influenced by political or other factors.
4. Remember the difference between income and wage, and their implications.
5. Think what kind of population contribute to the scheme, and what kind of people are eligible for benefits (pensioners, families of the employed, etc.).
6. Think in terms of transparency.

2.5 Community-Based Health Insurance Premiums

Community-based health insurance (CBHI) schemes primarily involve voluntary prepayments among group of people with common characteristics (geography, occupation, etc.). Under such schemes, a group of people or households come together and agree to contribute at a commonly agreed rate at which all would be contribute, and then that cumulative amount would be used to pay for the healthcare needs of all people. Membership premiums are often a flat rate and are not dependent on the risk of falling ill. The examples of CBHIs in India include the *Seva* scheme in Gujarat and Accord scheme in southern India. Interestingly, such schemes are geographically placed around the coastal belt of India in the southern, western, and eastern regions. These schemes are also called "health insurance for informal sector" or "micro-health insurance schemes" or "mutual health organizations" [16, 17].

The schemes are diverse in terms of amount of premium, and health benefits covered; however, as community is involved in the set-up and management of such schemes, they are likely to be more transparent and enhance community empowerment. Additionally, such schemes have been shown to have a positive impact on utilization rates, and to some extent, fill the risk protection gaps in countries with large workforce employed in informal sector [15, 16]. One of the biggest advantages of using CBHI is that it is kind of a prepayment mechanism and hence separates time of payment from the time-of-service use. This is important especially to rural households due to their seasonal variations of revenue and expenditures in the Indian context. Figure 2.5 depicts the advantages and disadvantages of such schemes.

Two factors, that is, low enrolment rates due to voluntary nature, and low community-rated premiums affect the financial sustainability of CBHI schemes. As a result, they tend to often depend on some kind of philanthropic aid or external funding to support the overall operations of the insurance [17]. The reasons for low enrolment rates have been affordability, perceived poor quality of health services, lack of health-seeking behavior, cultural beliefs, and perceived no benefits in

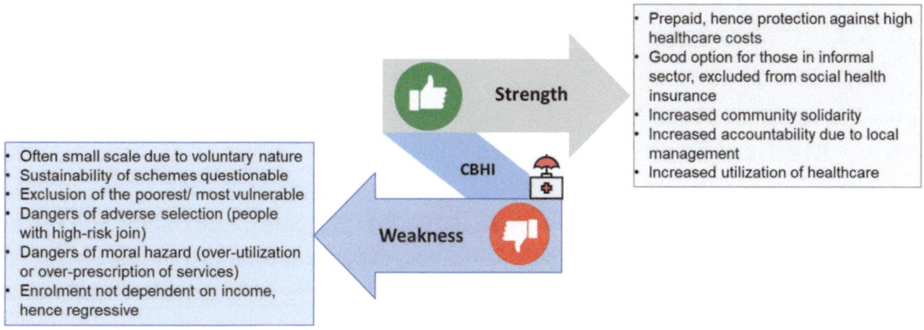

Fig. 2.5 Strengths and weaknesses of community-based health insurance premiums. Visual representation of the strengths and weaknesses of community-based health insurance premiums

joining the schemes. Additionally, studies have reported management issues in functioning of schemes, thereby creating distrust in the community. From a systems' perspective, CBHIs have limitations as individuals who cannot afford to pay premiums are often excluded from enrollment. Thus, the economically disadvantaged and vulnerable population groups often remain excluded. Furthermore, community-rated premiums are often regressive as they are not adjusted based on household income. The limited scale of CBHIs makes it challenging to achieve the goal of equitable resource mobilization. Additionally, the issue of "adverse selection" (more people with high risk may enroll at the same flat rate) may occur, thus impacting the sustainability of such schemes. Moreover, "moral hazard" is another problem that is reportedly faced while implementing CBHIs, that is, there is over-utilization of health services because people feel that insurance pays for services or over-prescription of services by the providers.

Two countries—Ghana and Rwanda—linked their CBHIs with their national scheme, thus expanding the pool of resources, and at the same time, retaining strong local management [18]. Therefore, in countries with established CBHI schemes, the government could benefit from its positive outcomes of local governance and public acceptance of prepaid payment models.

Activity Box 2.3

According to what you have learnt till now, consider that there is a national health insurance scheme, which provides mandatory free treatment to poor population of the country without any financial contributions from the eligible population. What do you think could be the source of revenue for the scheme?

Cues to Answers

- Think if the scheme is based on contributions from wages.
- Think if the scheme involves voluntary prepayments among the group of people.
- Think if the scheme could use tax revenue for financing.

2.6 Medical Saving Accounts

Medical Savings Accounts (MSAs) are individual accounts designated solely for the purpose of saving for future health-related expenses, thus providing a mechanism for managing healthcare costs over an individual's lifetime. These accounts enable individuals to allocate funds during periods of good health, which can be used during times of illness. MSAs have been implemented in various countries, including Singapore, the United States, China, South Africa, and Hong Kong [19]. However, these are not a source of revenue collection for healthcare in India.

The mechanics of MSAs differs significantly across nations. For instance, in Singapore, participation is mandatory for all citizens, while in the United States, the MSA program is voluntary and primarily available to self-employed individuals or employees of small businesses. To encourage participation in voluntary schemes, governments often offer additional incentives, such as tax exemptions. Typically, MSAs alone do not provide sufficient funds to cover the high costs of serious medical conditions. Consequently, these accounts are usually supplemented with additional insurance plans that offer coverage for catastrophic health events, albeit with high deductible payments that must be paid before insurance benefits become available.

Advocates of MSAs argue that they promote individual's responsibility in healthcare spending, so as to maximize the money left unspent in the account that can be carried over for future healthcare needs. However, critics contend that MSAs may lead individuals to defer medical care until hospitalization becomes unavoidable. Nonetheless, MSAs are considered to incur lower administrative costs compared to traditional third-party reimbursement systems in comprehensive health insurance models.

From an equity perspective, MSAs are often seen as suboptimal. These accounts tend to attract healthier, younger, wealthier, and better-educated individuals as they are more likely to have the financial means to contribute to the accounts and benefit from associated tax exemptions. In countries like the United States and Singapore, tax subsidies on MSAs tend to disproportionately benefit higher-income individuals, especially when exemptions are granted based on marginal tax rates, which offer greater relief to those in higher tax brackets. Additionally, individuals who do not pay taxes—such as the unemployed, nonworking dependents, and those with incomes below the tax threshold—do not benefit from these tax exemptions [1, 20].

Furthermore, because MSAs are individual accounts, they limit risk-sharing between the healthy and the sick, as well as between wealthier and poorer individuals. Those who experience long-term unemployment or suffer from chronic illnesses may struggle to accumulate sufficient savings in their MSAs, and the high deductibles may discourage low-income individuals from seeking necessary medical care. As a result, MSAs are often regarded as a relatively regressive method of revenue collection compared to other methods, such as taxation, SHI, and CBHI.

2.7 Private Health Insurance Premiums

The fourth type of source of revenue for healthcare is the private health insurance (PHI), which rests on the collection of voluntary and prepaid premiums. The premium under PHIs is not dependent on the ability to pay in terms of income or wage, but is related to the risk of falling ill, determined based on a range of factors, such as age, gender, occupation, family disease history, and past healthcare utilization. Therefore, such premium is called risk-rated premium and is actuarially determined. The formula to calculate premium is

$$\text{PR} = pL + l$$

where PR = premium, p = probability of falling ill, L = expected cost of treatment or the loss of income that you will have when you fall ill, and l = loading/administrative costs.

For example, if you have a 5% risk of falling ill (p), and there is a treatment expenditure (L) of ₹10,000. Additionally, there is a certain administrative cost to running the insurance, which are required to be recovered, so that insurance can sustain itself. Suppose l = ₹200. Therefore, premium is

PR= (0.05*10000) + 200 = ₹ 700

Activity Box 2.4
Consider probability of falling ill is 10% and expected cost of treatment is ₹50,000. Administrative cost is ₹500. Calculate the premium.

As you would have realized that revenue collection in this type of means has no relationship with the ability to pay but is dependent only on the risk of falling ill. In such a case, health insurers usually adopt risk rating system and charge higher premiums to individuals who have a greater probability of using care. The poor (due to poor social determinants and a higher risk of falling ill), elderly, and under-5-year-old children have a higher probability of them falling ill, and as a result, the premium would be higher if you are a poor person, an elderly person, or a child. Revenue collection methods, as PHI, that do not safeguard vulnerable populations (unemployed, dependent population, individuals with low income) tend to make the system regressive as these groups are typically economically disadvantaged. Moreover, private insurance may even exclude certain categories of individuals, with a high probability of falling ill. This phenomenon is called cream-skimming, by which insurers promote participation of individuals with low risk and discourage or refuse enrolment of individuals with a high risk of having disease [21]. These attributes of inclusion of low-risk individuals in PHI pose serious equity problems. The next chapter discusses more in detail the failure of voluntary private insurance in health.

The administration for delivering PHIs tends to be costlier due to the requirements to assess risk, set premiums, design complex benefit packages, and additional spending on advertising and marketing. It has been found that administrative costs range from 6% to 39% in middle-income countries and from 20% to 65% of the total costs in low-income countries, thus making it unaffordable for low-income groups.

Activity Box 2.5

Please attempt the questions and see if you have understood common concepts in private health insurance, which are likely to influence equity, and cost containment.

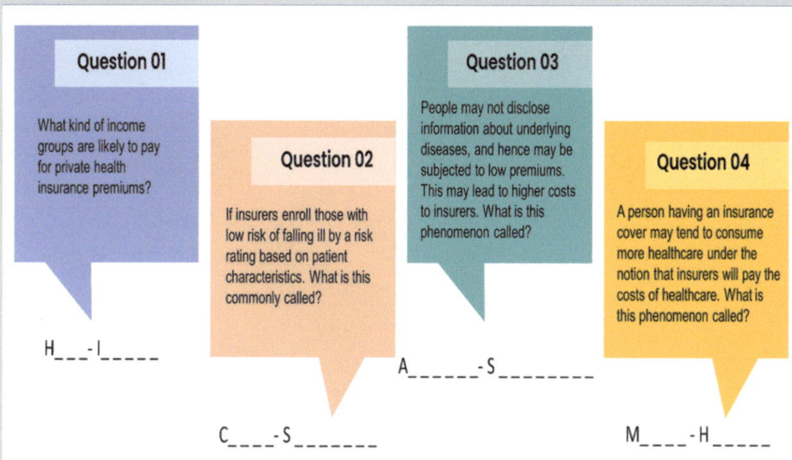

2.8 Out-of-Pocket Payments

Out-of-pocket (OOP) payments include all types of costs paid directly by the consumers at the time of accessing healthcare. Direct OOP payments from individuals/households occur in the absence of insurance cover or use of noninsured services or for insured services as diagnostics or medicines that were not available at the time-of-service use at the empaneled health facilities. In the Indian context, this is a significant source to fund healthcare. These payments are proportional to the use of care and are not related to income, therefore are regressive in nature. There are some arguments in favor of such payments as a means of revenue, under the belief that population may have a poor willingness to pay for insurance premiums ex ante in low-and-middle-income countries and because of existing informal payment arrangements, which are worse than formal payment mechanisms.

OOP payments can also occur on face of demand-side cost-sharing arrangements for services that are present in the benefit package but are not entirely covered (Fig. 2.6). Examples of formal cost-sharing include user fees, co-payments, co-insurance, deductibles, balance billing. Co-payments is a flat fee per service, while

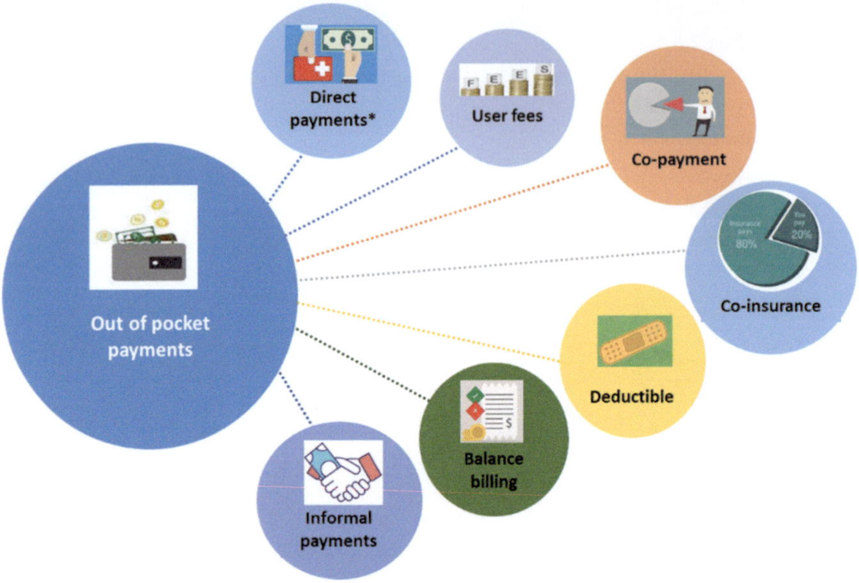

Fig. 2.6 Types of out-of-pocket payments. Visual representation of the types of out-of-pocket payment mechanisms in healthcare. *Direct payments are the payments that are made by the population in the absence of insurance cover or use of noninsured services or for insured services as diagnostics or medicines that were not available at the time-of-service use at the empaneled health facilities. These are exclusive from formal cost-sharing mechanisms and informal payments

co-insurance is a percentage of the total charge per service. Deductible implies a predefined payment before the insurance coverage starts. Balance billing refers to the practice where a healthcare provider bills a patient for the difference between the amount charged for a service and the amount covered by the patient's insurance in the form of provider payment or reimbursement rate [1]. Balance billing may occur both under formal contractual agreements and informally, where the provider invoices the patient for services that are otherwise included under the insurance coverage.

Activity Box 2.6

Instance I. Consider that you have an insurance cover but before the insurance cover starts you are required to pay ₹3000. Now, when you access a service costing ₹50,000, which is covered under your insurance, you pay ₹2000, and 10% of the treatment charges, i.e., ₹5000. After the treatment, you are required to pay ₹1000 as out-of-pocket for a diagnostic test, which is not covered under your insurance. Which of these is deductible, co-insurance, co-payment, and balance billing?

₹3000............................
₹2000............................
₹5000............................
₹1000............................

Instance II. Consider that you do not have an insurance cover. You visit a government facility and are required to pay ₹10 as a registration fee. Upon consultation, the doctor asks you for a diagnostic test, which is available in the government facility, but there is a long waiting time to access the test. You pay ₹500 to the radiographer for an early appointment and the radiographer conducts the test. You then show the test report to the doctor, and he prescribes you five medicines, out of which three were available free of cost in the facility. However, you spend ₹1000 for two medicines. Which of these payments is user fee, direct OOP, and informal payments?

₹10.................................
₹500................................
₹1000..............................

Existing literature reveals an inverse relationship between healthcare utilization and cost-sharing; specifically, increased cost-sharing is associated with a decline in healthcare utilization. For instance, studies have shown that patient visits to the physicians decreased by 20–30% in response to co-payments, and pharmaceutical prescriptions were reduced by 30% due to cost-sharing [1]. While this might suggest that cost-sharing could limit excessive service use and promote efficiency, evidence indicates that cost-sharing reduces both appropriate and inappropriate demand for services, thereby failing to enhance allocative efficiency. Furthermore, reductions in service utilization are disproportionately concentrated among low-income individuals, leading to higher unmet needs and poorer health outcomes in these groups [22].

While it may be expected that reduced utilization would result in cost containment in healthcare, this assumption is not always valid. Providers often respond by increasing the prescription of services that do not require cost-sharing, thereby limiting cost containment. Nonetheless, the primary objective of cost-sharing is not to diminish healthcare demand but to generate additional funds for healthcare financing (Fig. 2.7). While cost-sharing mechanisms, such as user fees, do contribute supplementary revenue, their overall share in total healthcare revenue remains relatively small.

Strengths	Weaknesses
• Additional source of funding healthcare • Effective means to encourage judicious use of healthcare • Increases choice of providers	• Leads to unmet need for healthcare • Disproportionately affects the poor • Most regressive among all means of revenue collection • Poor healthcare outcomes • Cost of healthcare usually higher, due to utilization of services in advanced stage of diseases

Fig. 2.7 Strengths and weaknesses of out-of-pocket payments. Visual representation of the strengths and weaknesses of healthcare revenue collection through out-of-pocket payments

To mitigate the adverse effects of demand-side cost-sharing on vulnerable populations, healthcare systems typically provide complete or partial exemptions for children, the elderly, and individuals from low-income households. Such exemptions are likely to reduce the regressivity of payments. However, cost-sharing mechanisms require substantial administrative capacity for implementation and are associated with increased administrative costs.

Informal payments also fall within the scope of direct cost-sharing mechanisms. These payments, which occur outside official payment channels or for services that are supposed to be provided free by the healthcare system, are directed to individual providers rather than the healthcare system as a whole. Unlike formal charges, informal payments are made directly to providers, often under the table, and remain unaudited and unreported due to their covert nature. Such payments tend to restrict access for individuals with limited financial means and can render essential services unaffordable. The lack of transparency surrounding informal payments complicates efforts to utilize this revenue and renders it an unacceptable method for financing healthcare.

2.9 Loans, Grants, and Donations

Donations and grants from donor agencies, along with loans from international financial institutions, constitute another supplementary revenue generation mechanism for healthcare. Numerous examples demonstrate how such development aid has expanded the revenue base and enhanced access to healthcare services. For instance, financial support from the Global Alliance for Vaccines and Immunization (GAVI) and other development assistance channels has significantly increased vaccination coverage across approximately 120 countries [23]. Similarly, the Global Fund to Fight AIDS, Tuberculosis, and Malaria (GFATM) has allocated substantial financial resources to various nations, contributing to an estimated 65 million lives saved since its inception [24].

In some low-income countries, this mechanism can account for up to 25% of total healthcare revenue. However, in India, it represents a much smaller share, contributing less than 1% of the country's total healthcare revenue. A significant drawback of heavy reliance on external aid is its vulnerability to shifts in donor priorities, which can adversely affect long-term financial sustainability. Donor transitions have been linked to a negative impact in terms of reduced resources for healthcare, leading to disruption in healthcare services [25].

Another limitation of over-reliance on loans, grants, and donations is that such aid is often earmarked for specific diseases and interventions that may not align with a country's national health needs, potentially resulting in expenditures on programs that do not address the most pressing health priorities. This misalignment can result in expenditures on programs that fail to address critical health priorities. Moreover, external funding in the form of loans imposes a future repayment burden on the nation, creating additional financial obligations.

However, a notable advantage of external funding is the direct link it establishes between revenue and expected outcomes. This fosters accountability by integrating monitoring and evaluation systems, ensuring that funds are used effectively to achieve health-related goals.

2.10 Critical Analysis of the Different Means of Revenue Collection

Different means of revenue collection have different implications in terms of

1. Population coverage: How much of the population is contributing to the revenue collection mechanism?
2. Vertical equity/progressivity: How does the revenue collection vary with individual's income?
3. Horizontal equity: Does the revenue collection vary in population with the same income level?
4. Access to healthcare: How does the funding system affect access to healthcare and choice of providers?
5. Cost containment: How do revenue generation mechanisms affect the overall costs of healthcare?
6. Transparency: How transparent are the revenue collection mechanisms?
7. Fiscal sustainability: How sustainable are the revenue generation mechanisms?
8. Efficiency: How efficient are the processes of different revenue collection mechanisms?

2.10.1 Population Coverage

Population coverage refers to the extent of individuals contributing to revenue through various mechanisms. Taxation, being universal, achieves the highest population coverage compared to other revenue collection methods. Social health insurance (SHI) contributions, however, are drawn from the formal labor workforce and their employers, resulting in limited population coverage within the Indian context. Similarly, the voluntary nature of community-based health insurance (CBHI) and private health insurance (PHI) premiums leads to their relatively small scale in India. As a result, taxation typically generates the highest amount of revenue, followed by SHI contributions, as illustrated in Fig. 2.8.

2.10.2 Vertical Equity/Progressivity

Vertical equity examines whether a revenue generation system is progressive (where high-income groups contribute a higher proportion of their income), proportional (where contributions are made in equal proportions by both rich and poor, regardless of income), or regressive (where low-income groups pay a higher proportion of their income). Direct taxes generally exhibit progressivity as they are typically

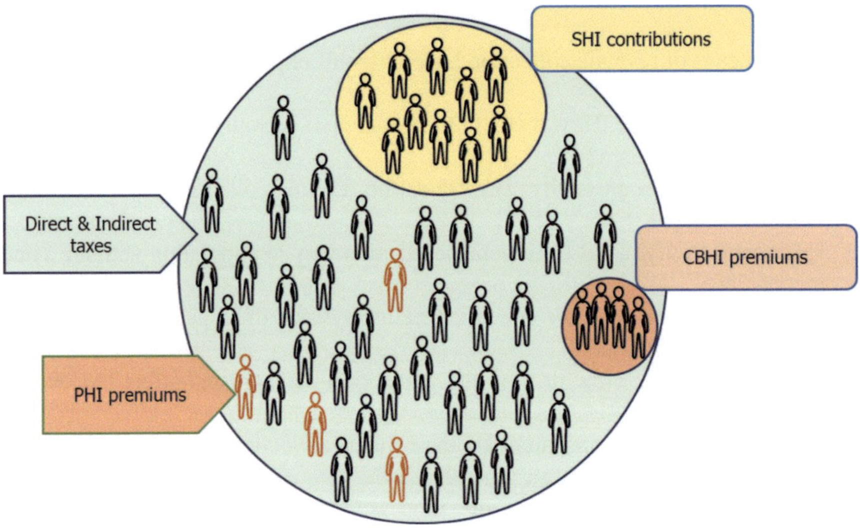

Fig. 2.8 Population coverage under different mechanisms of revenue collection involving risk pooling. SHI social health insurance, PHI private health insurance, CBHI community-based health insurance. Illustration of the relative size of population contributing to different mechanisms of revenue collection

levied on income or wealth. In contrast, indirect taxes, which are based on consumption rather than wealth, tend to be regressive.

Activity Box 2.7
Discuss, if tax subsidies are provided for the purchase of private health insurance, will it improve the progressivity of revenue generation system?

Overall, a tax system that includes both direct and indirect taxes is usually mildly progressive. SHI contributions are proportional to wages, making them less progressive. The degree of progressivity in tax-based and SHI systems of revenue collection can vary based on their operational frameworks. For instance, countries like the Netherlands and Cyprus, which have tax systems with greater variation depending on income and offer dependent and elderly tax credits for low-income individuals, score highly on the progressivity of their revenue generation. Similarly, France employs a progressive tax structure with five marginal tax brackets, ranging from 0% for incomes up to approximately €11,000 to 45% for incomes above €170,000. In contrast, some countries, like Slovak Republic, use only one or two tax brackets, with a small difference between marginal tax rates. Furthermore, if taxation policies allow for significant exemptions for the wealthy, the overall contributions generated from both rich and poor may not be as equitable, undermining the fairness of the system.

Similarly design of SHIs has an impact on equity. Two key factors in the structure of SHI contributions are whether there is a wage ceiling for the contributions and whether there is a difference in contribution rate between different wage groups. For instance, in Germany, there is a cap on the health insurance contributions, according to income threshold set at around €58,000 annually [26]. Once this threshold is reached, no additional contributions are deducted from their earnings. Another regressive design in some countries is mandatory contribution from all income levels, including those with low earnings. For example, in the United States, every individual must pay a payroll tax for the Medicare program, which provides health coverage for seniors and disabled individuals, regardless of their income.

On the other hand, countries like Israel and France provide good examples of progressive SHI design. Israel implemented wage-dependent rates, with 3.1% contribution from employees with salary up to 60% of the average pay, and 5% contribution from working groups above this salary band. France has also adhered to progressive design of contribution rates and compensations to low-salaried and vulnerable groups [27].

CBHI and PHI premiums are not income-dependent, which adversely affects vertical equity. Similarly, user fees can lead to vertical inequity if they are uniformly applied across all income groups. However, equity benefits may arise if exemptions are provided based on income or if the collected revenue is directed toward supporting low-income populations. Nonetheless, direct OOP payments are generally considered regressive because they are contingent on healthcare usage and instances of illness. Given the direct correlation between poor health and poverty, this mechanism tends to disproportionately impact lower-income individuals, making it highly regressive.

2.10.3 Horizontal Equity

Horizontal inequity arises when individuals with the same income levels incur differing payments for healthcare revenue collection. While direct taxes are generally proportional to income, ensuring a degree of equity, horizontal inequity can arise in situations where tax rates vary geographically without corresponding redistribution, such as in case of local taxes. This may require people with similar income levels across geographies to contribute differently to revenue collection. Similarly, exemptions from taxation, such as those for mortgage interest payments or PHI premiums, can also contribute to horizontal inequity.

In the context of SHI systems, the ethos of horizontal equity will be affected if membership is determined by location or occupation, or contributions vary according to the health risks of the occupations, despite a similar wage structure. PHI premiums form a classic source of horizontal inequity as they are often determined by an individual's actuarial risk of illness rather than their income, leading to differing premium amounts for individuals with similar economic status. However, in case PHI is supplementary in nature and utilized by high-income groups, it is more likely to lead to vertical inequity, than horizontal inequity. Similarly, OOP payments can become horizontally inequitable when user fees are waived or adjusted based on patient characteristics, such as age or gender, within the similar income groups. Additionally, variations in cost-sharing mechanisms across different regions can further exacerbate horizontal inequity.

2.10.4 Access to Healthcare

The means of revenue collection has the potential to affect access to healthcare as well as access to insurance. Revenue raising through prepayments improve access by reducing financial barriers to care. The access to insurance in India is dependent on income levels, formal employment status, and ability of population to afford voluntary premiums. Tax-funded systems usually have the responsibility to improve access to healthcare by providing healthcare free or at a low cost. SHI contributions, being earmarked deductions, improve access to healthcare for the formally employed population. However, SHIs are usually dependent on subsidies from the government since wage-based contributions are not enough to provide universal benefits. Similarly voluntary premiums also increase utilization of care and expand the choice of providers. However, systems majorly reliant on voluntary premiums lead to lower access to care at the population level due to affordability issues. In practice, access to services is dependent on other factors, especially in terms of time and earnings that are required to be foregone for seeking care. Therefore, any mechanism of revenue collection cannot guarantee access to care to population groups.

As discussed earlier in this chapter, OOP payments, including direct payments as well as cost-sharing arrangements, deter access to care (both appropriate and inappropriate) and lead to poor health outcomes. Such payments either put vulnerable population at higher risk of catastrophic expenditure or force them to forgo care. On the contrary, OOP payments improve the choice of providers for the affluent, who can afford expensive care. Apparently, such payments also result in inequities in access to healthcare.

2.10.5 Cost Containment

It has been observed that healthcare costs are generally lower in systems predominantly funded by taxation (Table 2.1). This phenomenon is often attributed to the monopsony purchasing power of the government, which exerts significant control over cost negotiations and enables stringent expenditure management. Additionally, political motivations in tax-funded systems often drive efforts to maintain lower costs. This principle also applies to systems reliant on SHI contributions, where funds are pooled centrally. In contrast, private health insurers typically focus on several administrative activities related to advertisements, determination of premium and settlement of claims, which in certain cases leads to relatively higher administrative costs. The risk of over-provision and its consequent effect on increasing the cost would influence all forms of risk pooling but have greater effect on voluntary rather than mandatory enrolment schemes. Consequently, voluntary insurance systems are less effective in containing healthcare costs.

2.10.6 Transparency

In terms of transparency, SHI, CBHI, and external funding generally exhibit higher levels of transparency compared to tax-funded systems, PHI, and informal payments. SHI contributions are managed through distinct structures for fund collection and administration, which enhances their transparency. CBHIs benefit from community involvement in their establishment and management, thereby increasing both transparency and accountability throughout the process. External funding is typically characterized by clear objectives, strict expenditure guidelines, and financial penalties for failing to meet these objectives. The funding process is often governed by legal agreements, ensuring a high degree of transparency.

In contrast, tax collection can be prone to evasion, depending on the administrative capacity of the country. PHI may lack transparency due to issues such as cream-skimming, adverse selection, and moral hazard. Informal payments are particularly nontransparent as they are hidden transactions that remain unreported in the official revenue accounts for healthcare.

Table 2.1 Critical analysis of different means of revenue collection

Means of revenue collection	Population coverage	Horizontal equity	Vertical equity	Access to healthcare	Cost containment	Transparency	Sustainability
Taxes	++++	+++	+++	++ (Based on allocation)	++++	++	Fluctuation of fiscal position
Social health insurance contributions	++	++	++	+++	++	++++	Quite stable
CBHI premiums	+	+	NA	++	+	++++	Low
PHI premiums	+	+	NA	+++	+	+	Unlikely to be sizeable and sustainable
Out-of-pocket payments	NA	+ (If exemption not based on factors as age, gender)	+ (If exemption is based on income)	+	NA	NA	Unsustainable
Loans, grants, and donations	NA	NA	NA	NA	NA	++++	Unsustainable

NA not applicable; strength of relation between type of revenue collection method and different implications in terms of population coverage, horizontal equity, vertical equity, access to healthcare, cost containment, transparency, and fiscal sustainability is presented by "+," where + implies low strength, while ++++ implies high strength

Table depicts the performance of different means of revenue collection in terms of population coverage, equity, access to healthcare, cost containment, transparency, and fiscal sustainability

2.10.7 Sustainability

The likelihood of revenue fluctuations is generally higher with taxation compared to SHI contributions. Tax revenue is influenced by the fiscal conditions of a country, which can vary over time. While SHI contributions are somewhat stable, they are still dependent on employment rates within the formal sector and can be affected by economic downturns. CBHI premiums often lack sustainability due to their limited scale and small fund pool. Although co-payments can enhance the sustainability of such schemes, they shift the financial burden onto individuals. PHI faces similar challenges in terms of size and sustainability, particularly in LMICs where the population's capacity and/or willingness to pay premiums is limited. Adverse selection exacerbates these issues, as high-risk individuals tend to enroll in schemes at lower-than-expected premiums, leading to higher costs for insurers and impacting their financial sustainability. External aid, including loans, grants, and donations, is typically short-term and earmarked for specific purposes, which limits its long-term sustainability.

2.10.8 Efficiency

Efficiency in revenue collection should be evaluated based on whether the processes results in avoidable expenditures. Administrative costs associated with various revenue generation mechanisms can differ based on factors such as competition and the number of collection agents involved. Mechanisms involving voluntary prepayments often exhibit higher levels of competition due to additional marketing expenses, rendering them relatively inefficient for revenue generation. Similarly, administrative costs can increase if different taxes are collected by separate organizations rather than a unified national tax authority. User fees and OOP payments are generally regarded as the most inefficient mechanisms for revenue generation due to their high collection costs. Beyond administrative efficiency, technical efficiency is more closely linked to the purchasing mechanisms rather than the collection processes. These aspects will be explored in greater detail in the subsequent chapters.

2.11 Summary

Most funding systems in the world are mixed and involve different types of revenue collection methods (Fig. 2.9). In order to improve the performance of resource collection, it is essential to evaluate the relative advantages and disadvantages of each funding collection mechanism in the country's context. The decisions on ideal means to fund healthcare should be based on discussions for raising resources for healthcare in an equitable and efficient manner, taking into consideration the political, social, and economic conditions in the country.

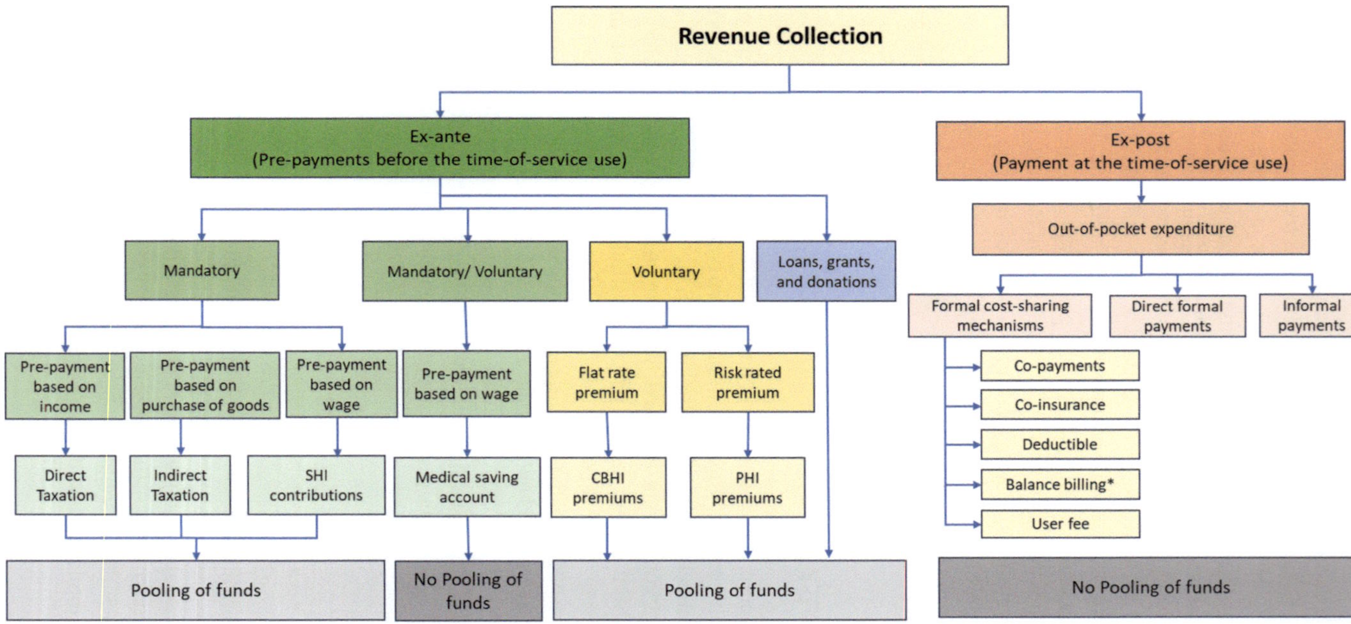

Fig. 2.9 Framework of the means of revenue generation for healthcare. *Can be a part of formal or informal payments. SHI social health insurance, PHI private health insurance, CBHI community-based health insurance. Illustration of the different mechanisms of revenue collection

References

1. World Health Organization, Regional Office for Europe, European Observatory on Health Systems and Policies, Mossialos E, Dixon A, Figueras J, Kutzin J. Funding health care: options for Europe. World Health Organization. Regional Office for Europe; 2002.
2. Jowett M, Kutzin J. Raising revenues for health in support of UHC: strategic issues for policy makers. Health Financing Policy Brief No. 1. World Health Organization; 2015. WHO/HIS/HGF/PolicyBrief/15.1.
3. Kutzin J, Witter S, Jowett M, Bayarsaikhan D. Developing a national health financing strategy: a reference guide. Geneva: World Health Organization; 2017. https://iris.who.int/handle/10665/254757. (Health Financing Guidance No 3) License: CC BY-NC-SA 3.0 IGO.
4. Gottret P, Schieber G. Health financing revisited: a practitioner's guide (English). Washington, DC: World Bank Group; 2006. [cited 2025 Jan 15]. Available from: http://documents.worldbank.org/curated/en/874011468313782370/Health-financing-revisited-a-practitioners-guide.
5. Deshmukh AK, Mohan A, Mohan I. Goods and Services Tax (GST) implementation in India: a SAP-LAP-twitter analytic perspective. Glob J Flex Syst Manag. 2022;23(2):165–83.
6. Assessing growth dividend – establishing linkage between GDP growth and indirect tax to GDP ratio. [Internet]. Available from: https://nacin.gov.in/resources/file/downloads/5698809e9a150.pdf. Accessed 08 Aug 2024.
7. Karnik A, Raju S. State fiscal capacity and tax effort: evidence from Indian states. South Asian J Macroecon Public Finance. 2015;4(2):141–77.
8. Doetinchem O. Hypothecation of tax revenue for health. World Health Report (2010) Background Paper, No. 51. Geneva: World Health Organization; 2010.
9. Reserve Bank of India. Handbook of statistics on Indian economy. 2021–22. [Internet] 2022. [cited 2024 Aug 8]. Available from: https://rbidocs.rbi.org.in/rdocs/Publications/PDFs/0HOS2022_F0D15432F09C8484FABECFC6577A541A9.PDF. Last accessed on 22 June 2023.
10. De S. Recent reforms in India's corporate income tax regime: rationale, impacts and improvements. NIPFP Working Paper Series. No. 393. New Delhi: National Institute of Public Finance and Policy; 2023.
11. Department of Economic Affairs, Ministry of Finance, Government of India. Economic survey 2021–22. [Internet] 2022. [cited 2024 Aug 8]. Available from: https://www.indiabudget.gov.in/economicsurvey/ebook_es2022/index.html#p=398. Last accessed on 22 June 2023.
12. Hemming R. [Internet] Increasing public health expenditure in India- challenges and opportunities. The Centre for Policy Impact in Global Health. Report: number 3. [Internet] 2020. [cited 2024 Aug 8]. Available from: https://centerforpolicyimpact.org/wp-content/uploads/sites/18/2020/02/India-public-health-expenditure-and-fiscal-space-report_Final-1.pdf.
13. National Portal of India. ESIC-2.0. Employees' State Insurance Corporation. [Internet]. 2024. [cited 2024 Aug 8]. Available from: https://www.india.gov.in/spotlight/employees-state-insurance-scheme#tab=tab-1.
14. Ministry of Health and Family Welfare, Government of India. [Internet] Central Government Health Scheme. [Internet] 2024. [cited 2024 Aug 8]. Available from: https://cghs.gov.in/CghsGovIn/faces/ViewPage.xhtml.
15. Regional Office for South-East Asia, World Health Organization. Social health insurance. Report of a regional expert group meeting. New Delhi, 13–15 March 2003; 2003.
16. Purohit B. Community based health insurance in India: prospects and challenges. Sci Res. 2014;6(11):1237–45.
17. Ranson MK. Community-based health insurance schemes in India: a review. Natl Med J India. 2003;16(2):79–89. PMID: 12816186.
18. Odeyemi IA. Community-based health insurance programmes and the National Health Insurance Scheme of Nigeria: challenges to uptake and integration. Int J Equity Health. 2014;13:20.

19. Hanvoravongchai P. Medical savings accounts: lessons learnt from limited international experience. Geneva: World Health Organization. [Internet]; 2002. [cited 2025 Jan 15]. Available from: https://iris.who.int/bitstream/handle/10665/69029/EIP_FER_DP_02.3.pdf.
20. Wouters OJ, Cylus J, Yang W, Thomson S, McKee M. Medical savings accounts: assessing their impact on efficiency, equity and financial protection in health care. Health Econ Policy Law. 2016;11(3):321–35. https://doi.org/10.1017/S1744133116000025. Epub 2016 Feb 17. PMID: 26883211.
21. Mathauer I, Kutzin J. Voluntary health insurance: its potentials and limits in moving towards UHC, Policy Brief, Department of Health Systems Governance and Financing. Geneva: World Health Organization; 2018. (WHO/HIS/HGF/PolicyBrief/18.5). Licence: CC BY-NC-SA 3.0 IGO.
22. Geruso M, Layton TJ. Selection in health insurance markets and its policy remedies. J Econ Perspect. 2017;31(4):23–50.
23. Ikilezi G, Augusto OJ, Dieleman JL, Sherr K, Lim SS. Effect of donor funding for immunization from Gavi and other development assistance channels on vaccine coverage: evidence from 120 low and middle income recipient countries. Vaccine. 2020;38(3):588–96. https://doi.org/10.1016/j.vaccine.2019.10.057. Epub 2019 Nov 1. PMID: 31679863.
24. The Global Fund. Results report 2024. [Internet]. 2024. [cited 2025 Jan 16]. Available from: https://www.theglobalfund.org/en/results/.
25. Huffstetler HE, Bandara S, Bharali I, Kennedy Mcdade K, Mao W, Guo F, Zhang J, Riviere J, Becker L, Mohamadi M, Rice RL, King Z, Farooqi ZW, Zhang X, Yamey G, Ogbuoji O. The impacts of donor transitions on health systems in middle-income countries: a scoping review. Health Policy Plan. 2022;37(9):1188–202. https://doi.org/10.1093/heapol/czac063. PMID: 35904274; PMCID: PMC9558870.
26. Rostampour M, Nosratnejad S. A systematic review of equity in healthcare financing in low- and middle-income countries. Value Health Reg Issues. 2020;21:133–40. https://doi.org/10.1016/j.vhri.2019.10.001. Epub 2019 Nov 28. PMID: 31786404.
27. Rice T, Vrangbæk K, Saunes IS, Bouckaert N, Bryndová L, Cascini F, Võrk A, Dimova A, Kocot E, Murauskiene L, Bricard D, Blumel M, Gaál P, Pažitný P. Can revenue collection for public funding in health care be progressive? An assessment of 29 countries. Health Policy. 2024;148:105147. https://doi.org/10.1016/j.healthpol.2024.105147. Epub 2024 Aug 10. PMID: 39178753.

Suggested Reading

Selvaraj S, Karan KA, Srivastava S, Bhan N, Mukhopadhyay I. India health system review. New Delhi: World Health Organization, Regional Office for South-East Asia; 2022.

Smith RD, Kara H. Health systems in low- and middle-income countries: an economic and policy perspective. Online ed. Oxford: Oxford Academic; 2012. https://doi.org/10.1093/acprof:oso/9780199566761.001.0001.

Risk Pooling

3

Prakash Singh, Shankar Prinja, and V. R. Muraleedharan

Abstract

Risk pooling is a fundamental function of health financing that helps spread financial risk associated with healthcare cost across a group, ensuring that individuals are protected from catastrophic health expenditures. This chapter begins by discussing the need for risk pooling in healthcare, highlighting its role in financial protection and improved access to healthcare services. It then explores the concept of risk pooling.

In the later sections, this chapter introduces the fundamental prerequisites for the effective functioning of voluntary private health insurance (VPHI). It then examines how violations of these conditions contribute to the failure of voluntary private insurance in healthcare and the resulting consequences for the health system. Finally, the chapter explores potential corrective measures to address these market failures and discusses the possible role of VPHI in financing health.

Keywords

Risk pooling · Universal health coverage (UHC) · Health financing · Health insurance · Voluntary private health insurance (VPHI)

P. Singh · S. Prinja (✉)
Department of Community Medicine and School of Public Health, Post Graduate Institute of Medical Education & Research, Chandigarh, India

V. R. Muraleedharan
Department of Humanities and Social Sciences, Indian Institute of Technology, Madras, Chennai, India

S. Prinja (ed.), *Healthcare Financing and Insurance*,
https://doi.org/10.1007/978-981-95-3513-2_3

Learning Objectives
After going through the chapter, you will be able to:

- Understand the concept of risk pooling
- Mechanism of risk pooling in Indian context
- The different approaches to risk pooling

Key Terms
- *Risk pooling*: The practice of combining multiple health risks into a single group to spread The financial burden of healthcare costs among all members, thereby reducing individual financial exposure.
- *Universal health coverage*: Universal health coverage (UHC) means that all people have access to the full range of quality health services they need, when and where they need them, without financial hardship [1].
- *Cream skimming*: The practice by insurers of selecting only the healthier individuals for coverage, thereby avoiding high-risk individuals to minimize costs.
- *Adverse selection*: A situation where individuals with higher health risks are more likely to purchase health insurance, leading to higher overall healthcare costs for the insurer.
- *Moral hazard*: The phenomenon where individuals who are insured may use more healthcare services than they actually need because they do not bear the full financial costs of their care.

3.1 Introduction

In contrast to many of the necessities of everyday life that may have a predictable course, an individual's need for healthcare is largely uncertain. As a result, the expenditure on healthcare is also unpredictable, both in magnitude and timing. It is therefore intrinsically difficult for an individual to make financial provision for episodes of sickness or even chronic healthcare needs. The older people tend to have higher spending needs than younger people (except for the very young), and people with chronic health conditions tend to have higher spending needs than healthy individuals [2].

In the previous chapter on revenue collection (Chap. 2), we explored the key functions of healthcare financing, focusing on revenue collection—the process of gathering funds to finance healthcare services. We examined different mechanisms for revenue collection, highlighting two fundamental approaches. The first approach involves individuals paying for healthcare services at the time of need, which carries two major uncertainties: the timing of healthcare needs and the extent of expenditure. The second approach involves collecting funds in advance when individuals are healthy, creating a financial risk pool from which health expenditures are covered when needed. This second method, known as *risk pooling*, helps mitigate the financial burden on individuals during health crises.

Risk Pooling

...accumulation and management of revenues in such a way as to ensure that the risk of having to pay for healthcare is borne by all members within the pool, not by each contributor individually [3].

Risk pooling is a crucial function of health financing, which allows for the redistribution of financial risk across a group of individuals. Without risk pooling, healthcare costs can become catastrophic for individuals facing unexpected and expensive treatments. For example, in a system where people pay directly for services, an accident or a severe illness could impose an overwhelming financial burden on a single household. However, with risk pooling, individuals contribute to a common fund, and this common fund is used to pay for expenditure of healthcare for those who fell sick. This ensures that financial risks are shared, and no single person bears the full cost of care alone. This chapter will explore the concept of risk pooling in depth, examining its role in health financing and its impact on financial protection and access to healthcare. The following sections will provide a detailed analysis of different risk pooling mechanisms in the context of voluntary private health insurance (VPHI), its advantages and limitations, and its application in the health systems.

3.2 Concept of Risk Pooling

Ensuring that all individuals can access quality healthcare based on their needs, without financial hardship, is the central goal of universal health coverage (UHC). However, in India, a significant portion of the population still faces unmet healthcare needs due to financial, geographic, and systemic barriers. Limited access to essential health services, especially among vulnerable groups, hampers progress toward achieving UHC. Therefore, the proportion of the population requiring healthcare that successfully receives effective and high-quality services serves as a critical measure of UHC progress [1].

Unmet healthcare need is a key indicator of barriers to healthcare access and health inequalities. It refers to persistent healthcare needs that remain unaddressed, often due to health system limitations. However, unmet need is not solely determined by systemic factors; it is also shaped by an individual's socioeconomic characteristics. Personal choices, attitudes, and financial constraints contribute to acceptability barriers, further restricting access to care. There are various sociodemographic factors that influence access to formal healthcare services. Beyond health system barriers, disparities in resources, information gaps, cultural factors, wage loss, and reliance on self-treatment—often mediated by socioeconomic conditions—play a crucial role in shaping healthcare access [4, 5].

In India, disparities in healthcare access are influenced by class, caste, gender, region, religion, and age. Among these, economic inequality, social exclusion, and gender discrimination are recognized as key drivers of unmet healthcare needs. Individuals from lower socioeconomic backgrounds use healthcare services far less than their more affluent counterparts [6]. One of the reasons for this unmet need among poor households is that a substantial share of health expenses is financed through out-of-pocket expenditure (OOPE), placing a heavy financial burden on households. Financial burden remains a significant factor contributing to unmet healthcare needs and the decision not to seek treatment. While the share of OOPE has declined significantly during recent years, it continues to impose a substantial burden on households [7].

Secondly, besides leading to poorer access and unmet need, the high OOPE also poses burden on those who access care. Evidence suggests a strong correlation between the proportion of healthcare costs paid out-of-pocket and the risk of impoverishment due to medical expenses. Countries with a high reliance on OOPE tend to experience greater financial hardship among their populations, pushing more individuals below the poverty line due to catastrophic health expenditures [8]. For instance, in India, where OOPE accounts for nearly half of current health expenditure, many households face financial distress when seeking medical care [9]. The absence of adequate risk pooling mechanisms—forces families to rely on savings, sell assets, or incur debt to afford treatment. In contrast, countries with strong risk pooling mechanisms, such as the United Kingdom's National Health Service (NHS) or Thailand's Universal Coverage Scheme (UCS), have significantly lower levels of catastrophic health expenditure and medical-induced impoverishment [10, 11].

Risk pooling helps mitigate challenges such as high unmet healthcare needs, limited access to care, and catastrophic health expenditure (CHE) among those seeking medical services. It operates on the principle that individuals contribute in advance, before falling ill, to cover potential future healthcare costs. These contributions are pooled together and subsequently used to finance the healthcare expenses of those who require medical care during a specified enrollment period.

The mechanism of risk pooling offers a kind of cushion to people who fall ill, and for their healthcare expenditures. It helps reduce the unmet need that is attributable to poor financial access; as a result, it increases access to healthcare. It also provides financial risk protection to those who access care, which does not let people go below the poverty line or face catastrophic consequences of healthcare expenditures. When it improves access, it improves healthcare outcomes that leads to better public welfare and it leads to efficiency. The fact is that it has a positive effect on offering financial risk protection that helps us move forward toward our aspiration of UHC. The rising expenditures disproportionately affect the poor more than the rich. As a result, any degree of risk pooling provides a greater degree of benefit to the poor. Risk pooling is traditionally viewed as an insurance function, where financial risk associated with health interventions for which the need is uncertain is equitably shared within the covered population.

Let us also better understand it with an example: Consider a group of ten individuals. If one of them falls sick and requires hospitalization, he/she must bear the entire cost out-of-pocket. This financial burden can be particularly devastating for low-income individuals, who may struggle to afford necessary care. Such a scenario highlights the need for a mechanism that protects people from incurring high out-of-pocket health expenditures.

This is where risk pooling plays a crucial role. Instead of each person facing unpredictable and potentially unaffordable healthcare costs alone, a system can be established where all individuals contribute to a common pool of funds. When someone in the group falls ill, their medical expenses are covered from this shared fund, preventing catastrophic financial consequences. This concept is illustrated in Fig. 3.1, which visually demonstrates how risk pooling distributes financial risk across a group, ensuring that no individual is solely responsible for the full cost of healthcare.

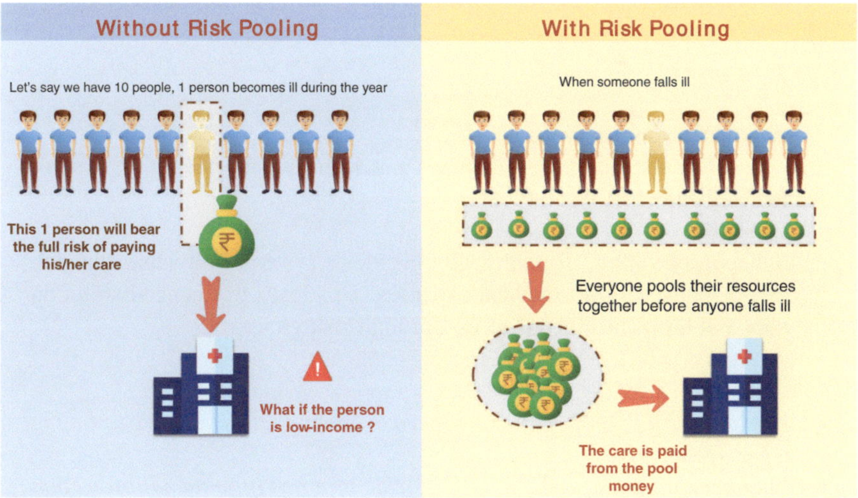

Fig. 3.1 Concept of risk pooling

There are three redistributive functions implicit in risk pooling (from healthy to sick, and from rich to poor and across life cycle) by means of three stylized scenarios:

1. *Healthy to sick*: Members might make equal financial contributions, but the pool effectively enables a transfer to be made from the relatively healthy to the sick (the risk pooling function). All forms of risk pooling—taxation, social health insurance (SHI), community-based health insurance (CBHI), and voluntary private health insurance (VPHI), have a feature of redistributing the resources from healthy to sick.
2. *Rich to poor*: Members might make equal use of healthcare, but by seeking differential financial contributions the pool effectively enables a transfer to be made from the rich to the poor (the income redistribution function). This is the aim of health financing systems that base contributions on income, wage, or ability to pay, which is true for taxation and social health insurance programs.
3. *Productive to nonproductive*: Individuals may contribute equally to a health financing pool and utilize healthcare services in equal measure over their lifetimes. However, the pooling mechanism allows for redistribution based on an individual's stage in the life cycle. Since younger adults who are more productive individuals are generally healthier and require less healthcare, as a result their contributions help finance the healthcare needs of older and less productive individuals, who experience higher rates of illness and may contribute less. This dynamic results in a transfer of resources from the young to the old and from the productive to the nonproductive, embodying the life cycle redistributive function of risk pooling [2] (Fig. 3.2).

Activity Box 3.1: Unravelling the Risk

Objective: Understand the key elements that determine the need for risk pooling in healthcare.

Scenario:

In a country with no formal health insurance system, individuals have to pay out-of-pocket for all medical expenses. This leads to financial strain on the poor and limits healthcare access for high-risk groups.

Question:

- *What are the top three challenges faced by individuals without risk pooling in this scenario?*
- *What benefits would risk pooling provide in terms of financial protection and access to healthcare?*

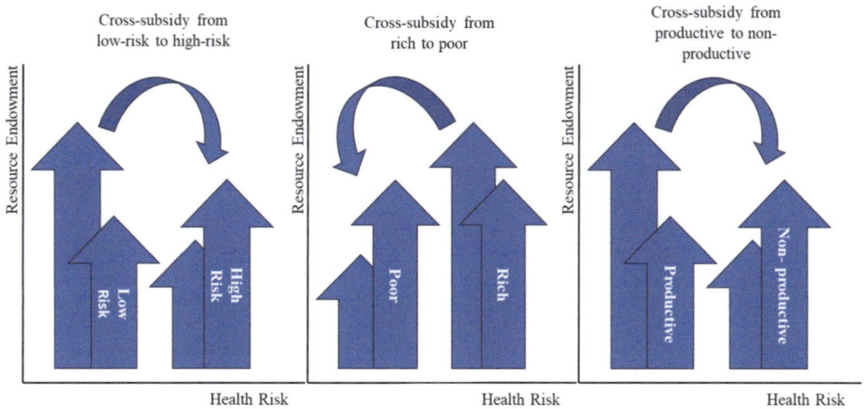

Fig. 3.2 Pooling of risks. (Source: Risk Pooling in Health Care Financing: The Implications for Health System Performance [2])

3.3 Emergence of Risk Pooling in the Indian Healthcare System

Risk pooling in healthcare financing in India has its roots in early efforts and initiatives aimed at addressing the financial risks associated with healthcare expenses. Even before the advent of modern healthcare systems, traditional forms of risk-sharing existed within communities. These informal mechanisms involved pooling resources to support individuals and families during times of illness or medical emergencies. Additionally, philanthropic organizations and voluntary initiatives played a significant role in providing financial support for healthcare. Charitable trusts, religious institutions, and community-driven initiatives would collect funds from donors and distribute them to individuals in need of medical assistance. These early initiatives laid the foundation for the concept of collective risk pooling and resource mobilization to meet healthcare expenses.

As discussed in the previous sections, both globally and in India, health insurance relies on four primary mechanisms of organized risk pooling to mitigate health and financial risks [12] (Table 3.1).

In Chap. 2 on revenue collection, we explored how, in India, contributions to tax-based and social health insurance systems are levied based on an individual's or household's income and wage, respectively. This means that the amount contributed is directly linked to the ability to pay, ensuring a more equitable distribution of financial responsibility. This mechanism of collecting and managing funds is referred to as "pooling of funds," as discussed earlier in this chapter. In contrast, community-based health insurance (CBHI) operates on a flat-rate contribution model. Regardless of the income level, all members of the community pay a fixed amount to participate in the scheme. While this approach promotes community solidarity, it may place a disproportionate financial burden on lower-income households

Table 3.1 Different mechanisms of risk pooling

Type of insurance	National health insurance (tax-based)	Social health insurance (SHI)	Community-based health insurance (CBHI)	Voluntary private health insurance (VPHI)
Size	Large size	Medium	Usually small	Small
Diversity	Highly diverse	Formal sector	Not usually diverse	Mostly affluent population
Participation	Universal, funded by general taxation	Mandatory for formal sector workers, financed through payroll deductions	Voluntary, typically at the community or cooperative level	Voluntary, individuals or employers decide to enroll
Subsidization	Highly subsided	Subsidized	Usually subsidized by donor or government	Not subsidized
Financing mechanism	Government revenue collected through taxes	Payroll contributions from employees and employers	Premiums collected from members within a community	Premiums paid by individuals or employers based on health risk
Premium structure	No direct premium: healthcare is funded through general taxes	Based on a percentage of wage/salary, ensuring progressive financing	Typically flat-rate contributions, sometimes subsidized by external donors or governments	Risk-rated, higher for those with pre-existing conditions or older age groups
Risk pooling	High, as all taxpayers contribute regardless of health status	Strong, as all formal sector workers contribute and share risk	Moderate, with risk-sharing within the community but limited financial sustainability	Limited, as healthier individuals may opt out, leading to adverse selection
Management and administration	Public sector, managed by government agencies (e.g., Ministry of Health, GOI)	Public or quasi-public organizations, often managed by statutory bodies	Community-based organizations, cooperatives, or NGOs	Private for-profit insurers, regulated by IRDAI
Coverage and equity	Universal coverage, ensuring access to all citizens	Covers formal sector workers, but informal sector often excluded unless subsidized	Targets informal sector and rural populations, but coverage is limited	Tends to cover middle- and upper-income groups; low-income individuals may find premiums unaffordable

(continued)

Table 3.1 (continued)

Type of insurance	National health insurance (tax-based)	Social health insurance (SHI)	Community-based health insurance (CBHI)	Voluntary private health insurance (VPHI)
Service provision	Public healthcare providers, with additional private sector involvement	Public and private providers contracted for service delivery	Primarily local healthcare providers, often with limited services	Private healthcare providers preferred, with varying coverage levels
Government role	Direct service provider and financier	Regulator, financier, and sometimes service provider	Supporter, sometimes providing subsidies or technical assistance	Regulator and policy oversight
Example	AB PM-JAY	CGHS, ESIS, etc.	SEWA, ACCORD, etc.	Care Health Insurance, Aditya Birla Health Insurance, etc.

Source: Author's contribution
Abbreviations: *AB PM-JAY* Ayushman Bhaarat-Pradhan Mantri Jan Arogya Yojana, *CGHS* Central Government Health Scheme, *ESIS* Employees' State Insurance Scheme, *SEWA* Self-Employed Women's Association, *ACCORD* Action for Community Organisation, Rehabilitation and Development, *IRDAI* Insurance Regulatory and Development Authority, *GOI* Government of India, *NGO* nongovernmental organization

compared to tax-based or income-linked contributions. Now, one of the fundamental differences between voluntary private health insurance (VPHI) and any other of the three risk pooling mechanisms is that in VPHI the amount that you collect from each individual as a premium is actually a measure of the extent of the risk that this individual has of falling ill. Hence, it is a risk-rated premium that is "actuarially determined" because it is based on the probability an individual to fall ill.

In the next section, we will explore in detail the factors that determine contributions in voluntary private health insurance, including key determinants and their implications for efficiency and equity. This discussion is central to the core objective of this chapter—pooling of risks—which ensures that financial burdens are distributed across individuals to enhance affordability and sustainability in healthcare financing.

Activity Box 3.2: Types of Risk Pooling

Objective: Match each risk pooling model with its description.

Match the pairs:

1. Tax-based health insurance	A. Mandatory contributions from workers and employers
2. Social health insurance (SHI)	B. Premium-based, mainly for higher-income groups
3. Community-based health insurance (CBHI)	C. Government-funded through taxes
4. Voluntary private health insurance (VPHI)	D. Small-scale, often rural, member-driven

Key:

- 1-C
- 2-A
- 3-D
- 4-B

3.3.1 Voluntary Private Health Insurance (VPHI): A Risk-Based Pooling Mechanism

VPHI can be defined as a prepaid pooling arrangement that receives voluntary contributions from individuals and pools them [13]. Unlike publicly funded or social health insurance schemes, VPHI is voluntary in nature, meaning individuals and families choose to enroll based on their personal preferences, financial capacity, and perceived need for coverage.

A defining feature of VPHI is that contributions, in the form of premiums, are risk-rated rather than linked to an individual's ability to pay. Insurers assess policyholders' health risks, demographic factors, and other actuarial variables to determine premium levels, often leading to higher costs for older individuals or those with preexisting conditions.

VPHI in India is predominantly managed by private, for-profit insurance companies that operate in a competitive market. These entities design and administer policies with the primary objective of maximizing returns while offering varying levels of coverage. The structure and functioning of VPHI are largely influenced by regulatory frameworks set by the Insurance Regulatory and Development Authority of India (IRDAI), which oversees aspects such as consumer protection, solvency norms, and policy design.

📌 **Understanding Premium Calculation in Voluntary Private Health Insurance**

In voluntary private health insurance, the *premium* an individual pay for coverage is determined by a well-defined formula. This formula takes into account *risk factors, expected healthcare costs, and administrative expenses*, ensuring that the pricing accurately reflects the financial burden on the insurer.

💡 *Indicative Formula for Premium Calculation*:

$$\boxed{\text{Premium} = pL + l}$$

🔍 *where*:

✅ p = probability of falling ill

✅ L = loss of income during illness (or expected treatment expenditure)

✅ l = loading cost (insurance company's administrative and operational expenses)

✨ *Breaking It Down with an Example*:

Imagine an individual has a *5% probability (p = 0.05) of falling ill*, and each time they do, the *average treatment cost is INR 50,000 (L = 50,000)*.

$$\text{Expected claim cost} = 0.05 \times 50{,}000 = \text{INR } 2500$$

🔹 *Adding the Loading Cost*: Since insurance companies incur operational, expenses (claims processing, policy administration, etc.), The final amount, after including this cost, becomes the total premium charged to the policyholder.

$$\text{Premium} : 2500 + 1000 = 3500$$

💰 *How the Nature of Illness Affects Premiums based on (L)?*

🔺 *Higher Premiums*: If the insured individual is at risk of costly treatments (e.g., *cardiac conditions, cancer treatments*), the premium increases since the *expected treatment expenditure (L) is significantly higher*.

🔻 *Lower Premiums*: If the individual is at risk of *common illnesses* (e.g., *seasonal flu, common cold*), the premium is lower, as the associated treatment costs are minimal.

💰 *How the Probability of Falling Ill Affects Premiums (p)?*

🔺 *Higher Probability (p ↑) → Higher Premium*: If an individual has a greater likelihood of falling ill (due to chronic conditions, old age, or high-risk lifestyle), their premium will be significantly higher.

🔻 *Lower Probability (p ↓) → Lower Premium*: If a person is generally healthy and less likely to make claims, their premium remains lower.

Thus, *insurance pricing reflects the financial risk insurers take on*, ensuring fairness and sustainability in voluntary private health insurance. 🚑💰

3.3.2 Conditions for Voluntary Private Insurance

For a voluntary private insurance to succeed four important conditions need to be satisfied. These conditions are important for any kind of voluntary private health insurance scheme to successfully operate in any kind of industry whether it is the automobile industry, agriculture, house insurance, or in healthcare. Let us discuss these in detail in the context of its applicability in the healthcare market.

3.3.2.1 Condition I: "p" Can Be Determined Accurately

One of the primary requirements for the successful operation of voluntary private insurance is the insurer's ability to accurately assess an individual's probability of falling ill. However, a key challenge in healthcare is the asymmetry of information between the insurer and the individual seeking voluntary health insurance. In such cases, individuals have a better understanding of their own health risks than the insurer. As a result, when a voluntary health insurance policy is introduced, those who choose to enroll are often the individuals who anticipate a higher likelihood of falling ill and requiring healthcare services. The insurer knows the risk at the population level but not at the individual level.

Let us understand this with an example:

Imagine an insurer designing a voluntary health insurance plan for a population. Based on a recent survey report, the insurer knows that

- 10% of the population is likely to fall ill in a given year (morbidity rate).
- 4% of the population is expected to require hospitalization (hospitalization rate).

However, a critical challenge arises—the insurer does not know in advance which specific individuals will fall into this 4% who will need hospital services. As the voluntary enrollment process begins, people make their own decisions about whether to purchase health insurance. Those who already suspect they have a higher risk of illness—such as individuals with chronic conditions, a family history of diseases, or recent health issues—are more likely to enroll at a higher rate than healthier individuals. This creates a situation where the insurance pool is disproportionately filled with high-risk individuals, leading to a phenomenon known as "*adverse selection*" [14]. Since the insurer has estimated the premium based on average population level risk or "*p*" of falling ill, which is lower than the risk ("p^o") of those who actually enroll in the scheme, the overall revenue that the insurer collects is lesser than required to pay the entire claims which arise from services utilized.

In the next year, the insurer raises the premium and again invites people to enroll voluntarily. Now that the insurer has raised the premium, the individuals who are at low risk feels that the premium is now way too high (marginal benefit is lower than the marginal cost) for them to consider being part of this insurance pool. When they opt out of this scheme, what is left within the pool of those who are insured is a higher proportion of those who are at high risk of falling ill and utilizing care, and this continues to go on and on. This is classically called a "*death spiral*" [15] (Fig. 3.3). So, the premiums keep rising because there is a higher proportion of

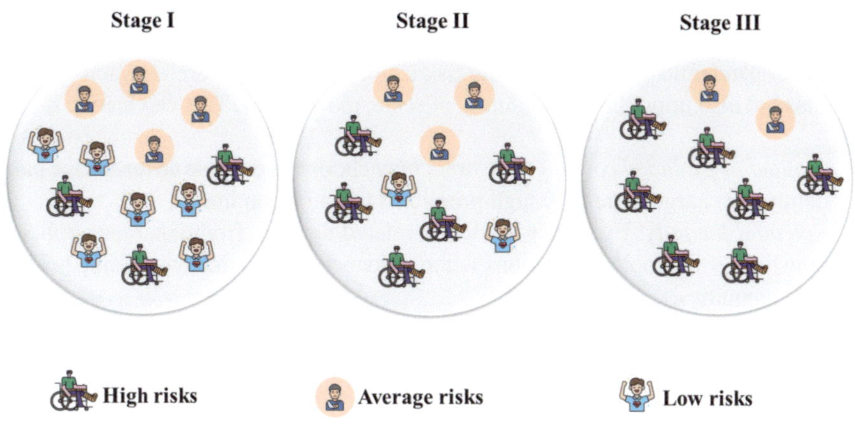

Fig. 3.3 The death spiral: a consequence of an adverse selection

high-risk people who join the insurance pool because of this problem of adverse selection. This means that voluntary private insurance becomes inefficient in the long run and unsustainable.

In order to countercheck adverse selection, the insurer starts to investigate each and every individual to ascertain their risk and their likelihood of falling ill. They collect information on family history or some risk factors, such as smoking, to determine additional risk of falling ill. In other cases, the insurer undertakes a preliminary medical assessment of the potential applicant before enrollment. The insurer also specifies certain exclusion from the policy for those who have preexisting illnesses and would not be taken into consideration. In all these, the insurer aims to selectively pick those who are at low risk of falling ill, i.e., "*cream skimming*" [16]. However, the practice of cream skimming introduces inequities as they start excluding the ones who need the healthcare the most, that is, the elderly, the poor, the ones who are very young, and the ones with the preexisting diseases. As a result, the violation of this assumption that there should be an ability to accurately determine "p" leads to certain practices, which are adverse selection and cream skimming and eventually lead to a drop in efficiency and equity.

3.3.2.2 Condition II: "p" Should Be Independent

For an insurance model to function optimally, the probability of an individual falling ill ("*p*") should be independent of others' health risks. In other words, one person's likelihood of illness should not be influenced by another's. However, this condition is often violated in the case of communicable diseases, where the probability of infection is inherently linked to the health status of others in the community.

Let us understand this with an example:

Consider the COVID-19 pandemic. If an individual's neighbor tests positive for COVID-19, the person living next door faces an increased risk of infection due to proximity. In such cases, the probability of falling ill is no longer independent—it is influenced by external factors such as community transmission and exposure levels. As a result, insurers are often hesitant to offer products that cover diseases of epidemic or pandemic proportions as the risk is not only highly correlated across individuals but also unpredictable in terms of scale and severity. This can lead to

- *Limited or excluded coverage*: Insurers may choose to exclude coverage for pandemics or charge extremely high premiums for such conditions.
- *Potential inequity*: Excluding epidemic-related diseases from insurance policies may leave vulnerable populations without financial protection, worsening healthcare inequities.
- *Financial unsustainability for insurers*: If such diseases are covered, insurers could face large-scale claims simultaneously, leading to significant financial losses and potential collapse of the insurance scheme.

To address this challenge, government and insurers in India have introduced specialized health insurance policies covering pandemics and infectious diseases. For instance, during COVID-19, the Insurance Regulatory and Development Authority of India (IRDAI) mandated insurers to offer *Corona Kavach* and *Corona Rakshak* policies, ensuring financial protection for affected individuals [17].

3.3.2.3 Condition III: "p" Should Be Probability and Not a Certainty

The fact that the probability reaches closer to one for several of these chronic diseases, congenital diseases, and maternity conditions, especially in the early reproductive age group. In old age, these are high-risk individuals, and their probabilities go more in the direction of 1 than in the direction of 0. So as a result, these insurers tend to offer lower coverage for these age groups. The closer the probability gets to 1, it would no longer be a viable option to run an insurance policy because if it is 1, then it means that every individual is definitely likely to fall ill and definitely going to seek healthcare, and it means that the company should be charging this individual an amount that would be equal to the actual cost of care that he will incur. If the premium is equivalent to the actual cost that the individual is supposed to pay at the time when he falls sick, then the individual also does not have any incentive to get into the insurance because he could pay that out of pocket (OOP) when he falls sick rather than paying up front only and that too at a time when he does not know whether or not he will fall sick or not. So, the probability should not be closer to 1, which gets violated in certain circumstances or conditions.

3.3.2.4 Condition IV: "p" Should Not Be Endogenous

This condition implies that an individual cannot influence their inherent risk of falling ill. However, while the probability of illness remains unchanged, the likelihood of seeking healthcare—and consequently incurring medical expenses—may increase among those who are insured. For instance, a person is insured then even on having a minor health condition, the person will rather seek a specialist consultation and get healthcare immediately. So, there is going to be "*moral hazard*" on the demand side or the consumer side [18]. The individual will be the one who is insured and is more likely to seek healthcare and in certain cases might even be frivolous and perhaps unnecessary. This moral hazard may also manifest on the provider side, and then it is labeled as "*supplier-induced demand.*" For a patient who does not necessarily require hospitalization, the healthcare provider may advise the patient to get hospitalized and get treated because the insurance covers hospitalization because the enrollment in an insurance does not cover outpatient treatment.

In the overall context of healthcare expenditure, it will increase the healthcare expenditure for the same set of utility that the individual can get from the treatment, whether the individual could have given it in an outpatient or inpatient setting. In certain cases, it goes in for frivolous use of diagnostics that may not be necessary, and as a result, supplier-induced demand raises health expenditure and leads to inefficiency.

So, the conclusion is that all these four preconditions for voluntary private insurance to succeed do not completely hold true in the context of the health sector, and it results in the outcomes that eventually lead to the overall health system becoming inefficient as well as inequitable. As a result, the key problems with voluntary private health insurance are

1. The premium is risk rated
2. The insurance is voluntary in nature

If the same insurance, even risk-created insurance is mandatory, it may not have created a problem because then everybody has to necessarily get insured. So, a lot of problems of adverse selection, cream skimming, etc., would go away. However, the problems of moral hazard and supplier-induced demand may still exist in that scenario as well. Moral hazard and supplier-induced demand are present even within tax-based health insurance, social health insurance (SHI), and community-based health insurance (CBHI) pooling mechanisms.

Activity Box 3.3: Identifying Market Failures

Objective: Recognize key challenges in health insurance markets.

Fill in the blanks:

1. When only sick people buy insurance, it leads to _________.
2. When insurers avoid high-risk patients, it's called _________.
3. When insured individuals overuse healthcare, it's _________.

Word Bank:

Cream Skimming | Moral Hazard | Adverse Selection

3.3.3 Solutions for Market Failure in Voluntary Private Health Insurance

The previous section examined the failure of the private healthcare market in the context of voluntary private health insurance. The following section will explore potential solutions to address market failures in the private health insurance sector (Table 3.2).

3.3.3.1 Regulatory Responses

If there is *adverse selection*, which means people who are more at risk of falling ill are the ones who are likely to get themselves insured, then the possible solution is to make the insurance scheme mandatory. This addresses the problem of the adverse selection. Alternatively, insurers can enroll the household instead of members, that is, all the members of the household get enrolled. Thirdly, the insurers may offer subsidies for people who enroll in insurance schemes. This incentivizes more people to get enrolled in the insurance schemes. Finally, people can be educated about the benefits of purchasing an insurance.

The second problem is *cream skimming or risk selection by insurers*. One possible regulatory solution that has been tried in some countries as well, is having open enrollment periods. So, the insurer is allowed to keep an exclusion policy with the condition that there will be a window of defined period in which an individual who walks in to buy an insurance policy cannot be refused from buying insurance policy, irrespective of the characteristic of the individual.

Moral hazard is a significant challenge in healthcare financing, referring to the overuse or oversupply of services from both the demand and supply sides. This issue arises when patients consume more healthcare services than necessary because they are insulated from the full cost, or when providers deliver excessive services to maximize revenue. To mitigate moral hazard, various cost-sharing mechanisms are implemented on both the demand and supply sides. On the demand side, patients bear a portion of treatment costs to discourage unnecessary utilization. Common forms of demand-side cost sharing include copayments, where patients pay a fixed fee for each service; coinsurance, where patients pay a percentage of the total cost; and deductibles, where patients must cover a minimum amount before insurance coverage begins. These are explained in the previous chapter (Chap. 2) on revenue collection.

Table 3.2 Solutions for market failure in voluntary private health insurance (VPHI)

Problem	Consequences	Possible solutions?
Adverse selection	Little risk pooling, no market, only some insured	Education, subsidies, compulsion
Risk selection	No insurance for some groups	Open enrollment, community rating
Moral hazard	Overuse, oversupply	Cost sharing (demand and supply), "managed care"
Info asymmetry	No price competition	Standardized benefits

On the supply side, providers are incentivized to avoid unnecessary service provision through alternative payment mechanisms. For instance, bundled payments replace traditional fee-for-service reimbursements by providing a fixed payment for an entire episode of care, while capitation offers a fixed per-person enrolled payment, encouraging cost-effective care instead of excessive service delivery. By shifting from fee-for-service to case-based or capitation-based payments, providers have a financial incentive to reduce inefficiencies and avoid unnecessary interventions. Further regulatory strategies for addressing moral hazard and optimizing provider payment mechanisms will be explored in the subsequent chapter on (Chap. 4) *Strategic purchasing.*

Finally, to bridge this problem of *information asymmetry*, which may happen because the consumers are not very well aware of the structure of the scheme, the design of the scheme, etc, there could be a policy that every scheme would have standardized benefits, so the benefit package would be the same across all schemes. This means that the changes in prices now have to reflect any other additional features that the scheme wants to incorporate, like improved quality.

3.3.4 The Role of Voluntary Private Health Insurance Amid Market Failures

In the preceding sections, the failure of voluntary private health insurance in the healthcare market has been examined. To address certain effects of this market failure, various regulatory mechanisms have been discussed. However, despite these challenges, voluntary private health insurance can still play a role in bridging gaps in healthcare financing in several ways: [19]

The Substitutive Role In some countries, private health insurance has been utilized in a substitutive function, allowing individuals to opt out of government or employer-sponsored insurance. Under this model, health insurance contributions are not mandatory, and those who choose to opt out—typically wealthier individuals—can purchase voluntary private insurance instead. As a result, public funds, primarily derived from tax revenues, are allocated to finance healthcare for lower-income populations, ensuring a risk pool for them. While this approach offers individuals greater choice, it may also lead to unintended consequences, particularly in terms of equity in healthcare financing. When wealthier individuals opt out, their contributions to the public system cease, potentially reducing overall resources available for healthcare. However, if public healthcare financing is primarily tax-based, these negative equity effects are minimized, as funding remains progressive. On the other hand, if healthcare financing relies on mandatory, earmarked contributions, allowing wealthier individuals to opt out restricts the risk pool to lower-income populations alone. This can lead to financial instability within the system and exacerbate inequities in healthcare access and quality.

The Complementary Role The second possible role could be the complementary role of a private insurance company. So, the government's publicly funded health insurance, for example, the *Ayushman Bharat Pradhan Mantri Jan Arogya Yojana* (AB PM-JAY) in India, may be able to create a scheme that offers a defined benefit package that includes coverage for the treatment of certain diseases and surgical procedures. For example, in AB PM-JAY, about 1949 procedures are covered, but the range of healthcare conditions or interventions could be even greater than 1949 [20]. So, what about health services or conditions that are not covered by a publicly funded or tax revenue-driven scheme for health and health financing? In that case, private insurance could help cover those services that are excluded from public coverage.

The Supplementary Role One key role of private insurance is as a supplementary mechanism. Despite the existence of schemes like AB PM-JAY, certain procedures may only be covered when provided in public facilities. In such cases, individuals seeking greater choice and access to private providers can utilize private insurance for these supplementary services. Similarly, while AB PM-JAY covers treatment in general wards and sets provider payment rates accordingly, private health insurance can be used to cover expenses for private wards or additional amenities (e.g., hotel services). Furthermore, voluntary private health insurance can facilitate faster access to care, reduce or eliminate waiting times, and provide direct access to specialist services, thereby enhancing overall healthcare access and patient experience. This approach has gained significant traction as it promotes efficiency in the use of public resources by ensuring that funds are allocated only to necessary and cost-effective services. Additionally, it allows individuals the flexibility to opt for more comprehensive coverage beyond what is provided by publicly funded insurance.

So, to summarize, there is every theoretical merit in having a risk pooling arrangement. There are different mechanisms for risk pooling, one of which is voluntary private insurance. The four fundamental principles of voluntary private insurance that are necessary for such an insurance to be viable in healthcare do not successfully operate and are violated in the healthcare market. As a result, voluntary private insurance cannot be a sustainable mechanism to finance universal healthcare. So, we are either left with making some corrections through regulatory options or we have to identify some other possible role, either a substitutive, complementary, or supplementary role for private insurance.

Activity Box 3.4: Designing a Fair System

Objective: Identify key principles of an effective risk pooling system.

Select the best approach:

1. To make risk pooling equitable, should contributions be based on.
   - ☐ A. *Income*
   - ☐ B. *Health status*
2. To avoid adverse selection, should insurance be.
   - ☐ A. *Mandatory*
   - ☐ B. *Voluntary*

Key:

1. Income
2. Mandatory

3.4 Approaches to Risk Pooling

The design of risk pooling arrangements is a policy decision influenced by a country's priorities and circumstances. In many Western European nations, risk pools typically encompass entire regions or the entire country, aligning with the principle of solidarity to achieve universal health coverage. In contrast, the United States has a more segmented approach, with risk pools structured around factors such as age (Medicare), income level (Medicaid), or employment status. Despite concerns regarding fairness and efficiency, many developing countries make little effort to establish formal risk pools. Instead, healthcare financing largely depends on direct household contributions, either through informal payments—unregulated but often integral to the health system—or user fees, which are officially sanctioned out-of-pocket expenditure. While government funding may provide some subsidies to public healthcare facilities, it remains limited in many cases.

There are four major classes of approach to risk pooling, considered in turn (Fig. 3.4):

- No risk pool
- Unitary risk pool
- Fragmented risk pool
- Integrated risk pools

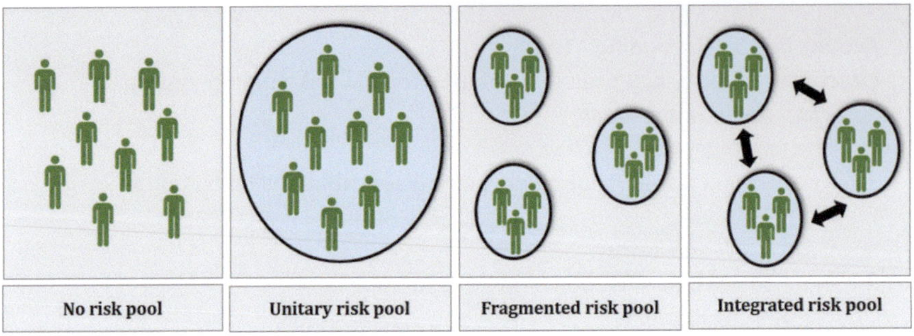

Fig. 3.4 Approaches to risk pooling

3.4.1 No Risk Pool

In the absence of risk pooling, individuals must bear the full cost of their medical expenses, leading to significant financial burdens. This system operates on a pay-as-you-go basis, where patients are required to cover healthcare costs at the time of service, with no financial protection for those unable to afford treatment. A stark example of this can be seen in India, where a substantial portion of healthcare spending—approximately 45.1%—is out-of-pocket (National Health Accounts 2021–22) [9]. Many low-income households face catastrophic health expenditures, often leading to delayed or forgone care. This lack of risk pooling exacerbates health inequities, disproportionately affecting economically disadvantaged populations who may be denied essential treatment due to their inability to pay.

3.4.2 Unitary Risk Pool

In a unitary risk pool, all revenue—whether generated through general taxation, social health insurance, private health insurance, or user fees—is consolidated into a single central fund. This pooled fund is then used to finance a defined package of healthcare services, with payments made to providers based on patient needs. For this model to function effectively, participation must be mandatory, ensuring that affluent and healthier individuals cannot opt out of contributing. Mandatory risk pooling serves as a policy mechanism to mitigate inefficiencies and inequities arising from adverse selection, cream-skimming, and high transaction costs. In India, the AB PM-JAY exemplifies certain aspects of the unitary risk pool approach. Funded through general taxation, AB PM-JAY consolidates financial resources to provide health coverage to economically disadvantaged populations, ensuring equitable access to healthcare while reducing financial barriers.

3.4.3 Fragmented Risk Pools

Implementing a fully unified risk pool presents significant practical challenges. While a nationwide risk pool can, in theory, ensure comprehensive risk-sharing and reduce variations in expected healthcare expenditures, it also introduces complex issues related to managerial oversight and coordination. As a result, most countries delegate healthcare purchasing responsibilities to smaller entities, leading to the fragmentation of risk pools. Fragmentation occurs whenever multiple risk pools operate within a system, each managing a subset of the population. Under these arrangements, individuals might be assigned to a particular pool depending on criteria such as

- Where they live (geographical risk pools)
- The nature of their employment
- Their personal characteristics such as age, health status, or socioeconomic status
- Their personal choice (e.g., competing insurance funds)

Membership in a risk pool can either be voluntary, as seen in competitive insurance markets, or mandatory, as is common with geographically defined pools. However, many health systems ensure that all individuals are enrolled in at least one risk pool to promote broad coverage. Fragmented risk pools often vary in population size, leading to differences in per capita expected healthcare expenditure.

One prominent example is the coexistence of the AB PM-JAY and various state-specific health insurance chemes. AB PM-JAY, launched by the central government, aims to provide financial protection to economically vulnerable households across India. Several states operate their own parallel insurance programs, while some states have integrated their schemes with AB PM-JAY, others continue to run independent programs with separate risk pools. This fragmentation results in variations in population coverage, benefit packages, and reimbursement rates across different schemes. Consequently, individuals in different states or economic categories experience differing levels of financial protection, leading to inefficiencies and disparities in healthcare access.

3.4.4 Integrated Risk Pools

Decentralizing healthcare purchasing can lead to fragmented risk pools, which may result in inefficiencies and inequities in resource allocation. To mitigate these challenges, many health systems adopt integrated risk pooling mechanisms, where financial transfers between pools help reduce disparities caused by fragmentation. If the goal is to provide a standard package of healthcare services to all citizens, one of the key factors influencing variations in spending needs across fragmented pools is the size of the covered population. A fundamental step toward integration is the adoption of capitation-based funding, where each risk pool receives a fixed amount per individual for a specified period. In its simplest form, this method allocates an equal per capita amount to all risk pools. However, this approach does not account for differences in healthcare needs across populations. To address these disparities, many countries use risk-adjusted capitation models, which modify payments based on individual characteristics such as age, socioeconomic status, and health conditions. These adjustments help ensure that risk pools receive adequate funding based on their population's healthcare needs, promoting financial sustainability and equitable access to care.

In India, an example of movement toward integrated risk pooling is the central government's AB PM-JAY, which encourages states to merge their health insurance schemes into a unified framework. While full integration remains a challenge due to the coexistence of multiple state-specific programs, risk adjustment mechanisms and financial transfers between central and state pools can help create a more balanced and efficient health financing system.

3.5 Conclusion

In conclusion, risk pooling in healthcare financing is a crucial mechanism for ensuring affordable and equitable access to healthcare services in India. India has made significant strides in implementing various initiatives to pool healthcare risks and provide financial protection to its population. The introduction of national health insurance schemes, such as AB PM-JAY, has played a pivotal role in expanding health insurance coverage and reducing the financial burden of healthcare expenses for vulnerable households. These schemes have provided a safety net for millions of individuals, particularly those from low-income backgrounds, who previously had limited or no access to healthcare services. The concept of universal health coverage has gained prominence in India, emphasizing the importance of risk pooling in achieving equitable healthcare. By sharing risks across a larger population, risk pooling ensures that the financial burden of healthcare is distributed more fairly, preventing catastrophic health expenditures, and protecting individuals from falling into poverty due to medical expenses. In addition to government-led initiatives, community-based health insurance programs have emerged as an effective way to pool resources and provide coverage to specific population groups. These initiatives leverage the collective strength of communities and address their unique healthcare needs, particularly in rural areas and among informal sector workers. Private health insurance companies also play a significant role in risk pooling by offering a variety of health insurance products. These companies enable individuals and organizations to pool their healthcare risks, collect premiums, and utilize the pooled funds to pay for healthcare expenses when required. The presence of private insurers enhances the diversity and flexibility of health insurance options available to the population.

Collaborative efforts involving the government, insurance companies, healthcare providers, and civil society organizations are necessary to develop comprehensive strategies that foster sustainable risk pooling mechanisms and support the goal of universal health coverage. In conclusion, risk pooling in healthcare financing has the potential to transform the healthcare landscape in India. By pooling resources and sharing risks, individuals can access affordable and quality healthcare services while being protected from the financial hardships associated with medical expenses. Continued efforts to strengthen risk pooling mechanisms and address the challenges will contribute to a more inclusive and resilient healthcare system in India.

References

1. Universal Health Coverage (UHC). https://www.who.int/news-room/fact-sheets/detail/universal-health-coverage-(uhc). Accessed 28 Mar 2025.
2. Risk pooling in health care financing: the implications for health system performance. 2004. https://hdl.handle.net/10986/13651. Accessed 28 Mar 2025.
3. Pooling financial resources for universal health coverage: options for reform. https://www.who.int/publications/i/item/pooling-financial-resources-for-universal-health-coverage-options-for-reform. Accessed 28 Mar 2025.
4. Wu L, Liu Q, Fu R, et al. Unmet healthcare needs, health outcomes, and health inequalities among older people in China. Front Public Health. 2023;11:1082517.
5. Chung W. Changes in barriers that cause unmet healthcare needs in the life cycle of adulthood and their policy implications: a need-selection model analysis of the Korea health panel survey data. Healthcare. 2022;10:2243.
6. Mahapatro SR, James KS, Mishra US. Intersection of class, caste, gender and unmet healthcare needs in India: implications for health policy. Health Policy Open. 2021;2:100040.
7. Yadav R, Yadav J, Shekhar C. Unmet need for treatment-seeking from public health facilities in India: an analysis of sociodemographic, regional and disease-wise variations. PLOS Global Public Health. 2022;2:e0000148.
8. Rahman MM, Islam MR, Rahman MS, et al. Forgone healthcare and financial burden due to out-of-pocket payments in Bangladesh: a multilevel analysis. Health Econ Rev. 2022;12:5.
9. National Health Accounts | National Health Systems Resource Centre. https://nhsrcindia.org/national-health-accounts-records. Accessed 25 Mar 2025.
10. Tangcharoensathien V, Tisayaticom K, Suphanchaimat R, et al. Financial risk protection of Thailand's universal health coverage: results from series of national household surveys between 1996 and 2015. Int J Equity Health. 2020;19:1–12.
11. Fenn P, Egan T. Risk management in the NHS: governance, finance and clinical risk. Clin Med. 2012;12:25.
12. Health financing revisited: a practitioner's guide. https://documents.worldbank.org/en/publication/documents-reports/documentdetail/874011468313782370/health-financing-. Accessed 28 Mar 2025.
13. Voluntary health insurance: potentials and limits in moving towards UHC. https://www.who.int/publications/i/item/WHO-HIS-HGF-Health-Financing-Policy-Brief-18.5. Accessed 28 Mar 2025.
14. Powell D, Goldman D. Disentangling moral hazard and adverse selection in private health insurance. J Econ. 2020;222:141.
15. Bertens RM, Vonk RAA. Small steps, big change. Forging a public-private health insurance system in the Netherlands. Soc Sci Med. 2020;266:113418.

16. Barros PP. Cream-skimming, incentives for efficiency and payment system. J Health Econ. 2003;22:419–43.
17. Home – IRDAI. https://irdai.gov.in/home. Accessed 25 Mar 2025.
18. Einav L, Finkelstein A. Moral hazard in health insurance: what we know and how we know it. J Eur Econ Assoc. 2018;16:957.
19. Implementing health financing reform: lessons from countries in transition. https://www.who.int/publications/i/item/9789289042116. Accessed 28 Mar 2025.
20. About PM-JAY – National Health Authority | GOI. https://nha.gov.in/PM-JAY. Accessed 28 Mar 2025.

Strategic Purchasing

4

Gaurav Jyani, Shankar Prinja, and Pankaj Kumar Arora

Abstract

Strategic purchasing in healthcare is an approach for optimizing resource use, improving service quality, and promoting equity within health systems. While extensive literature exists detailing various aspects of strategic purchasing in healthcare, this chapter is specifically designed to address the unique perspectives and needs of health insurers, providing tailored insights and strategies to optimize purchasing decisions in alignment with insurer objectives. This chapter explores the core principles and mechanisms of strategic purchasing, addressing its significance in the context of rising healthcare costs, variable service quality, and the need for sustainable health financing. Strategic purchasing centers on three fundamental domains: what to purchase, from whom to purchase, and how to purchase, all of which are discussed with respect to maximizing value and aligning with population health needs. In addition, in this chapter we bring an additional fourth domain of monitoring and evaluation and use of data for improving the efficiency of the health system. Key strategies, such as selective contracting, value-based purchasing, and performance-based incentives, enable health insurers to establish efficient provider networks and promote high-quality care. The chapter also examines the role of stakeholders, including health insurers, healthcare providers, regulatory bodies, and the public, in creating an environment that supports effective strategic purchasing. The chapter also describes how the cost evidence plays a pivotal role in strategic purchasing by enabling health insurers to design benefit packages, set provider payment rates, and make

G. Jyani · S. Prinja (✉)
Department of Community Medicine and School of Public Health, Post Graduate Institute of Medical Education and Research (PGIMER), Chandigarh, India

P. K. Arora
National Health Authority, Government of India, New Delhi, India

S. Prinja (ed.), *Healthcare Financing and Insurance*,
https://doi.org/10.1007/978-981-95-3513-2_4

informed purchasing decisions that balance quality with financial sustainability. By utilizing a variety of payment mechanisms such as capitation, bundled payments, and risk-sharing agreements-insurers can drive cost-effectiveness, encourage preventive care, and support financial sustainability.

Keywords

Strategic purchasing · Health insurance · Value-based care · Provider payment mechanisms · Universal health coverage

Learning Objectives

After going through the chapter, you will be able to

1. Understand the key principles and objectives of strategic purchasing in healthcare and its role in enhancing health system performance
2. Identify the core components of strategic purchasing, including benefit package design, provider selection, and payment mechanisms
3. Recognize the roles and responsibilities of various stakeholders, including health insurers, providers, government, and the public, in supporting effective strategic purchasing
4. Explain the importance of cost data, value-based purchasing, and performance-based incentives in achieving sustainable and high-quality healthcare
5. Appreciate the significance of government regulation and accountability measures in fostering a transparent and equitable healthcare purchasing environment

Key Terms

1. *Strategic purchasing:* Strategic purchasing is an active approach to health financing in which purchasers of health services (e.g., health insurers) deliberately decide what services to buy, from whom, and how, using evidence and data. The goal is to maximize health system performance in terms of efficiency, quality, equity, and financial protection.
2. *Passive purchasing:* Passive purchasing refers to a situation where purchasers simply reimburse bills or follow a fixed budget without actively shaping which services are bought or how providers are paid. It does not use purchasing power to influence quality, efficiency, or alignment with population health needs.

3. *Health benefit package (HBP):* A health benefit package is the defined set of healthcare services that an insurance scheme or purchaser agrees to cover for its beneficiaries.
4. *Health technology assessment (HTA):* HTA is a systematic evaluation of the clinical effectiveness, costs, and broader impacts of health technologies (drugs, devices, procedures, programs). In strategic purchasing, HTA evidence is used to design benefit packages, set coverage limits, and ensure that purchased services provide good value for money.
5. *Empanelment:* The formal process of selecting and accrediting healthcare providers that meet defined service quality and infrastructure standards to deliver care under an insurance program.
6. *Selective contracting:* Selective contracting is a purchasing strategy in which insurers contract only with providers that meet specific criteria related to quality, cost, and accessibility. By choosing a network of "preferred" or empaneled providers, purchasers can negotiate better prices, set quality standards, and influence provider behavior.
7. *Value-based care/value-based purchasing:* Value-based purchasing links provider payment to the quality and outcomes of care rather than the sheer volume of services delivered. Under value-based care, providers are rewarded for improving health outcomes, patient experience, and efficiency, aligning financial incentives with 'value for money'.
8. *Capitation:* Capitation is a provider payment method where a healthcare provider receives a fixed amount per enrolled person for a given period, regardless of how many services that person uses. It encourages efficiency and preventive care but requires strong monitoring to avoid under-provision of necessary services.
9. *Fee-for-service (FFS):* Under fee-for-service, healthcare providers are paid for each individual service or procedure they deliver. While FFS can encourage comprehensive service provision, it may also incentivize over-prescription.
10. *Diagnosis-related groups (DRGs):* DRGs are a case-based hospital payment system in which patients admitted to hospitals are classified into clinically similar groups that are expected to require comparable levels of resources. Under DRGs, hospitals receive a fixed, predetermined payment based on the patient's assigned diagnosis group, regardless of the actual length of stay or services used. This encourages hospitals to improve efficiency, reduce unnecessary procedures, and better manage costs, while still maintaining quality care.
11. *Bundled payment:* Bundled payment is a method where a single, comprehensive payment is made for all services related to an episode of care (e.g., surgery plus implant plus post-operative care).

12. *Blended (mixed) provider payment model:* A blended payment model combines multiple payment methods, such as capitation and fee-for-service, to balance incentives for efficiency, volume, and quality. Strategic purchasers use blended payment models to harness the strengths and mitigate the weaknesses of individual payment methods.
13. *Risk-sharing arrangements:* Risk-sharing arrangements are contracts where financial risk for the cost of care is shared between purchasers and healthcare providers (e.g. gainsharing, loss-sharing, or outcome-based contracts). These mechanisms aim to align incentives for cost control and quality, while avoiding one party bearing all the financial risk.
14. *Standard treatment guidelines (STGs):* Evidence-based protocols for diagnosis and treatment that providers must follow while delivering care. They reduce unnecessary variations in care and promote effective and standardized clinical practice.
15. *Formulary/essential medicines list and essential diagnostics list:* Standardized lists of approved medicines and diagnostic tests used to ensure availability of essential healthcare inputs.
16. *Performance-based incentives:* Financial rewards provided to providers when they meet established quality or outcome benchmarks. These incentives help align provider behavior with the goals of strategic purchasing.
17. *Health information systems (HIS) for purchasing:* Digital systems used by insurers to collect, analyze, and act on data related to utilization, claims, and provider performance. They support decision-making, fraud detection, and accountability.
18. *Regulatory framework for strategic purchasing:* Policies, rules, and enforcement mechanisms set by government to guide insurers and providers, uphold quality standards, and protect patient rights, enabling purchasing to improve system performance.
19. *Performance monitoring and evaluation:* A continuous process of reviewing provider performance, service utilization, and health outcomes to improve decision-making. In AB PM-JAY, claims and utilization data are regularly analyzed to detect inefficiencies and fraud while improving purchasing strategies. Provider accountability is enforced through audits, performance-linked payments, and regulatory oversight.

4.1 Strategic Purchasing in Healthcare and Its Importance for Health Insurers

Rising healthcare costs are straining health insurance systems worldwide, challenging the financial viability of insurers and limiting access to necessary care for many individuals [1, 2]. Health insurers frequently face the dilemma of balancing the cost of comprehensive coverage with the need to keep premiums and overall costs affordable. This challenge is compounded by inefficiencies in service delivery, variations in provider quality, and the growing demand for high-cost treatments [3]. The insurers sometimes find themselves covering services with minimal health benefits or shouldering costs for avoidable hospitalizations, all of which undermine the effectiveness and sustainability of their programs [4]. In this landscape, there is a pressing need for a more proactive approach to healthcare financing, one that can optimize resource use, improve quality, and address inequities in access. Strategic purchasing offers a solution to this challenge by enabling insurers to make deliberate, evidence-based choices about healthcare spending. Passive purchasing implies following a predetermined budget or simply paying bills when presented [5]. Strategic purchasing involves a continuous search for the best ways to maximize health system performance by deciding which interventions should be purchased, how, and from whom [5].

Purchasing refers to the process by which funds are allocated to healthcare providers to obtain services on behalf of identified groups (e.g., insurance scheme members) or the entire population [6]. Strategic purchasing is a transformative approach to healthcare financing that enables payers or health insurers to make targeted, data-driven decisions on where and how to allocate resources for optimal impact [7]. Unlike traditional purchasing, which often involves passively reimbursing healthcare providers for services rendered, strategic purchasing seeks to actively shape the healthcare landscape by determining which services should be provided, by whom, and under what conditions [8]. At its core, strategic purchasing is about maximizing value by aligning financial resources with population health priorities, cost-efficiency goals, and quality benchmarks.

At the heart of strategic purchasing in healthcare are three critical questions that determine the effectiveness, efficiency, and equity of healthcare delivery: *What to purchase? From whom to purchase? and how to purchase?* [9–11] In addition, in this chapter we bring an additional fourth question of *how to use monitoring and evaluation and data for improving the efficiency of the health system?* Each of these questions requires a deliberate and evidence-based approach to ensure that healthcare spending directly contributes to better health outcomes and system sustainability. **The first question, "What to purchase?"**, focuses on identifying which health services and interventions provide the most value for a given population. This involves assessing the population's health needs, prioritizing services that address prevalent conditions, and investing in cost-effective, preventive, and high-impact interventions that can improve health outcomes and contain future healthcare costs [12, 13]. Insurers and policymakers consider factors such as the cost-effectiveness of interventions and their potential to improve health equity [14]. By carefully defining the benefit package, strategic purchasers ensure that resources are allocated to services with the greatest potential for positive health impact, ultimately maximizing the value derived from healthcare spending.

Case Study: Cost Saving in India's National Health Insurance Scheme Using Strategic Purchasing

In the national health insurance scheme of India, Ayushman Bharat Pradhan Mantri Jan Arogya Yojana (AB PM-JAY), the principle of "What to purchase?" has been operationalized through the rational selection of benefit packages that prioritize cost-effective and high-impact interventions. The package selection process is driven by evidence-based decision-making, incorporating health technology assessments (HTA) to ensure that interventions offer maximum health benefits relative to cost (for details, please refer to chapter on Use of HTA for Strategic Purchasing of Healthcare Services). Additionally, AB PM-JAY emphasizes equity considerations by specifically covering vulnerable populations that otherwise face significant barriers to accessing healthcare. By aligning strategic purchasing with epidemiological priorities and cost-effectiveness analyses, AB PM-JAY ensures that limited resources are directed toward services that yield the highest value in terms of health outcomes and financial risk protection, thereby strengthening the overall efficiency and sustainability of India's health system. To maximize value for money in AB PM-JAY resource allocation, improve accessibility, enhance financial protection, and reduce health disparities, the National Health Authority (NHA) established the Health Financing and Technology Assessment (HeFTA) unit. This unit facilitates the use of HTA evidence to ensure the efficient distribution of AB PM-JAY funds. One of its key initiatives, horizon scanning, has played an important role in refining the Health Benefit Packages (HBPs). A significant example of this impact is the revision of oncology packages. The incorporation of the targeted monoclonal antibody trastuzumab alongside chemotherapy as part of adjuvant treatment for HER2/neu-positive breast cancer has substantially improved both disease-free and overall survival rates. Initially, PM-JAY's breast cancer oncology package capped trastuzumab treatment at four cycles. However, between 2019 and 2022, numerous appeals from stakeholders—including private hospitals, individual patients, advocacy groups, state health authorities, and elected state representatives—called for an expansion of the approved cycles from four to 18 per year. This demand underscored the necessity of evaluating the cost-effectiveness of such an extension. In a recent study evaluating the cost-effectiveness of adjuvant trastuzumab therapy for HER2/neu-positive women in India, treatment durations of one year and six months were compared. The findings indicated that a six-month regimen was more cost-effective than the full-year treatment. During a horizon-scanning review of HTA evidence, the HeFTA unit identified this study as relevant for updating the Standard Treatment Guidelines (STG) for trastuzumab. Consequently, the STGs were revised to increase the maximum number of approved cycles from four to eight. This revision had two key implications. First, expanding the approved cycles from four to eight improved patient access to trastuzumab therapy, enhanced clinical outcomes, and reduced out-of-pocket expenses, as patients were no longer required to self-fund the final four cycles of treatment. Second, utilizing HTA evidence while limiting the approved cycles to 8 rather than extending them to 18 resulted in an estimated annual cost saving of ₹4160 million (50 million USD) for the payer (NHA).

The second question, "From whom to purchase?", addresses the selection of providers who are equipped to deliver high-quality, accessible, and efficient care. This involves evaluating providers based on criteria such as their clinical expertise, quality of care, geographic accessibility, and commitment to continuous improvement [7]. Insurers may engage in selective contracting, forming partnerships with providers who meet specific performance standards and align with the goals of the purchasing organization [15]. Through selective contracting, insurers ensure that they are working with a network of providers who can deliver reliable, cost-effective care, often incentivized to uphold quality and efficiency standards.

The third question, "How to purchase?", centers on the mechanisms and strategies used to pay for healthcare services. Strategic purchasers must decide on payment methods that align provider incentives with desired outcomes. Options include fee-for-service, capitation, bundled payments, or value-based purchasing, each with different implications for cost, quality, and provider behavior. For example, value-based models reward providers for achieving quality benchmarks and patient satisfaction, while capitation promotes efficient use of resources by providing fixed payments per individual covered for provision of care [16]. Chapter 5 discusses each of the provider payment method in detail. By choosing payment mechanisms that promote quality and cost control, insurers can create a system where financial incentives support both patient-centered care and sustainable healthcare delivery.

Finally, **the fourth key question** in strategic purchasing focuses on leveraging **monitoring, evaluation, and data analysis** to enhance the efficiency of the health system. It deals with the exploration of how data-driven insights can be used to refine purchasing decisions and improve overall healthcare delivery. By systematically analyzing health data, insurers can assess service utilization trends, patient outcomes, and emerging health challenges, enabling them to make informed adjustments to their purchasing strategies. For example, in the context of PM-JAY, data-driven decision-making is integral to optimizing resource allocation and ensuring the scheme's effectiveness. The NHA continuously monitors claims data, treatment patterns, and beneficiary demographics to identify inefficiencies, detect fraud, and enhance the appropriateness of care. For example, real-time analysis of hospital claims helps flag overutilization or underutilization of specific treatments, guiding policy refinements to prevent unnecessary expenditure while ensuring essential services reach those in need. This continuous cycle of data collection, evaluation, and strategic adaptation ensures that PM-JAY not only optimizes value for money but also advances its mission of universal, equitable healthcare coverage.

Check Your Learning by Answering These Questions:

1. Health insurers often struggle to balance cost containment with providing comprehensive coverage. How can strategic purchasing help resolve this tension, and what trade-offs might insurers face in implementing it effectively?
2. Consider two health insurance schemes: one that passively reimburses all healthcare providers and another that selectively contracts with high-performing providers. What potential advantages and risks does the latter approach present in terms of cost, quality, and access to care?

From the perspective of strategic purchasing, it is important to understand that HTA determines the value-based price of interventions, that is a price that reflects the health outcomes and benefits achieved relative to the resources invested. This value-based price then serves as the foundation for strategic purchasing mechanisms such as price negotiation and price regulation. However, translating this into practice requires strong institutional structures and governance capacity (Fig. 4.1). Through strategic purchasing, health insurers can identify high-value services, select providers based on performance and quality metrics, and implement payment mechanisms that reward efficient and effective care [17]. Rather than reimbursing services passively, insurers can leverage their purchasing power to shape the market, incentivize quality improvements, and focus on preventive care, ultimately aligning healthcare spending with broader value-based goals of health improvement, equity, and sustainability [18, 19]. This proactive approach helps insurers to manage costs while enhancing patient outcomes, making strategic purchasing an essential tool in today's complex healthcare environment.

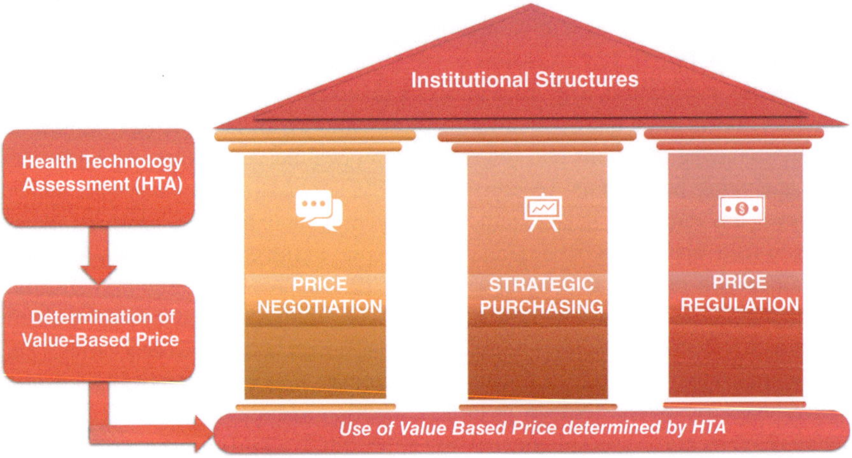

Fig. 4.1 Using HTA to determine value-based price and strengthen strategic purchasing mechanisms within health systems

4.2 Key Stakeholders in Strategic Purchasing

Strategic purchasing in healthcare involves a diverse array of stakeholders, each playing a unique role in shaping effective, equitable, and sustainable healthcare delivery. At the forefront are the payers and health insurers, who act as the primary agents of strategic purchasing [20]. By deciding what services to cover, selecting providers, and negotiating payment mechanisms, insurers have significant influence over the quality, cost-effectiveness, and accessibility of care. Insurers are also responsible for gathering and analyzing data on service utilization and outcomes, which enables them to make informed purchasing decisions that align with both population health needs and financial constraints [20].

In addition to the payers and insurers, healthcare providers, including hospitals, clinics, and individual practitioners, are also the important stakeholders in this process [21]. They directly deliver the services purchased by insurers and thus have a substantial impact on the quality and efficiency of care [22]. Providers play a key role in implementing quality standards and participating in payment models that incentivize high-quality, cost-effective services [23]. Their collaboration is essential for aligning clinical practices with the goals of strategic purchasing, such as reducing unnecessary care and improving patient outcomes [24]. Likewise, regulatory bodies and government agencies are pivotal stakeholders, overseeing the implementation of policies that support strategic purchasing. These entities set guidelines and quality standards, ensure compliance, and create an enabling environment for insurers and providers to collaborate effectively. By enforcing regulations and monitoring performance, they ensure that strategic purchasing practices are equitable, transparent, and focused on improving health outcomes [18].

4.3 Health Insurers as Strategic Purchasers: Scope, Responsibilities, and Actions

Health insurers occupy a central role as strategic purchasers in healthcare, bearing the responsibility of making decisions that can significantly impact both the health system's performance and the well-being of the insured population. Their scope extends beyond simply financing care, as insurers actively shape healthcare delivery by deciding what services are covered, who delivers those services, and how providers are reimbursed [25]. Through strategic purchasing, insurers can influence a range of outcomes, from improving care quality and patient satisfaction to controlling costs and expanding access to essential services. This proactive role enables insurers to align their purchasing decisions with population health needs, ensuring that resources are directed toward interventions and providers that offer the best value and outcomes for patients.

In fulfilling these responsibilities, health insurers employ a variety of mechanisms to achieve efficient and high-quality care. This includes designing benefit packages (a set of healthcare services, defined by the insurance provider, that are available to beneficiaries, and outlines what services are covered) that prioritize high-impact, evidence-based interventions, implementing value-based payment models that reward providers for achieving quality metrics, and fostering partnerships with selected providers based on performance criteria [26]. Additionally, insurers are responsible for monitoring and evaluating healthcare delivery to ensure compliance with contractual standards and quality benchmarks. By analyzing health data, insurers can continuously assess service utilization patterns, patient outcomes, and emerging health trends, allowing them to refine their purchasing strategies over time.

Another fundamental responsibility of health insurers as strategic purchasers is to select and accredit providers based on a comprehensive assessment of their capacity to deliver quality care across a range of services [7]. This process involves evaluating providers' infrastructure, clinical expertise, patient safety records, and geographical location to ensure accessible, high-quality services that meet the needs of the insured population. By accrediting providers, insurers establish a network of trusted facilities and practitioners who are well-equipped to deliver essential healthcare services. Once providers are selected, insurers establish service agreements or contracts that outline the terms of engagement, specifying the scope of services, quality standards, and mutual expectations. These contracts serve as a framework for accountability, ensuring that providers adhere to agreed-upon standards and that insurers uphold their commitment to timely payments and supportive oversight. For example, to be empaneled under PM-JAY, the hospitals must fulfill specific eligibility criteria set by the NHA, which include maintaining a minimum number of inpatient beds, ensuring adequate staffing, and complying with the standards outlined in the Clinical Establishment Act and relevant State government regulations [27]. Healthcare providers are incentivized to achieve quality benchmarks through PM-JAY Certification, which is awarded at three levels: Bronze, Silver, and Gold. These certifications not only signify adherence to quality standards but also offer corresponding financial incentives under the scheme. Furthermore, healthcare facilities must undergo a renewal process, which is subject to their compliance with the minimum standards set by PM-JAY Certification or the guidelines of the National Accreditation Board for Hospitals and Healthcare Providers (NABH) [28]. Further details on this aspect is provided in the chapter of Publicly Financed Health Insurance Schemes in India.

Another key action in strategic purchasing is to provide guidance on creating an essential drug list or formulary, and standard treatment guidelines that accredited providers are required to follow. These guidelines should cover not only the use of medicines but also diagnostic tools, surgical supplies, and other necessary equipment. In India, National List of Essential Medicines (NLEM) and National Essential Diagnostic Lists (NEDL), along with Medical Services Corporations, play an important role in strategic purchasing by guiding insurers in cost-effective procurement and ensuring the availability of essential medicines and medical supplies [29]. By standardizing drug procurement, these lists help insurers optimize spending and prevent unnecessary expenditures on non-essential or high-cost alternatives. Medical Services Corporations further enhance efficiency by enabling bulk purchasing and centralized distribution, reducing costs while ensuring a steady supply of essential medicines and equipment. This approach not only enhances financial sustainability but also improves patient outcomes by ensuring timely access to standardized treatments. Formularies, which typically include lists of approved generic drugs, surgical supplies, and prostheses, should ensure that cost-effective, evidence-based options are available for patients. Standard treatment guidelines help harmonize care delivery by presenting providers with a structured approach to diagnosis and treatment, which can reduce unnecessary variations in care and improve outcomes.

Health insurers are also responsible for designing and implementing provider-payment methods such as capitation, bundled payments, or performance-based incentives to promote efficiency and encourage high-quality care [30, 31]. Payment methods are strategically selected and regularly modified to discourage over-servicing, prevent cost escalation, and reward value rather than volume. Alongside this, insurers work to establish appropriate payment rates that are fair and sustainable for both providers and the insurer, balancing cost containment with provider motivation [32].

Effective provider management also requires insurers to secure timely information on services provided, monitor provider performance, and act on any cases of poor performance. This entails continuous assessment of service quality, patient outcomes, and adherence to established guidelines [33]. Monitoring mechanisms such as periodic audits and performance reviews allow insurers to detect and address issues early, ensuring that substandard care is corrected promptly. In cases where fraud or corruption is suspected, insurers implement protective measures to safeguard the integrity of their funds, which may include regular audits of provider claims and rigorous verification processes. Ensuring regular and timely payment to providers builds trust and fosters a stable relationship that ultimately benefits patients. Additionally, strategic purchasers are tasked with allocating resources equitably across regions, implementing policies that promote equitable access, and managing user payment policies to reduce financial barriers to care [34]. Underpinning these actions is the development and use of robust information systems that provide the data needed for effective decision-making, resource allocation, and continuous improvement of purchasing strategies.

4.4 Key Strategic Purchasing Actions Related to Citizens and Government

An important aspect of strategic purchasing is to align healthcare services with the needs, preferences, and values of the population [22, 35]. Assessing service needs and preferences involves analyzing epidemiological data, conducting community health surveys, and gathering direct input from the population to understand their health priorities and challenges [22]. This assessment enables insurers to tailor service entitlements and benefit packages that are relevant and responsive to the population's specific health requirements, ensuring that resources are directed toward high-priority services. By developing health benefit packages that reflect the real needs of the population, insurers not only improve health outcomes but also enhance the perceived value of health coverage, fostering greater trust and satisfaction among beneficiaries [36].

Equally important is informing the population about their entitlements and obligations. Clear communication is essential to ensure that citizens are aware of the services they are entitled to receive, any cost-sharing mechanism such as a co-payment or deductible requirements, and their rights and responsibilities as beneficiaries [36]. This information must be accessible, transparent, and regularly updated so that individuals understand how to access services and what they can expect from the health system. To support equitable access, insurers also need to ensure that all population segments can access their entitlements, regardless of socioeconomic status, geographic location, or other barriers. This may involve establishing networks of accessible providers, offering transportation subsidies for remote areas, or using digital health platforms to reach underserved communities. By actively working to remove barriers to care, insurers fulfill a fundamental obligation to the insured population, promoting inclusivity and fairness in healthcare access.

Furthermore, strategic purchasing requires establishing effective mechanisms for receiving and responding to complaints and feedback from the population [20]. This feedback loop enables insurers to gain insights into beneficiaries' experiences, identify service delivery gaps, and make continuous improvements to enhance the quality and responsiveness of care. Feedback mechanisms might include surveys, helplines, or online portals where beneficiaries can voice their concerns and suggestions. The NHA's helpline number and call center facility for PM-JAY beneficiary serves as an important mechanism for strategic purchasing by providing a structured platform to receive and address complaints, grievances, and beneficiary feedback. This real-time responsiveness helps identify service gaps, prevent fraud, and improve provider accountability, ensuring more efficient and patient-centered healthcare delivery.

Additionally, publicly reporting on resource use and performance measures demonstrates accountability and transparency, building public trust in the health system. Regular performance reports should cover aspects such as expenditure patterns, health outcomes, service coverage, and provider quality metrics. By keeping the public informed, insurers reinforce their commitment to responsible resource stewardship and provide the population with valuable information that empowers them to make informed choices about their healthcare.

Likewise, the government plays an essential role in fostering an environment where strategic purchasing can effectively improve healthcare access, quality, and efficiency. One of its primary actions is to establish clear regulatory frameworks for both purchasers and providers. By defining the roles, responsibilities, and operational standards for health insurers and healthcare providers, the government sets the foundation for a transparent and coordinated system. This regulatory framework may include licensing standards, quality benchmarks, and patient rights, along with mechanisms for monitoring and enforcement [37]. A well-defined framework creates consistency across the healthcare sector, allowing insurers to make purchasing decisions confidently and empowering providers to align with best practices. It also ensures that strategic purchasing initiatives are in sync with broader health system goals, such as universal health coverage and equity in access.

Another vital government responsibility is to fill gaps in service delivery infrastructure to ensure that healthcare facilities are available, especially in underserved areas [38]. Infrastructure gaps can pose significant barriers to access, especially in rural or remote regions where private providers may be less willing to establish services due to high costs or limited demand. The government can address these gaps through targeted investments in public healthcare facilities, subsidies for private providers willing to operate in these areas, initiatives to train and retain healthcare workers in underserved communities, and setting differential pricing based on the type of city and level of care [39]. For instance, in aspirational districts, hospitals empaneled under PM-JAY receive a 10% incentive on the base package rate, ensuring fair compensation for healthcare providers serving these underserved areas [27, 39]. This approach enhances strategic purchasing by improving healthcare accessibility where it is needed most. In addition, the government of India has launched the viability-gap funding scheme with the aim of promoting public–private partnership in the development of health infrastructure, wherein the government provides subsidies to make the socially essential projects commercially viable [38]. The scheme prioritizes Aspirational Districts and encourages private investment in Tier 2 and Tier 3 cities to expand access to affordable healthcare. With this scheme, the government aims to promote the establishment of hospitals in locations where there are no/minimal empaneled hospitals under the PM-JAY. By strengthening the healthcare infrastructure, the government enhances the effectiveness of strategic purchasing efforts, as health insurers can contract with a robust network of providers and ensure that benefits reach all segments of the population [40].

Finally, the government is responsible for mobilizing adequate resources to meet the health service entitlements of the population and ensuring the accountability of purchasers. Resource mobilization may involve generating funds through taxation, social health insurance contributions, or donor support to meet health service demands without imposing excessive financial strain on individuals [10]. The aspects pertaining to mobilizing resources for healthcare have been described in detail in the chapter on revenue collection (Chap. 2). The government must allocate these resources efficiently, ensuring that strategic purchasing is financially sustainable and can fulfill its commitments. Additionally, holding purchasers accountable is crucial for maintaining transparency and trust in the system. The government can establish accountability mechanisms, such as performance audits and regular reporting requirements, to ensure that health insurers uphold their contractual obligations, provide quality services, and manage funds responsibly [41]. This oversight encourages prudent use of resources and safeguards public interests, making strategic purchasing a powerful tool for advancing national health objectives.

Check Your Learning by Answering These Questions:

1. Health insurers can have substantial influence over healthcare delivery through strategic purchasing. However, their decisions can sometimes create conflicts with providers or regulators. What are some potential areas of misalignment between these stakeholders, and how can insurers navigate these challenges to maintain both efficiency and equity?
2. Selective contracting allows insurers to engage with high-performing providers, but it may also lead to access barriers for some populations. How should insurers balance quality-driven provider selection with the need to ensure equitable healthcare access?
3. Governments play a critical role in creating a regulatory framework that enables effective strategic purchasing. In what ways can weak governance or inadequate regulation undermine the intended benefits of strategic purchasing for both insurers and beneficiaries?
4. Robust data systems are essential for insurers to monitor provider performance and ensure accountability. However, excessive reliance on performance metrics can sometimes lead to unintended consequences. What potential risks might arise from a heavily data-driven approach to provider management, and how can insurers mitigate them?

4.5 Mechanisms and Tools for Strategic Purchasing

Strategic purchasing encompasses a variety of models, each designed to optimize healthcare spending and improve outcomes by aligning financial incentives with health system goals. One common model is selective contracting, where insurers establish partnerships with a limited network of high-quality providers based on performance metrics and cost-effectiveness [15]. By selectively contracting with providers who meet specific standards, insurers can control costs while ensuring quality care for their beneficiaries. Selective contracting also allows insurers to negotiate favorable rates, implement quality assurance protocols, and incentivize providers to focus on high-value care.

Another key approach within strategic purchasing is value-based purchasing (VBP), which ties provider reimbursement to the quality of care delivered rather than the volume of services [18, 24, 42, 43]. In VBP models, payments are often linked to measurable outcomes, such as patient satisfaction, readmission rates, or adherence to clinical guidelines [18]. This shift from fee-for-service to value-based reimbursement encourages providers to focus on patient-centered care, preventive services, and chronic disease management, ultimately improving health outcomes and reducing unnecessary expenditures. Population-based payment models are an extension of this approach, where providers receive a set payment for managing a defined population's health, incentivizing preventive care and integrated services. Together, these models illustrate the versatility of strategic purchasing and its potential to transform healthcare systems by promoting efficiency, accountability, and high-quality care.

Effective strategic purchasing relies on a range of provider payment mechanisms designed to align provider incentives with healthcare goals, such as cost control, quality improvement, and equitable access. The different provider payment methods have been described in detail in the Chap. 5 on "Provider payment methods." To mention briefly, one common payment method is capitation, where providers receive a fixed payment per enrolled individual over a specific period, regardless of the services used [16]. Capitation encourages providers to focus on preventive care and efficient resource use as they assume financial risk if patients require extensive services. However, it also requires careful monitoring to prevent under-provision of care. Fee-for-service (FFS), another payment model, reimburses providers for each service delivered [44]. While FFS can incentivize comprehensive care, it may lead to overutilization as providers are compensated for volume rather than outcomes. Strategic purchasing aims to balance different payment mechanisms to encourage efficiency without compromising quality.

To further address these challenges, many health systems utilize diagnosis-related groups (DRGs) and bundled payments. DRGs assign a fixed payment based on the patient's diagnosis and the expected cost of treatment, encouraging hospitals to optimize care processes for specific conditions and reduce unnecessary interventions [45]. Similarly, bundled payments provide a single, comprehensive payment for all services associated with a treatment episode, such as surgery and postoperative care. Bundled payments incentivize providers to coordinate care across different settings, improve care continuity, and avoid complications that could lead to additional costs. Both DRGs and bundled payments hold providers accountable for the cost and quality of care within a defined scope, aligning incentives with efficient, high-quality service delivery. Global experience therefore suggests that the successful health financing models have attempted to use multiple payment methods that are characterized by a layering of individual provider payment method (e.g., FFS, capitation, DRGs) and/or "add-on" incentives that are applied to individual or multiple providers [46]. This type of provider payment mechanism is known as blended payment model.

Beyond payment mechanisms, VBP and performance-based incentives are important tools for promoting quality and patient-centered care. VBP models link provider payments to the achievement of specific performance targets, such as reduced hospital readmissions, improved patient satisfaction, or adherence to clinical guidelines [18, 24, 35, 42, 43]. By rewarding providers who deliver high-quality care, VBP shifts the focus from quantity to value, encouraging providers to invest in preventive services, chronic disease management, and patient education. Performance-based incentives extend this concept by offering additional financial rewards for providers who meet or exceed established benchmarks. For example, providers may receive bonuses for achieving high scores in areas like patient safety or care coordination. These tools enable strategic purchasers to drive improvements in care quality while maintaining financial accountability, making them essential components of an effective purchasing strategy.

Check Your Learning by Answering These Questions:

1. Selective contracting allows insurers to control costs and improve care quality by working only with high-performing providers. However, this approach can limit patient choice and access to care. What strategies can insurers use to ensure that selective contracting balances cost-efficiency with equitable access for all beneficiaries?
2. Blended payment models combine different payment methods to achieve a balance between cost control, quality improvement, and provider incentives. What are the potential advantages and challenges of using a blended payment approach, and how can strategic purchasers mitigate the risks associated with this model?
3. Risk-sharing arrangements create financial accountability for both insurers and providers. However, these agreements may discourage providers from treating high-risk patients due to potential financial losses. What mechanisms can be implemented to prevent risk-averse behavior while ensuring that providers remain financially sustainable?

4.6 Summary

Strategic purchasing represents a transformative approach in healthcare that empowers health insurers to manage resources with precision, efficiency, and a strong focus on quality. By moving away from passive reimbursement models, strategic purchasing enables insurers to selectively invest in high-value services, negotiate performance-based contracts, and engage in risk-sharing arrangements that align provider incentives with health outcomes. This approach is instrumental in tackling pressing challenges such as rising healthcare costs, variable service quality, and disparities in access, all of which have profound implications for achieving universal health coverage (UHC). Strategic purchasing, therefore, not only drives improvements in care but also enhances system sustainability by ensuring that healthcare spending directly contributes to population health goals.

The chapter emphasizes the integral roles of various stakeholders—insurers, providers, government bodies, and the population—in creating a successful strategic purchasing environment. Insurers lead the way by designing benefit packages, implementing robust provider payment mechanisms, and fostering provider partnerships that emphasize accountability and performance. Providers, for their part, play a crucial role by adhering to quality standards and participating in payment models that reward efficiency. Government agencies provide the essential regulatory and financial support needed to uphold the framework within which strategic purchasing operates, ensuring that insurers and providers act in the public's best interest. Finally, a commitment to transparency and feedback from the population is vital for building trust and refining purchasing practices to better meet healthcare needs.

The use of varied payment mechanisms—such as capitation, bundled payments, and value-based purchasing—demonstrates the flexibility and adaptability of strategic purchasing. Each mechanism brings unique advantages and is tailored to encourage different aspects of provider behavior, whether through cost-control measures, preventive care, or quality improvement initiatives. Risk-sharing contracts further strengthen the system by distributing financial responsibility between insurers and providers, fostering a shared commitment to delivering cost-effective and high-quality care. Together, these mechanisms form a toolkit that allows insurers to respond effectively to the complex and evolving healthcare landscape.

As health systems continue to evolve, strategic purchasing remains a powerful tool for driving meaningful improvements in health outcomes and system efficiency. However, to maximize its potential, ongoing collaboration among stakeholders and continuous adaptation of purchasing practices will be essential. Strategic purchasing offers a path forward that not only meets immediate healthcare demands but also builds a resilient, equitable, and sustainable foundation for the future of healthcare delivery.

References

1. World Health Organisation. Out-of-pocket health expenditure (% of private expenditure on health). World Health Organization Global Health Expenditure Database 2016. Availalble from: https://apps.who.int/nha/database/Select/Indicators/en
2. Yu H, Dick AW. Impacts of rising health care costs on families with employment-based private insurance: a national analysis with state fixed effects. Health Serv Res. 2012;47(5):2012–30.
3. Bazyar M, Rashidian A, Alipouri Sakha M, Vaez Mahdavi MR, Doshmangir L. Combining health insurance funds in a fragmented context: what kind of challenges should be considered? BMC Health Serv Res. 2020;20:1–4.
4. Angell BJ, Prinja S, Gupt A, Jha V, Jan S. The Ayushman Bharat Pradhan Mantri Jan Arogya Yojana and the path to universal health coverage in India: overcoming the challenges of stewardship and governance. PLoS Med. 2019;16(3):e1002759.
5. World Health Organization. The World Health Report 2000. Health systems: improving performance. Geneva: World Health Organozation; 2000. [Cited on 07 Nov 2024]. Available at: https://apps.who.int/iris/handle/10665/42281
6. Kutzin J. A descriptive framework for country-level analysis of health care financing arrangements. Health Policy. 2001;56(3):171–204.
7. RESYST. What is strategic purchasing for health? Health financing research theme, Resilient and Responsive Health Systems (RESYST). 2014. http://resyst.lshtm.ac.uk/sites/resyst.lshtm.ac.uk/files/docs/reseources/Purchasing20brief.pdf
8. Sanderson J, Lonsdale C, Mannion R. What's needed to develop strategic purchasing in healthcare? Policy lessons from a realist review. Int J Health Policy Manag. 2019;8(1):4–17.
9. World Health Organization. The World Health Report 2010. Health systems financing: the path to universal coverage. Geneva: World Health Organization; 2010. [Cited on 28 October 2024]. Available from: https://www.who.int/publications/i/item/9789241564021
10. Kutzin J. Health financing for universal coverage and health system performance: concepts and implications for policy. Bull World Health Organ. 2013;91(8):602–11.
11. Mathauer I, Dale E, Jowett M, Kutzin J. Purchasing health services for universal health coverage: how to make it more strategic? Geneva: World Health Organization; 2019. [Cited 01 Nov 2024]. Available from: https://apps.who.int/iris/handle/10665/311387

12. Prinja S, Jyani G, Gupta N, Rajsekar K. Adapting health technology assessment for drugs, medical devices, and health programs: Methodological considerations from the Indian experience. Expert Rev Pharmacoecon Outcomes Res. 2021;21(5):859–68. https://doi.org/10.1080/14737167.2021.1921575.
13. Gupta N, Jyani G, Rajsekar K, Gupta R, Nagar A, Gedam P, et al. Application of health technology assessment for oncology care in India: implications for Ayushman Bharat Pradhan Mantri Jan Aarogya Yojana. Indian J Med Paediatr Oncol. 2021;42(05):479–83.
14. Prinja S, Chugh Y, Gupta N, Aggarwal V. Establishing a health technology assessment evidence ecosystem in India's Pradhan Mantri Jan Arogya Yojana. Health Syst Reform. 2023;9(3):2327097.
15. Bes RE, Wendel S, Curfs EC, Groenewegen PP, de Jong JD. Acceptance of selective contracting: the role of trust in the health insurer. BMC Health Serv Res. 2013;13:375.
16. Mills A, Bennett S, Siriwanarangsun P, Tangcharoensathien V. The response of providers to capitation payment: a case-study from Thailand. Health Policy. 2000;51(3):163–80.
17. Rezapour A, Hakimzadeh SM, Panahi S, Teymourzadeh E, Bahadori M, Bastani P, et al. Designing a pragmatic model for strategic purchasing of health services in health insurance companies: the feasible pivot of strategic purchasing in a developing country. Int J Health Govern. 2019;24(1):42–55.
18. Volume-based to value-based care: Ensuring Better Health Outcomes and Quality Healthcare under AB PM-JAY. [Internet]. National Health Authority, Government of India. Official website of Ayushman Bharat Digital Mission. [cited 30 October 2024]. Available from: https://abdm.gov.in:8081/uploads/VBHC_Policy_Document_For_Upload_a20f871a55.pdf
19. Hanson K, Barasa E, Honda A, Panichkriangkrai W, Patcharanarumol W. Strategic purchasing: the neglected health financing function for pursuing universal health coverage in low- and middle-income countries comment on "What's needed to develop strategic purchasing in healthcare? Policy lessons from a realist review". Int J Health Policy Manag. 2019;8(8):501–4.
20. Cashin C, Gatome-Munyua A. The strategic health purchasing progress tracking framework: a practical approach to describing, assessing, and improving strategic purchasing for universal health coverage. Health Syst Reform. 2022;8(2):e2051794.
21. Prinja S, Singh MP, Aggarwal V, Rajsekar K, Gedam P, Goyal A, et al. Impact of India's publicly financed health insurance scheme on public sector district hospitals: a health financing perspective. Lancet Reg Health Southeast Asia. 2022;9:100123.
22. Prinja S, Jyani G, Goyal A, Sharma S, Kaur T, Sundararaman T. Framework for responsive financing of district hospitals of India. Front Public Health. 2024;12:1398227.
23. Jha A, Zeng W, Farag M, Nandakumar A, Gonzalez-Pier E. Editorial: organizing and financing universal primary health care systems – best practices and blueprints for low- and middle-income countries. Front Public Health. 2024;12:1422873.
24. Teisberg E, Wallace S, O'Hara S. Defining and implementing value-based health care: a strategic framework. Acad Med. 2020;95(5):682–5.
25. Provider payments and price setting under PMJAY: Improving efficiency, acceptability, quality and sustainability. [Internet]. National Health Authority, Government of India. Official website of Ayushman Bharat Digital Mission. [cited 30 October 2024]. Available from: https://abdm.gov.in/sites/default/files/2022-03/AB%20PM-JAY%20Price%20Consultation%20Paper.pdf
26. Honda A, Obse A. Payment arrangements for private healthcare purchasing under publicly funded systems in low- and middle-income countries: issues and implications. Appl Health Econ Health Policy. 2020;18(6):811–23.
27. Government of India. Ayushman Bharat- Pradhan Mantri Jan Arogya Yojana. Guidelines on Hospital Empanelment and De- Empanelment (Version – 3.0). [Cited on 19 March 2025]. Available from: https://nha.gov.in/img/resources/Revised-Empanelment-and-De-empanelment-Guideline.pdf
28. National Health Authority. Ayushman Bharat Pradhan Mantri –Jan Arogya Yojana Operation Manual [Internet]. 2022 [cited 2024 Nov 11]. Available from: https://nha.gov.in/img/resources/Operation%20Manual%20for%20AB%20PM-JAY.pdf

29. National Essential Diagnostics List. New Delhi: Indian Council of Medical Research; 2019. [cited 19 March 2025]. Available from: https://www.nhp.gov.in/NHPfiles/NEDL_2019_Final_V2.pdf
30. Soeters R, Habineza C, Peerenboom PB. Performance-based financing and changing the district health system: experience from Rwanda. Bull World Health Organ. 2006;84(11):884–9.
31. Witter S, Chirwa Y, Chandiwana P, Munyati S, Pepukai M, Bertone MP, et al. Results-based financing as a strategic purchasing intervention: some progress but much further to go in Zimbabwe? BMC Health Serv Res. 2020;20(1):180.
32. Prinja S, Singh MP, Rajsekar K, Sachin O, Gedam P, Nagar A, Bhargava B, CHSI Study Group. Translating research to policy: setting provider payment rates for strategic purchasing under India's National Publicly Financed Health Insurance Scheme. Appl Health Econ Health Policy. 2021;19(3):353–70.
33. Hirth RA, Turenne MN, Wheeler JR, Pan Q, Ma Y, Messana JM. Provider monitoring and pay-for-performance when multiple providers affect outcomes: an application to renal dialysis. Health Serv Res. 2009;44(5p1):1585–602.
34. Prinja S, Bahuguna P, Singh MP, Guinness L, Goyal A, Aggarwal V. Refining the provider payment system of India's government-funded health insurance programme: an econometric analysis. BMJ Open. 2023;13(10):e076155.
35. Porter M. Value-based health care delivery. Harvard Business School; 2012.
36. Oortwijn W, Jansen M, Baltussen R. Evidence-informed deliberative processes for health benefit package design. Part II: A practical guide. Int J Health Policy Manag. 2022;11(10):2327–36.
37. Bauhoff S, Sudharsanan N. The insurance cascade framework to diagnose bottlenecks and improve the effectiveness of health insurance programs: an application to India. CGD Working Paper 583. Washington, DC: Center for Global Development; 2021. [Cited on 16 October 2024] Available from: https://www.cgdev.org/publication/insurance-cascade-frameworkdiagnose-bottlenecks-and-improve-effectiveness-health
38. Cabinet approves Continuation and Revamping of the Scheme for Financial Support to Public Private Partnerships in Infrastructure Viability Gap Funding VGF Scheme [Internet]. Pib.gov.in. 2020 [cited 19 March 2025]. Available from: https://pib.gov.in/PressReleasePage.aspx?PRID=1671914
39. Health Benefit Package 2.2 [Internet]. National Health Authority. Pmjay.gov.in. 2021 [Cited 27 October 2020]. Available from: https://nha.gov.in/img/resources/HBP-2.2-manual.pdf
40. Jyani G, Gedam P, Sharma S, Dixit J, Prinja S. Financial Viability of Private Hospitals Operating Under India's National Health Insurance Scheme Ayushman Bharat Pradhan Mantri-Jan Arogya Yojana (AB PM-JAY). Appl Health Econ Health Policy. 2025;23(5):841–53. https://doi.org/10.1007/s40258-025-00966-9. Epub 2025 Apr 11.
41. Shwartz MI, Restuccia JD, Rosen AK. Composite measures of health care provider performance: a description of approaches. Milbank Q. 2015;93(4):788–825.
42. Gentry S, Badrinath P. Defining health in the era of value-based care: lessons from England of relevance to other health systems. Cureus. 2017;9(3):e1079.
43. Porter ME, Teisberg EO. Redefining health care: creating value-based competition on results. Boston: Harvard Business School Press; 2006.
44. Camara BS, Delamou A, Grovogui FM, de Kok BC, Benova L, El Ayadi AM, et al. Interventions to increase facility births and provision of postpartum care in sub-Saharan Africa: a scoping review. Reprod Health. 2021;18(1):16.
45. Kotherová Z, Caithamlová M, Nemec J, Dolejšová K. The Use of diagnosis-related group-based reimbursement in the Czech Hospital Care System. Int J Environ Res Public Health. 2021;18(10):5463.
46. Feldhaus I, Mathauer I. Effects of mixed provider payment systems and aligned cost sharing practices on expenditure growth management, efficiency, and equity: a structured review of the literature. BMC Health Serv Res. 2018;18:996.

Suggested Readings for Further Learning

World Health Organization. Strategic Purchasing for UHC: Unlocking the potential. Global meeting summary and key messages. Geneva: World Health Organization; 2017.

Mathauer I, Dale E, Meessen B. Strategic purchasing for Universal Health Coverage: key policy issues and questions. A summary from expert and practitioners' discussions. Geneva: World Health Organization; 2017.

Prinja S, Singh MP, Rajsekar K, Sachin O, Gedam P, Nagar A, CHSI Study Group, et al. Translating research to policy: setting provider payment rates for strategic purchasing under India's national publicly financed health insurance scheme. Appl Health Econ Health Policy. 2021;19(3):353–70.

Provider Payment Methods

5

Navneet Kaur, Gaurav Jyani, Sudha Chandrashekar, and Shankar Prinja

Abstract

This chapter introduces the landscape of provider payment methods (PPMs), offering a comprehensive overview of various types, key characteristics, as well as potential benefits and inherent risks associated with each method. It contextualizes these payment systems within the complexities of the healthcare market, examining how different PPMs impact healthcare delivery and outcomes. The chapter provides an in-depth analysis of prevalent provider payment methods, including fee-for-service, capitation, and case-based payments, among others. Special attention is given to the methods employed in India, along with global examples. Additionally, the chapter builds on the concept of strategic purchasing in chapter 4 by introducing the innovative concept of blended payments. Through this exploration, the chapter aims to equip readers with an understanding of how provider payment methods can influence healthcare quality, efficiency, and equity.

Keywords

Provider payment methods · Global budget · Strategic purchasing · Blended payments · PPM

N. Kaur · G. Jyani · S. Prinja (✉)
Department of Community Medicine and School of Public Health, PGIMER, Chandigarh, India

S. Chandrashekar
Senior Consultant, World Bank and Advisor, Health System Transformation Platform, Bengaluru, Karnataka, India

S. Prinja (ed.), *Healthcare Financing and Insurance*,
https://doi.org/10.1007/978-981-95-3513-2_5

Learning Objectives

After going through the chapter, you will be able to

- Understand and differentiate between various types of provider payment methods, their characteristics, and the associated benefits and risks with each method
- Understand provider payment methods employed in India and globally

Key Terms

- *Purchaser* may be an individual seeking healthcare, government purchasing healthcare for the population or insurance companies purchasing on behalf of those who insured.
- *Healthcare provider* refers to any individual or organization that delivers healthcare services, thus including doctors, nurses, laboratories, hospitals, pharmacy, and primary care units.
- *Provider payment* is a mechanism through which purchaser pays the service provider for the delivery of healthcare services.
- *Global budget*: Fixed lump-sum amount allocated to a provider for overall expenditure to provide a set of services for a defined period.
- *Line-item budget*: Fixed amount is allocated to the provider to cover certain input costs for a specific period.
- *Salary*: Fixed regular payment to the provider.
- *Capitation*: Per-person amount paid to the providers prospectively to provide a defined set of services for a fixed period to a defined population.
- *Fee-for-service*: Payment paid to providers for each individual service they deliver.
- *Case-based payments or Case-based bundled payments*: Healthcare providers receive a fixed amount per admission (or per outpatient consultation), inclusive of all services provided during a given patient-provider contact (hospitalization or outpatient consultation).
- *Pay for performance*: Payment to the provider tied to quality or certain performance metrics.
- *Upcoding*: Deliberately assigning a patient's case to a higher-cost code or group than its actual code, usually associated with higher payment rates.

5.1 Introduction

As we have learnt in Chap. 1, healthcare financing includes three key functions, namely revenue collection, risk pooling, and purchasing. Revenue generation and risk pooling have been discussed previously in Chaps. 2 and 3, respectively. This chapter deals with the third function of healthcare financing, that is, "*Purchasing*." Within purchasing, this chapter addresses the specific questions: How to pay provider? And at what rate/price?

Healthcare provider refers to any individual or organization that delivers healthcare services, thus including doctors, nurses, laboratories, hospitals, pharmacy, and primary care units. Purchaser may be an individual seeking healthcare, government purchasing healthcare for the population, or insurance companies purchasing on behalf of those insured. Provider payment methods (PPMs) refer to the methods through which purchaser pays the healthcare provider for the delivery of services [1]. PPMs play a crucial role in determining how healthcare is financed and delivered. They play an important role in ensuring quality services and influencing provider behavior. Globally, different PPMs have been used in combination for strategic purchasing and achieving universal health coverage goals.

This chapter explores the various types of provider payment methods, highlighting their key characteristics through examples and case studies from different countries. It examines the advantages and disadvantages of each payment model, leading to the concept of blended payments as a strategy to balance benefits and risks. Additionally, the chapter provides a detailed discussion on provider payment methods prevalent in India.

5.2 Types of Provider Payment Methods

PPMs can be categorized based on two key characteristics:

- **Time for payment to the providers (prospective/retrospective)**: It refers to whether the payment to the provider is made before the delivery of the service (prospectively) or after the service has been delivered (retrospectively). In prospective payment methods, the financial risk is on the provider as if the costs of delivering services turn out to be higher than the preset prices, the healthcare provider bears the consequences. However, in retrospective methods financial risk lies with the payer. In prospective methods, there is an incentive to reduce the costs and improve the efficiency; however, quality may get compromised. Retrospective methods provide no incentive to reduce costs, thus may lead to over-provision of services.
- **Ground for payment** (input based or output based): This refers to whether the payment to providers is linked to the quantity and value of inputs used (such as doctor consultation, medicines, and investigations) or the volume and/or quality of outputs produced (like services delivered).

Table 5.1 presents the different PPMs and their categorization based on the three key characteristics described above. Different types of PPMs include global budget, line-item budget, salary-based payments, capitation, fee-for-service, case-based payments, and pay for performance. These various types of PPMs are often used in combination to enhance efficient service delivery.

In the next sections, different types of provider payment methods have been explained in detail, along with the benefits and risks associated with each method.

5.2.1 Global Budget

A global budget is a fixed lump sum amount allocated prospectively to a provider to cover the overall expenditures incurred in providing a set of services over a specific period [2]. In this method, there is a flexibility in the utilization of various input resources as the amount is not necessarily tied up to certain line items (Table 5.2). The amount of global budget allocated is likely to be dependent on the historical precedence, which means the amount of money that was budgeted last year, as well as some incremental changes over and above to that. Another way to ascertain the

Table 5.1 Different types of provider payment methods (PPMs) and their key characteristics

Provider payment methods	Time for payment to providers	Ground for payment
Global budget	Prospective	Inputs and outputs
Line-item budget	Prospective	Inputs
Salary-based payments	Retrospective	Inputs
Capitation	Prospective	Outputs
Fee-for-service	Retrospective	Inputs
Case-based payments	Retrospective	Outputs
Pay for performance	Retrospective	Outputs

Table 5.2 Representation of a global budget

Proposed global budget for Primary Health Centres (PHCs) (in hundred thousands ₹)	
Health facility A	30.2
Health facility B	32.6
Health facility C	28.1
Health facility D	33.9

Note: figures are for illustration purpose, not actual budgeting estimates global budget amount is to determine the need for healthcare services, and the corresponding amount of resources required to deliver the services. So, in any case, it is eventually tied to the cost of inputs that are likely to be utilized for the delivery of healthcare services.

5.2.2 Line-Item Budget

A line-item budget is a type of provider payment method in which fixed amounts are allocated to the provider to cover a certain set of different input costs for a specific period. In this, the providers are paid prospectively. It is a typical kind of budget that can be seen in India's public healthcare delivery system. The ability to transfer funds between line items is somewhat restricted, providing strong administrative controls and cost containment. However, this system lacks incentives for enhancing efficiency. Since providers receive a fixed allocation, they may respond to perceived funding shortages by either reducing service provision or increasing referrals to other providers. Additionally, budget allocations for the following year are based on expenditures from the current year. Unspent funds are often considered an indication of overallocation or reduced absorption capacity, potentially leading to budget cuts in the following year. Consequently, this creates an incentive for providers to spend funds quickly to secure future allocations, often at the expense of efficiency. Table 5.3 represents an example of line-item budget that is allocated to a health facility.

Table 5.3 Proposed line-item budget approved for a hospital

Detailed head description	Total amount (in thousands ₹)
Salaries	261,218
Professional services	20,947
Electricity charges	25,369
Medical reimbursement	1981
Other charges	11,511
Water charges	1421
Petrol, oil, and lubricants	183
Office expenses	194
Domestic travel expenses	25
Telephones	40
Wages	0

Note: this is an illustration of budget estimates for a hospital

5.2.3 Salary-Based Payments

The salary payment method is a widely used approach to compensate healthcare providers, particularly in public health systems such as in India and large healthcare organizations. Under this model, providers receive a fixed, regular payment, regardless of the number of patients they see or the volume of services they deliver. This ensures financial stability for providers and simplifies administrative processes by eliminating the need for per-service billing. However, this may also reduce the motivation to maximize efficiency or productivity, as payment is decoupled from the volume or complexity of services delivered.

5.2.4 Capitation

In capitation, a fixed amount is paid to the providers in advance to provide a defined set of services for each person enrolled for a fixed period. The amount is paid at the beginning of the period, irrespective of the actual volume of services delivered thereafter. In simplest form, capitation-based payment could be determined based on per-capita rate, which is multiplied with the total population covered for service provision by the healthcare provider, and the total payment per month or per year can thus be calculated. Table 5.4 illustrates an example of a capitation-based payment model. In this model, a fixed per-capita rate of ₹350 is assigned for each individual per month. The total monthly payment for each health facility is then calculated based on the total population it covers.

Table 5.4 Representation of a capitation-based payment method

Facility	Capitation rate (per person, per month in ₹)	Total population	Payment per facility, Per month (in ₹)
Health facility-1	350	75,000	26,250,000
Health facility-2	350	100,000	35,000,000
Health facility-3	350	96,450	33,757,500
Health facility-4	350	86,190	30,166,500

Formula for Capitation-Based Payment

Total Payment to Provider = Base Capitation rate* Number of people enrolled with the provider

Illustration 1:
Two healthcare providers, **Provider A** and **Provider B**, each serve 1000 patients under a capitation-based payment system. Both providers receive the same fixed rate of ₹350 per patient per month, resulting in a monthly payment of ₹350,000.

Sounds good! Fair distribution? What are your thoughts?

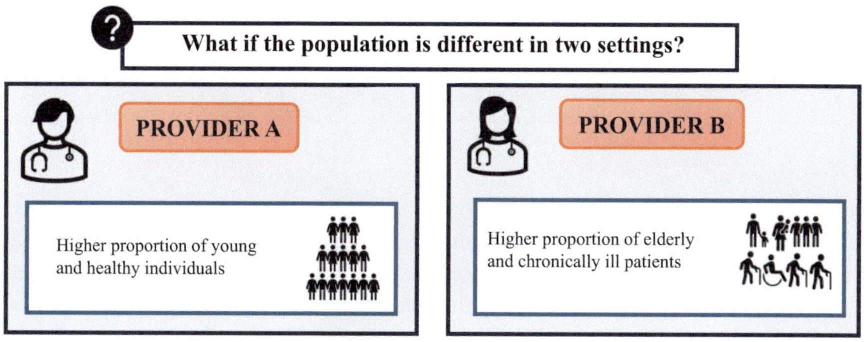

What could be the problem?
Provider A's population is mostly healthy, thus requiring minimal care, and Provider B has higher proportion of elderly and chronically ill patients who need frequent and expensive medical care. So, Provider B would face financial challenges because their patients require more resources, despite receiving the same payment as Provider A.

So, in situations like above, the providers may avoid enrolling high-risk or high-cost patients, leading to inequitable access to care for vulnerable populations. This brings us to an alternative approach of risk adjustment that modifies the per-capita rate to account for expected cost differences. Risk adjustments are made because the differences in the populations in terms of the absolute number of people in the catchment area may not be sufficient to reflect the differences in the healthcare needs in the different regions. And these differences in need are attributable to differences in the characteristics of population that determine the need for healthcare, example age, gender, socioeconomic status, risk factors, etc. So, as a result, we need some kind of additional risk adjustment to be made based on certain factors that can predict the need for healthcare services.

Risk Adjustment

Now, reconsider the case study in illustration 1 once again.

What if in the above illustration payments are adjusted to reflect the higher healthcare needs of Provider B's population?

For instance, Provider A continues to receive ₹350 per patient, but Provider B's rate is increased to ₹500 per patient due to the higher risk. This results in Provider B receiving ₹500,000 monthly, ensuring they can meet the healthcare demands of their patient population with relatively higher risk.

Risk adjustment ensures providers are fairly compensated for serving sick or higher-risk populations, promoting equity and reducing the incentive to avoid high-cost patients.

This concept, sometimes referred to as weighted capitation, was first introduced in England, where a formula was introduced to allocate resources based on an initial capitation rate. While the capitation rates were initially calculated based on population size (patient list registered under the practitioner), these were later adjusted by standardized mortality rates (SMRs) representing the burden of disease, population size, gender distribution, and socioeconomic status [3]. So, what this means is that, in addition to the per-person rate calculated by multiplying the predetermined rate by the population size of a given region or facility, the final payment is further adjusted to reflect differences in population risk profiles. Thus, a region that is having more of the elderly population perhaps will get a higher payment compared to a region that is having a much younger population. Similarly, adjustments could be made based on various factors such as patient demographic (age/gender/ethnicity), place of residence (urban/rural), and health status indicators of the population (crude mortality rate). Table 5.5 presents the list of factors that have been used for risk adjustment in different countries.

So, a capitation-based payment formula can be as simple as coming up with just one rate per person per year to be paid, multiplied by the population, to then further adjusting it by all these factors that are likely to determine the healthcare need. For risk adjustments in capitation-based payment systems, we require robust data on population demographics, health status, and resource utilization. The lack of such data may limit one's ability to do accurate risk adjustment, ensuring payments reflect the varying healthcare needs and complexities of different patient populations.

Formula for Capitation-Based Payment with Risk Adjustment

Total Payment to Provider = Base rate*Number of people enrolled with the provider*Risk adjustment coefficient

Table 5.5 Factors for risk adjustment considered in different countries

Factor	Countries
Age	Australia, Belgium, Canada, England, Finland, France, Germany, Israel, Italy, the Netherlands, New Zealand, Northern Ireland, Norway, Scotland, Stockholm, Switzerland, the United States
Sex	Australia, Belgium, Canada, England, Germany, the Netherlands, New Zealand, Switzerland, the United States
Marital status	Norway, Stockholm
Housing	Stockholm
Ethnicity	Australia, Canada, Finland, New Zealand
Homelessness	Australia
Private hospital care	Australia
Rurality	Australia, the Netherlands, Northern Ireland
Hospital expenditure	Australia, France
Geographical location	Australia, Belgium, France, Italy
Unemployment	Belgium, the Netherlands, Stockholm
Income	Belgium, Canada, Germany, New Zealand
Mortality	Belgium, England, Italy, Northern Ireland, Norway, Scotland
Morbidity	England, Finland, Israel

5.2.5 Fee-for-Service

The fee-for-service (FFS) model is a payment system where providers are paid for each individual service they deliver. These services can include things like consultations, medical tests, drugs prescribed, or surgical procedures. Under this model, every service has a specific fee, and providers are reimbursed based on the number and type of services they provide. The more services a provider performs, the more they are paid. This could be an incentive for providers to provide more services to increase payments, even if not all of them are necessary. This can lead to higher healthcare costs and overuse of medical services. In Fig. 5.1, Invoice reflects the typical FFS model where each service billed separately based on the hospital's fee schedule. The charges are based on individual services like consultation fees, blood test, and X-ray along with other services provided during the visit.

However, FFS models of payment are sometimes preferred by payer/purchasers for those services that need to be incentivized for provision. For example, in case of preventive services such as immunization, several countries prefer to pay FFS.

5.2.6 Case-Based Payments

In case-based payment models, healthcare providers receive a fixed amount per episode of care, that is, hospitalization or a daycare treatment or an outpatient consultation. These payments are often considered a form of bundled payment and are primarily applied to inpatient care, although they can also be used in

Fig. 5.1 Invoice for representation of fee for service

Invoice for Fee for Service

ABC Multi-Speciality Hospital

Patient Name: XYZ
Patient ID: 12345
Date of Visit: 26th January 2025

Service Provided	Description	Amount (₹)
Doctor Consultation	General Physician Visit	1200
Blood Test	Complete Blood Count (CBC)	800
X-Ray	Chest X-Ray	1500
Ultrasound	Abdominal Ultrasound	2000
Medication	Prescribed Medicines	900
Wound Dressing	Minor Dressing Procedure	1000
Total Amount Payable		**7400**

certain outpatient services. This approach encourages providers to avoid overuse of resources, as a predetermined lump sum is allocated for each case. For instance, the payment could cover specific conditions or procedures, such as malaria treatment, diarrhea management, percutaneous transluminal coronary angioplasty (PTCA), or hernia surgeries. Each fully treated episode whether admission, hospitalization, or disease-specific treatment is compensated as a bundled payment. A notable example of this approach is India's *Ayushman Bharat Pradhan Mantri Jan Arogya Yojana* (AB PM-JAY) scheme, which establishes predefined package rates for various procedures within its Health Benefit Package [4]. The treatment package covers all costs, including pre- and post-hospitalization expenses explained in detail in Chap. 9.

Bundled payments refers to single fixed payment for treatment of entire episode of care including medicines, diagnosis, any procedure or hospital stay, etc., rather than billing for individual service provided. This approach incentivizes efficiency and coordination among healthcare providers while controlling costs.

A further refinement of the case-based payment model is the diagnosis-related group (DRG). This concept was started from United States in the 1970s [5]. This system classifies conditions or services that share similar clinical and resource consumption characteristics into distinct groups. The grouping is based on two main criteria: clinical homogeneity, meaning the conditions that are clinically similar, and resource consumption homogeneity, indicating that these conditions require roughly the same level of healthcare resources. As a result, each DRG group receives the same total payment, regardless of the specific disease or procedure. Using a predefined classification method, patients are grouped into categories based on their diagnosis, known as DRGs. Each group is assigned a weight reflecting its cost compared to the average cost of all cases. A hospital's payment for a case is determined by multiplying a base rate by the weight of the group the patient belongs to (Box 5.1).

Box 5.1: Steps to Calculate Payments for a Provider Using a Diagnostic-Related Group (DRG) System

1. *Classification of the cases*: Establish the categories based on diagnoses, procedures, and resource use. Group the cases into categories either medical or surgical, or using classification system for diseases. Patient cases need to be grouped into appropriate DRGs considering the severity and complexity of the conditions.
2. *Calculate cost weights*: First determine the average base cost per case. Analyze hospital costs to establish relative weights (RWs) for each DRG, reflecting the resources typically used. Assign relative weights to each DRG that represents the estimated resource intensity needed to treat a patient within that group compared to the average across all DRGs.
3. *Set payment rates*: Develop payment rates based on DRG cost weights and average cost per case (base rate).

Formula for Diagnostic-Related Group (DRG) System

$$\text{Percase Payment to Provider} = \text{Base rate}^{*} \text{Relative case weight for the case group}\left(\text{DRG relative weight}\right)$$

Determining payment rates using the DRG system is technically complex and requires a structured approach. First, clinical data must be collected to classify patients into appropriate DRGs. This step needs standardized clinical information on morbidity as per the International Classification of Diseases (ICD). Secondly, robust cost data is essential for calculating base rates and cost weights. Since the introduction of DRGs is a dynamic process, continuous monitoring is necessary to ensure the accuracy and relevance of disease classifications and payment rates.

Regular reviews of DRGs and their associated tariffs, including base rates and cost weights, are crucial. This process relies on a robust information system with unique patient identifiers to enable accurate data linking and analysis.

Case Study 5.1: Evolution of the Diagnosis-Related Group (DRG) Classification System in Thailand [6]

The journey of Thailand's DRG classification system began in 1993, focusing on accident and emergency cases. Initially they used the U.S. Health Care Financing Administration (HCFA) DRG classification system, which was based on the International Classification of Diseases, Ninth Revision (ICD-9-C). However, at that time Thailand had already adopted the more advanced International Classification of Diseases, Tenth Revision (ICD-10) classification system. This led to Thailand's initiatives to develop its own DRG system. The first version of the Thai DRG (Version 1) faced criticism for not accounting for all combinations of diseases and medical procedures. Therefore, a revised version Thai DRG Version 2 was introduced after two years, which intended to accommodate all possible combinations of diseases and procedures. However, complexity of certain diseases was still not addressed properly.

A significant turning point came in 2002 with the launch of Thailand's Universal Coverage Scheme (UCS) that adopted DRG system. By then, Thai DRG Version 3 had been developed, incorporating the Australian Refined DRG model to better capture disease severity. This version allowed up to 12 diagnosis codes and 12 operating room procedure codes, expanding its ability to reflect complex medical cases. As Thailand's health system evolved, so did its DRG system. The continuous improvements in Thai DRG system were done with consultation from clinical experts. Thai DRG Version 4 introduced innovative features such as recognizing conditions that affected both sides of the body (bilaterality) and accounting for multiple surgeries during a single treatment. This version expanded the classification system to 1920 groups, ensuring more precise categorization of medical cases. By Version 5, the number of DRG categories had grown to nearly 2500, but this was later reduced to 1500 in Version 6 to streamline the system while maintaining its effectiveness.

The Thai DRG system's development highlights the importance of adapting healthcare tools to suit local needs. By building on international models and tailoring them to fit the Thai healthcare environment, the system has evolved to improve both healthcare delivery and financial management.

Although DRG-based payments are an advanced form of case-based payment systems, they require robust mechanisms for continuous monitoring to ensure effectiveness. One potential drawback of the DRG system is the risk of "upcoding," also referred to as "code creep." Upcoding occurs when healthcare providers deliberately assign a patient's case to a higher-cost code or group than it actually belongs to. For example, simpler and less expensive procedures may be deliberately reported as more complex and costly ones. This practice of code creep undermines the efficiency of the DRG system by inflating costs and diverting resources away from its primary goal of promoting cost-effective healthcare. Without proper oversight, upcoding can lead to inefficiencies, excessive financial burden, and a failure to achieve the intended benefits of the DRG system.

5.2.7 Pay for Performance

The mechanism of pay for performance ties payment to the quality or performance of healthcare providers. It rewards providers based on certain performance metrics, such as patient outcomes, adherence to best practices, or patient satisfaction. For example, if a hospital achieves lower readmission rates or higher patient satisfaction scores, they may receive additional financial incentives. The performance may be measured based on the volume of services (outcome-based), quality benchmarks of the services (quality-based), or any other value connotation such as the extent to which provision of care improves population health. A classic example of pay for performance is payments given to the village-level health worker, that is, Accredited Social Health Activist (ASHA) in India. These incentives are linked to the number of different services delivered at the grassroot level such as ensuring antenatal care for women, full immunization of a child under one year, ensuring birth spacing and others. On the contrary, there could be certain quality-based pay for performance measurement frameworks. In certain other context, the providers receive additional payments for achieving specific quality benchmarks, such as reducing hospital-acquired infections or improving certain infrastructure standards/process of care. For instance, under AB PM-JAY, incentives are paid to hospitals for maintaining quality standards. Another example of quality-based pay for performance is Estonia's quality bonus schemes, in which additional bonus payment that should be given to provider is decided based on a certain set of primary care indicators such as childhood vaccination, cancer screening, chronic disease management, along with some quality indicators [7].

Case Study 5.2: Estonia's Quality Bonus Scheme in Primary Healthcare
In 2006, the Estonian Health Insurance Fund (EHIF), in collaboration with the Society for Family Doctors, developed the Quality Bonus Scheme (QBS) to align financial incentives with health priorities. QBS was introduced as a pay-for-performance (P4P) mechanism aimed at incentivizing family physicians to enhance service quality, focus on chronic disease management, and actively participate in preventive care. The scheme operates on a stepwise target-setting approach, where each year's performance benchmark is set at the previous year's average plus 10%. Physicians achieving these targets receive annual lump-sum bonuses.

Key Features of the QBS: The QBS is structured around three performance domains:

Disease prevention	Chronic disease management	Other quality indicators
Child vaccination coverage full bonus for 100% coverage, maximum 90 points) Completing preventive health check-ups for children at key ages (70 points available) Colon cancer screening	Prevention of cardiovascular disease Management of type II diabetes Management of hypertension Secondary prevention after myocardial infarction and Hypothyroidism	Patients follow-up and monitoring Comprehensive management of high-risk patients Better use of healthcare resources—proper prescriptions and diagnostic tests

Impact of QBS

1. Significant improvement in Estonia's primary healthcare system
2. Improvement in indicators of chronic diseases
3. Declined hospitalization rates and specialist referrals among patients treated by QBS enrolled physicians.

Adapted from World Health Organization, Good Practice Brief: Pay for Performance in Estonia [8]

Check Your Learnings

1. What are some unintended consequences associated with different provider payment methods discussed above?
2. If you were to design a new provider payment model, what key principles would you prioritize to ensure fairness, efficiency, and quality?
3. Would your proposed model be applicable globally, or would it need to be tailored to a specific healthcare system?

5.3 Comparison of the Benefits and Risks of PPMs

Designing an effective provider payment system is a crucial task for any strategic purchaser of healthcare services. The incentives created by the PPMs, payment rates, and the accountability mechanisms established between providers and purchasers could significantly influence the providers' behavior and determine the way of service delivery. This section explains the impact of method of provider payment on provider's behavior and provision of services. For instance, to contain the costs of healthcare delivery one may argue to choose global budget as the PPM. However, such a system lacks incentives for efficiency. On the contrary, pay for performance can incentivize efficiency, but it comes with comparatively more administrative burden for measuring performance. Moreover, the services that are not monitored may receive lesser attention for provision. Such a phenomenon of "crowding-out" of services not included in performance measurement framework of a pay-for-performance payment model, and "crowding-in" of services that are monitored, is not an uncommon phenomenon. Therefore, it is important to carefully design PPMs keeping in mind the advantages and disadvantages of each method. The payment mechanisms should ideally encourage the access to high-quality healthcare services for patients, improve equity, and promote efficient use of the resources. Table 5.6 presents the detailed description of possible advantages and disadvantages associated with each PPM.

By incentivizing specific aspects of care, PPMs influence what services are provided, who receives them, and how effectively they are delivered. Designing suitable PPMs is crucial for any health system as they can drive or discourage the desired provider behaviors.

Table 5.6 Description of advantages, disadvantages, and potential regulatory mechanisms to prevent unintended consequences

	Advantages	Disadvantages	Regulatory mechanisms to prevent unintended consequences
Global budget	Reduces oversupply of services Cost containment Low administrative costs	No incentives for efficiency	Periodic budget reviews and audits Ensure the fund allocation reflects population health needs
Line-item budget	Administrative ease Cost containment Reduces oversupply of services	No incentives for efficiency Limited flexibility	Periodic budget reviews and audits Ensure the fund allocation reflects population health needs
Salary-based payment	Administrative ease Provider retention Cost containment	No incentives for efficiency Low responsiveness to demand	Provider monitoring for efficiency and outputs
Capitation	Encourages efficiency Reduction in unnecessary provision of services Low administrative costs Incentivize preventive care to keep population healthy	Risk of adverse selection	Good management system for beneficiary tracking Quality assurance to prevent under-treatments and over-referrals Modified design of capitation payment rates (risk-adjusted payments)
Fee-for-service	Increased supply of services Improves access to healthcare High patient responsiveness	Supplier induced demand (overutilization of services) High administrative costs	Demand-side cost-sharing mechanisms for rationing the overutilization of healthcare
Case-based payments	Enhances efficiency Improve transparency of hospital funding	Higher admission/readmission rate Reduced intensity of care	Activity ceilings, adjustments to average prices, data audits Patient satisfaction monitoring
Pay for performance	Promotes efficiency, fairness and transparency Improves uptake of intended services	Administrative burden of measuring performance Crowding-out of services not measured for performance assessment	Strong monitoring system for fair performance metrics

5.4 Factors Shaping Provider Behavior: Achieving the Right Balance

Apart from the type of PPMs, other important characteristics influencing provider behavior are accountability mechanisms, payment rate, payment schedule, and performance requirements (Fig. 5.2) [9]. The payment rate or level of payment should ideally reflect the cost of resources used to provide services while also incentivizing the provision of services. Aligning provider payments with the actual cost of care is crucial for ensuring financial sustainability, maintaining service availability, and improving healthcare quality. Well-structured pricing encourages positive provider behavior, leading to efficient resource use, better patient outcomes, and increased accessibility. In contrast, inappropriate pricing or cost price differential (whether too high or too low) can lead to inefficiencies, reduced quality, and disparities in healthcare access. Various field experiments have demonstrated the role of appropriate PPMs on the provider's behavior and treatment decisions [10, 11]. An analysis of the real-world data from utilization of services within the India's health insurance scheme *Ayushman Bharat Pradhan Mantri Jan Arogya Yojana* (AB PM-JAY), demonstrated that the pricing reforms in the health benefit packages of the previously underpriced packages significantly improved their utilization [12]. Differential incentives for different services could also impact the volume of the services provided. The providers may be willing to only provide services having higher rates relative to the costs, and the one with high cost-price differential may be denied. Thus, it is important to consider all possibilities while designing payment rates.

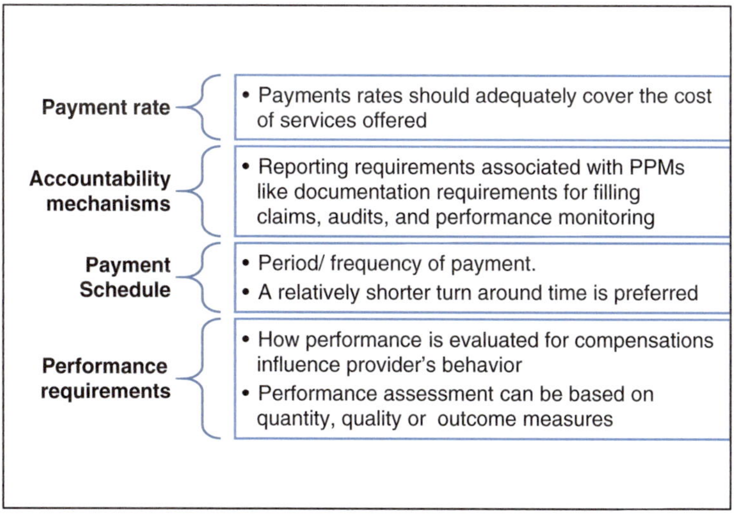

Abbreviations: *PPMs: Provider payment methods*

Fig. 5.2 Characteristics of provider payment methods (PPMs)

Similarly, payment schedule and the turnaround time (TAT) are also important factors to be considered. TAT refers to the time taken from when a healthcare provider submits a claim to when they receive payment from the payer. Delayed payment may discourage the providers to provide quality services and negatively impact the provider's behavior. For example, in Nigeria, delays in payments and dissatisfaction with payment rates have led to healthcare providers being less motivated to offer timely and adequate care to members of the Formal Sector Social Health Insurance Programme (FSSHIP) [13]. In some cases, beneficiaries have even been denied treatment [13].

5.5 Provider Payment Methods in India

In India, various provider payment methods are employed to pay providers of healthcare services (Fig. 5.3). In government healthcare facilities, line-item budgets are primarily used, allocating funds for specific expenses and services. On the other hand, the private sector primarily operates on a fee-for-service, where patients or insurers pay providers based on the services delivered. In the context of the public health insurance scheme AB PM-JAY, both public and private hospitals that are empaneled receive payments through case-based bundled payments, where hospitals receive a fixed amount per treatment episode, promoting cost efficiency. In addition to the above, India has also implemented pay-for-performance method in various healthcare programs to improve service delivery and health outcomes. Under the National Health Mission (NHM) performance-based incentives have been introduced for ASHAs. Under AB PM-JAY, empaneled hospitals receive incentives for providing quality care and maintaining patient satisfaction.

5.6 Toward Strategic Payment Mechanisms: Blended Payments

In the previous chapter, you have been introduced to the concept of strategic purchasing and its importance. By now, you must be able to differentiate between passive and strategic purchasing. Passive purchasing involves simply reimbursing providers for services delivered without actively influencing how care is provided, while strategic purchasing focuses on aligning payments with health system goals to improve efficiency, quality, and equity in healthcare delivery. As countries shift from passive to strategic purchasing to support universal health coverage (UHC), blended payments are becoming an important tool, in which a mix of PPMs is used to balance efficiency, provider incentives, and patient outcomes, instead of relying on single payment method.

Blended payments combine different payment methods (discussed in Sect. 2) to achieve healthcare goals. This involves layering various payment methods, like capitation and fee-for-service, and may include additional incentives for individual or multiple providers. The objective of blended payments is to maximize the

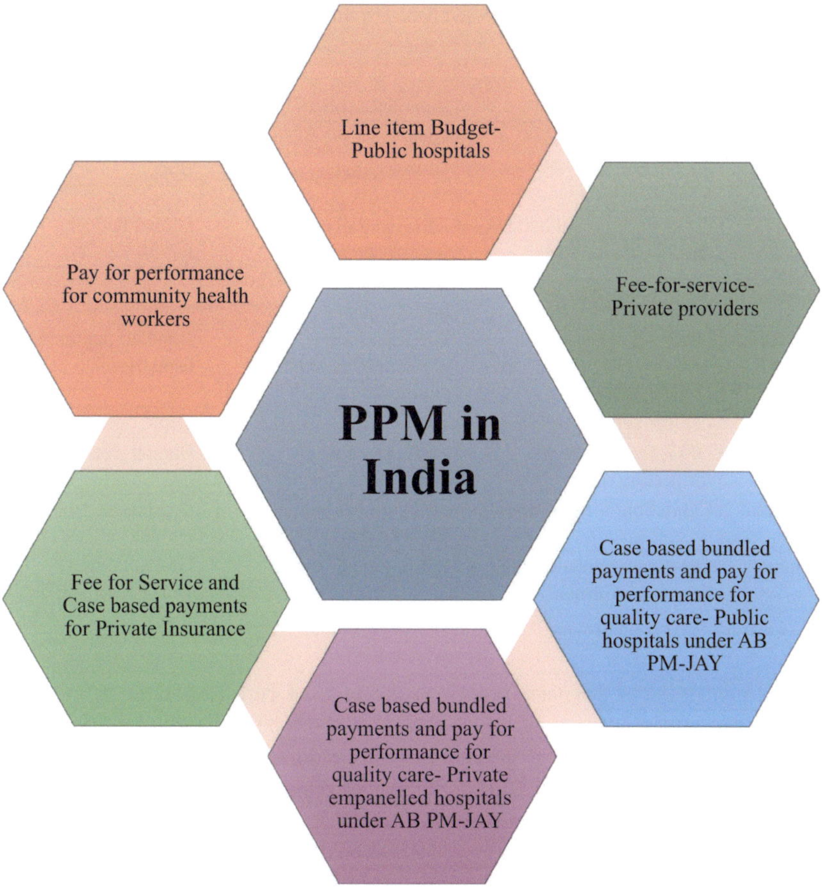

Abbreviations: PPM: Provider Payment Methods; AB PM-JAY: Ayushman Bharat Pradhan Mantri Jan Arogya Yojana

Fig. 5.3 Description of various provider payment methods (PPM) employed in India

benefits of each provider payment method while minimizing their drawbacks by balancing the incentives they create. This approach creates a mix of incentives and offers flexibility to align payment structures with healthcare priorities. For example, global budgets and capitation are effective at controlling costs but may risk reducing productivity or quality. On the other hand, case-based payments (like DRGs) and fee-for-service encourage providers to deliver more services and improve quality but lack strong cost-containment measures unless paired with strict budgets or competitive environments. Using multiple payment methods wisely can create complementary systems—such as capitation for routine primary care, fee-for-service for priority interventions (emergency care), and DRGs or global budgets for episodic care. The key is to balance incentives, improve quality, and coordinate care to build a payment model that aligns financial goals with better health outcomes.

Table 5.7 Provider payment methods established by different countries to pay for their healthcare services

Setting	Outpatient services	Inpatient services	Preventive/promotive/ public health services
Australia	Line-item budget	DRG	Line-item budget
Canada	Global budget, fee-for-service	Global budget	Budget, salary
China	Capitation, global budget, fee-for-service	DRG, global budget, fee-for-service	Global budget, fee-for-service
England	Global budget, weighted capitation	DRG, pay for performance	
France	DRG	DRG, pay for performance, bundled payments	Bundled payments, capitation
Germany	Fee-for-service	DRG	Capitation, budget
Poland	DRG, fee-for-service, pay for performance	DRG, pay for performance	Budget, fee-for-service
Thailand	Capitation, fee-for-service	DRG, global budget, fee-for-service	Capitation, global budget
Spain	Capitation, global budget, pay for performance	DRG, global budget	Global budget

DRG diagnostic-related groups

Payment models can vary based on the type of care (inpatient or outpatient), level of care (primary, secondary, tertiary), or the type of health facility (public or private). Many countries use blended provider payment systems to improve healthcare delivery (Table 5.7). In China, outpatient services are funded through capitation, a global budget, and fee-for-service, while inpatient care is covered by DRGs, a global budget, and fee-for-service. Public health services rely on fee-for-service and a global budget. In England, outpatient services operate under a fixed global budget that includes salaries and capitation payments, adjusted for factors like patient demographics (sex/age/location of patients), the number of new patients, the morbidity profile of the population, and the market forces factor. Inpatient care is funded through DRG and pay-for-performance. Thailand combines adjusted capitation and fee-for-service for outpatient care, while inpatient services use DRG, a global budget, and FFS. Public health services are supported through capitation and a global budget. Many countries adopting these blended payment models have reported improvements in equity, accessibility, affordability, and healthcare efficiency.

5.7 Conclusion

To conclude, setting provider payment methods is a complex task. This requires both science and art to balance the outcomes effectively. Each PPM has its own advantages and disadvantages associated with them. No single method is perfect, so it is important to be flexible and willing to adapt continuously. This is reflective in the journey of many countries that have experimented with the different PPMs and continuously evolved during the process of setting PPMs in their countries. Ultimately, the goal is to respond to the behavior of demand and supply, so a combination of different PPMs can be used in a health system depending upon the context and need. When designing a provider payment method, several critical questions must be addressed. What incentives will it create for healthcare providers, and how might these impact patient outcomes? Should payments be adjusted based on factors like patient complexity, geographic differences, or specialized care needs? How can the system balance cost control with quality care? Additionally, what infrastructure is needed for data collection, implementation, and monitoring? A well-structured payment model must align financial incentives with healthcare goals, ensuring efficiency, equity, and sustainability.

References

1. Kutzin J, Yip W, Cashin C. Alternative financing strategies for universal health coverage. World Scientific Handbook of Global Health Economics and Public Policy; 2016. p. 267–309. Available from: https://www.worldscientific.com/doi/pdf/10.1142/9789813140493_0005
2. Guo K, Gu X. Dealing with the issue of supplier-induced over-consumption: price regulation, competition, or provider-payment reforms. Soc Sci Guangdong. 2017;5:176–85.
3. Smith PC. Resource allocation and purchasing in the health sector: the English experience. Bull World Health Org. 2008;86(11):884–8.
4. National Health Authority, Government of India. Pradhan Mantri Pradhan Mantri Jan Arogya Yojana (PM-JAY). Available from: https://nha.gov.in/PM-JAY. Accessed 15 July 2024.
5. Bredenkamp C, Bales S, Kahur K, editors. Transition to diagnosis-related group (DRG) payments for health: Lessons from case studies. World Bank Publications; 2019.
6. Khiaocharoen O, Zungsontiporn C, Cheyprasert S, Pannarunothai S. Major changes in Thai Diagnosis Related Group Version 6.2. J Health Sci Thailand. 2020;29(5):954–62. Available from: https://thaidj.org/index.php/JHS/article/view/9488
7. Kasekamp K, Habicht T, Kalda R. The milestones of reforming primary health care in Estonia. Lancet Global Health Commission on Financing Primary Health Care. Working Paper No. 3. 2022.
8. World Health Organization, Good Practice Brief. Pay for performance in Estonia: a transformative policy instrument to scale up prevention and management of noncommunicable diseases. Accessed from: https://iris.who.int/bitstream/handle/10665/375099/WHO-EURO-2015-8732-48504-72063-eng.pdf?sequence=1&isAllowed=y
9. Kazungu JS, Barasa EW, Obadha M, Chuma J. What characteristics of provider payment mechanisms influence health care providers' behaviour? A literature review. Int J Health Plan Manag. 2018;33(4):e892–905.
10. Xi X, Wang E, Lu Q, Chen P, Wo T, Tang K. Does an economic incentive affect provider behavior? Evidence from a field experiment on different payment mechanisms. J Med Econ. 2019;22(1):35–44.
11. Green EP. Payment systems in the healthcare industry: an experimental study of physician incentives. J Econ Behav Org. 2014;106:367–78.
12. Prinja S, Dixit J, Nimesh R, Garg B, Khurana R, Paliwal A, Aggarwal AK. Impact of health benefit package policy interventions on service utilisation under government-funded health insurance in Punjab, India: analysis of Ayushman Bharat Pradhan Mantri Jan Arogya Yojana (PM-JAY). Lancet Reg Health Southeast Asia. 2024;28:100462.

13. Etiaba E, Onwujekwe O, Honda A, Ibe O, Uzochukwu B, Hanson K. Strategic purchasing for universal health coverage: examining the purchaser-provider relationship within a social health insurance scheme in Nigeria. BMJ Glob Health. 2018;3(5):e000917.

Suggested Readings

Joint Learning Network for Universal Health Coverage. Assessing health provider payment systems: a practical guide for countries working toward universal health coverage. Washington, DC: Results for Development Institute; 2015.

Langenbrunner JC, Cashin C, O'Dougherty S, editors. Designing and implementing health care provider payment systems: how-to manuals. World Bank; 2009.

Use of Health Technology Assessment (HTA) for Strategic Purchasing of Healthcare Services

6

Yashika Chugh, Nidhi Gupta, and Shankar Prinja

Abstract

This chapter explores the pivotal role of health technology assessment (HTA) in strategic purchasing of healthcare, with a focus on its application in the context of India's *Ayushman Bharat Pradhan Mantri Jan Arogya Yojana* (AB PM-JAY). It underscores the necessity of HTA for prioritizing healthcare technologies and services, ensuring efficient use of resources. The chapter begins with an overview of healthcare economics and the challenges associated with resource allocation in systems constrained by limited budgets. It then delves into the definition and purpose of HTA, highlighting its importance in evaluating clinical, economic, social, and ethical dimensions of health technologies. The chapter explains the institutionalization of HTA in India through HTAIn and its coordination with the National Health Authority's Health Financing and Technology Assessment (HeFTA) Unit. Case studies demonstrating the role of HTA in evidence-informed decision-making, including the formulation of standard treatment guidelines, inclusion and exclusion decisions for health benefits packages, and others, are presented. The chapter concludes with recommendations for enhancing the use of HTA in healthcare purchasing.

Keywords

Priority setting · Health benefits package · Health technology assessment · Economic evaluations · Health Financing and Technology Assessment (HeFTA)

Y. Chugh · S. Prinja (✉)
Department of Community Medicine and School of Public Health, Post Graduate Institute of Medical Education and Research, Chandigarh, India

N. Gupta
Department of Radiation Oncology, Government Medical College and Hospital, Chandigarh, India

S. Prinja (ed.), *Healthcare Financing and Insurance*,
https://doi.org/10.1007/978-981-95-3513-2_6

Learning Objectives

After working through this chapter, you will be able to

- Discuss the importance of priority setting in healthcare decision-making
- Describe what HTA is and its significance in healthcare decision-making
- Explain different types of economic evaluations
- Develop an understanding of the HTA ecosystem in India
- Explain how HTA provides evidence to support the strategic purchasing process

Key Terms

Priority setting: Priority setting in healthcare refers to the process of making informed decisions regarding the allocation of limited resources to various health interventions, programs, or services based on their relative importance and potential impact.

Strategic purchasing: It involves the evidence-based process of deciding what to purchase; from whom to purchase; how to pay the providers, at what level, and what quality.

Health benefits package: A defined set of healthcare services, medicines, treatments, and interventions that are covered or provided to individuals or populations under a specific government program, health insurance plan, or healthcare system. It outlines the services and treatments that are included, how they are accessed, and the conditions under which they are provided, including the level of reimbursement and co-payment, aiming to ensure access to essential healthcare while managing costs and resources effectively.

Health technology assessment: HTA refers to a multidisciplinary process that uses explicit methods to determine the value of a health technology at different points in its lifecycle.

Efficiency: The extent to which resources (inputs) are used optimally to achieve maximum health outcomes (outputs). Efficiency in healthcare is typically categorized into technical efficiency (producing maximum output with minimum resources) and allocative efficiency (resources are allocated to produce the highest societal benefit).

Economic evaluation: Economic evaluation involves an analysis of costs and outcomes of alternative interventions or health programs.

Cost-effectiveness analysis: It is one of the types of economic evaluation design where outcomes are measured in terms of diseases prevented, persons cures, lives saved, years of life gained, or any disease specific outcome measures.

6.1 The Economics of Healthcare

Healthcare systems worldwide operate within the constraints of limited resources while striving to meet the diverse and evolving health needs of their populations. Governments, as the primary providers and regulators of healthcare services, face the ongoing challenge of ensuring that available resources are distributed efficiently, equitably, and sustainably [1]. However, the demand for healthcare services frequently surpasses what can be feasibly provided, necessitating a structured approach to decision-making—commonly referred to as priority setting.

6.1.1 What Is Priority Setting in Healthcare?

Did You Know?

What is a health benefits package (HBP): A defined set of healthcare services, medicines, treatments, and interventions that are covered or provided to individuals or populations under a specific government program, health insurance plan, or healthcare system. It outlines the services and treatments that are included, how they are accessed, and the conditions under which they are provided, including the level of reimbursement and co-payment, aiming to ensure access to essential healthcare while managing costs and resources effectively [2].

Priority setting in healthcare refers to the formal and informal processes by which decision-makers determine how to allocate scarce resources among competing health needs. These decisions involve evaluating the relative importance of different healthcare interventions, treatments, and services to maximize health benefits while ensuring fairness and cost-effectiveness [3].

Healthcare prioritization occurs at multiple levels within a health system:

- Macro-Level (National and Policy Level)—At the highest level, national governments and health ministries establish broad policies, define essential health benefit packages (HBPs), and allocate budgets for public health programs, disease control initiatives, and hospital funding.
- Meso-Level (Regional and Institutional Level)—At the intermediate level, state or regional health authorities, hospital administrators, and insurance schemes decide how to distribute funds within specific geographic areas or healthcare institutions. This may involve determining hospital capacities, funding specific medical specialties, or purchasing essential medical technologies.
- Micro-Level (Clinical and Community Level)—At the grassroots level, physicians, nurses, and local health providers must make real-time decisions on individual patient care, prioritizing treatments based on urgency, clinical guidelines, and ethical considerations.

Box 6.1: Some examples of how healthcare prioritisation occurs at each level of the health system are given below. Can you identify the level of prioritisation (macro/meso/micro)? Secondly, can you identify the criteria being used to prioritize?

A. For the *Ayushman Bharat Pradhan Mantri Jan Arogya Yojana* (PM-JAY) scheme, the government decided to provide health insurance coverage to **the bottom 40% of the population.**
B. In primary health centres (PHCs), the caregiver must decide which patients receive priority for referrals to higher-level facilities based on severity. For instance, healthcare workers at the community level use triaging methods to prioritize high-risk pregnancies for referral to better-equipped hospitals. For high-risk pregnancies, triaging is guided by key criteria. Pregnant women with severe anaemia, hypertension, diabetes, or heart disease are referred early to prevent complications. Obstetric conditions such as pre-eclampsia, heavy bleeding, or a history of caesarean sections also warrant priority. If the facility lacks essential services like C-sections, blood transfusions, immediate referral is ensured to prevent adverse outcomes.

6.1.2 Why Is Prioritization Essential?

The necessity of prioritization stems from the fundamental reality that healthcare resources—including financial budgets, healthcare workforce, hospital infrastructure, and medical supplies—are finite. The demand for healthcare services, whether driven by medical necessity (such as life-saving treatments) or personal preferences (such as elective procedures), consistently exceeds what health systems can provide. This creates an imperative for decision-makers at all levels to carefully assess which interventions deliver the most significant impact for the population's health and well-being. Effective priority setting requires a delicate balance between multiple considerations, such as [4]

- Clinical effectiveness—Clinical effectiveness ensures that only treatments and interventions with proven health benefits are prioritized. This implies focusing on interventions that prevent diseases and improve long-term health for large populations.
- Cost-effectiveness—This implies prioritizing interventions that provide the best health outcomes for the lowest cost. This is crucial in resource-constrained settings where every healthcare rupee needs to be spent wisely.
- Equity and fairness—Equity in healthcare ensures that vulnerable populations—such as low-income groups, rural communities, and marginalized groups—receive the care they need without financial or geographic barriers. It prioritizes resources to reduce healthcare disparities.
- Reduction in out-of-pocket (OOP) expenditure—Prioritizing healthcare interventions that reduce the financial burden on patients, ensuring that cost is not a barrier to accessing essential services.

Given the complexities involved, prioritization in healthcare is not merely a technical or economic exercise but also a deeply ethical and social justice question. Policymakers, healthcare providers, and the public must engage in a transparent and evidence-based decision-making to ensure that healthcare systems function efficiently and equitably for all.

6.1.3 Priority Setting in Low- and Middle-Income Countries (LMICs)

In low- and middle-income countries (LMICs) like India, priority setting is a particularly complex task due to limited resources, inadequate infrastructure, and a significant disease burden. A real-world example of strategic priority setting in India is the *Ayushman Bharat Pradhan Mantri Jan Arogya Yojana (PM-JAY),* launched in 2018 [5]. As the world's largest publicly funded health insurance scheme, PM-JAY aims to provide low-income families with financial coverage of up to ₹500,000 annually for hospitalizations for a list of specific conditions or procedures. As of March 2025, the PM-JAY ecosystem consists of approximately 31,809 empaneled hospitals, with about half (14,400) belonging to the private sector. For the provisioning of care, these empaneled healthcare providers are reimbursed based on a case-based bundled payment system, where patients are grouped based on different criteria such as diagnosis and required treatment procedures. Hospital providers are paid a fixed rate per category per admission (or case treated).

Did You Know?
Socio-Economic and Caste Census, 2011: The SECC-2011 is a study assessing the socio-economic status of rural and urban households in India, enabling the ranking of households based on predefined vulnerability criteria. These criteria extend beyond traditional financial indicators like income, wealth, or expenditure to identify vulnerability more comprehensively. The SECC-2011 considers seven key parameters: (i) housing material and size, (ii) absence of an adult member aged 18–59 years, (iii) female-headed households, (iv) households led by individuals with disabilities, (v) households from historically marginalized castes and tribes, (vi) lack of a literate adult above 25 years, and (vii) landless households primarily dependent on manual labor for income.

The PM-JAY scheme exemplifies priority setting through key decisions on population coverage, the service packages it provides, and the cap on overall risk cover. The scheme determines eligible families based on income and vulnerability criteria derived from the Socio-Economic and Caste Census (2011). The scheme is focused on delivering healthcare to the bottom 40% of India's population—approximately 500 million people—the scheme thus prioritizes the provision of care to this targeted population group aligning with efforts to satisfy the "equity" criteria [6].

Secondly, the scheme defines a structured HBP, selecting essential secondary and tertiary care services to ensure cost-effective and high-impact interventions. The initial design of the HBP was guided by key factors such as disease burden, service utilization patterns, and OOP expenditures, along with clinical expertise in determining service inclusion. Over time, the use of health economic evidence expanded, with later updates incorporating evidence on cost-effectiveness for selected packages and reimbursement rates increasingly based on empirical cost data [7]. Thirdly, the financial cap of ₹500,000 per family per year, without any limit on the number of family members or any age cap, reflects a balance between expanding coverage and maintaining fiscal sustainability.

6.1.4 The Role of Strategic Purchasing

To make PM-JAY more effective in achieving universal health coverage (UHC), insurers must use resources efficiently while maintaining fairness and quality. Strategic purchasing offers a solution to this challenge by enabling insurers to make deliberate, evidence-based choices about healthcare spending. Strategic purchasing is an ongoing process of optimizing healthcare system performance by carefully selecting which services to fund, how they should be financed, and which providers should deliver them (refer to Chap. 4 on strategic purchasing) [8].

Health technology assessment (HTA) serves as a key tool in this process, providing an evidence-based platform for decision-making, enabling the selection of cost-effective interventions, setting reimbursement rates, and prioritizing healthcare services in line with national health goals. The subsequent sections will delve deeper into the components of HTA, provide insights into India's HTA framework and processes, and discuss its influence on strategic purchasing decisions under the PM-JAY.

6.2 Leveraging Health Technology Assessment (HTA) for Strategic Purchasing

6.2.1 Definition and Purpose of HTA

HTA refers to a multidisciplinary process that uses explicit methods to determine the value of a health technology at different points in its lifecycle, where a health technology is an intervention developed to prevent, diagnose, or treat medical conditions; promote health; provide rehabilitation; or organize healthcare delivery. This intervention can be a test, device, medicine, vaccine, procedure, program, or system. The purpose is to inform decision-making in order to promote an equitable, efficient, and high-quality health system [9–11].

HTA assesses healthcare interventions across multiple dimensions. The dimensions of value for a health technology may be assessed by examining the intended and unintended consequences of using a health technology compared to existing alternatives. These dimensions often include clinical effectiveness, safety, costs and economic implications, ethical, social, cultural and legal issues, organizational and environmental aspects, as well as wider implications for the patient, relatives, caregivers, and the population [11]:

- Safety—Ensures that a medical intervention's benefits outweigh its potential risks. A treatment might be effective, but if it has severe adverse effects, its overall usefulness may be limited.
- Clinical effectiveness—Determines how well a treatment or medical procedure works in real-world conditions. For example, does a new cancer drug significantly prolong survival compared to existing standard treatments?
- Costs and economic implications—Analyzes cost-effectiveness and budget impact to determine whether the intervention provides value for money within a given healthcare system. This helps policymakers decide whether an expensive new drug or medical technology is worth funding compared to other available options. In addition, the budget impact is assessed to determine financial feasibility and sustainability.
- Ethical issues—Examines considerations such as patient autonomy, fairness in access, and implications for vulnerable populations.
- Social and cultural aspects—Considers societal attitudes, cultural beliefs, and acceptability of the technology among different population groups, influencing adoption and adherence.
- Legal issues—Reviews regulatory requirements, liability concerns, intellectual property rights, and compliance with national or international health laws.
- Organizational aspects—Evaluates how the technology affects healthcare infrastructure, workforce needs, training requirements, and service delivery models.
- Environmental aspects—Assesses the ecological impact, including waste production, energy consumption, and sustainability concerns related to the technology.
- Wider implications for patients, relatives, and caregivers—Examines the broader impact on quality of life, caregiving burden, and psychosocial well-being of patients and their families.
- Population-level implications—Considers the public health impact, such as the potential to reduce disease burden, improve equity, and contribute to long-term health system sustainability.

The overall value may vary depending on the perspective taken, the stakeholders involved, and the decision context. In priority setting, where some individuals may gain access to certain treatments while others may not, the ethical justification for following and accepting decisions made by governments becomes crucial. These decisions are inherently difficult because they create winners and losers. To make this process fair and justifiable, HTA integrates scientific evidence with societal values through a structured and transparent deliberation process [12].

One way to simplify this is to assume that value can be solely encapsulated into clinical outcomes generated from well-designed clinical trials [13]. However, relying solely on clinical outcomes presents several limitations. First, clinical trial results may not fully capture a patient's real-world experience, as aspects like quality of life, compliance to treatment, and long-term consequences might be overlooked. Second, decisions based purely on clinical outcomes do not always provide clear guidance on how best to allocate healthcare resources to maximize overall population health. Third, clinical measures fail to account for broader social and economic factors, such as the financial burden of illness on families, the productivity impact on the workforce, or the societal preference for certain treatments based on ethical and cultural considerations. These shortcomings have led health system stakeholders to adopt methods that account for broader dimensions of value in their decision-making [4].

6.2.2 Economic Evaluations for Resource Allocation Decisions

Drummond et al. (2015) describe economic evaluation as the process of comparing two or more interventions in terms of their costs and outcomes [4]. Various types of economic evaluations help answer different decision-making questions in healthcare. While all approaches measure costs in monetary terms, they differ in how they incorporate consequences. Cost-effectiveness analysis (CEA) is one of the most widely used methods in the health sector. In this type of economic evaluation design, the outcomes are measured in terms of diseases prevented, persons cures, lives saved, years of life gained, or any disease specific outcome measures. For example, reduction in blood pressure following administration of drug A versus drug B. However, a limitation of CEA is that it is difficult to compare interventions that address different health issues as outcome measures are either disease specific or do not capture all aspects of benefits.

To address some of these limitations, cost-utility analysis (CUA) was developed. CUA uses standardized health measures such as quality-adjusted life-years (QALYs) and disability-adjusted life-years (DALYs) to account for both the quantity and quality of life gained from an intervention. This makes CUA more versatile than CEA as it allows for the comparison of diverse healthcare programs that impact quantity and quality of life in different ways. A CEA and CUA measure the relative efficiency of interventions by examining the cost per unit of outcome achieved. In both methods, the outcome is typically represented as an incremental cost-effectiveness ratio (ICER), which reflects the additional cost required to gain an additional unit of outcome, such as a life-year or a QALY [4].

In contrast, cost–benefit analysis (CBA) is unique among economic evaluation methods because it expresses both costs and benefits in monetary terms. This allows for comparisons not only within the health sector but also across different sectors. CBA can help determine the overall financial value of investing in a particular program. In CBA, as both costs and benefits are expressed in monetary terms, enabling straightforward comparisons. The decision rule in CBA is simple: policy options should be implemented if their benefits exceed the costs. A summary of the different types of economic evaluation and their defining features can be found in Table 6.1.

Table 6.1 Types of economic evaluations

Type of analysis	Description	Costs	Consequences	Interpretation
Cost-effectiveness analysis	Compares the costs and effectiveness of interventions. Outcomes are measured in natural units	Monetary	Effectiveness is measured in natural units such as life-years gained, cases prevented, or reduction in disease burden	Results are typically expressed as cost per unit of outcome (e.g., cost per life-year gained). The intervention with the lower cost for the same or better effectiveness is preferred
Cost-utility analysis	A form of CEA that uses QALYs or DALYs to measure outcomes	Monetary	Outcomes are measured in QALYs or DALYs, which incorporate both the length and quality of life	Results are expressed as cost per QALY gained or DALY averted. The decision rule is based on whether the cost per QALY gained is within an acceptable threshold, indicating cost-effectiveness
Cost–benefit analysis	Compares the costs of interventions to their benefits, where both are expressed in monetary terms	Monetary	Benefits are valued in monetary terms	Results are expressed as net benefits (benefits minus costs). If the net benefits are positive, the intervention is considered economically justified
Cost-minimization analysis	Compares the costs of interventions that have been shown to have equivalent outcomes	Monetary	Outcomes are assumed to be identical	The intervention with the lowest cost is deemed the most efficient, assuming outcomes are equal

USD US dollar, *QALY* quality-adjusted life-year, *DALY* disability-adjusted life-year

Box 6.2: Below are some real-world scenarios. For each scenario, determine which type of economic evaluation it represents:

Scenario 1:

A health system is considering two equally effective treatments for hypertension. Drug A costs ₹300 more per patient as compared to Drug B. The effectiveness of both drugs is identical in terms of reducing blood pressure. What type of economic evaluation design should be used here?

Answer:

Scenario 2:

A country is evaluating a new vaccine for influenza against no vaccination. The vaccine costs ₹1200 per dose, and it is expected to prevent 1000 cases of influenza in a population of 100,000. What type of economic evaluation design should be used here?

Answer:

Scenario 3:

A public health organization is considering whether to introduce a program for childhood obesity prevention or to invest in a mobile vaccination program to increase immunization rates in a remote rural district. What type of economic evaluation design should be used here?

Answer:

6.2.3 Institutionalization of HTA in India

In India, Health Technology Assessment in India (HTAIn) was institutionalized by the Indian government to facilitate transparent and evidence-driven decision-making in the healthcare sector [14, 15]. HTAIn is responsible for evaluating health technologies, including medicines, medical devices, and health programs, to assess their cost-effectiveness, clinical effectiveness, and impact on equity. Its key objectives include

- Facilitate evidence-based decision-making in healthcare at both central and state levels by providing scientifically reliable information.
- Establish transparent and inclusive systems for evaluating new and existing health technologies.
- Disseminate research findings and policy outcomes to educate and empower the public for better-informed healthcare choices.

6.2.3.1 Structure of HTAIn

The Government of India established HTAIn in 2017, which is currently an attached office of the Ministry of Health within the Department of Health Research (DHR) [16]. The HTAIn Secretariat, located within the DHR, serves as a coordinating body, linking the user departments, Technical Appraisal Committee (TAC), regional resource hubs and centers, technical partners, and the HTAIn Board (Fig. 6.1). The HTAIn Board, the apex decision-making authority, is chaired by a member (Health) of National Institution for Transforming India (NITI) Aayog and includes ex-officio members and domain experts, such as policymakers, clinicians, bureaucrats, and representatives from various government departments. The TAC is a multidisciplinary body with experts from different areas, viz., economists, clinicians, researchers, social scientists, and health policy experts. HTAIn responds to requests from user departments, who identify candidate topics, and works alongside

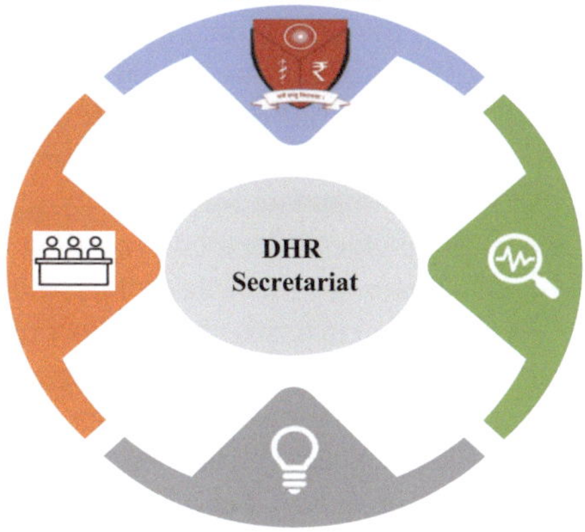

Fig. 6.1 Framework of HTAIn [17]. (Note: *HTAIn* Health Technology Assessment in India, *DHR* Department of Health Research)

a network of regional resource hubs and centers to conduct HTA studies and make recommendations regarding the adoption of the respective technology.

HTAIn is organized into four specialized divisions:

Clinical Effectiveness Assessment Division: Evaluates the clinical effectiveness of medical devices, vaccines, drugs, diagnostics, intervention procedures, and digital health technologies.

Economic Assessment Division: Analyzes the cost-effectiveness of medical devices, vaccines, drugs, diagnostics, intervention procedures, and digital health technologies.

Technology Integration in Public Health Programs Division: Facilitates the incorporation of health technologies recommended by the HTA Board into public health programs, ensuring accessibility, affordability, and equity. It also identifies the appropriate levels of the health system for technology implementation.

Coordination, Communication, and Administration Division: Manages communication and coordination with various stakeholders, including nonhealth ministries and departments, academia, and the private sector.

6.2.3.2 Processes Under HTAIn [16]

The process of conducting HTA in India begins with the submission of topics by user departments, which include budget-holding and decision-making entities such as the Ministry of Health and Family Welfare (MoHFW), State Health Departments, the National Health Mission (NHM), etc.; payer agencies like the National Health Authority (NHA), Employees' State Insurance Scheme (ESIS), and Central Government Health Scheme (CGHS); and regulatory bodies such as the National

Pharmaceutical Pricing Authority (NPPA). More recently, HTAIn has expanded its scope to accept submissions from the private sector innovators and industry partners as well. Upon receiving the submissions, the HTAIn Secretariat evaluates them using a structured selection and prioritization process, which is a two-stage approach. In the initial stage, the primary focus is on determining whether the proposed research aligns with HTAIn's mandate for a priority topic and qualifies for an HTA study. The second stage involves a detailed evaluation by the HTAIn Topic Prioritization Committee, which assesses multiple factors, including the extent of the affected population, disease burden in terms of prevalence and severity, potential clinical benefits, economic implications for households, relevance to national health policy goals, and the strength of available evidence. Topics are then scored and assigned for priority. If more data is expected from ongoing research or the topic is considered a lower priority, it may be deferred to a waiting list.

Once prioritized, the selected topics are assigned to the relevant resource hubs or centers, which then develop a study proposal that is then presented to the TAC for approval. This proposal outlines the policy question(s) that the HTA study aims to address, the research question(s) to be investigated, the objectives, and the PICO framework (Population, Intervention, Comparator, Outcome). It also details the study methodology and timelines. This proposal is then presented to the TAC for appraisal. Once the TAC reviews and approves the proposal, the resource hub or center can proceed with conducting the HTA study as outlined in the approved plan.

These resource centers, which are entrusted with the responsibility to conduct the HTA study, are located within academic and research institutions, chosen for their technical capacity to conduct HTA studies. To further strengthen the HTA ecosystem in India, the HTAIn has recently created HTA resource hubs in regions across the country, including the northern, western and central, western, southern, northeastern, and union territories. These hubs play a vital role in facilitating HTA studies, enhancing the capacity of regional resource centers, organizing sensitization workshops for state and central government programs, and promoting the use of HTA evidence in program and policy. They are also responsible for quality assurance during ongoing studies, providing technical support, and contributing to the preparation of policy briefs aimed at guiding healthcare decision-making.

Upon completion of the study, the resource center submits the outcome report to the TAC for review. This report, which contains the findings and recommendations of the HTA study, is subjected to a thorough evaluation by the TAC. If the report meets the necessary standards, it is forwarded to the HTAIn Board for final approval. The Board ensures that the report's findings align with national health priorities and standards before providing its approval. After receiving Board approval, a policy brief is prepared that summarizes the key findings and actionable recommendations of the HTA study. This policy brief is then disseminated to the relevant central or state government authorities for implementation, ensuring that evidence-based decisions are made to improve healthcare delivery and policy in India. The entire process, from submission of topics to dissemination of results, is designed to be transparent, rigorous, and responsive to the healthcare needs of the population. The process is demonstrated in Fig. 6.2.

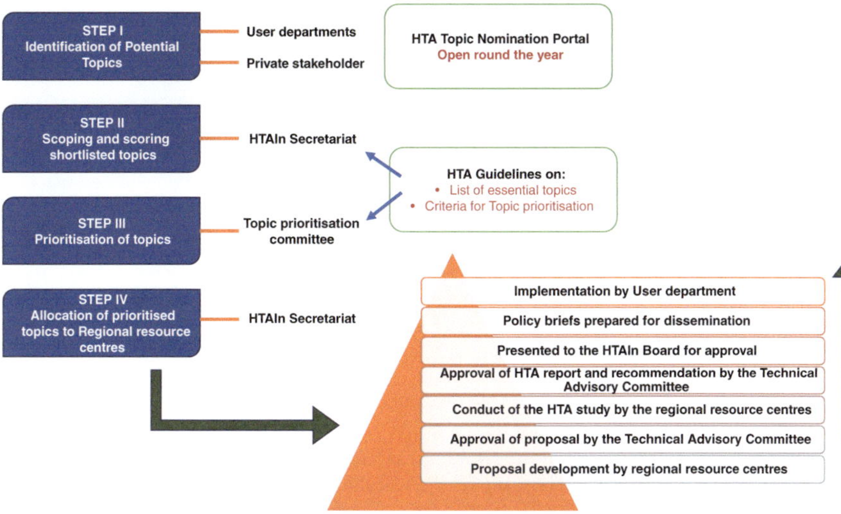

Fig. 6.2 Process of decision-making under HTAIn [16]. (*HTAIn* Health Technology Assessment in India)

6.2.3.3 Establishment of HTA Unit Under the National Health Authority [18]

The NHA is an autonomous body under the Ministry of Health and Family Welfare, responsible for the design and implementation of the PM-JAY scheme [19]. In addition to this central role, the NHA is tasked with developing and updating the HBP, formulating policy and operational guidelines, and establishing treatment and quality standards. One of its key functions is to design mechanisms for purchasing healthcare services under the PM-JAY, determining which services to purchase, from which providers, at what cost, and for which population groups [20]. For details on NHA's roles and responsibilities, please refer to Chap. 9 on "Government-funded health insurance schemes in India."

In 2022, the NHA established the Health Financing and Technology Assessment (HeFTA) unit to enhance the evidence-based decisions on allocation of financial resources, improve accessibility, provide financial protection, and address health disparities within the PM-JAY (Fig. 6.3) [18]. The HeFTA unit aims to optimize resource allocation by incorporating HTA evidence into the decision-making process. The formation of the HeFTA unit and the collaboration with HTAIn arose from two important considerations. First, at the time when HeFTA was established in 2022, the HTAIn accepted HTA topic nominations from public entities and payers only. On the other hand, PM-JAY ecosystem encompasses around 31,809 empaneled hospitals, with nearly half being private sector institutions—key stakeholders in the scheme. As a result, the HeFTA unit, functioning under the NHA, provided a platform for private sector entities, such as hospitals, pharmaceutical companies, and the medical device industry, to submit nominations for inclusion in the HBP. Second, in order to develop capacity for using HTA evidence, as well as undertaking a horizon scanning for emerging evidence, provided further justification

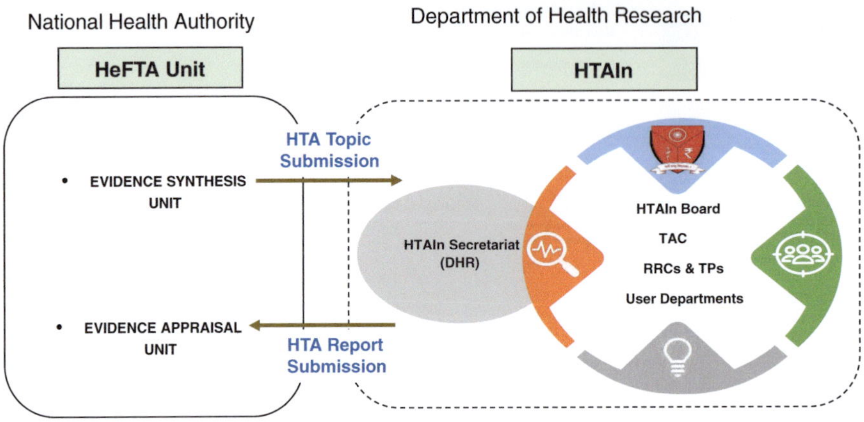

Fig. 6.3 Operational framework of the Health Financing and Technology Assessment (HeFTA) unit, National Health Authority (NHA) [18]. (*HeFTA* Health Financing and Technology Assessment Unit; *HTAIn* Health Technology Assessment in India, *DHR* Department of Health Research, *TAC* Technical Appraisal Committee, *RRC* Regional Resource Centers, *TP* technical partners)

to establish HeFTA. This team is tasked with reviewing existing evidence and prioritizing it based on the needs of the population served by the program.

A major objective of the HeFTA unit is to create a structured, transparent process for selecting technologies to be included in the HBP. To achieve this, the NHA launched a dedicated portal on its website that allows stakeholders—pharmaceutical companies, the medical device industry, healthcare professionals, patient advocacy groups, payer agencies, regulatory bodies, and others—to submit nominations for new technologies to be considered for inclusion in the PM-JAY HBP. The portal is open year-round, with the assessment and prioritization process occurring concurrently. The prioritization process plays a critical role in identifying the most relevant topics for evaluation. The key criteria for prioritization include the burden of the health issue, its economic and clinical impact, the feasibility of its implementation, the availability of evidence on clinical effectiveness, potential ethical and equity implications, and its policy relevance. This approach ensures that resources are allocated efficiently, focusing on topics with the highest potential value.

In addition to managing technology nominations, the HeFTA unit is also responsible for gathering and analyzing health economic evidence. To support this, it conducts horizon scanning—an ongoing process that identifies and monitors emerging HTA evidence related to health technologies, treatments, and interventions. While horizon scanning traditionally focuses on identifying new technologies for inclusion in the HBP, the HeFTA unit uses it more broadly to evaluate the quality and generalizability of emerging HTA evidence. This evidence is then assessed for its suitability within the PM-JAY framework, guiding decisions on HBP inclusion, the formulation of STGs, pricing, and the development of quality guidelines.

The HeFTA unit works closely with HTAIn, which is responsible for producing high-quality HTA evidence. Through this collaboration, HTAIn fulfills the evidence

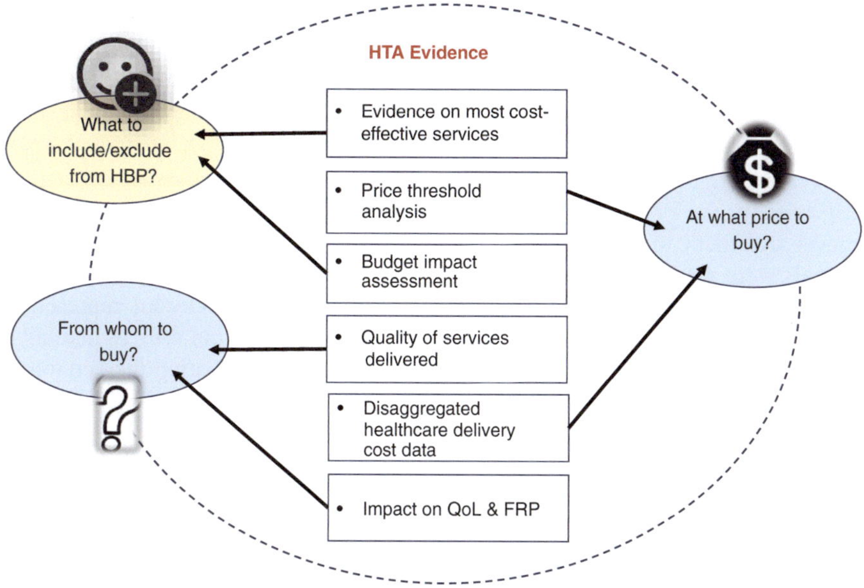

Fig. 6.4 Integration of HTA evidence into the strategic purchasing framework for PM-JAY (*Qol* quality of life, *FRP* financial risk protection, *HBP* health benefit package, *HTA* health technology assessment)

requirements of HeFTA by conducting detailed HTA studies on prioritized topics for HBP evaluation. Initially, each submission to the HeFTA unit undergoes a preliminary review. Topics deemed suitable for full economic assessment are referred to HTAIn for further evaluation. This collaboration between the HeFTA unit and HTAIn ensures a robust, comprehensive evaluation of healthcare topics, facilitating informed, evidence-based decisions.

Integrating HTA into PM-JAY's decision-making ensures evidence-based and cost-effective healthcare purchasing (Fig. 6.4) [8]. It aids the refinement of STGs by identifying clinically and economically viable interventions, prioritizes high-value treatments in HBPs through cost-effectiveness analysis, and informs price negotiations by assessing affordability thresholds. Costing studies help set fair package rates, ensuring sustainable pricing, while HTA also evaluates the impact of interventions on patients' quality of life. The next section discusses several examples where HTA has informed strategic purchasing for PM-JAY.

6.3 Examples of the Use of HTA Evidence for Strategic Purchasing Under PM-JAY

Next, three examples are discussed, highlighting the instances where recent HTA evidence has led to cost-effective policymaking, revision of STGs, and informed decisions regarding the inclusion requests for the HBPs [18].

6.3.1 Using HTA for Improving HBP Construct

The inclusion of the targeted monoclonal antibody trastuzumab alongside chemotherapy for women with breast cancer has shown substantial benefits, significantly enhancing both disease-free and overall survival rates [21]. However, trastuzumab is an expensive drug, limiting its utilization for treatment in LMICs like India [22, 23]. Initially, the PM-JAY scheme limited coverage for trastuzumab-based breast cancer treatment to four cycles. However, between 2019 and 2022, numerous appeals were made by various stakeholders—including private hospitals, patient advocacy groups, individuals, state health authorities, and elected representatives—urging an increase in the covered treatment cycles from 4 to 18 annually. These persistent demands underscored the necessity of evaluating the economic viability of such an expansion, prompting a thorough review of cost-effectiveness evidence.

In a recent evaluation published in 2020, the cost-effectiveness of adjuvant trastuzumab therapy in HER2/neu-positive Indian women was assessed, comparing a 1-year duration of treatment to 6 months [24]. The analysis demonstrated that using trastuzumab for 6 months was cost-effective compared to 1 year. As part of the review of HTA evidence through horizon scanning, the HeFTA unit identified this evidence for application to revise the STG for the trastuzumab package. This led to increasing approved treatment cycles from four to eight, eventually resulting in enhanced treatment access, improved health outcomes, and reduced out-of-pocket expenses for patients. Furthermore, adhering to 8 cycles rather than 17 results in an annual cost saving of approximately ₹4160 million (US$ 50 million) for the payer.

6.3.2 Using HTA Evidence for Revising STGs

Another example highlighting the utilization of HTA in defining STGs involves radiation therapy (RT) packages for breast cancer, among the most frequently used treatments. There is variability in clinical practices exists regarding the indications for RT, such as the number of nodes involved, and the optimal number of radiation fractions delivered. While hypofractionated RT (42.5 Gy in 16 fractions) is considered safe and effective, it is not widely practiced despite its recommendation in STGs. This discrepancy prompted an evaluation [25–27].

The HeFTA unit, through horizon scanning, identified evidence on the cost-effectiveness of post-mastectomy RT (PMRT) in India, considering modalities of radiotherapy delivery, laterality, nodal burden, and fractionation [28]. The evidence favored PMRT for node-positive disease, but not for those with node-negative disease. Additionally, adopting hypofractionated therapy as the standard of care could notably reduce treatment costs [28]. Consequently, the STGs for breast cancer radiation were revised, recommending a hypofractionated regimen over the conventional approach. This adjustment is estimated to yield substantial savings, as around 67% of patients were undergoing unnecessary fractions, costing ₹418 million (US$ 5 million) annually. Moreover, the revised STGs withdrew use of PMRT indications for node-negative patients previously receiving radiotherapy, potentially saving ₹528–1056 million (US$ 6–12 million) annually for PM-JAY. These changes aim to enhance cost-effectiveness while ensuring quality care for breast cancer patients.

6.3.3 Deciding on the Inclusion Requests Based on HTA Evidence

Among the numerous inclusions proposed for HBPs, a request was made to include cyclin-dependent kinase 4/6 inhibitors (CDK4/6i), specifically ribociclib and palbociclib, for metastatic breast cancer patients, showcasing enhanced survival rates [29, 30]. This request was directed to the HTAIn for a comprehensive assessment. The analysis compared the cost-effectiveness of ribociclib or palbociclib combined with fulvestrant against fulvestrant monotherapy (presently part of the PM-JAY HBP) and other existing treatments. Results indicated that using ribociclib or palbociclib in combination with fulvestrant was not cost-effective, at the then available prices of ribociclib and palbociclib, within the Indian context [31]. Consequently, based on this evidence, the request to include these agents was rejected due to concerns about their cost-effectiveness, implying that the treatment costs outweigh their potential benefits within the Indian healthcare system.

Generation of evidence for HTA is a dynamic process based on the evolution of data on the efficacy of drugs, depending on long-term follow-up of published trials and changing drug prices. The prices of the drugs continue to evolve, particularly with the introduction of the generic molecules, subsequent to the expiry of the patent for the original molecules. Currently one of the CDK4/6i palbociclib is available in a generic version in India, at a price that is 7% of the price of the original drug, which was used in the above CEA. Hence, there is a need to continuously update the evidence from HTA while the processes are institutionalized or integrated for evidence-based decision-making in insurance context.

6.4 To Summarize: What Next for PM-JAY?

Evidence-informed decision-making is fundamental to achieving UHC. As PM-JAY continues to evolve, the integration of HTA into its strategic purchasing decisions is pivotal to ensure that healthcare resources are allocated efficiently. Health economic evidence helps address pricing challenges, preventing services from being underpriced, leading to compromised quality, informal out-of-pocket payments, or denial of care. It also prevents overpriced provider payment rates, which leads to inefficiencies. HTA thus plays a key role in setting optimal procurement prices, ensuring that services offer value for money. However, to enhance evidence-based decision-making, there is a need to strengthen collaboration between the HTA ecosystem and regulatory bodies such as the NPPA. This would enable more effective price negotiations, pooled procurement, and continuous refinement of HBPs.

At the same time, HTA evidence can be leveraged to improve service quality by integrating adherence to STGs informed by economic evaluations. Linking these guidelines to performance benchmarks can incentivize providers to maintain high standards of care through performance-linked payments.

Finally, strengthening institutional capacity for HTA within the NHA and the wider HTA ecosystem is critical. Building capacity to generate and interpret HTA evidence is equally important, equipping policymakers and decision-makers with the skills to use this evidence effectively. This can be supplemented by expanding the role of the HeFTA unit and fostering closer collaboration between HTAIn and its network of regional resource centers.

For health insurance practitioners, understanding and applying these principles can drive improvements in the wider healthcare ecosystem in India.

6.5 Answers

Activity Box 6.1:

A. Macro level
B. Micro level

Activity Box 6.2:

A. Cost-minimization analysis
B. Cost-effectiveness analysis
C. Cost–benefit analysis

References

1. Chalkidou K, Glassman A, Marten R, Vega J, Teerawattananon Y, Tritasavit N, Gyansa-Lutterodt M, Seiter A, Kieny MP, Hofman K, Culyer AJ. Priority-setting for achieving universal health coverage. Bull World Health Org. 2016;94(6):462.
2. World Health Organization. Principles of health benefit packages; 2021.
3. Glassman A, Chalkidou K. Priority-Setting in Health Building institutions for smarter public spending. Center for Global Development's Priority-Setting Institutions for Global Health Working Group; 2012.
4. Drummond MF, Sculpher MJ, Claxton K, Stoddart GL, Torrance GW. Methods for the economic evaluation of health care programmes. Oxford University Press; 2015.
5. National Health Authority, Ministry of Health and Family Welfare, Government of India. Pradhan Mantri Jan Arogya Yojana (PM-JAY) [Internet]. 2024 [cited 2024 Aug 4]. Available from: https://pmjay.gov.in/about/pmjay
6. UIDAI. Unique Identification Authority of India. Government of India; 2019. http://uidai.gov.in
7. Prinja S, Chugh Y, Garg B, et al. National hospital costing systems matter for universal healthcare: the India PM-JAY experience. BMJ Glob Health. 2023;8:e012987. https://doi.org/10.1136/bmjgh-2023-012987.
8. RESYST. What is strategic purchasing for health? Health financing research theme, Resilient and Responsive Health Systems (RESYST). 2014. http://resyst.lshtm.ac.uk/sites/resyst.lshtm.ac.uk/files/docs/reseources/Purchasing20brief.pdf

9. O'Rourke B, Oortwijn W, Schuller T, International Joint Task Group. The new definition of health technology assessment: a milestone in international collaboration. Int J Technol Assess Health Care. 2020;36(3):187–90.
10. Institute for Clinical and Economic Review. ICER guide to understanding health technology assessment [Internet]. 2018 Jun 19 [cited 2024 Aug 14]. Available from: https://icer.org/wp-content/uploads/2020/10/ICER-Guide-to-Understanding-Health-Technology-Assessment-6.19.18.pdf
11. O'Rourke B, Oortwijn W, Schuller T. The new definition of health technology assessment: a milestone in international collaboration. Int J Technol Assess Health Care. 2020;36(3):187–90.
12. Gruskin S, Daniels N. Process is the point: justice and human rights: priority setting and fair deliberative process. Am J Public Health. 2008;98(9):1573–7.
13. Alonso-Coello P, Schunemann HJ, Moberg J, Brignardello-Petersen R, Akl EA, Davoli M, et al. GRADE Evidence to Decision (EtD) frameworks: a systematic and transparent approach to making well informed healthcare choices. Gac Sanit. 2018;32(2):166 e1–10.
14. Prinja S, Downey LE, Gauba V, Swaminathan S. Health technology assessment for policy making in India: current scenario and way forward. Pharmacoecon Open. 2018;2(1):1–3. https://doi.org/10.1007/s41669-017-0037-0.
15. Downey LE, Mehndiratta A, Grover A, Gauba V, Sheikh K, Prinja S, Singh R, Cluzeau FA, Dabak S, Teerawattananon Y, Kumar S, Swaminathan S. Institutionalising health technology assessment: establishing the Medical Technology Assessment Board in India. BMJ Glob Health. 2017;2:e000259. https://doi.org/10.1136/bmjgh-2016-000259.
16. Health Technology Assessment in India (HTAIn)—Framework [Internet]. Htain.icmr.org.in. 2022. https://htain.icmr.org.in/index.php/about-us/framework. Accessed 4 May 2022.
17. Chugh Y, Bahuguna P, Sohail A, Rajsekar K, Muraleedharan VR, Prinja S. Development of a health technology assessment quality appraisal checklist (HTA-QAC) for India. Appl Health Econ Health Policy. 2023;21(1):11–22.
18. Prinja S, Chugh Y, Gupta N, Aggarwal V. Establishing a health technology assessment evidence ecosystem in India's Pradhan Mantri Jan Arogya Yojana. Health Syst Reform. 2023;9(3):2327097.
19. National Health Authority (NHA). About the National Health Authotity. Available at: https://pmjay.gov.in/about/nha. Accessed 27 May 2023.
20. Provider Payments and Price Setting under Ayushman Bharat Pradhan Mantri Jan Arogya Yojana Scheme (PM-JAY) In India: Improving Efficiency, Acceptability, Quality & Sustainability. New Delhi: National Health Authority; 2022. p. 1–51.
21. Patnayak R, Jena A, Rukmangadha N, Chowhan AK, Sambasivaiah K, Phaneendra BV, Reddy MK. Hormone receptor status (estrogen receptor, progesterone receptor), human epidermal growth factor-2 and p53 in South Indian breast cancer patients: a tertiary care center experience. Indian J Med Paediatr Oncol. 2015;36(02):117–22.
22. Romond EH, Perez EA, Bryant J, Suman VJ, Geyer CE Jr, Davidson NE, Tan-Chiu E, Martino S, Paik S, Kaufman PA, Swain SM. Trastuzumab plus adjuvant chemotherapy for operable HER2-positive breast cancer. N Engl J Med. 2005;353(16):1673–84.
23. Cameron D, Piccart-Gebhart MJ, Gelber RD, Procter M, Goldhirsch A, de Azambuja E, Castro G, Untch M, Smith I, Gianni L, Baselga J. 11 years' follow-up of trastuzumab after adjuvant chemotherapy in HER2-positive early breast cancer: final analysis of the HERceptin Adjuvant (HERA) trial. The Lancet. 2017;389(10075):1195–205.
24. Gupta N, Verma RK, Gupta S, Prinja S. Cost effectiveness of trastuzumab for management of breast cancer in India. JCO Glob Oncol. 2020;6:205–16.
25. McGale P, Taylor C, Correa C, et al. Effect of radiotherapy after mastectomy and axillary surgery on 10-year recurrence and 20-year breast cancer mortality: meta-analysis of individual patient data for 8135 women in 22 randomised trials, vol. 383. Lancet (London, England); 2014. p. 9935.
26. Huang EH, Tucker SL, Strom EA, et al. Postmastectomy radiation improves locoregional control and survival for selected patients with locally advanced breast cancertreated with neoadjuvant chemotherapy and mastectomy. L Clin Oncol. 2004;22:4691–9.

27. Liu L, Yang Y, Guo Q, et al. Comparing hypofractionated to conventional fractionated radiotherapy in postmastectomy breast cancer: a meta-analysis and systematic review. Radiat Oncol. 2020;15(1):1–5.
28. Gupta N, Chugh Y, Chauhan AS, Pramesh CS, Prinja S. Cost-effectiveness of Post-Mastectomy Radiotherapy (PMRT) for breast cancer in India: An economic modelling study. Lancet Reg Health-Southeast Asia. 2022;4:100043.
29. Slamon DJ, Neven P, Chia S, Fasching PA, Laurentiis MD, Im S-A, et al. Overall survival with ribociclib plus fulvestrant in advanced breast cancer. N Engl J Med. 2020;382(6):514–24. Available at: https://www.nejm.org/doi/10.1056/NEJMoa1911149
30. Turner NC, Slamon DJ, Ro J, Bondarenko I, Im S-A, Masuda N, et al. Overall survival with palbociclib and fulvestrant in advanced breast cancer. N Engl J Med. 2018;379(20):1926–36.
31. Gupta N, Gupta D, Dixit J, Mehra N, Singh A, Krishnamurthy MN, Jyani G, Rajsekhar K, Kalaiyarasi JP, Roy PS, Malik PS. Cost effectiveness of Ribociclib and Palbociclib in the second-line treatment of hormone receptor-positive, HER2-negative metastatic breast cancer in post-menopausal indian women. Appl Health Econ Health Policy. 2022;20(4):609–21.

Suggested Readings

Cangelosi M, Chahar A, Eggington S. Evolving use of health technology assessment in medical device procurement – a global systematic review: an ISPOR Special Interest Group Report. Value in Health; 2023.

EUnet HT. An analysis of HTA and reimbursement procedures in EUnetHTA partner countries: final report. 2017.

Patcharanarumol W, Panichkriangkrai W, Sommanuttaweechai A, Hanson K, Wanwong Y, Tangcharoensathien V. Strategic purchasing and health system efficiency: a comparison of two financing schemes in Thailand. PLoS One. 2018;13(4):e0195179.

Part II

Health Financing: Indian Perspective

Health Financing in India

7

Yashika Chugh and Basant Garg

Abstract

This chapter provides an overview of India's health financing landscape, drawing on insights from the National Health Accounts Estimates. It examines the structure, composition, and trends in healthcare expenditures by analyzing successive National Health Accounts rounds from 2013–14 to 2020–21. The chapter explores the allocation of financial resources across public and private sectors, with a particular focus on key indicators such as total health expenditure (THE), government health expenditure (GHE), and out-of-pocket expenditure (OOPE). Finally, it traces financing trends over the past decade and compares India's performance with other countries in the Southeast Asia region to provide insights into the evolving dynamics of health financing in India.

Keywords

Health financing · National Health Accounts · Total Health Expenditure · Government Health Expenditure · Out-of-Pocket Expenditure

Y. Chugh (✉)
Department of Community Medicine and School of Public Health, Post Graduate Institute of Medical Education and Research, Chandigarh, India

B. Garg
Secretary, Health and Family Welfare, Government of Punjab, Punjab, India

S. Prinja (ed.), *Healthcare Financing and Insurance*,
https://doi.org/10.1007/978-981-95-3513-2_7

Learning Objectives
After working through this chapter, you will be able to

- Understand various indicators of health financing
- Understand India's current health financing landscape
- Understand the framework of National Health Accounts
- Compare the financing situation in India with other countries in the Southeast Asia region

7.1 Introduction

Health financing plays a critical role in determining access to healthcare, financial protection, and overall health system performance. In India, where healthcare is financed through a mix of public and private sources, understanding the composition, flow, and impact of health expenditures is essential for effective policymaking. While several earlier chapters in Part I of the textbook provide a theoretical understanding of health systems, health financing, and its various functions, this chapter aims to present an overview of the current state of health financing in India, drawing insights from the National Health Accounts Estimates 2021–22—the ninth round of such estimates for the country [1]. Health Accounts describe health expenditures and flow of funds for a financial year. They provide critical insights into key policy questions, including the sources of healthcare financing, the entities responsible for managing these funds, the providers delivering healthcare services, and the types of services utilized by the population.

To ensure international comparability, health expenditure estimates are compiled using the System of Health Accounts 2011 (SHA 2011) framework [2]. This standardized methodology categorizes expenditures into two broad classifications: current health expenditures (CHE) and capital expenditures. The primary focus is on CHE, which captures the ongoing costs associated with healthcare delivery. These expenditures are systematically analyzed across four dimensions:

1. *Revenue Sources for Healthcare Financing Schemes*—identifying the entities that contribute financial resources to support healthcare services.
2. *Healthcare Financing Schemes*—examining the mechanisms that receive and manage these funds to purchase or pay for healthcare goods and services.
3. *Healthcare Providers*—understanding which institutions or entities receive financial resources to produce and deliver healthcare services.
4. *Healthcare Functions*—assessing how funds are allocated across different types of healthcare services and interventions.

Before delving into the specifics of India's health financing landscape, it is essential to first understand the key indicators that help assess and compare health expenditures both internationally and across different rounds of National Health Accounts within the country. The most commonly used health financing indicators, along with their descriptions, are as follows:

- *Total Health Expenditure (THE) as a Percentage of Gross Domestic Product (GDP)*: THE represents the sum of the current and capital expenditures on healthcare from both government and private sources, including external funds. THE as a percentage of GDP indicates health spending relative to the country's economic development.
- *THE* per Capita: THE per capita indicates health expenditure per person in the country.
- *Current Health Expenditures (CHE) as a Percentage of THE*: The SHA 2011 framework disaggregates expenditures into current and capital expenditures. CHE includes all recurrent expenditures on healthcare, excluding capital investments. CHE is expressed as proportion within THE indicates the operational spending on healthcare services that directly impact population health outcomes in a given year.
- *Government Health Expenditure (GHE) as a Percentage of THE*: GHE includes the spending under all schemes funded and managed by union, state, and local governments, including quasi-governmental organizations and donors in case funds are channeled through government organizations. GHE as a percentage of THE represents the share of government in the overall health financing of the country.
- *Out-of-Pocket Expenditures (OOPE) as a Percentage of THE*: OOPE refers to direct payments made by households at the time of receiving healthcare services. This indicator reflects the extent of likely financial hardship for the households.
- *Social Security Expenditure on Health as a Percentage of THE*: Social Security Expenditures include finances allocated by the government toward payment of premiums for the government-financed health insurance schemes, including the *Ayushman Bharat Pradhan Mantri Jan Arogya Yojana* (AB PM-JAY), *Rashtriya Swasthya Bima Yojana* (RSBY), and other state-specific health insurance schemes, employer-based health benefits schemes, or any reimbursements made to government employees for healthcare purposes. This indicates the extent of pooled funds available for specific categories of population.
- *Private Health Insurance Expenditures as a Percentage of THE*: Private health insurance expenditures constitute spending through health insurance companies where households or employers pay a premium to be covered under a specific health plan. This indicates the extent to which there are private voluntary prepayment plans to provide financial protection.
- *External/Donor Funding for Health as a Percentage of THE*: This includes all financial assistance received from international donors and external agencies to support healthcare in the country.

- *GHE as a Percentage of General Government Expenditure (GGE)*: This represents the share of government spending allocated to healthcare in the GGE. It serves as an indicator of the government's prioritization toward health.
- *Household Health Expenditure as a Percentage of THE*: This comprises both direct OOPE and indirect expenses such as insurance premiums paid by households. A higher proportion suggests a greater reliance on individual financial resources (income/savings) to meet healthcare expenses.
- *Union and State Government Health Expenditures as a Percentage of GHE*: Union Government Health Expenditures refer to the financial resources allocated by various ministries and departments of the central government for healthcare services, both for the general population and government employees, including transfers to local bodies. In a similar manner, State Government Health Expenditures encompass the health-related allocations made by different departments across all state governments, covering services for the public and government staff, as well as contributions from and to local bodies using their own funds. These expenditures together reflect the respective roles and financial contributions of the union and state governments in overall public health spending—an essential aspect of India's federal structure.
- *Ayurveda, Yoga, Naturopathy, Unani, Siddha, and Homeopathy (AYUSH) Expenditure as a Percentage of THE*: AYUSH, referred to the traditional and alternative medical systems, stands for Ayurveda, Yoga, Naturopathy, Unani, Siddha, and Homeopathy. This indicator captures all the financial allocation for non-allopathic healthcare practices within the THE. This comprises a range of long-standing and still-evolving practices based on diverse beliefs and theories.
- *Pharmaceutical Expenditures as a Percentage of CHE*: This includes spending on prescribed medications, over-the-counter drugs, and pharmaceuticals consumed as part of inpatient and outpatient treatments. It highlights the share of pharmaceutical expenditures in the CHE [1].

7.2 National Health Accounts Estimates for India

7.2.1 Trends in Health Financing: Indicators for India

7.2.1.1 Total and Current Health Expenditure

- Based on the estimates available for 2021–22, the total health expenditure (THE) had risen to ₹9,04,461 crores, constituting 3.83% of GDP, with THE per capita spending increasing to ₹6602 (Figs. 7.1 and 7.2). In 2020–21, India's THE was ₹7,39,327 crores, accounting for 3.73% of GDP, with per capita health spending at ₹5436. This has been an increasing trend since 2018–19 where THE stood at 3.2% of the GDP [1, 3, 4].
- The per capita CHE also increased to 1.5 times from 2017–18 to 2021–22. The CHE remained the dominant component of the THE, amounting to ₹7,89,760 crores (87.32% of THE), while capital spending grew to ₹1,14,701 crores (12.68%) from ₹75,910 crores (10.27%) of THE in 2020–21 [1, 3–6].

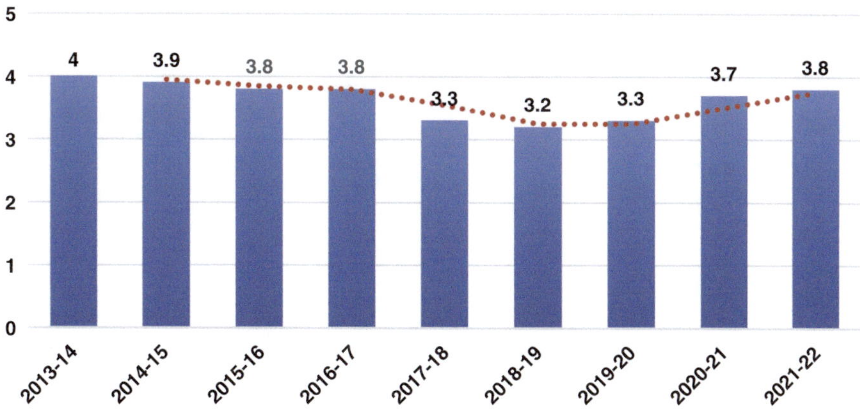

Fig. 7.1 THE as a percentage of GDP

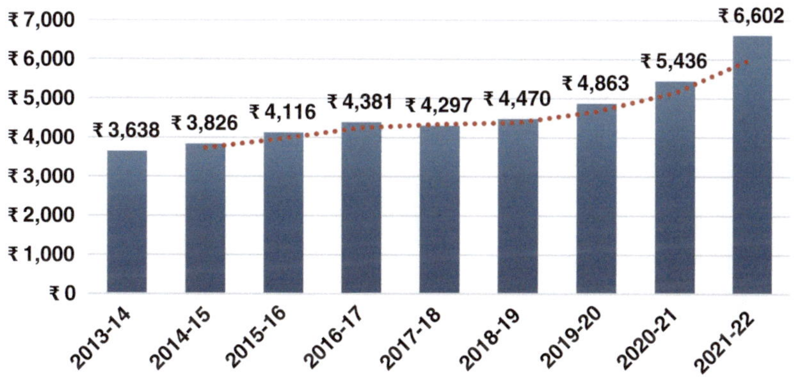

Fig. 7.2 THE per capita (₹) at current prices

- GHE also saw a substantial increase, reaching ₹4,34,163 crores, covering 48% of THE and 41.1% of CHE, which has increased from 40.8% of THE and 33.2% of CHE, respectively (Figs. 7.3 and 7.4). This shift indicates reduced reliance on OOP payments and an expansion of publicly funded health services. Enhanced government allocations have contributed to improved infrastructure, service delivery, and financial protection for citizens [1, 3–6].

7.2.1.2 Trends in Government Health Expenditure

- Over the years, public expenditure on healthcare has increased significantly, reflecting the government's commitment to strengthening the health system. In 2020–21, government health spending amounted to ₹3,16,554 crores, accounting for 1.60% of GDP and ₹2328 per capita (Fig. 7.5). This expenditure saw a notable rise in 2021–22, reaching ₹4,34,163 crores, which represented 1.84% of

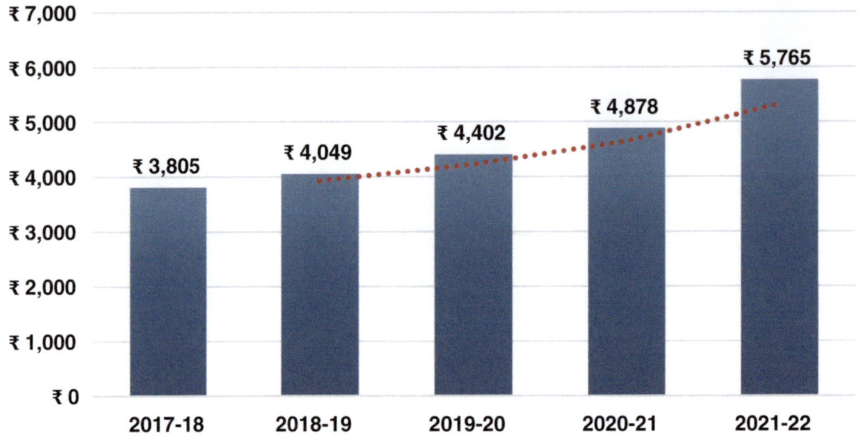

Fig. 7.3 CHE per capita (₹) at current prices

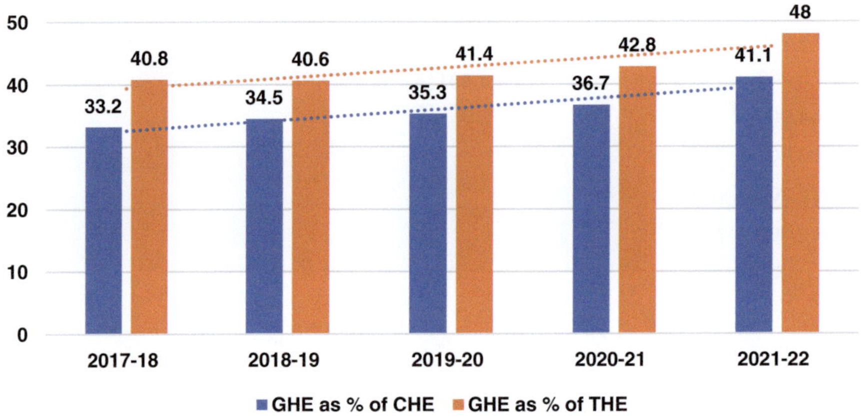

Fig. 7.4 Trends in GHE as a percentage of THE and CHE

GDP. The shares of GHE as a percentage of GDP increased from 1.13% in 2014–15 to 1.84% in 2021–22 (Fig. 7.5). Similarly, GHE as a proportion of GGE grew from 3.94% to 6.12% over the same period.

- Within the GHE, in the year 2020–21 state governments contributed the majority share at 64.3%, while the union government accounted for 35.7%, primarily funding major public health programs such as the National Health Mission and the Central Government Health Scheme. In the following year (2021–22), the union government's share in GHE increased to 41.8%, while the states' contribution declined to 58.2%. Key union government programs, including the National Health Mission, Defense Medical Services, and the Central Government Health Scheme, continued to play a vital role in public health spending [1, 3–6].

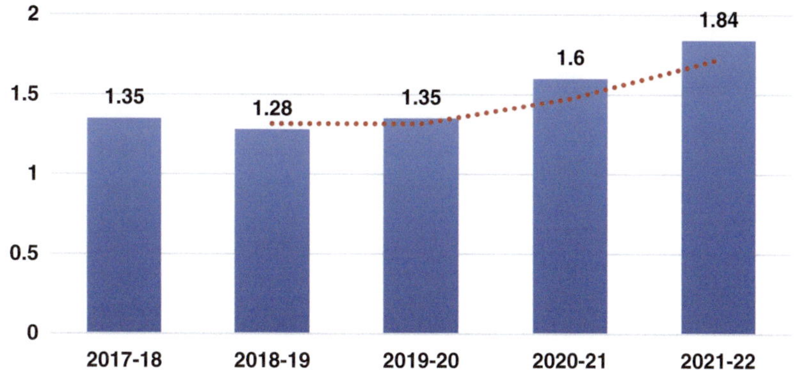

Fig. 7.5 GHE as a percentage of GDP

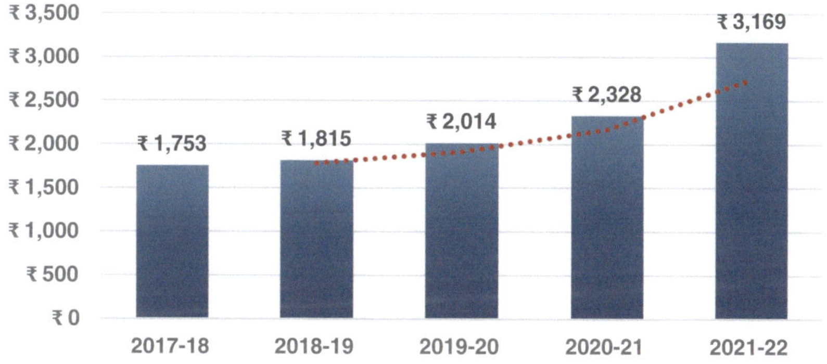

Fig. 7.6 Trends in per capita GHE

- In per capita terms, GHE has nearly tripled, rising from Rs. 1108 in 2014–15 to ₹3169 in 2021–22, signifying a significant increase in healthcare investments (Fig. 7.6) [1, 3–7].

7.2.1.3 Trends in OOPE

- OOPE has traditionally been a major contributor to the financial burden for households in India. Although the per capita OOPE has increased from ₹2096 to ₹2600 over the previous 5 years; however, its share in THE fell from 62.6% in 2014–15 to 39.4% in 2021–22, reflecting the impact of enhanced public healthcare funding (Fig. 7.7). This decline suggests improved financial protection for individuals, reducing the need for direct payments at the point of care [1, 3–6].
- Further, the share of OOPE as a percentage to the CHE has also decreased from 55% to 45% over the previous 5 years from 2017–18 to 2021–22 [1, 3–10] (Fig. 7.8).

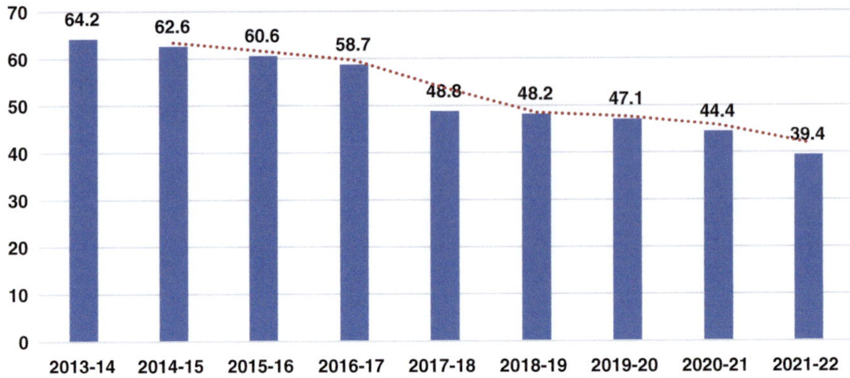

Fig. 7.7 Trends in OOP expenditure as a percentage of THE

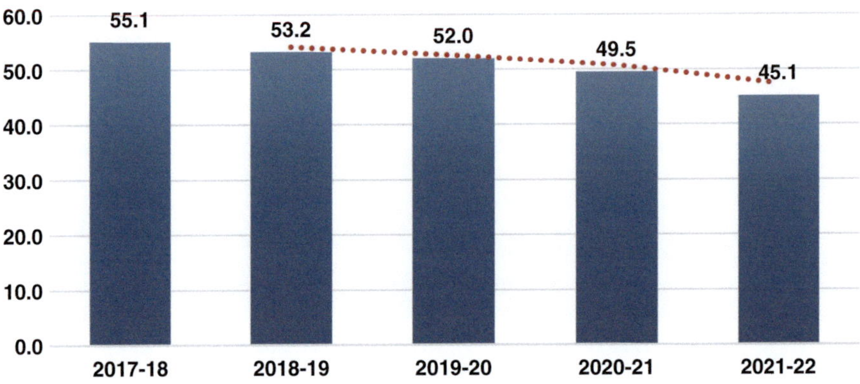

Fig. 7.8 OOPE as a percentage of the CHE

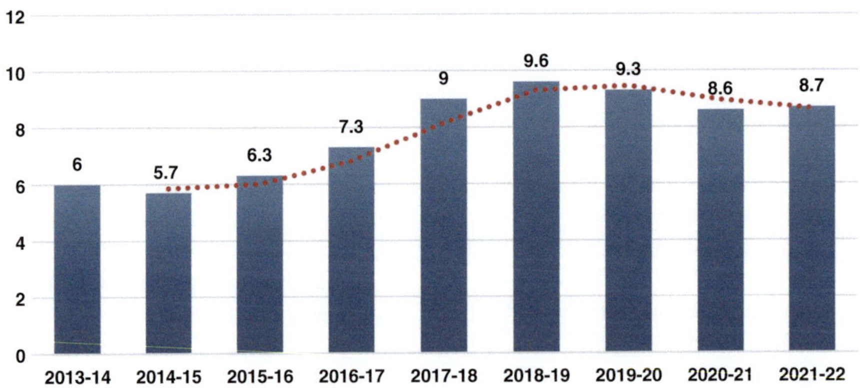

Fig. 7.9 Trends in share of SSE as a percentage of THE

7.2.1.4 Growth in Social Security Expenditure (SSE) on Health

- A key development in India's health financing landscape is the increase in SSE, which plays a crucial role in lowering direct medical costs for individuals. SSE includes government-backed health insurance, medical reimbursements for public sector employees, and social health insurance programs. The proportion of SSE within THE grew from 5.7% in 2014–15 to 8.7% in 2021–22 (Fig. 7.9) [1, 7].

7.2.2 Estimates by the National Health Accounts Classifications

This section outlines the allocation of CHE based on the National Health Accounts classification. These categories, originally defined under the SHA 2011, have been adapted to align with the Indian healthcare system. The total healthcare expenditure for 2021–22 amounted to ₹7,89,760 crores, distributed across key components: healthcare financing schemes, sources of financing (revenues of healthcare financing schemes), healthcare providers, and healthcare functions [1, 2].

7.2.2.1 Expenditure Estimates by the Healthcare Financing Schemes

Healthcare financing schemes form the foundational elements of healthcare financing systems, outlining the mechanisms through which financial resources are collected and allocated for providing healthcare services. These schemes ensure the efficient distribution of funds to support population health needs.

Table 7.1 Current health expenditures (2021–22) by healthcare financing schemes

National Health Accounts Code[a]	Healthcare financing schemes	Amount (crores)	%
HF.1.1.1.1	Union government schemes (nonemployees)	₹1,11,126	14.07
HF.1.1.1.2	Union government schemes (employees)	₹20,718	2.62
HF.1.1.2.1.1	State government schemes (nonemployees)	₹1,16,267	14.72
HF.1.1.2.1.2	State government schemes (employees)	₹9694	1.23
HF.1.1.2.2.1	Urban local bodies	₹12,630	1.6
HF.1.1.2.2.2	Rural local bodies	₹7856	1
HF.1.2.1	Social health insurance (not including 1.2.1.4)	₹25,626	3.24
HF.1.2.1.4	Government-financed health insurance	₹20,808	2.63
HF.2.1.1.1	Employer-based insurance (private group health insurance)	₹36,890	4.67
HF.2.1.1.3	Other primary coverage schemes (private individual health insurance)	₹30,085	3.81
HF.2.1.2.1	Community-based insurance	₹16	0
HF.2.2.1	Non-Profit Institutions Serving Households (NPISH)	₹13,893	1.76
HF.2.2.2	Resident foreign agencies schemes	₹1239	0.16
HF.2.3.1.2	Enterprises	₹26,658	3.38
HF.3.3	All household out-of-pocket payment	₹3,56,254	45.11
	Total	**₹7,89,760**	**100**

[a]Refer to the National Health Accounts 2021–22 for a description of these categories

Table 7.1 details the expenditure distribution across various healthcare financing schemes.

In 2021–22, CHE in India amounted to ₹7,89,760 crores, with household out-of-pocket payments accounting for the largest share (45.11%). Government health schemes, including both union and state programs, contributed significantly, with state government schemes (nonemployees) making up 14.72% and union government schemes (nonemployees) 14.07%. Private health insurance accounted for 8.48% and included employer-based insurance and other primary coverage schemes (private individual health insurance) while social health insurance including the government-financed health insurance accounted for 5.87% of the total [1].

7.2.2.2 Sources of Revenues of Healthcare Financing Schemes

Of the total CHE, the union government accounts for ₹1,25,854 crores, representing 15.94% of CHE, while state governments contribute ₹1,71,952 crores, making up 21.77% of CHE. Local bodies allocate ₹8601 crores, constituting 1.08% of CHE. Households, including contributions toward insurance, bear the largest share at ₹3,99,136 crores, accounting for 50.55% of CHE, with OOPE alone comprising 45.11% of CHE. Enterprises, inclusive of insurance contributions, contribute ₹64,206 crores (8.13% of CHE), while nongovernmental organizations (NGOs) provide ₹12,013 crores (1.52% of CHE). External and donor funding amounts to ₹7998 crores, making up 1.01% of CHE (Fig. 7.10) [1].

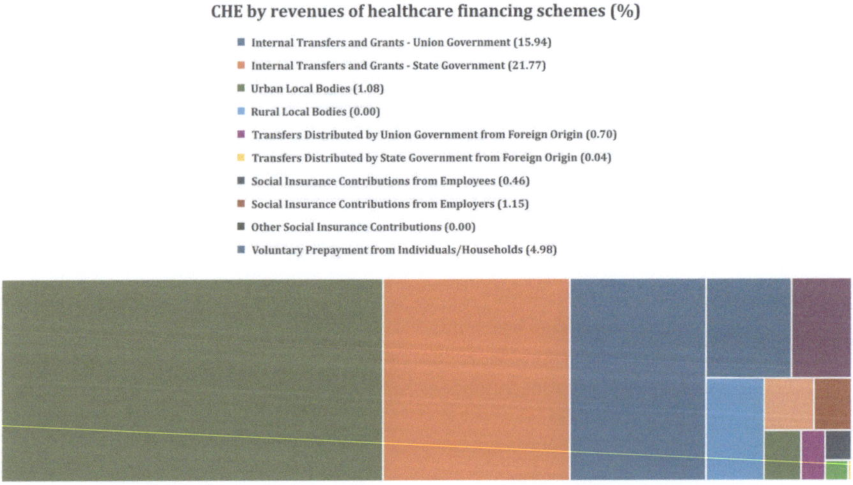

Fig. 7.10 Current health expenditures (2021–22) by revenues of healthcare financing schemes

7.2.2.3 Expenditure Estimates by Healthcare Providers

Government hospitals account for ₹1,49,900 crores, representing 18.99% of the total CHE, while private hospitals account for ₹2,12,948 crores, making up 26.96% of CHE. Expenditure on other government healthcare providers, including primary health centers (PHCs), dispensaries, and family planning centers, amounts to ₹56,477 crores (7.15% of CHE). Other private providers, such as private clinics, account for ₹30,080 crores (3.81% of CHE).

Spending on patient transport and emergency rescue services stands at ₹28,906 crores (3.65% of CHE), while medical and diagnostic laboratories receive ₹26,238 crores (3.32% of CHE). Pharmacies constitute a significant portion, with ₹1,52,910 crores (19.35% of CHE), whereas other retailers contribute ₹837 crores (0.11% of CHE). Providers of preventive care account for ₹82,325 crores (10.42% of CHE).

Additionally, ₹27,380 crores (3.48% of CHE) is allocated to providers responsible for health system administration and financing, while ₹21,759 crores (2.76% of CHE) is attributed to other healthcare providers not classified elsewhere [1].

7.2.2.4 Expenditure Estimates by Healthcare Functions

Inpatient curative care accounts for ₹2,99,587 crores, representing 37.94% of CHE, while spending in day curative care accounts for ₹7327 crores (0.93% of CHE). Outpatient curative care expenditure stands at ₹1,20,816 crores, making up 15.30% of CHE. Patient transportation services incur ₹28,906 crores (3.65% of CHE), and laboratory and imaging services amount to ₹26,238 crores (3.32% of CHE).

Spending on prescribed medicines totals ₹1,26,225 crores (15.98% of CHE), while over-the-counter (OTC) medicines account for ₹25,458 crores (3.22% of CHE).

Preventive care accounts for ₹1,07,048 crores, comprising 13.55% of CHE, and other healthcare expenditures total ₹20,686 crores (2.63% of CHE). Additionally, governance, health system administration, and financing are attributed ₹26,632 crores (3.37% of CHE).

Total pharmaceutical expenditure (TPE), which includes prescribed medicines, OTC drugs, and medications provided in inpatient, outpatient, or other healthcare settings, constitutes 30.84% of CHE. Spending on Traditional, Complementary, and Alternative Medicine (TCAM) accounts for 3.59% of CHE [1].

7.2.3 Expenditure Estimates by Primary, Secondary, and Tertiary Care

In terms of care levels, 46% of CHE is allocated to primary care, 33% to secondary care, and 16% to tertiary care, while governance and supervision account for 3%. Within government health expenditure, 50% is attributed to primary care, 28% to secondary care, and 12% to tertiary care. The trends from 2017–18 to 2021–22 are demonstrated in Fig. 7.11 [1, 3–6].

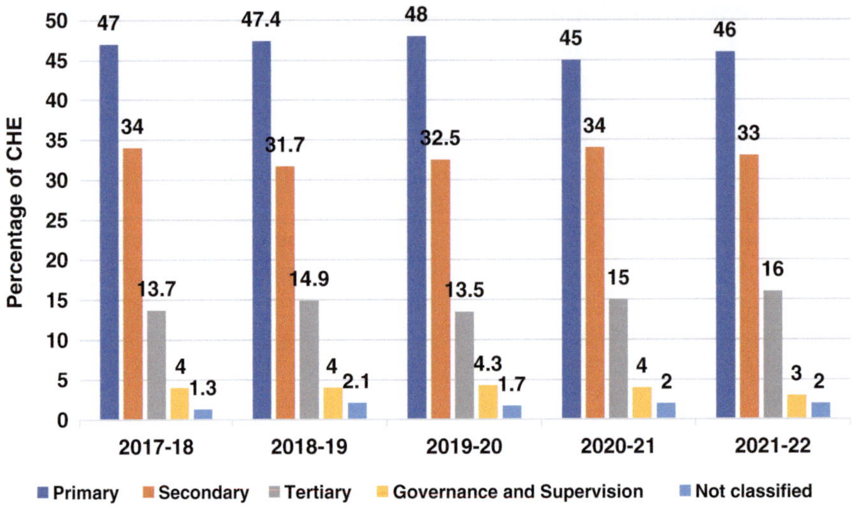

Fig. 7.11 Current health expenditure in India by primary, secondary, and tertiary care levels

7.2.4 Health Insurance Expenditures

Health insurance encompasses healthcare financing schemes that are funded through contributions or premiums collected from individuals or the government. These pooled funds are then utilized to actively purchase healthcare services from providers, either through government entities (such as health departments or government-managed corporations, trusts, or societies) or insurance companies. In the context of India's National Health Accounts, health insurance expenditures are classified under four key categories:

- Social health insurance, including schemes such as the Central Government Health Scheme (CGHS), Employees' State Insurance Scheme (ESIS), and Ex-Servicemen Contributory Health Scheme (ECHS).
- Government-financed health insurance schemes, covering programs run by both union and state governments, employer-based insurance, excluding enterprise schemes, such as private group health insurance.
- Other primary coverage schemes, which include private individual health insurance.
- Community-based health insurance, which relies on collective risk-sharing within specific communities.

The expenditure estimated from 2018–19 to 2021–22 is tabulated in Table 7.2 [1, 3, 4, 6].

It is important to note that health insurance expenditures do not account for medical reimbursements provided to union government employees under the Central Services Medical Attendance (CSMA), healthcare services delivered through

Table 7.2 Health insurance expenditure (2021–22) under different schemes

		Expenditure (crores)			
S. no.	Health insurance schemes	2018–19	2019–20	2020–21	2021–22
1	Social health insurance schemes	₹21,795	₹25,401	₹25,905	₹27,250
2	Government-financed health insurance	₹12,680	₹13,809	₹13,459	₹20,808
3	Private health insurance	₹39,201	45,838	53,948	₹66,975
4	Community-based health insurance	₹13	₹39	₹16	₹16

defense and railways, state government reimbursements for employee medical expenses, or emergency medical relief funds disbursed by union and state governments to financially vulnerable individuals for secondary and tertiary care.

7.3 India's Health Financing Situation Compared to Other Countries

According to the Global Health Expenditure Database, India's CHE stood at about 3.3% of its GDP for the year 2022, which is relatively lower than those in comparable low- and middle-income economies. Data from a set of five comparator countries in the Southeast Asian region show that India lies somewhere in the middle of the pack, spending less than Thailand and Sri Lanka on healthcare as a proportion of GDP, but more than Bangladesh and Indonesia. (Fig. 7.12) [11].

An analysis of long-term trends in CHE shows that India's health spending as a share of GDP has remained relatively stable and has not increased significantly compared to other countries. In contrast, Thailand and Sri Lanka have exhibited a rising trend over time (Fig. 7.13) [11].

The allocation of health spending has been a long-standing concern in India, as private expenditure accounts for over two-thirds of total health spending, while the central and state governments contribute only about one-third. In 2022, India's per capita current health expenditure (CHE) stood at USD 80, making it the second lowest among the Southeast Asian comparator countries, surpassing only Bangladesh (Fig. 7.14) [11].

Figure 7.15 presents data on the proportion of public and private spending in CHE. Unlike Thailand, where nearly 70% of health spending comes from public sources, government spending on healthcare in India accounts for only about

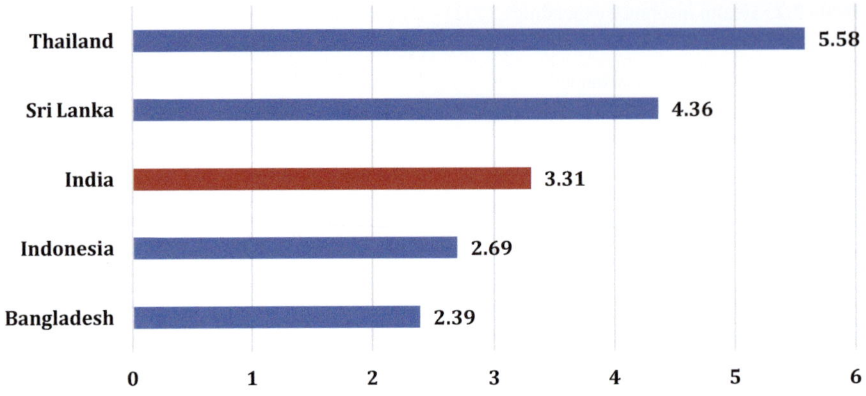

Fig. 7.12 CHE as a share of GDP (%) in selected Southeast Asian countries for the year 2022

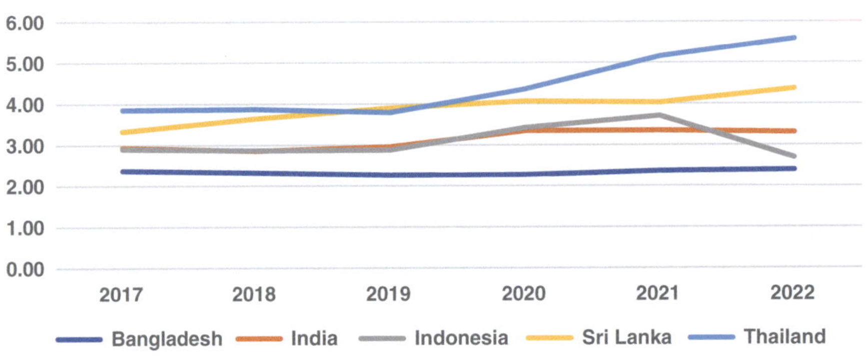

Fig. 7.13 Trends in CHE as a share of GDP (%) in selected Southeast Asian countries for the year 2022

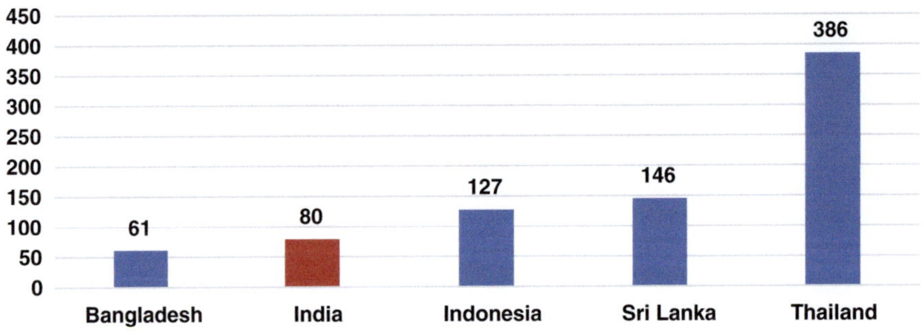

Fig. 7.14 CHE per capita at international USD (US dollar) ($) in selected countries in 2022

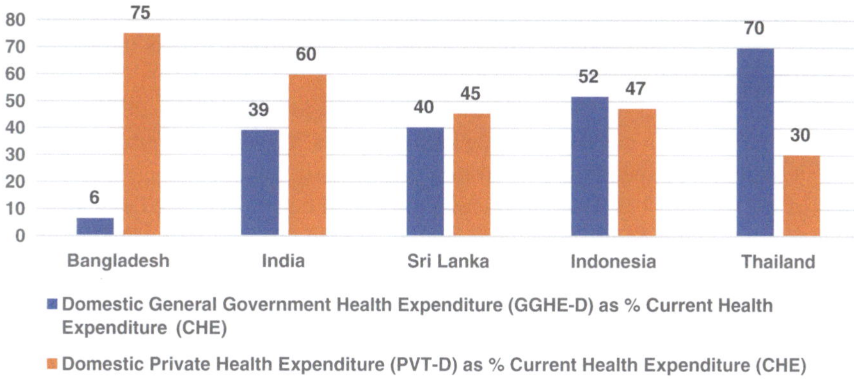

Fig. 7.15 Domestic general government health expenditure and private health expenditure (% of current health expenditure) 2022

one-third of total health expenditures. Similarly, both Indonesia and Sri Lanka have a higher share of government health spending and lower private expenditures compared to India. These spending patterns highlight the varying degrees of reliance on risk-pooled funds across countries, which in turn influence the efficiency and equity of resource distribution [11].

7.4 Summary

India's health financing landscape has evolved significantly over the years, with increasing efforts to strengthen financial protection and expand healthcare access. Government initiatives have contributed to a decline in OOPE, which fell from 64% of total health spending in 2013–14 to 39% in 2021–22 [1, 8]. Public health expenditure has also grown, reaching 1.8% of GDP in 2021–22, up from less than 1% in the early 2000s [12].

Despite these advancements, there remain challenges such as fragmentation in financing, limited risk pooling, and a continued reliance on private spending. Currently, India's total health expenditure, including both public and private sources, stands at 3.8% of GDP, which is lower than the middle-income countries (MIC) average of 5.2% [1, 11]. Government funding, contributed by both the central and state governments, constitutes approximately half of total health spending, with states accounting for nearly two-thirds of this expenditure in line with their constitutional responsibilities for healthcare.

To improve financial risk protection, India has made concerted efforts to expand health insurance coverage, particularly for low-income and informal sector workers. Initially, social health insurance schemes covered a limited segment of the population, primarily central government employees and select formal sector workers—about 137 million people in total. However, with the introduction of the RSBY in 2008 and the subsequent launch of the AB PM-JAY, government-backed insurance has played an increasing role in facilitating access to secondary and tertiary hospital care.

Since the launch of the National Rural Health Mission (NRHM) in 2005, government health spending has seen notable improvements. The share of public expenditure in total health spending rose from approximately 23% in the early 2000s to 48% in 2021–22 [1, 12]. The introduction of NRHM helped enhance flexibility and predictability in financing, with funds initially routed through off-budget societies until 2014. From 2015 onward, central government funds have been directed via state treasuries, ensuring greater alignment with state-level health priorities.

While government-sponsored health insurance schemes, including AB PM-JAY and RSBY, currently account for 2.63% of total public health spending, the overall financing of public healthcare services remains largely reliant on general revenues [1]. Salaries form a major component of these allocations, and historical spending patterns continue to shape funding decisions. Publicly financed health insurance has also introduced a third-party payer mechanism, enabling beneficiaries to access both public and private hospital care, thus expanding choices for patients.

Despite these efforts, household OOP expenditures remain a concern, particularly for outpatient services and medicines, which account for nearly two-thirds of total OOP spending. As a result, over 55 million people in India experience financial hardship due to healthcare costs each year. Data on government health spending patterns indicate that approximately 50% of current health expenditure (CHE) is directed toward primary care, while secondary and tertiary care receive 28% and 12%, respectively, with the remainder allocated to administrative and other costs [1].

Overall, while India's health financing system continues to face structural challenges, ongoing policy initiatives and increasing public investments are driving improvements in financial risk protection, insurance coverage, and access to essential healthcare services.

References

1. National Health Accounts for India 2021–2022. National Health Systems Resource Centre. New Delhi: Ministry of Health and Family Welfare, Government of India. https://nhsrcindia.org/national-health-accounts-records.
2. World Health Organization. A System of Health Accounts 2011 Revised edition: Revised edition. OECD publishing; 2017. https://www.who.int/publications/i/item/9789240042551.
3. National Health Accounts for India 2018–2019. National Health Systems Resource Centre. New Delhi: Ministry of Health and Family Welfare, Government of India. https://nhsrcindia.org/national-health-accounts-records.
4. National Health Accounts for India 2020–2021. National Health Systems Resource Centre. New Delhi: Ministry of Health and Family Welfare, Government of India. https://nhsrcindia.org/national-health-accounts-records.
5. National Health Accounts for India 2017–2018. National Health Systems Resource Centre. New Delhi: Ministry of Health and Family Welfare, Government of India. https://nhsrcindia.org/national-health-accounts-records.

6. National Health Accounts for India 2019–2020. National Health Systems Resource Centre. New Delhi: Ministry of Health and Family Welfare, Government of India. https://nhsrcindia.org/national-health-accounts-records.
7. National Health Accounts for India 2014–2015. National Health Systems Resource Centre. New Delhi: Ministry of Health and Family Welfare, Government of India. https://nhsrcindia.org/national-health-accounts-records.
8. National Health Accounts for India 2013–2014. National Health Systems Resource Centre. New Delhi: Ministry of Health and Family Welfare, Government of India. https://nhsrcindia.org/national-health-accounts-records.
9. National Health Accounts for India 2015–2016. National Health Systems Resource Centre. New Delhi: Ministry of Health and Family Welfare, Government of India. https://nhsrcindia.org/national-health-accounts-records.
10. National Health Accounts for India 2016–2017. National Health Systems Resource Centre. New Delhi: Ministry of Health and Family Welfare, Government of India. https://nhsrcindia.org/national-health-accounts-records.
11. World Health Organization. Global health expenditure database. Geneva: World Health Organization. https://apps.who.int/nha/database.
12. Selvaraj S, Karan KA, Srivastava S, et al. India: health system review. Health Syst Transit. 2022;11(1). World Health Organization Regional Office for South-East Asia. https://iris.who.int/handle/10665/352685.

Universal Health Coverage: How to Finance It?

8

Shankar Prinja, Prakash Singh, and Jyoti Dixit

Abstract

This chapter explores the concept of universal health coverage (UHC) and the strategies for financing it. It begins by defining UHC and introducing the UHC cube, outlining its three key dimensions: population coverage, service coverage, and financial risk protection. The chapter then traces the global and Indian evolution of UHC, highlighting its integration into the Sustainable Development Goals (SDGs) and the measurement of progress through the UHC Coverage Index.

One of the pathways to achieving UHC is through publicly financed health insurance schemes, which have played a crucial role in India's health system. The chapter examines their impact, leading to the emergence of the *Ayushman Bharat Pradhan Mantri Jan Arogya Yojana* (AB PM-JAY). The chapter explores the expansion of the dimensions of the UHC cube, highlighting the challenge of the "missing middle" in population coverage and identifying possible strategies for their inclusion. It further argues for expanding the benefit package, particularly through the inclusion of outpatient care, to enhance service coverage. The chapter also presents evidence on financial risk protection, supporting the adequacy of AB PM-JAY's current coverage and demonstrating its effectiveness in reducing out-of-pocket expenditure (OOPE). Finally, it underscores the essential role of the public sector in achieving UHC, emphasizing the need for its continued strengthening as the foundation of an equitable and sustainable health system.

Keywords

Universal Health Coverage (UHC) · Health Financing · Health Insurance · Out-of-pocket expenditure (OOPE) · *Ayushman Bharat Pradhan Mantri Jan Arogya Yojana* (AB PM-JAY)

S. Prinja (✉) · P. Singh · J. Dixit
Department of Community Medicine and School of Public Health, Post Graduate Institute of Medical Education & Research, Chandigarh, India

S. Prinja (ed.), *Healthcare Financing and Insurance*,
https://doi.org/10.1007/978-981-95-3513-2_8

Learning Objectives

After working through this chapter, you will be able to

- Understand the concepts of universal health coverage
- Understand the evolution of universal health coverage: global and Indian
- Understand the measurement of universal health coverage
- Understand the strategies for financing universal health coverage

Key Terms

1. *Universal health coverage (UHC):* A health system goal in which all individuals and communities receive the health services they need—of sufficient quality—without suffering financial hardship. It includes the entire spectrum of care, from promotion and prevention to treatment, rehabilitation, and palliative care.
2. *UHC cube:* A conceptual framework that visualizes progress toward UHC across three dimensions: Breadth: population coverage (who is covered); Depth: service coverage (which services are included); Height: financial risk protection (what proportion of costs are covered).
3. *Out-of-pocket expenditure (OOPE):* Direct payment made by individuals to healthcare providers at the time-of-service use, not reimbursed by any insurance scheme. High OOPE increases the risk of financial hardship and poverty.
4. *Catastrophic health expenditure (CHE):* Health spending that exceeds a predefined proportion of a household's income or consumption expenditure (commonly ≥10% of total income or ≥40% of non-food consumption expenditure), resulting in financial distress.
5. *Government-funded health insurance (GFHI):* Publicly financed insurance schemes that pay for healthcare services for eligible populations, particularly low-income or vulnerable groups.
6. *Ayushman Bharat Pradhan Mantri Jan Arogya Yojana* (AB PM-JAY): India's flagship government-funded insurance program launched in 2018, providing up to ₹500,000 per family per year for secondary and tertiary inpatient care. It aims to improve both access and financial protection for the poorest 40% of the population.
7. *Ayushman Arogya Mandirs* (AAMs): The upgraded primary healthcare facilities under *Ayushman Bharat*, providing comprehensive primary care including preventive, promotive, and basic curative services.
8. *Missing middle*: A population segment that is not poor enough to qualify for government-subsidized insurance and not rich enough to afford private insurance. This group largely works in the informal sector, remains uninsured, and is highly vulnerable to OOPE.

8.1 Introduction

Universal health coverage (UHC) is a broad and comprehensive concept, encompassing the entire health system. The World Health Organization (WHO) defines UHC in terms of "*all individuals and communities receive the health services they need without suffering financial hardship. It includes the full spectrum of essential, quality health services, from health promotion to prevention, treatment, rehabilitation, and palliative care*" [1]. UHC refers to ensuring that every individual has access to the health services they require without facing financial distress due to high out-of-pocket expenditure (OOPE) [2]. It encompasses a full spectrum of services—ranging from health promotion and disease prevention to treatment, rehabilitation, and palliative care—while also providing mechanisms for financial protection against medical costs. A key principle of UHC is inclusivity, meaning that coverage should extend to the entire population. While no country has achieved complete UHC, most nations are progressively working toward this goal, with improving access to essential services being a crucial step in the process [2, 3].

UHC is attained when individuals are able to receive the health services they require while being safeguarded from financial hardship. In contrast, access refers to the ability or opportunity to utilize these services and benefit from such protection. Therefore, although UHC cannot be achieved without ensuring universal access, the two concepts remain distinct. Access to healthcare can be understood through three key dimensions [4–6]: (i) physical accessibility: health services should be available within a reasonable distance and offered at convenient times, with appropriate systems such as appointments and service delivery arrangements that enable people to use them when needed. (ii) Financial affordability: individuals should be able to pay for health services without experiencing financial strain. This includes not only the direct cost of care but also indirect and opportunity costs, such as transportation expenses and loss of income due to time away from work. Affordability is shaped both by household income and the structure of the health financing system. (iii) Acceptability: people must be willing to seek care, which depends on their perception of service quality and cultural compatibility. Acceptability tends to be low when services are viewed as ineffective or when barriers such as language, gender, ethnicity, religion, or social norms discourage people from accessing care.

So, the health services must be physically accessible, financially affordable, and acceptable to public if UHC is to be attained [5, 7].

Physical accessibility is achieved when health services are of adequate quality, available, and located within reasonable proximity to the population. Service readiness refers to the presence of essential inputs—such as infrastructure, equipment, skilled health workers, medicines, and technologies—necessary to deliver those services effectively. Financial affordability can be strengthened by reducing reliance on direct out-of-pocket spending, for example, through prepaid financing and pooling mechanisms such as tax-based funding or health insurance contributions, as well as demand-side approaches like vouchers and conditional cash transfers. Social and cultural accessibility improves when health systems and providers consistently treat individuals and their families with dignity, respect, and sensitivity to cultural contexts [5].

8.1.1 The UHC Cube

Over the past two decades, UHC has gained significant global prominence, with governments increasingly demonstrating their commitment to achieving healthcare for all. It is now one of the most widely recognized global health policy priority formally incorporated into the Sustainable Development Goals (SDGs) in 2015. The concept of UHC is typically represented through three key dimensions: breadth, referring to population coverage; depth, indicating the range of health services included and height which reflects the proportion of health service costs covered by public financing, minimizing out-of-pocket expenditures, and ensuring financial risk protection. These dimensions are best visualized through the UHC cube (see Fig. 8.1). Originally conceived in the early 2000s, the UHC cube was later refined as a foundational framework in the European Observatory's Health Systems in Transition reports. It gained further recognition through the World Health Reports of 2008 and 2010 and has since become widely known as the coverage cube. Today, it remains a fundamental tool for illustrating UHC and supporting related policy analyses worldwide [8].

Now that we have explored the concept of UHC and its key dimensions, it is essential to understand its evolution before delving into the next sections on measuring and financing UHC. A historical perspective provides valuable insights into how UHC has developed over time, the factors that have shaped its progress, and the challenges that remain.

In the following section, we will examine the evolution of UHC from both a global and an Indian perspective. This discussion will highlight the milestones, policy shifts, and strategic initiatives that have contributed to the advancement of UHC worldwide and within India. Understanding this trajectory will help contextualize the approaches to measuring and financing UHC, which will be explored in the subsequent sections.

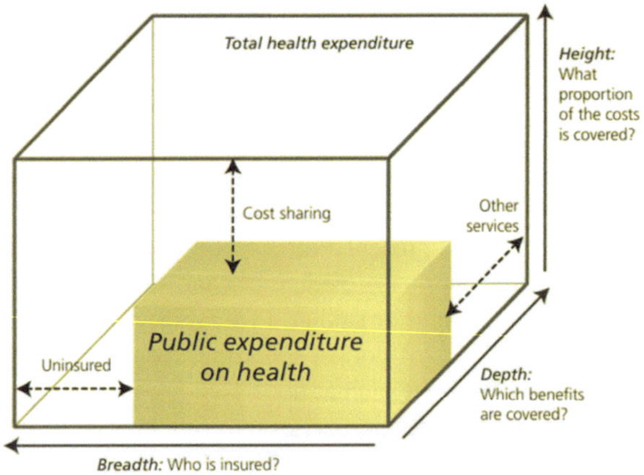

Fig. 8.1 The three dimensions of universal health coverage

8.2 Evolution of the Concept of Universal Health Coverage

Global Let us explore some key historical events from the past two centuries that have contributed to the growing momentum and renewed focus on UHC. The origins date back to the nineteenth century when several Scandinavian countries (e.g., Germany) began institutionalizing mandatory health insurance and risk coverage for healthcare needs. Two pivotal moments stand out in this history, shaped by the broader context of their times. The first was around the period of the First World War, coinciding with the development of the National Insurance Act in the United Kingdom. The second occurred after the Second World War, with the establishment of the National Health Service (NHS). These developments were influenced by two major factors: war and industrialization. As industries expanded and nations needed strong, able-bodied workers and soldiers, the demand for a healthy workforce became essential. This need drove efforts to ensure that citizens remained healthy to maintain productivity and safeguard national security. Additionally, global conventions over time began articulating the right to the highest attainable standards of physical and mental health. A notable milestone was the "Health for All" declaration at the Alma Ata conference. Finally, in 2005, the World Health Assembly officially adopted the term "universal health coverage." More recently, UHC has become a key part of the SDGs, and in 2019, the United Nations (UN) issued a political declaration and a foreign policy outlook prioritizing health. These events reflect the evolving global commitment to ensuring health for all (Fig. 8.2).

India The concept of UHC in India is not new, dating back to the pre-independence era with aspirations to provide comprehensive healthcare, as articulated in the Bhore Committee report in 1946 (Fig. 8.3). The Indian Constitution also plays a role in

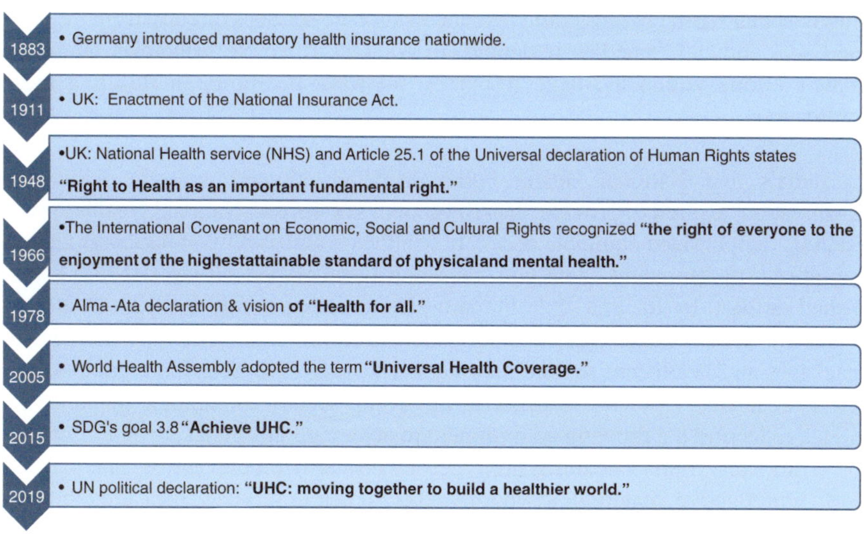

Fig. 8.2 Evolution of UHC globally. (*UK* United Kingdom, *SDG* Sustainable Development Goals, *UN* United Nations, *UHC* universal health coverage)

1946
- **Bhore Committee-** Comprehensive preventive and curative allopathic services through a rural-focused multi-level public system, financed by the government, through which all citizens would receive care irrespective of their ability to pay.

1950
- **Constitution of India-** Article 21: Protection of life and personal liberty to every citizen.

1983
- **National Health Policy-** Health for All by 2000 through the comprehensive primary health care services.

2002
- **National Health Policy-** Equitable access to health services across the social and geographical expanse of the country.

2010
- Planning Commission of India constituted a High-Level Expert Group (HLEG) on UHC.

2012
- **Twelfth five-year plan** - includes 47 pages on health and 13 pages directed towards UHC.
- Inclusion of curative care and NCDs in the benefit packages.
- Outcome indicator- Reduction of household's OOPE.

2017
- **National Health Policy**- Progressively achieve UHC.

2018
- **Ayushman Bharat-** Providing CPHC through AAMs and reducing financial hardship through AB PM-JAY.

2022
- **Right to Health Care Act** – Rajasthan.

Fig. 8.3 Evolution of UHC in India (*UHC* Universal Health Coverage, *NCDs* Non-communicable diseases, *OOPE* Out-of-pocket expenditure, *CPHC* Comprehensive Primary Health Care, *AB PM-JAY Ayushman Bharat Pradhan Mantri Jan Arogya Yojana*)

shaping this vision, particularly through Article 21, which guarantees the protection of life and personal liberty. While this article does not explicitly mention health, it implies a state's obligation to ensure the well-being of its citizens. Although health is not explicitly stated as a fundamental right, several directive principles address the state's responsibility to improve public health, including provisions for workers' health, maternity relief, nutrition, and living standards. However, the distinction between a fundamental right and a directive principle is crucial. If health were a fundamental right, citizens could demand healthcare services directly from the state and seek judicial remedies if denied. In contrast, directive principles guide the state's efforts within available resources, allowing flexibility in fulfilling these obligations.

India's first National Health Policy in 1983, aligned with the Alma Ata Declaration, aspired to provide "health for all." The second National Health Policy, in 2002, emphasized equitable access to healthcare across all population groups. A significant development came with the High-Level Expert Group (HLEG) established in 2010 by the erstwhile Planning Commission before the 12th Five-Year Plan. The HLEG made specific recommendations on UHC, including entitlement packages and healthcare service providers. The 12th Five-Year Plan, published in 2012, dedicated 13 of its 38 pages in the health section to strategic planning for UHC, reflecting the growing commitment to achieving this goal.

Historically, India's health system focused primarily on preventive care, particularly reproductive, maternal, newborn, and child health services, measured through coverage indicators. However, the push for UHC brought a needed shift toward including curative care in monitoring framework and addressing non-communicable diseases (NCDs). The second critical change was the introduction of indicators for OOPE reduction in the Twelfth Five-Year Plan, marking the first time financial risk protection was formally monitored in India's planning process. A third fundamental shift in India's approach to UHC was the recognition of healthcare financing as a key driver for achieving UHC. While financing is not the end goal, the strategies used to fund healthcare services significantly impact health system outcomes. The 2017 National Health Policy explicitly prioritized UHC as its primary objective, aiming for population coverage, financial risk protection, improved access, affordability, and reduced OOPE.

To support this, the Government of India introduced the *Ayushman Bharat* program in 2018, focusing on comprehensive primary care through *Ayushman Arogya Mandirs* (AAMs) and the *Ayushman Bharat Pradhan Mantri Jan Arogya Yojana* (AB PM-JAY) for secondary and tertiary care. Additionally, states have begun enacting their own Right to Healthcare Acts, moving toward making health a statutory right for individuals. AB PM-JAY encompasses two broad domains: service coverage and financial risk protection, reinforcing the commitment to UHC through both accessible healthcare services and financial security for citizens.

8.2.1 UHC in Sustainable Development Goals (SDGs)

In recent years, global initiatives and stakeholders have increasingly emphasized UHC, particularly following its explicit recognition under SDG target 3.8. UHC is a critical component of the SDGs, which include a specific health goal:

> "Ensure healthy lives and promote well-being for all at all ages" (SDG 3). Within this health goal, target 3.8 is specifically to "Achieve UHC, including financial risk protection, access to quality essential health care services and access to safe, effective, quality and affordable essential medicines and vaccines for all." [9]

UHC means ensuring that everyone can access the health services they require at an acceptable quality, without suffering financial hardship from high medical expenses. Progress toward achieving SDG Target 3.8 on UHC is monitored through two key indicators: SDG 3.8.1, which measures coverage of essential health services, and SDG 3.8.2, which assesses the incidence of catastrophic health expenditure. The following section focuses on how UHC is measured [10].

8.2.2 How to Measure Universal Health Coverage?

To measure UHC, two primary indicators are used: service coverage and catastrophic health expenditure (CHE). These indicators assess both access to essential health services and the financial protection available to individuals [11].

Service Coverage SDG indicator 3.8.1 measures the coverage of essential health services, calculated as the average level of access to key services across the general population as well as among disadvantaged groups. The measure is based on tracer interventions spanning reproductive, maternal, newborn and child health, infectious diseases, NCDs, and overall health system capacity and access. It is expressed as an index ranging from 0 to 100, derived using the geometric mean of 14 tracer indicators. These tracers provide a representative picture of service coverage but are not intended to capture every health service or intervention required for achieving UHC [12] (Table 8.1).

Catastrophic Healthcare Spending serves as the second major indicator of UHC. Ensuring financial protection is central to UHC and represents one of its ultimate objectives. The design of health financing policies has a direct influence on the extent of such protection. When financial safeguards are weak, households are exposed to economic strain from high out-of-pocket payments, which can also restrict their ability to seek essential care. SDG 3.8.2 reflects this concern by measuring both the incidence of catastrophic spending on health and the degree to which OOPE push families into poverty.

Spending is considered catastrophic when it exceeds a certain percentage of a household's income, signaling financial distress. Thresholds vary, commonly set at 40% of non-food expenditure or 10% of overall income. In Fig. 8.4, two specific indicators are used here: catastrophic out-of-pocket spending (often measured at the 10% threshold) on the Y-axis, and the Service Coverage Index on the X-axis. Ideally, a country's progress should move diagonally from the bottom left to the top right in

Table 8.1 UHC service coverage indicators

Tracer area	Tracer indicator
Reproductive, maternal, newborn, and child health	
Family planning	Demand satisfaction with modern methods
Pregnancy and delivery care	ANC, 4+ visits
Child immunization	DPT3 immunization
Child treatment	CSB for suspected pneumonia
Infectious disease	
Tuberculosis treatment	TB treatment coverage
HIV therapy	HIV ART coverage
Malaria prevention	ITN use
Water and sanitation	Population with access to at least basic sanitation
Non-communicable disease	
Prevention of CVDs	Prevalence of raised blood pressure
Management of diabetes	Mean FPG
Tobacco control	Tobacco use
Service capacity and access	
Hospital access	Hospital beds density
Health workforce	Health worker density
Health security	IHR capacity index

ANC antenatal care, *DPT* diphtheria, pertussis, and tetanus, *CSB* care-seeking behavior, *TB* tuberculosis, *HIV* human immunodeficiency virus, *ITN* insecticide-treated nets, *CVD* cardiovascular disease, *FPG* fasting plasma glucose, *IHR* International Health Regulations

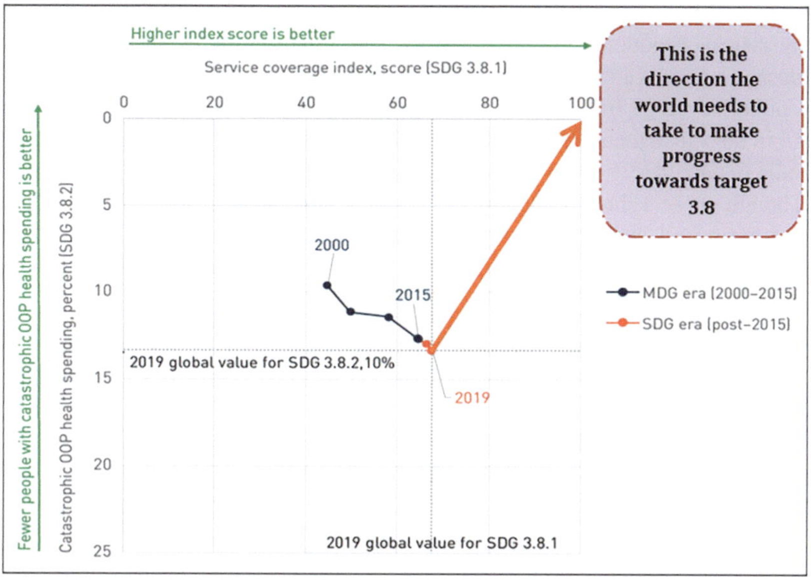

Fig. 8.4 The UHC coverage. (*MDG* Millennium Development Goals, *SDG* Sustainable Development)

this graph, indicating improvement in both service coverage and financial risk protection. Global Trends (2000–2018) show a general increase in service coverage across most regions. However, reliance on out-of-pocket spending has also grown, leading to greater financial hardship [11].

One of the effective approaches to achieving UHC is through publicly financed health insurance schemes. India has made significant progress in developing and expanding government-funded health insurance (GFHI) programs, playing a crucial role in this effort. The following section explores the evolution of GFHIs in India and their contribution to advancing UHC.

8.2.3 Health Insurance as a Means of Attaining UHC

India's journey toward institutionalizing government-funded and social health insurance began post-independence with the Employees' State Insurance Scheme (ESIS) for factory workers and the Central Government Health Scheme (CGHS) for government employees—remaining the only social insurance schemes until the 1990s. Economic liberalization in the 1980s and 1990s facilitated Voluntary Private Health Insurance (VPHI) and led to the formation of the Insurance Regulatory and Development Authority of India (IRDAI), but government-funded schemes remained limited. From 2003 onward, state-specific initiatives like Karnataka's *Yashaswini* Scheme and Andhra Pradesh's *Rajiv Aarogyasri* paved the way for broader coverage. The 2007 Unorganized Sector Workers Act led to the *Rashtriya*

Swasthya Bima Yojana (RSBY), providing a basic health risk cover of ₹30,000, with many states introducing "top ups" to expand benefits. States such as Himachal Pradesh, Kerala, Karnataka, Uttarakhand, and West Bengal further innovated by enhancing coverage limits and eligibility. These developments will be explored in detail in the subsequent chapter on Government-Funded Health Insurance Schemes in India (Chap. 9).

Though these schemes mentioned above contributed to increased healthcare access but raised questions about the balance between needed care and supplier-induced demand. The impact evaluations of these schemes highlighted two main outcomes:

- **Increased Access and Utilization**: The schemes led to greater healthcare utilization, though it remains unclear if this utilization addressed genuine health needs or was driven by provider incentives.
- **Limited Financial Risk Protection**: Despite the increased access, there was limited evidence that these schemes reduced OOPE or provided significant financial protection [13, 14].

8.2.3.1 Launch of Ayushman Bharat–AB PM-JAY (2018)

So, to overcome these barriers, in 2018, a major milestone was reached with the launch of AB PM-JAY under the *Ayushman Bharat* initiative. AB PM-JAY expanded both the benefit package and financial coverage, offering enhanced population protection and aiming for broader financial risk protection. This shift represented a new era in GFHIs in India, targeting deeper and more equitable health access and financial security for a large segment of the population. A detailed discussion on the construct of AB PM-JAY is provided in the subsequent chapter on GFHIs in India (Chap. 9). In the next section, we will discuss how AB PM-JAY finance UHC.

8.3 Financing Universal Health Coverage

Financing is the backbone of UHC, ensuring that essential healthcare services are accessible without financial hardship. In the Indian context, financing UHC revolves around three essential principles: equity, efficiency, and sustainability. Let us explore how each principle applies within India's healthcare landscape and why they are crucial for achieving UHC.

8.3.1 Key Principles of Financing Universal Health Coverage

- **Equity**: The principle of equity in healthcare emphasizes that all individuals, regardless of their socioeconomic status, should have access to essential health services without experiencing financial hardship. In India, where disparities in healthcare access are stark—particularly between rural and urban areas and across economic groups—achieving equity is a critical policy objective.

Initiatives such as *Ayushman Bharat* aim to address healthcare disparities through a two-pronged approach. The first component, AAMs—formerly known as Health and Wellness Centres (HWCs)—provides free and universally accessible primary healthcare services. The second component, AB PM-JAY, offers financial protection for secondary and tertiary healthcare, specifically targeting economically vulnerable populations at risk of catastrophic health expenditures. While these programs represent significant strides toward a more equitable healthcare system, true equity requires continuous efforts to expand coverage, enhance service quality, and ensure that healthcare improvements reach all regions and socioeconomic groups.

- **Efficiency**: Efficiency in healthcare financing means optimizing resources to deliver the highest value and effectiveness. In India, public healthcare resources are limited, so maximizing efficiency is vital to meet the needs of such a vast population. AB PM-JAY, for example, uses a strategic purchasing approach to contain costs by setting fixed prices for a range of services, preventing providers from overcharging patients. By standardizing costs, AB PM-JAY ensures that funds are used judiciously while still providing necessary care. Efficiency also involves reducing administrative costs, eliminating waste, and ensuring that every penny spent translates into effective health outcomes. Implementing digital health initiatives and streamlined data systems can help further improve the efficiency of India's healthcare system by reducing redundancies and improving decision-making, which will further be discussed in the chapters on fraud management (Chap. 12) and applications of digital technologies for healthcare financing (Chap. 13).
- **Sustainability**: For UHC to be successful, India must establish long-term, sustainable financial mechanisms that protect against excessive OOPE. Currently, OOPE account for a significant portion of healthcare spending in India, pushing many families into poverty. Reducing these OOPE is essential for sustainability as high personal expenses discourage people from seeking timely healthcare and can lead to catastrophic financial burdens. Through *Ayushman Bharat*, the government seeks to reduce OOPE by providing coverage for a broad range of health services. However, establishing a more robust insurance system and expanding coverage for primary and preventive care can also help ensure long-term financial sustainability for UHC in India.

8.3.2 How to Finance UHC?

As discussed in the sections above, UHC is often visualized as a three-dimensional cube, representing the key dimensions that must be expanded to achieve comprehensive healthcare access for all. These dimensions include population coverage (who is covered), service coverage (which services are covered), and financial protection (to what extent costs are covered). In the Indian healthcare context, addressing these dimensions requires targeted policies and reforms to ensure equitable, high-quality, and affordable healthcare for all citizens.

In the following sections, we will examine each dimension of the UHC cube in detail and discuss strategies to expand coverage effectively within India's healthcare system.

8.3.2.1 Filling the Breadth of UHC Cube: Expanding the Population Coverage

With the AB PM-JAY providing coverage to the bottom 40% of India's population, a significant challenge emerges—the issue of the "missing middle." This segment consists of individuals who are not poor enough to qualify for government-subsidized schemes but also not covered under employer-sponsored or private health insurance. Neither are they rich enough to easily afford high-cost medical care OOPE when the need arises. As a result, they remain vulnerable to high OOPE, which can lead to financial distress.

In the following section, we will explore the missing middle in detail—who they are, why they remain uninsured, and what policy options could be considered to bridge this gap. Achieving UHC requires ensuring that this population is not left behind. Expanding coverage to the missing middle is essential for a more inclusive and equitable health system in India. Let us examine the possible pathways to address this challenge effectively.

The Issue of Missing Middle Imagine a vast segment of the population caught in a gap—too well-off to qualify for government-subsidized health insurance yet not covered by social or private health insurance like those in the formal workforce. This group, often referred to as the "missing middle," sits between the most vulnerable, who receive government support, and the relatively affluent, who can afford private or employer-sponsored insurance. The missing middle is not a uniform group. It includes individuals from various expenditure quintiles across both urban and rural areas, with a higher concentration in the top two or three quintiles. While many in the lower quintiles benefit from government-funded schemes, some remain excluded due to challenges in identification and enrollment. Figure 8.5 provides a broad visualization of the missing middle population in India.

Despite having the financial ability to contribute to health insurance, the missing middle often remains vulnerable to catastrophic health expenditures. Data from the NSSO's 75th Round (2017–18) offer insights into their consumption patterns, health spending, and demographic distribution. A significant portion of this group lacks formal health coverage, especially in rural areas and among lower expenditure quintiles.

India is not alone in facing this challenge. Many developing countries that rely on social health insurance (SHI) as a pathway to UHC struggle with a missing middle. But is this group truly "missing," or is it just underserved due to structural barriers? The persistence of a large informal sector complicates efforts to include the missing middle in contributory insurance schemes. Simply mandating health insurance premiums for informal workers is not a viable solution—voluntary enrollment often results in low uptake, making financial sustainability a challenge. Expanding tax-financed, noncontributory health coverage and delinking entitlement

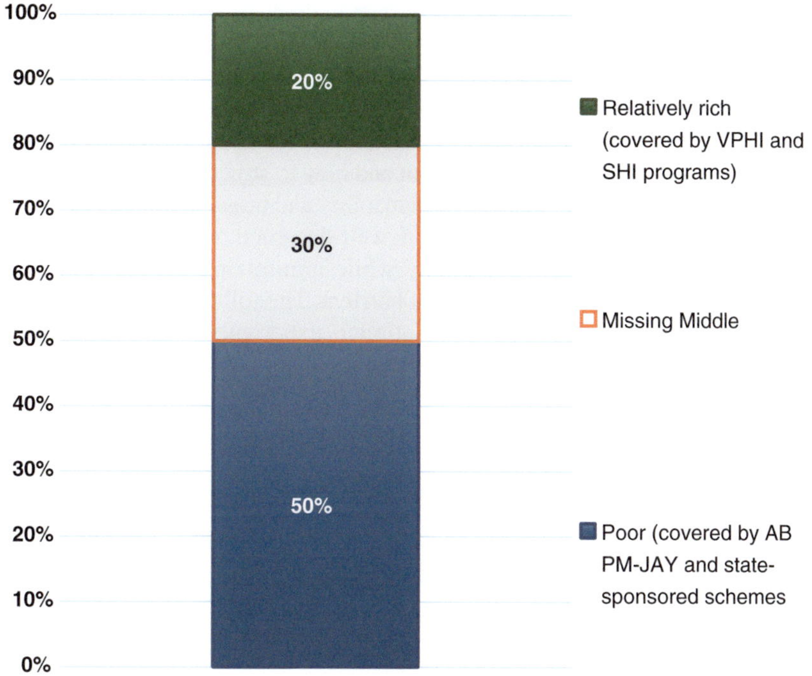

Fig. 8.5 Schematic for the missing middle population segment uncovered by health insurance. (*VPHI* Voluntary Private Health Insurance, *SHI* Social Health Insurance, *AB PM-JAY Ayushman Bharat Pradhan Mantri Jan Arogya Yojana*)

from contributions are potential policy options that countries like India could explore to bridge this gap. However, this would imply expanding the fiscal space. Addressing the missing middle is crucial for achieving true universal health coverage [15].

Solution Integrating the missing middle into UHC presents several complex challenges, particularly regarding their willingness and ability to pay for health insurance. Unlike the poorest segments covered under government-subsidized schemes, this group may not have a strong inclination to voluntarily purchase health insurance, making their inclusion a policy dilemma.

A key question arises: should the government fully finance their coverage, or should contributions be collected from individuals? If the government bears the financial burden, sustainability becomes a major concern. On the other hand, if individuals are required to contribute, determining the appropriate level of contribution and collection mechanism is crucial.

If mandatory contributions are imposed, political resistance may emerge, particularly from the large informal sector. If enrollment remains voluntary, adverse selection could pose a significant risk, where only those with a high likelihood of needing healthcare opt in, leading to financial instability in the insurance pool. To mitigate this, enrolling households rather than individuals has been suggested as a potential solution.

Another critical consideration is the structure of contributions. Should the model be fully cashless for beneficiaries, or should a co-payment system be introduced, where individuals contribute a smaller amount upfront? Determining the right balance—how much to charge as a premium and how to structure payments—will be essential for ensuring both financial sustainability and broad participation.

Addressing these issues requires a well-designed strategy that balances affordability, sustainability, and equity while minimizing the risks associated with voluntary enrollment and financial barriers. The following box explores the potential policy options and international experiences in tackling these challenges.

International Approaches to Including the Missing Middle in UHC

Countries worldwide have employed different strategies to extend health coverage to populations outside the formal sector, addressing the challenge of the missing middle. The experiences of Thailand, China, and several Latin American nations offer valuable insights.

I. **Thailand: Universal Coverage Through Multiple Schemes**

Thailand ensures universal health coverage through three major schemes:

(a) Civil Servant Medical Benefit Scheme (CSMBS)—covers public sector employees and their families
(b) Social Security Scheme (SSS)—covers formal private sector employees
(c) Universal Coverage Scheme (UCS)—covers all others, including informal sector workers, rural populations, and the poor, accounting for nearly 75% of the population

UCS provides a comprehensive benefits package with inpatient, outpatient, and preventive care. It employs strategic purchasing, using a mix of provider payment methods such as capitation, diagnosis-related groups (DRGs), and fee schedules for high-cost treatments. However, UCS relies on government budget allocations, making it vulnerable to economic downturns.

II. **China: Expanding Coverage Through Merging Schemes**

China historically operated three main schemes:

(a) Urban Employment-Based Medical Insurance (UEMBI)—a compulsory scheme for formal sector workers
(b) Urban Resident Basic Medical Insurance (URBMI)—a voluntary scheme for non-formal urban workers, students, and the unemployed
(c) New Rural Cooperative Medical Scheme (NRCMS)—a voluntary scheme for rural residents

(continued)

To address inequities, China merged URBMI and NRCMS into the Urban and Rural Resident Basic Medical Insurance (URRBMI) in 2016, aiming for better risk pooling and harmonized benefits. However, challenges remain, such as inadequate financing, unclear cost-sharing between central and local governments, and the need for a more progressive contribution system. Some cities have piloted a further merger with UEMBI to create a uniform social health insurance scheme.

III. **Latin America: Targeted Subsidized Schemes**

Several Latin American countries—including Mexico, Colombia, Peru, and Costa Rica—have expanded insurance beyond the poor by introducing partially subsidized contributory schemes for informal sector workers. These countries classify populations based on income and use targeted enrollment methods:

(a) Active enrollment (requiring individuals to register) is used in Mexico, Peru, and Colombia.

(b) Automatic enrollment (using national databases) is implemented in Costa Rica.

Some countries, such as Costa Rica and Uruguay, integrate contributory and non-contributory groups into a single risk pool, enabling cross-subsidization. Others, like Peru and the Dominican Republic, face challenges such as high exclusion errors, fragmented risk pools, and disparities in benefit packages between subsidized and contributory members.

Lessons for India

International experiences highlight key strategies for including the missing middle:

- Integrating risk pools to ensure financial sustainability and reduce disparities
- Blended financing models combining government subsidies with contributory payments
- Targeted enrollment using a mix of active and automatic identification
- Strategic purchasing to improve efficiency and expand coverage

8.3.2.2 Filling the Depth of UHC Cube: Expanding the Service Coverage

UHC aims to ensure that all individuals have access to essential, high-quality healthcare without facing financial difficulties. However, no health system can provide every possible service to all individuals. Therefore, UHC necessitates prioritizing a specific set of services to ensure broad and equitable access. This process of prioritization should be guided by clear and transparent criteria, taking into account practical aspects of service delivery. The WHO emphasizes the importance of explicit decision-making frameworks to achieve fair and effective health coverage [16].

India's AB PM-JAY has made significant strides in providing inpatient care to vulnerable populations. However, any expansion of inpatient services must be guided by rigorous assessments, including health technology assessment (HTA), cost-effectiveness analysis (CEA), and budget impact analysis (BIA), with efficiency as a key consideration. When extending inpatient coverage, priority should be given to conditions that are both common and disproportionately affect the poor and vulnerable populations.

One of the major challenges in achieving comprehensive UHC in India is the lack of coverage for outpatient care. Evidence suggests that not only hospitalization but also outpatient expenses contribute significantly to household impoverishment. For daily wage earners, hospitalization is often a last resort due to both direct medical expenses and indirect costs such as lost wages for multiple family members. Additionally, seeking healthcare can lead to further financial burdens due to the need for ongoing treatment, medications, and diagnostic services—many of which are currently not covered under health insurance schemes. The focus of AB PM-JAY on secondary and tertiary inpatient care, while neglecting comprehensive outpatient services, could inadvertently increase OOPE for households. With rising life expectancy and an ongoing epidemiological shift toward NCDs such as hypertension, diabetes, and mental health conditions, the demand for long-term care is increasing. These conditions are best managed through strong primary and outpatient care rather than hospitalization. A health insurance scheme that prioritizes hospitalization over preventive and outpatient care may not fully address the healthcare needs of the population. Lessons from the RSBY indicate that benefit packages should be designed with a deep understanding of the social and economic realities of beneficiaries. To make AB PM-JAY more comprehensive, the inclusion of outpatient care, medicines, diagnostics, travel allowances, and wage-loss compensation should be considered. Special provisions could also be made for groups with specific needs, such as elderly individuals requiring long-term medication, children with disabilities, patients needing rehabilitation, and victims of road traffic accidents [17].

Expanding strategic purchasing of outpatient care coverage will require robust governance and monitoring mechanisms. Potential models for inclusion include:

- **Voucher Scheme**: providing beneficiaries with 5–6 consultation vouchers annually to access outpatient care.
- **Capitation-Based Payment**: establishing a fixed per-person payment system for outpatient services, ensuring financial sustainability.
- **Bundled Payment Model**: integrating outpatient care services into existing insurance mechanisms by covering consultations, diagnostics, and essential medications under a single bundled payment.

From the supply-side perspective, a more plausible solution lies in establishing a robust continuum of care through AAMs and strengthening the delivery of primary healthcare services within the public sector. Additionally, in areas where the public sector remains weak or certain services are unavailable, care can be strategically purchased from the private sector to ensure comprehensive service coverage.

8.3.2.3 Filling the Height of UHC Cube: Reducing the OOPE

The AB PM-JAY provides health coverage of up to ₹500,000 per family per year for secondary and tertiary hospitalization. Within the UHC framework, this financial protection primarily addresses the height dimension—which refers to the depth of coverage, or the extent of financial protection provided to beneficiaries.

Evidence on Reduction of OOPE Empirical studies have demonstrated that AB PM-JAY has contributed to reducing OOPE for covered households [18]. Prior to its implementation, a large proportion of healthcare costs, particularly for hospitalizations, were borne directly by patients, often pushing families into poverty. With AB PM-JAY's introduction, the financial burden on low-income households has decreased, leading to improved healthcare utilization without the deterrent of high costs. Several evaluations indicate a decline in OOPE among AB PM-JAY beneficiaries.

Is AB PM-JAY's Coverage Sufficient While AB PM-JAY effectively addresses hospitalization costs, a critical analysis is needed to determine whether its coverage of ₹500,000 per family per year is truly sufficient within the broader UHC framework. Several factors support the argument that this coverage is adequate for significantly reducing OOPE. Studies show that households enrolled in AB PM-JAY are less likely to experience catastrophic health expenditure—defined as health spending exceeding 10% of total household consumption or income—compared to non-enrolled households [18].

Despite its strengths, AB PM-JAY primarily focuses on secondary and tertiary inpatient care, leaving outpatient services, diagnostics, and medicines largely uncovered. As discussed in the section above, the outpatient care also contributes significantly to OOPE, expanding the benefit package to include primary healthcare services would further enhance financial risk protection. Additionally, targeted policy measures, such as integrating outpatient consultations, diagnostic tests, and medicines into AB PM-JAY, could further strengthen its impact on reducing OOPE.

In the context of UHC's height dimension, the ₹500,000 coverage provided by AB PM-JAY represents a substantial financial safeguard against catastrophic medical expenses, effectively reducing OOPE for beneficiaries. However, to achieve comprehensive UHC, future policy directions should focus on addressing remaining gaps, particularly in outpatient care and essential medicines, and better monitoring to prevent balance billing by the providers to ensure sustained financial protection across all levels of healthcare.

Activity Box 8.1: Mapping the UHC Cube

Objective: To help readers apply the UHC cube framework to their own country/state.

Instructions:

- Using the three dimensions of the UHC cube (population coverage, service coverage, financial risk protection), fill in the following for your country/state:
  1. **Population Coverage**—Who is currently covered by government schemes, private insurance, or social insurance? Who is left out?
  2. **Service Coverage**—List at least three services included in the current benefit packages and identify any critical services that are excluded.
  3. **Financial Risk Protection**—Estimate how much out-of-pocket expenditure still contributes to household financial distress.

Reflective Question:

- Based on your mapping, which dimension of the UHC cube needs the greatest attention in your context, and why?

8.4 Conclusion

Achieving UHC requires a strategic and comprehensive approach that ensures equitable access to essential health services without financial hardship. This chapter has explored the expansion of the UHC cube along its three critical dimensions—population coverage, service coverage, and financial risk protection—each of which plays a vital role in strengthening health systems and ensuring that no one is left behind.

Expanding population coverage remains a fundamental challenge, particularly in addressing the "missing middle"—a segment of the population that falls outside both government-sponsored schemes and private insurance. Bridging this gap is crucial to making UHC truly universal. Several mechanisms, including targeted subsidies, contributory models, and innovative financing strategies, can be leveraged to integrate this group into the broader health system. Without such inclusion, a significant portion of the population remains vulnerable to catastrophic health expenditures, limiting the overall success of UHC initiatives.

Enhancing service coverage is another key pillar of UHC expansion. While hospital-based inpatient care has been the focus of many government-funded schemes, comprehensive health coverage must also include outpatient care, which constitutes a substantial proportion of healthcare needs. Outpatient care services, including consultations, diagnostics, medications, and chronic disease management, are essential to preventing disease progression and reducing the need for costly hospitalizations. Without outpatient care coverage, patients face high OOPE, leading to delayed care-seeking and potential long-term economic burdens on households. Therefore, strengthening the provision of primary and outpatient care through the public sector, ensuring a robust continuum of care, and adopting selective and strategic purchasing of these services through innovative demand-side financing mechanisms—along with the integration of outpatient services into benefit packages—represent not merely an expansion of coverage, but a critical step toward reinforcing primary healthcare and preventive services.

Financial risk protection is the third and equally important dimension of UHC. The effectiveness of any health coverage scheme is ultimately measured by its ability to shield individuals from excessive financial strain due to healthcare expenses. In India, the AB PM-JAY provides coverage of ₹500,000 per family per year, which has significantly contributed to reducing OOPE for inpatient care. While evidence suggests that AB PM-JAY has led to financial relief for many households, ensuring its sustainability and expanding its scope remain ongoing challenges. Moving forward, financing mechanisms must evolve to accommodate rising healthcare costs while maintaining fiscal feasibility. Strengthening public sector healthcare facilities and leveraging strategic purchasing mechanisms will be critical in optimizing healthcare spending and maximizing the impact of financial protection measures.

In conclusion, UHC is not just a policy aspiration but a necessary commitment toward equitable healthcare. Expanding population coverage, enhancing service inclusion, and strengthening financial risk protection are interconnected strategies that require sustained political will, innovative financing approaches, and strong health system governance. The public sector must remain the backbone of UHC efforts, ensuring that health services are accessible, affordable, and of high quality. A well-financed and efficiently managed UHC system will not only improve health outcomes but also contribute to broader economic and social development, reinforcing the principle that healthcare is a fundamental right, not a privilege.

References

1. Universal Health Coverage. https://www.who.int/health-topics/universal-health-coverage#tab=tab_1. Accessed 6 Nov 2024.
2. WHO. The World Health Report HEALTH SYSTEMS FINANCING The path to universal coverage. World Health Rep. 2010:1–128.
3. Kutzin J. Health financing for universal coverage and health system performance: concepts and implications for policy. Bull World Health Org. 2013;91:602.
4. Tanahashi T. Health service coverage and its evaluation. Bull World Health Org. 1978;56:295.
5. Evans DB, Hsu J, Boerma T. Universal health coverage and universal access. Bull World Health Org. 2013;91:546.
6. Shengelia B, Tandon A, Adams OB, et al. Access, utilization, quality, and effective coverage: an integrated conceptual framework and measurement strategy. Soc Sci Med. 2005;61:97–109.

7. Evans D, Saksena P, Elovainio R, et al. Measuring progress towards universal coverage. Geneva; 2012.
8. Universal health coverage and the role of evidence-based approaches in benefit basket decisions. https://iris.who.int/handle/10665/332568. Accessed 24 Aug 2025.
9. THE 17 GOALS | Sustainable Development. https://sdgs.un.org/goals. Accessed 26 Mar 2025.
10. Gostin LO. The legal determinants of health: how can we achieve universal health coverage and what does it mean? Int J Health Policy Manag. 2021;10:1–4.
11. UHC Index (3.8). https://www.who.int/data/gho/indicator-metadata-registry/imr-details/4834. Accessed 6 Nov 2024.
12. SDG 3.8.2 Catastrophic health spending (and related indicators). https://www.who.int/data/gho/data/themes/topics/service-coverage. Accessed 24 Aug 2025.
13. Prinja S, Chauhan AS, Karan A, et al. Impact of publicly financed health insurance schemes on healthcare utilization and financial risk protection in India: a systematic review. PLoS One. 2017;12 https://doi.org/10.1371/JOURNAL.PONE.0170996.
14. Reshmi B, Unnikrishnan B, Rajwar E, et al. Impact of public-funded health insurances in India on health care utilisation and financial risk protection: a systematic review. BMJ Open. 11 https://doi.org/10.1136/BMJOPEN-2021-050077.
15. Health Insurance for India's Missing Middle | NITI Aayog. https://www.niti.gov.in/node/352. Accessed 26 Mar 2025.
16. Reynolds T, Wilkinson T, Bertram MY, et al. Building implementable packages for universal health coverage. BMJ Glob Health. 2023;8:e010807.
17. Zodpey S, Farooqui HH. Universal health coverage in India: progress achieved & the way forward. Indian J Med Res. 2018;147:327.
18. Prinja S, Dixit J, Gupta N, et al. Financial toxicity of cancer treatment in India: towards closing the cancer care gap. Front Public Health. 2023;11:1065737.

Government-Funded Health Insurance Schemes in India

9

Shuchita Sharma, V. R. Muraleedharan, Sudha Chandrashekar, and Shankar Prinja

Abstract

This chapter explores the evolution and implementation of Government-Funded Health Insurance Schemes (GFHIS) in India, with a specific focus on *Ayushman Bharat Pradhan Mantri Jan Arogya Yojana* (AB PM-JAY), the country's largest health insurance scheme. It provides a historical overview of GFHIS, beginning with the launch of schemes such as the Central Government Health Scheme (CGHS) and Employees' State Insurance Corporation (ESIS) in the late 1940s and early 1950s, and progressing to the introduction of various national and state-level insurance programs designed for different population groups. This chapter highlights the significant shift from supply-side to demand-side financing in India's healthcare system, marked by the introduction of various state initiatives and national schemes like *Rashtriya Swasthya Bima Yojana* (RSBY) and ultimately AB PM-JAY. This transition aims to enhance healthcare accessibility and promote a patient-centered approach where funds follow the patient, thereby incentivizing service provision. This chapter describes various aspirational aspects for the implementation of AB PM-JAY and explores the significant reforms in the scheme's design and implementation to achieve universal health coverage.

S. Sharma · S. Prinja (✉)
Department of Community Medicine and School of Public Health, Post Graduate Institute of Medical Education and Research, Chandigarh, India

V. R. Muraleedharan
Centre for Technology and Policy, Indian Institute of Technology (IIT), Chennai, India

S. Chandrashekar
The World Bank and Health System Transformation Platform, Bengaluru, Karnataka, India

S. Prinja (ed.), *Healthcare Financing and Insurance*,
https://doi.org/10.1007/978-981-95-3513-2_9

Keywords

Publicly funded health insurance · *Pradhan Mantri Jan Arogya Yojna* · *Ayushman Bharat Yojana* · Universal health coverage · Health insurance

Learning Objectives

After completing this chapter, the readers will understand:

- The historical evolution of the Government-Funded Health Insurance Scheme (GFHIS) in India
- Key features of the Government-Funded Health Insurance Schemes in India
- Recent reforms and challenges in the implementation of Government-Funded Health Insurance schemes
- Coverage, financing, payment mechanisms, and implementation mode of the world's largest Government-Funded Health Insurance Scheme—*Ayushman Bharat Pradhan Mantri Jan Arogya Yojana* (AB PM-JAY)

Key Terms

Empanelled Healthcare Providers

Empanelled healthcare providers are public and private healthcare facilities that have been authorized by the National Health Authority to offer cashless healthcare services to beneficiaries under the *Pradhan Mantri Jan Arogya Yojana.*

International Classification of Diseases (ICD)

The International Classification of Diseases is a standardized system developed by the World Health Organization for classifying and coding diseases, injuries, and causes of death worldwide, making it possible to research diseases, their causes, and their treatments.

International Classification of Health Interventions (ICHI)

The International Classification of Health Interventions is a system developed by the World Health Organization to classify and code health interventions globally. It aims to provide a standardized framework for describing and recording health interventions across various healthcare systems.

9.1 Introduction

Health financing is an inherent component and a facilitator of Universal Health Coverage (UHC). The health financing landscape in India encompasses a multifaceted blend of demand- and supply-side financing mechanisms. The supply-side financing involves allocating funds for health infrastructure development, staffing, medical supplies, and consumables. These allocations are generally determined by predefined payment norms based on the level of healthcare facilities. Notably, within the supply-side financing framework, a direct correlation between the allocated funding and the quantum of services delivered is often not explicitly established. On the other hand, in a demand-side financing system, a patient-centric approach is adopted, where money follows the patient/consumer. The provider is compensated based on the volume of services or the number of services provided to patients. This payment approach in all government-funded insurance systems in India exemplifies demand-side financing.

Traditionally, public healthcare financing in India has been primarily driven by a supply-side approach. However, this approach has posed significant challenges. Limited government health spending, uneven distribution of health infrastructure and human resources, and weak referral linkages have contributed to major inequities in access, utilization, and financial protection. In response, governments worldwide have increasingly shifted toward demand-side financing to enhance access and financial security. Aligning with this global shift, the Government of India has introduced various demand-side financing initiatives through centrally and state-funded health programs. The most recent and significant step in this direction is the launch of *Ayushman Bharat Pradhan Mantri Jan Arogya Yojana* (AB PM-JAY). By strengthening healthcare accessibility and incentivizing service provision, demand-side financing—particularly through public health insurance schemes—marks a decisive move toward a more patient-centered and service-driven healthcare system in India.

9.2 Origin of Demand-Side Financing Initiatives

9.2.1 Early Initiatives

The origin of demand-side financing schemes dates to the early 1950s when formal sector workers and civil servants were enrolled under the Employees' State Insurance Corporation (ESIS), 1952 and the Central Government Health Scheme (CGHS), 1954, respectively. These schemes are generally called Social Health Insurance (SHI) schemes. For details related to the basic structure and design of SHIs, please refer to Chaps. 2 and 3 on revenue collection and risk pooling, respectively. Both schemes offered extensive medical coverage and followed a traditional social insurance risk-pooling model, where funds were sourced from employer and employee contributions, supplemented by government subsidies specific to each scheme [1]. Table 9.1 presents the key features of the CGHS and the ESIS scheme.

Table 9.1 Key features of Social Health Insurance Schemes—CGHS and ESIS

Category	Central Government Health Scheme (CGHS)	Employee's State Insurance Scheme (ESIS)
Population covered	3.4 million individuals	3.42 million individuals
Premium collection	Monthly contributions vary based on the pay matrix level, ranging from ₹250 to ₹1000 [2]	Monthly contributions are shared by employees and employers based on wages [3] *Employer Contribution*: 3.25% of the employee's wages *Employee Contribution*: 0.75% of their wages
Services covered	Outpatient and inpatient treatment, hospitalization, diagnostic and radiology services, and specialist consultations	Outpatient and inpatient treatment, imaging and laboratory services, specialist consultations, free supply of drugs, dressings, artificial limbs, aids and appliances, ambulance services
Per capita expenditure	₹11,871	₹1245

9.3 Recent Government-Funded Health Insurance Schemes

Since the late 1990s, the Government of India has introduced numerous government-funded health insurance schemes at both the central and state levels. Driven by the National Health Policy (1983) and its vision of "Health for All by 2000," these Government-Funded Health Insurance Schemes (GFHIS) schemes grew to 48 by 2018. Initially, national schemes like the *Retired Employees Liberalized Health Scheme* (1997) and *Delhi Government Employee Health Scheme* (1997) were launched for the organized sector employees. Moving forward in the same year, for the first time, poor people from the unorganized sector were insured under the *Rashtriya Arogya Nidhi Scheme*. The scheme covered services availed for life-threatening diseases at public hospitals.

In the 1990s, political turmoil, market-oriented reforms, and reduced government health investments weakened the public health sector, while economic reforms accelerated the expansion of the private sector. As a result, the share of private healthcare facilities in total healthcare provision surged, with private sector contributions rising to 82% of outpatient care and 58% of inpatient care by 2005, compared to just 5–10% at the time of independence [4, 5]. This shift prompted a policy approach that leveraged public funding to purchase private healthcare services through insurance. This model emerged from the *Jeevandayee Yojana* in Maharashtra in 1997, the first state-level GFHIS, covering health treatments (heart, kidney, brain, and nervous system disorders) in public and select private hospitals for those living below the poverty line. The scheme quickly gained traction, culminating in 48 such schemes nationwide by 2018. The timeframes of different social health insurance and government-funded health insurance schemes are provided in Fig. 9.1.

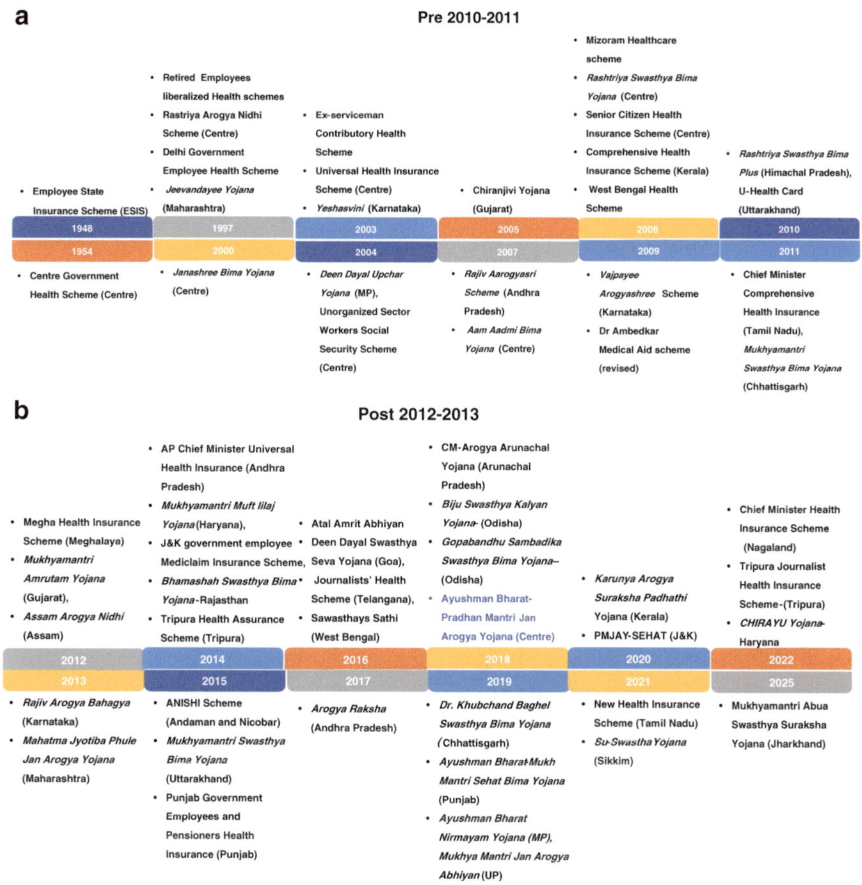

Fig. 9.1 Timeline of social and government-funded health insurance schemes in India

The National Health Policy (NHP) 2002 marked a significant shift by emphasizing financial protection for the poor, leading to the launch of the Universal Health Insurance Scheme (UHIS) in 2003. Following UHIS, the government introduced the Unorganized Sector Workers' Social Security Scheme in 2004 to enhance health security for low-income workers [6]. This scheme was designed to be co-funded by employees, employers, and the government. However, due to low enrollment during the pilot stage, both these schemes were discontinued.

Despite their limited uptake (3.5 million till 2008–2009), these early initiatives provided valuable lessons that shaped subsequent government-funded health insurance programs, including the centrally launched *Rashtriya Swasthya Bima Yojana (RSBY)*.

9.4 Launch of RSBY

Until 2008, the extent of coverage provided by various insurance schemes in India was limited, primarily concentrated within the formal sector. For instance, schemes like ESIS had a very narrow reach, encompassing only a marginal segment of the population (4%). This was further exacerbated by issues on both the supply and demand sides, such as reduced bed availability, decreased hospitalization rates, and fewer visits to outpatient facilities [6].

At the same time, India's unorganized sector, which constituted approximately 93% of the total workforce, remained largely uninsured. Recognizing the need for social security and welfare measures for this vast segment, the government enacted the Unorganized Workers' Social Security Act of 2008 [7]. This legislation aimed to extend social security benefits—including life and disability cover, health and maternity benefits, and old-age protection—to workers outside the formal economy. Despite various state and central government health insurance initiatives, many failed to achieve their intended objectives due to limited reach, inadequate funding, and poor implementation.

To address these gaps, the *Rashtriya Swasthya Bima Yojana* (RSBY) was launched in 2008 by the Ministry of Labor and Employment. The scheme specifically targeted below poverty line (BPL) families engaged in the unorganized sector, providing them with financial protection against hospitalization expenses. RSBY offered coverage of up to ₹30,000 per family per year, enabling beneficiaries to access over 725 procedures at empanelled hospitals. By 2013, the scheme had been rolled out across 27 states [8, 9].

While RSBY marked a significant step toward demand-side healthcare financing, there is mixed evidence of its overall impact. By September 2016, approximately 41 million families (around 150 million individuals) had enrolled in the scheme, covering 63% of the targeted 65 million families. Despite its ambitious goals, RSBY faced several gaps and challenges that limited its overall effectiveness. While it successfully expanded insurance coverage to millions of poor families, its impact on reducing out-of-pocket expenditure (OOPE) was limited. Evidence suggests that, despite using RSBY, 58% of patients still incurred OOPE, with studies indicating that beneficiaries were more likely to face catastrophic health expenses than non-beneficiaries [10]. Similarly, a systematic review found that although the introduction of various GFHIS increased service utilization, there was no impact on the reduction of OOPE [11].

The scheme's static coverage limit of ₹30,000 per family proved inadequate for high-cost treatments, particularly for tertiary care, placing financial strain on beneficiaries. Compared to several state-run schemes that offered higher financial coverage and included advanced medical procedures, RSBY's benefits were relatively limited. For instance, *Rajiv Aarogyasri* in Andhra Pradesh provided coverage of ₹2 lakhs per year, *Rajiv Gandhi Jeevandayee Arogya Yojana* (RGJAY) in Maharashtra covered ₹1.5 lakh per year, Chief Minister's Comprehensive Health Insurance Scheme (CMCHIS) in Tamil Nadu offered ₹1 lakh per year, *Vajpayee Aarogyasri* in Karnataka provided ₹2 lakhs per year, and *Bhamashah Swasthya Bima Yojana*

Box 9.1 Key features and design of the RSBY scheme
RSBY—Key Features and Scheme Design

1. Covered below poverty line (BPL) population (approximately 350 million people).
2. Included both public and private empanelled hospitals, led by the central government and implemented in collaboration with State and Union Territory authorities, insurance companies, public and private hospitals.
3. The scheme's premium was jointly funded by the central and state governments in a 75:25 ratio, with a 90:10 ratio for Northeastern states.
4. The central government also covered the cost of membership cards at ₹60 per card, while an additional ₹30 registration fee was collected at the state level to manage administrative expenses.
5. RSBY offered insurance coverage for selected hospitalization and inpatient procedures up to ₹30,000 (approximately US$500) annually for a family of up to five members on a floater basis.
6. The scheme covered all preexisting conditions from the first day and had no age restrictions.
7. The scheme covered
   - Hospitalization expenses
   - Diagnostic tests
   - Medications 1 day prior to admission and up to 5 days post-discharge
8. Outpatient department expenses or costs incurred in hospitals that did not result in hospitalization were not covered.

Source: Rashtriya Swasthya Bima Yojana|National Portal of India, Available at: https://www.india.gov.in/spotlight/rashtriya-swasthya-bima-yojana

(BSBY) in Rajasthan extended coverage up to ₹3.3 lakh per year. In contrast, RSBY's ₹30,000 per family per year coverage was significantly lower, limiting access to costly treatments and comprehensive care [11].

Additionally, low awareness and enrollment rates hindered utilization, as many eligible families remained unaware of their entitlements. Institutional weaknesses and inconsistent implementation across states further hampered its success [12, 13]. Moreover, some healthcare providers exploited loopholes in the system by inflating claims through unnecessary procedures, raising concerns about fraud and provider-induced demand.

These gaps highlighted the need for a more comprehensive health insurance model, ultimately influencing the design of *Ayushman Bharat Pradhan Mantri Jan Arogya Yojana* (AB PM-JAY) in 2018. PM-JAY expands upon the foundation laid by these schemes, enhancing its benefits while extending coverage to a broader segment of the population.

9.5 Overview of AB PM-JAY

Ayushman Bharat Pradhan Mantri-Jan Arogya Yojana, a flagship scheme of the Government of India was launched to accelerate the country's journey toward UHC. The scheme aims to ensure financial protection against Catastrophic Health Expenditure (CHE), reduce unmet needs, and provide access to affordable, quality healthcare.

9.5.1 Coverage

The scheme offers health insurance coverage of ₹500,000 per family per year, benefiting approximately 500 million people, or the bottom 40% of the population, making it one of the world's largest tax-funded health insurance programs. It is entitlement-based, ensuring coverage for identified groups under the Socio-Economic Caste Census (SECC), existing RSBY beneficiaries, and state-designated categories, eliminating the need for separate enrollment.

Key features include the following:

- Coverage for 1949 procedures and medical conditions across 27 specialties in both secondary and tertiary healthcare facilities.
- Treatment costs covered from 3 days before hospitalization to 15 days post-discharge.
- Cashless and paperless implementation.
- Portability of benefit, i.e., benefits can be accessed by any beneficiary from any state across empanelled hospitals in India.

9.5.2 Key Statistics (as of April 5, 2025)

1. The PM-JAY scheme is currently active in most States and Union Territories (UTs) across the country. Odisha became the 34th state to join on January 13, 2025, followed by Delhi (as the 35th state/UT) to implement the scheme from April 05, 2025.
2. So far, a total of 35 crore beneficiary cards have been distributed.
3. The scheme has established partnerships with a considerable number of hospitals—31,809 in total—of which 14,400 fall within the private sector.
4. The scheme shows a near-equal gender distribution in both enrollment and treatment, with females making up 49% of the total beneficiaries, as highlighted in Fig. 9.2.

Fig. 9.2 Key statistics of AB-PMJAY. (Source: PM-JAY Public Dashboard at www.pmjay.gov.in and www.ab-hwc.nhp.gov.in as of 30-10-2024)

9.5.3 Implementation Structure of PM-JAY

PM-JAY follows a hierarchical implementation framework, with the National Health Authority (NHA) at the top, overseeing execution through State Health Agencies (SHAs), as illustrated in Fig. 9.3.

National Health Authority: The NHA functions under the supervision of a governing body led by the Union Minister of Health and Family Welfare [14]. Some of the roles and responsibilities of the National Health Authority are mentioned below.

Roles and Responsibilities

- Set and periodically review the central premium ceiling or maximum contribution for States/UTs based on field data and actuarial analysis.
- Develop and periodically revise the health benefits package (HBP), Standard Treatment Guidelines, policy for provider payments and pricing, and Quality Guidelines to set provider payment rates.
- Maintain regular coordination with state governments for smooth PM-JAY execution and continuously build the capacity of State Health Agencies and other stakeholders.
- Collaborate with the Insurance Regulatory and Development Authority on health insurance regulations for insurers, third-party administrators (TPAs), hospitals, and stakeholders.
- Establish streamlined and effective payment processes for healthcare providers.
- Integrate PM-JAY with state and central health insurance and assurance schemes.
- Build an advanced health information technology framework to support PM-JAY and other health systems.
- Ensure the effective implementation of PM-JAY nationwide, regularly monitor its progress, and make necessary adjustments when required

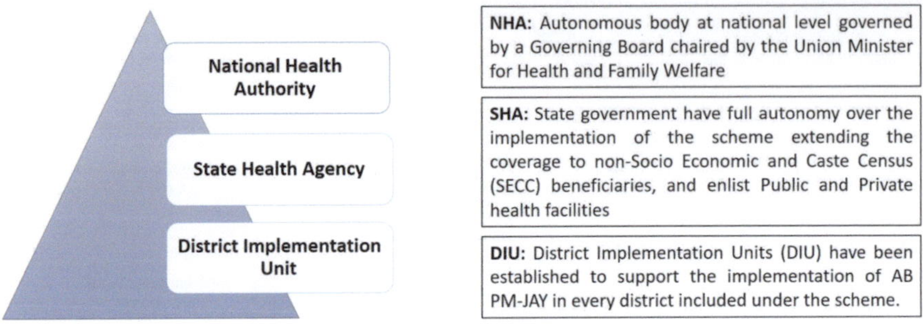

Fig. 9.3 Implementation structure of PM-JAY. (Source: www.pmjay.gov.in)

- Promote cross-learning among states, facilitate the sharing of best practices, and document successful implementation strategies.
- Conduct policy-relevant research and evaluations and facilitate knowledge sharing at national and international levels to improve scheme outcomes.

State Health Agency: At the state level, the SHA is a nodal agency, with the Chief Executive Officer in charge of it. Each participating state has a single SHA responsible for empaneling public and private hospitals within its jurisdiction. The SHA is also tasked with responsibilities such as data sharing; verifying and validating family member details; conducting Information, Education, and Communication (IEC) activities; and monitoring the overall progress of the scheme [14]. Some of the additional roles and responsibilities of the State Health Agency are mentioned below.

Roles and Responsibilities

- Adapting PM-JAY treatment protocols, package prices, and operational guidelines to meet state-specific needs.
- Selecting insurance companies through tendering (if applicable) or implementation support agencies (ISAs) under trust/hybrid mode.
- Undertaking and/or monitoring healthcare service delivery, approving pre-authorizations, and administering hospital claims.
- Implementing fraud control measures and taking disciplinary actions against fraudulent or corrupt practices.
- Conducting awareness campaigns.
- Setting up grievance redressal committees and overseeing their functioning.

District Implementation Unit (DIU): It is headed by the District Commissioner or District Magistrate. These units function alongside the state-level agency and complement the efforts of teams deployed by the insurance company or the ISA.

Roles and Responsibilities

- The primary responsibilities include coordinating between the implementing agency (ISA or insurer) and empanelled hospitals to facilitate efficient service delivery
- The DIU plays a critical role in monitoring the scheme's progress within the district, addressing operational challenges, and ensuring compliance with guidelines.
- The DIU is also tasked with submitting periodic review reports to higher authorities, highlighting performance metrics, and identifying areas for improvement.
- Additionally, the DIU also collaborates closely with the District Chief Medical Officer and their team to streamline healthcare services and beneficiary management.

Pradhan Mantri Arogya Mitras

A *Pradhan Mantra Ayushman Mitra* (PMAM) is a qualified frontline healthcare professional responsible for being the initial point of contact for beneficiaries at empanelled hospitals. To optimize the provision of healthcare services and ensure a smooth and efficient experience for beneficiaries, *Pradhan Mantri Arogya Mitras* are assigned to each Empanelled Healthcare Provider (EHCP).

The specific number of PMAMs to be stationed is determined by the average number of cases attended to each day. An indicative allocation of PMAMs based on the daily registered cases is provided below:

(a) 1 PMAM for 0–10 cases
(b) 2 PMAMs for 10–20 cases
(c) 3 PMAMs for 20–30 cases
(d) 4 PMAMs for 30–40 cases

Roles and Responsibilities

- Verify eligibility, manage the Beneficiary Identification System, and handle pre-authorization, treatment updates, and claims in the Transaction Management System.
- Ensure privacy and confidentiality of beneficiary data within PM-JAY IT systems.
- Guide beneficiaries on accessing timely treatment at EHCPs.

9.5.4 Implementation Model

The NHA grants states the freedom to select their preferred implementation models, and each SHA can select from three distinct implementation modes: the assurance/trust model, the insurance model, or the mixed model.

(a) *Assurance/trust model*: This is the most widely adopted implementation model across states. In this approach, the state government directly reimburses healthcare providers without the involvement of an insurance company. To manage claims and related processes, the State Health Agency (SHA) engages an ISA. Additionally, the SHA is responsible for overseeing the scheme's daily operations and administration, including hospital empanelment, beneficiary identification, claims processing, audits, fraud control, and other critical functions.

(b) *Insurance model*: Under this model, the SHA partners with an insurance company to manage PM-JAY. The insurance company manages claim payouts, while the SHA is responsible for paying premiums to the insurer for each eligible family during the policy period.

(c) *Hybrid/mixed model*: In the hybrid model, claim settlements are processed through a joint effort between the state and the insurance company. The insurance company covers claims up to a certain threshold (usually less than 100,000), while claims exceeding that limit are directly managed by the SHAs.

As of April 2025, out of the 35 states/UTs, 23 opted for the trust mode of implementation, 7 chose the insurance model, and only 3 followed the hybrid mode of implementation, as shown in Fig. 9.4.

9.5.5 Financing

PM-JAY is a fully tax-funded scheme, with costs shared between the Central and State Governments. The Government of India establishes a national ceiling amount (₹1052/ family) [15], which sets the maximum central contribution, funded through tax revenue collected at the national level. The generation of revenue from national and state taxes has been covered in Chap. 2.

The costs are shared between the Central Government and the States/UTs based on the ratio established by the Ministry of Finance, aligning with overall revenue collection and budget allocation strategies. Currently, most states follow a 60:40 cost-sharing ratio, while the Northeastern states and three Himalayan states (Jammu and Kashmir, Himachal Pradesh, and Uttarakhand) have a 90:10 ratio. For Union Territories without legislatures, the Central Government may fund up to 100% on a case-by-case basis.

9.5.6 Health Benefits Package (HBP)

An essential element of the scheme's design is its health benefits package (HBP), outlining the range of medical and surgical procedures, and health conditions for which eligible households under PM-JAY can receive cashless treatment. The PM-JAY HBP includes a comprehensive list of services, treatments, and medications that patients can access without payment at empanelled hospitals. As mentioned earlier, PM-JAY covers expenses 3 days before hospitalization, the costs

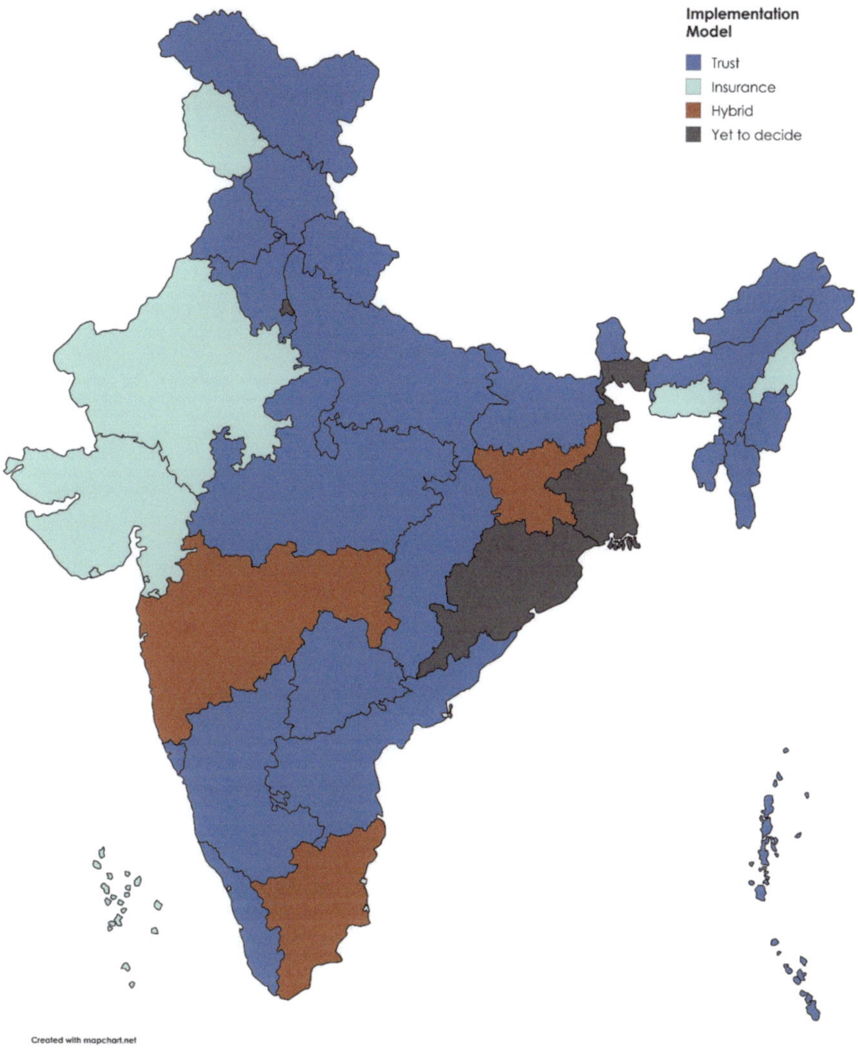

Fig. 9.4 Different implementation models adopted by all states in India. (Source: National Health Authority. About Pradhan Mantri Jan Arogya Yojana (PM-JAY) [Internet]. [cited 2024 Oct 31]. Available from: https://nha.gov.in/PM-JAY)

during hospital stay, and the cost of medicines lasting up to 15 days post-hospitalization, encompassing various surgical and medical packages. The key features of HBP are discussed in Fig. 9.5.

Since the scheme's launch, the HBP has undergone several revisions over time. Over the past 4 years, this transition has seen an expansion from 1393 packages spanning 24 specialties to approximately 1949 procedures, covering 27 medical and surgical specialties. Beyond the augmentation in covered procedures, each revision

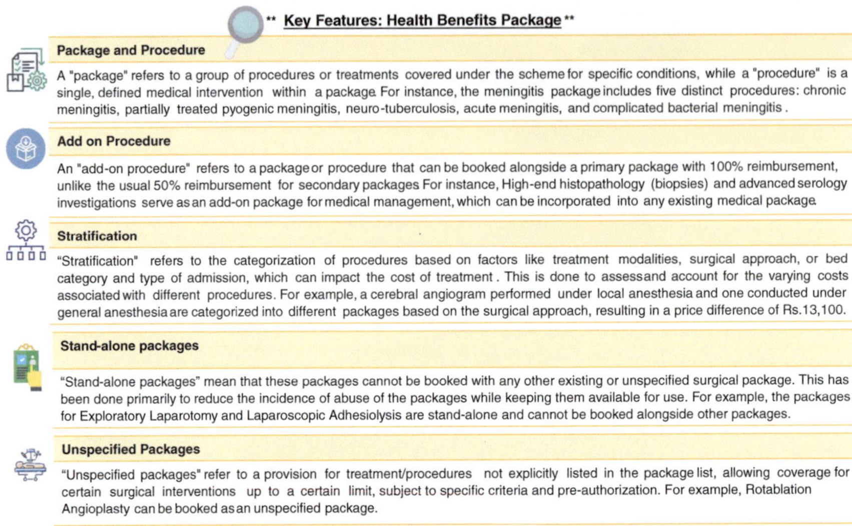

Fig. 9.5 Key features: health benefit packages. (Source: National Health Authority. Health Benefit Package 2.2. Available from: https://nha.gov.in/img/resources/HBP-2.2-manual.pdf)

has also updated the reimbursement rates within the HBP, as shown in Fig. 9.6. The most recent revision has seen price increases for 832 packages, incorporating differentiated pricing based on the city type (Tier I, II, or III), as well as the procedure type (tertiary vs. secondary).

9.5.7 Provider Payment Methods

An appropriate provider payment method (PPM) is a crucial tool for a strategic purchaser of healthcare services, ensuring both quality care and appropriate provider behavior. The chapter on provider payment discusses different methods of provider payment mechanisms. As outlined in Chap. 5, provider payment is determined by two key factors: the payment method used and the amount paid for each service provided.

PM-JAY uses a system of case-based bundled payment, where providers receive a fixed rate for a set of services listed under its HBP. For all medical packages, a per-bed-day rate is set and stratified according to the admission bed category, such as General Ward, High-Dependency Unit (HDU), and Intensive Care Unit (ICU). The final reimbursement to providers for medical packages is calculated according to the length of stay during hospitalization and patient's bed-day category. The per-bed-day prices for different bed categories are as follows:

- General ward: ₹2300
- High Dependency Ward: ₹3630
- Intensive Care Unit (without ventilator support): ₹9350
- Intensive Care Unit (with ventilator support): ₹9900

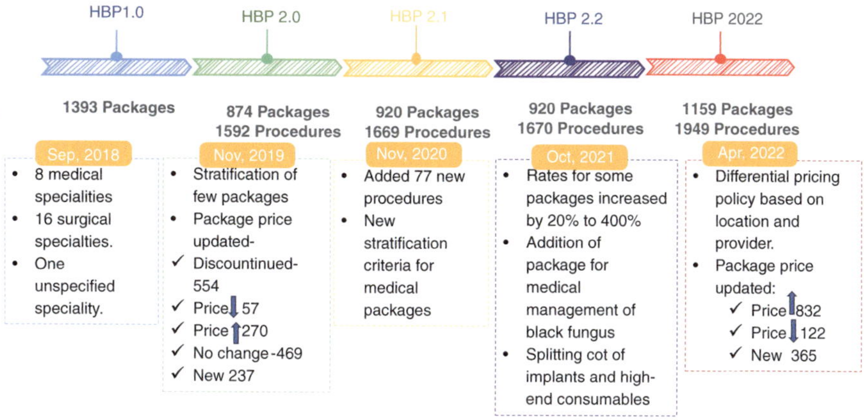

Fig. 9.6 Different health benefit package updates from 2018 to 2022. (Adapted from: Prinja et al. National hospital costing systems matter for universal healthcare: the India PM-JAY experience)

Each HBP under PM-JAY covers comprehensive hospitalization expenses, including all costs associated with the treatment, such as:

- Charges for registration, bed, nursing, and boarding.
- Fees for surgeons, anesthetists, medical practitioners, and consultants.
- Operational costs such as anaesthesia, blood transfusions, oxygen, surgical appliances, and OT charges.
- Medicines, drugs, prosthetic devices, and implants. The cost of implants is unbundled and is paid separately.
- Diagnostic tests, including basic radiology (X-ray, ultrasonography) and pathology (haematology, biopsies). High-end diagnostics can be added as separate procedures, but surgical packages are all-inclusive and exclude additional diagnostic costs.
- Patient meals during hospitalization.
- Pre- and post-hospitalization expenses for consultations, diagnostics, and medications incurred 3 days before admission and up to 15 days after discharge for the same condition.
- Any other costs directly related to the patient's treatment during hospitalization.

When PM-JAY was launched, the rates were determined based on an extensive review of prices under existing health insurance schemes, followed by multiple consultations with experts and consideration of limited available cost data. Subsequently, as shown in Fig. 9.6 as more evidence of cost became available through the Costing of Health Services in India (CHSI) study, the scheme witnessed four sets of revisions. The first set of refinement of the rates from HBP 1.0 to HBP 2.0, was based on a nationally representative CHSI study [16]. Consecutively, the prices under PM-JAY further evolved under HBP versions 2.1 and 2.2. Under HBP 2.2, the package rates for more than 400 treatment procedures were increased, in some cases by as much as 100%. Additionally, the current PPM system includes incentives for empanelled providers to compensate them for delivering higher-quality care, as identified through quality accreditations. The HBP 2022 introduced the concept of differential pricing, which adjusts hospital payments based on the tier of the city where the hospital is located and its specialty level (tertiary or secondary)—two key variables influencing resource utilization and costs [17].

The case-based payment system under PM-JAY is continuously evolving as the scheme gains insights from its implementation. Currently, reimbursement rates follow a constant bundled price for each procedure, without considering individual patient severity or complexity, and lack flexibility for cost adjustments based on patient-specific factors. The NHA aims to transition toward a more refined approach that accounts for patient characteristics. As a result, a cost-surveillance pilot was launched in April 2022, aimed at developing a sustainable, hospital-based, patient-level cost monitoring system [18].

As PM-JAY continues to evolve, another key focus of proposed reform is the transition from a volume-based to a value-based care model [19]. This transition focuses on incentivizing healthcare providers based on patient outcomes and the quality of care they deliver, rather than the absolute number of services provided. By aligning financial incentives with health outcomes, the scheme aims to improve treatment effectiveness, enhance patient satisfaction, and promote efficient use of resources. This approach is expected to drive better health results across the board, ensuring that beneficiaries receive not just more care, but better care. Detailed strategies and implementation frameworks for this model are discussed in Chap. 10 on Value-Based Care.

9.5.8 Hospital Empanelment

In the last 8 years of the scheme's implementation, more than 80 million hospital admissions have been authorized, worth ₹1.2 trillion. This could only be achieved through a vast network of public and private healthcare providers. Empanelled hospitals or healthcare providers (EHCPs) under PM-JAY are those enlisted by the State Health Agency to deliver cashless medical treatments to the scheme's beneficiaries [20]. To qualify for empanelment, hospitals must meet specific standards related to infrastructure, facilities, and service quality. This process is essential for improving access to healthcare services and ensuring beneficiaries receive optimal care. Establishing a network of empanelled hospitals that adhere to stringent quality benchmarks is critical to achieving the program's objectives effectively.

Two sets of empanelment criteria have been established, considering state-specific regulations on quality of care and the Clinical Establishments Act, 2011. These criteria are designed based on insights gained from existing practices in the Government-Funded Health Insurance Scheme, state-specific regulations related to quality of care, and the Clinical Establishment Act 2011 [21].

1. *General criteria*—Applies to hospitals offering general medical and surgical care, with or without ICU and emergency services.
2. *Special criteria -for clinical specialties*—Specific criteria have been outlined for each medical specialty. Hospitals must commit to providing all specialties available within the scope to PM-JAY beneficiaries; partial specialty applications are not permitted.
3. *Criteria for aspirational districts*—For the aspirational districts identified by National Institution for Transforming India (NITI) Aayog, special minimum criteria have been established for hospitals to meet before providing care under PM-JAY in these regions.

9.5.9 Process of Empanelment

Under PM-JAY, hospitals are empanelled through an online IT platform known as the Hospital Empanelment Module (HEM) (https://hospitals.pmjay.gov.in/empApplicationHome.html). The approval process follows predefined criteria and requires approvals from empanelment committees at the district and State/UT levels. Careful selection of providers is essential for the strategic procurement of healthcare services from both public and private sectors. This approach is frequently encouraged to promote competition and improve service quality. Figure 9.7 describes the process of empanelment for Empanelled Healthcare Providers in states under PM-JAY and those not following PM-JAY. To fast-track hospital empanelment under PM-JAY, a hospital can explore options like achieving National Accreditation Board for Healthcare accreditation, utilizing existing state scheme empanelment status, or applying for quality certification like the PM-JAY Quality Certification by Quality Council of India. These quality certifications or accreditation essentially demonstrate high-quality standards and compliance with PM-JAY guidelines to qualify for a faster empanelment process.

How can you check if the nearby facility is empanelled under Ayushman Bharat?

Steps:

- **Visit the website**: Visit the official Ayushman Bharat website: https://pmjay.gov.in/
- **Find Hospital option**: Click on the "Find Hospital" option on the homepage.
- **Select location**: Choose your state and district from the dropdown menus.
- **Search for facility**: Enter the name of the healthcare facility you want to check.
- **Check results**: The website will display if the facility is listed as an empanelled Ayushman Bharat hospital

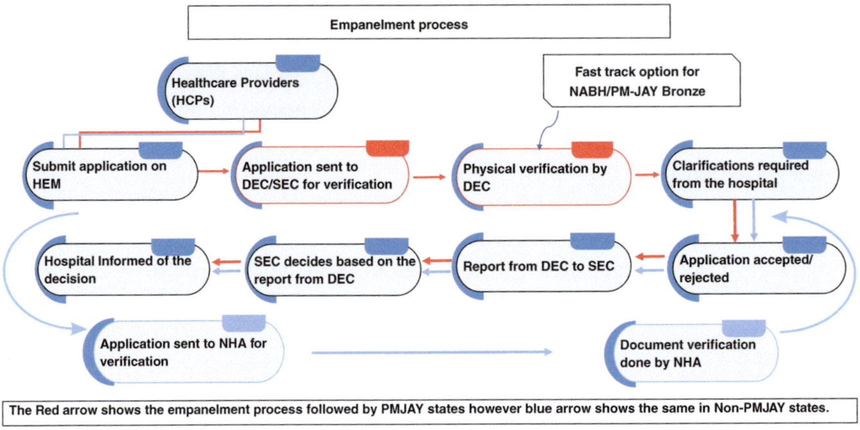

Fig. 9.7 Flowchart illustrating the empanelment process for healthcare providers, showing usual and fast-track application modes. (Source: National Health Authority. About Pradhan Mantri Jan Arogya Yojana (PM-JAY). [cited 2023 Aug 30]. Available from: https://nha.gov.in/PM-JAY) (DEC/SEC: District Empanelment Committee / State Empanelment Committee, HCP: Health Care Providers, HEM: Hospital Empanelment Module, NABH: National Accreditation Board for Hospitals & Healthcare Providers, NHA: National Health Authority)

Distribution of Empanelled Hospitals: As of March 2025, a total of 31,809 hospitals had been empanelled under the scheme, including 17,409 public hospitals. The state-wise distribution of empanelled hospitals is shown in Fig. 9.8.

9.5.10 Quality Assurance

The NHA encourages EHCPs to obtain PM-JAY quality certifications (Bronze, Silver, Gold), a move aimed at improving the quality of services provided to beneficiaries. NHA, with the Quality Council of India (QCI), has formulated criteria to uphold quality care and enhance patient safety, which States/UTs are advised to adhere to, thus reinforcing the maintenance of well-defined quality standards [22]. Moreover, quality cells have been established in 18 states to guide empanelled hospitals in improving care quality. Quality cell at NHA conducts analyses to determine the root causes of identified issues. They work with healthcare providers (HCPs) and other stakeholders to develop and implement solutions that aim to improve the quality of care. Similarly, in addition to the above-mentioned certifications, the National Quality Assurance Standards (NQAS), developed by the Ministry of Health & Family Welfare, serve as a structured set of guidelines and criteria to assess and enhance the quality of healthcare services in public health facilities, ensuring compliance with both national and global standards. Details are presented in Table 9.2.

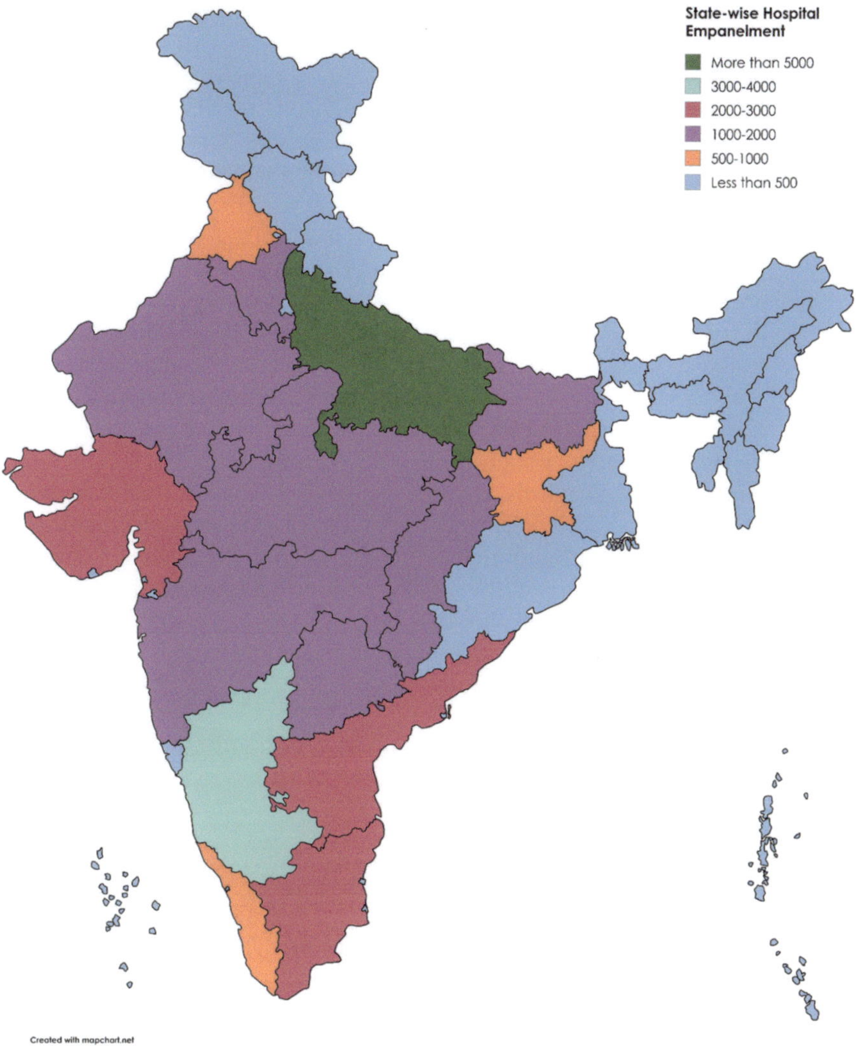

Fig. 9.8 Number of empanelled hospitals in different Indian States. (Source: PM-JAY Public Dashboard at https://pmjay.gov.in/ as of 05-03-2025)

Activity Box

Scenario: A private eye hospital, *Eye Care Clinic*, is a standalone facility with no inpatient beds. The hospital wants to apply for PM-JAY Quality Certification to enhance its credibility and provide services under the scheme. However, the facility is non-empanelled and wants to apply for empanelment after quality certification.

Task: As a hospital administrator, research and answer the following:

- Can *Eye Care Clinic* apply for PM-JAY Quality Certification despite not having inpatient beds?
- Based on the hospital's specialty, size, and available facilities, which certification should *Eye Care Clinic* apply for?
- What are the key requirements in terms of documents or certifications the hospital must fulfill to get empanelled under the PM-JAY?

Ans: The clinic is eligible to apply for PM-JAY Quality Certification even if it does not have inpatient beds. Depending on the clinic's size, if all required criteria—such as documentation and permissions—are met, the clinic can apply for Bronze Certification. For information on key requirements, documents, complete information is available on the guidebooks, please visit: https://pmjay.qcin.org/guide-book

To apply for the empanelment, you should visit and apply: https://hospitals.pmjay.gov.in/empApplicationHome.htm

Table 9.2 Features of AB-PMJAY quality certification

	Bronze quality certification	Silver quality certification	Gold quality certification
Who can apply?	Non-certified Hospitals	HOPE[a]/NQAS[b] certified Hospitals	NABH[c] Full/JCI[d] Accredited Hospitals
Financial incentive	5%	10%	15%
Validity of the certificate	2 years	Co-terminus with existing certificate validity	Co-terminus with existing certificate validity

Source: Guidebook for AB PM-JAY Quality Certification for Empanelled Hospitals [22]

[a]HOPE: Healthcare Organization for Platform for Entry-level Certification

[b]NQAS: National Quality Assurance Standards

[c]NABH: National Accreditation Board for Hospitals

[d]JCI: Joint Commission International

9.5.11 Standard Treatment Guidelines

Standard Treatment Guidelines (STGs) were developed by the National Health Authority to establish uniform patient care, enhance treatment efficiency, and provide healthcare professionals with structured clinical guidance. These guidelines define key clinical parameters and mandatory documentation for specific treatment packages, streamlining pre-authorization and claims processing by Pre-authorization Processing Doctors (PPDs) and Claims Processing Doctors (CPDs). While countries in Europe, North America, and Australia have long leveraged clinical guidelines, India has faced significant challenges, including fragmented documentation, irregular updates, and a lack of contextualization to its diverse healthcare landscape, often leading to dependence on international evidence.

To bridge these gaps, STGs were developed and initially piloted in six states for high-risk, abuse-prone packages. A dedicated medical cell, comprising domain experts, was also established to provide specialized insights, ensuring the guidelines were comprehensive and practical. Multiple revisions and approvals followed, culminating in their integration into the Transaction Management System (TMS) to enforce consistency across empanelled healthcare providers while effectively mitigating fraud and abuse. The development and implementation of STGs are a collective effort involving all key stakeholders, ensuring a robust framework for high-quality, standardized healthcare delivery. Currently, 678 STGs are in place, serving as indispensable references for different procedures for treating doctors, EHCPs, TPAs, Implementing Support Agencies (ISAs), State Health Agencies (SHAs), and medical auditors. The structure of STGs is divided into an introduction and four parts, as discussed in Fig. 9.9.

9.5.12 Advancements in PM-JAY

9.5.12.1 e-RUPI Integration: A Digital Payment Solution

Launched in August 2021, e-RUPI is a digital, voucher-based payment system designed to facilitate cashless transactions. It is a prepaid, person- and purpose-specific voucher, which means that a beneficiary (to whom the voucher has been given) can use it only for a specific purpose, such as diagnostics at empanelled facilities, without needing a card, digital payment app, or internet banking [23, 24].

9.5.12.2 How Does It Work?

Beneficiaries receive a prepaid voucher via SMS or QR code, which can be redeemed for specific services, such as diagnostic tests, under PM-JAY. Currently, diagnostic tests related to 459 surgical packages have been included under e-RUPI.

9.5.12.3 How Are Vouchers Issued?

The National Payments Corporation of India (NPCI), in collaboration with the Department of Financial Services, and the National Health Authority, developed e-RUPI on the UPI platform. Partner banks serve as issuing entities, allocating

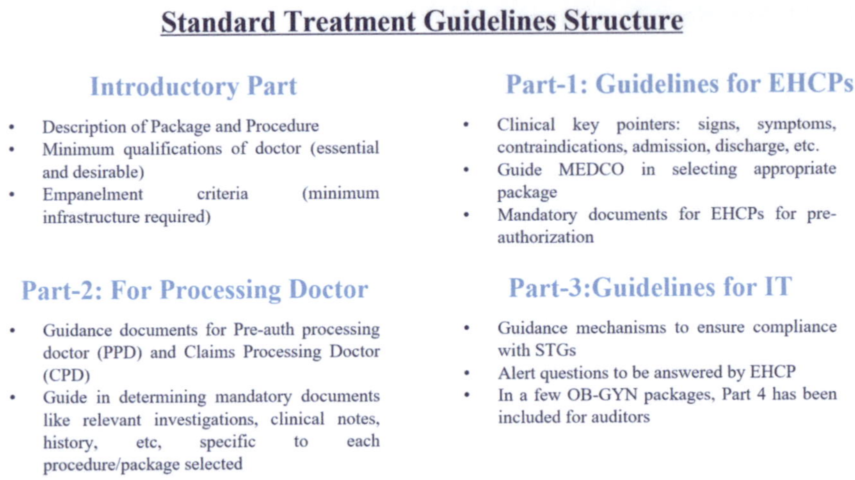

Fig. 9.9 Structure of standard treatment guidelines. (Source: National Health Authority. Documentation of process for customization of Standard Treatment Guidelines. National Health Authority; 2024) (CPD: Claim Processing Doctor, EHCP: Empanelled Health Care Provider, IT: Information Technology, MEDCO: Medical Coordinators, PPD: Pre-auth Processing Doctor, STG: Standard Treatment Guidelines)

vouchers to service providers for designated beneficiaries, identified via mobile numbers [25].

9.5.12.4 How to Redeem It?

The beneficiary visits an empanelled hospital or lab, avails the service, and redeems the e-RUPI voucher for payment. Figure 9.10 shows how e-RUPI is generated and redeemed.

Key Features

- e-RUPI is a QR code or SMS-based e-voucher sent directly to the beneficiary's mobile. It requires no physical card, digital payment app, or internet access.
- It is secure and ensures complete confidentiality of beneficiary details.
- The maximum value of an e-RUPI voucher is set at INR 1,00,000 per voucher for government schemes, while for private entities, the limit is restricted to INR 10,000 per voucher.
- Pilot testing has been conducted in Chandigarh, Jammu & Kashmir, and Madhya Pradesh for diagnostic packages [26]. A specialized e-RUPI variant has also been introduced for oncology diagnostic payments in outpatient settings.

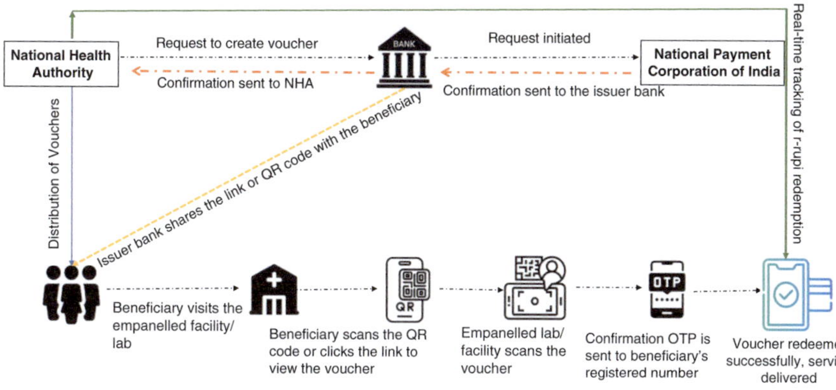

Fig. 9.10 Flowchart depicting the steps for generating and redeeming an e-RUPI voucher. (Source: National Payments Corporation of India. e-RUPI product Booklet. National Payments Corporation of India; Available from: https://www.npci.org.in/PDF/npci/e-rupi/Product-Booklet.pdf)

9.5.13 ICD-11 and ICHI Integration

The International Classification of Diseases (ICD) is the global standard for recording, analyzing, and comparing mortality and morbidity data. It helps countries identify key health challenges using a clinically relevant classification system, enabling informed public health policies and impact assessment, and clinical documentation. Similarly, the International Classification of Health Interventions (ICHI) standardizes the reporting and analysis of health interventions across various providers. It allows users to include additional details alongside the ICHI code, enhancing clinical documentation with more precise information. Their integration into PM-JAY marks a significant step toward standardizing disease classification and medical interventions in India's healthcare system. Historically, the lack of an integrated and standardized morbidity classification system led to inconsistencies in health data, vague diagnoses, multiple diagnostic listings per case, misuse of surgical packages, and fraudulent claims. While surveys like National Family Health Survey (NFHS) and National Sample Survey Office (NSSO) provided valuable health insights, the absence of a uniform coding framework affected their reliability [27].

To address these gaps, ICD-11 and ICHI have been integrated into PM-JAY's TMS, ensuring precise disease coding. This move enhances clinical documentation, data interoperability, claims management, and fraud detection, while also aligning India's health system with global standards. Additionally, this integration supports the *Ayushman Bharat Digital Mission* (ABDM) by fostering data-driven policymaking, improved health analytics, better patient safety, and comprehensive quality assessment, ultimately leading to a more efficient and transparent healthcare system.

9.5.14 Conclusion

India's approach to providing health-related financial risk protection began with the establishment of a large network of public healthcare facilities and setting up of social health insurance schemes. The coverage of social health insurance was restricted to employees of the organized sector. Over time, coverage was extended to financially vulnerable populations in the unorganized sector through Government-Funded Health Insurance Schemes. These policies have continually evolved, with PM-JAY now covering not only below poverty line (BPL) populations but also socially disadvantaged groups and, more recently, individuals above the age of 70. The network of service providers has also expanded beyond the public sector to include nonprofit and for-profit private providers. However, across various schemes, coverage has remained focused on secondary and tertiary inpatient care, while outpatient services have largely been overlooked. PM-JAY is envisaged to play a transformative role in expanding financial protection, improving access to quality healthcare, and reducing out-of-pocket expenditures, thereby contributing to India's UHC goals. By providing cashless and paperless treatment for millions of beneficiaries, it has mitigated catastrophic health expenditures, particularly among economically vulnerable populations. The scheme has also increased hospitalization rates among the poor, ensuring timely care at both public and private healthcare facilities.

Despite its successes, PM-JAY faces several implementation challenges, like variability in empanelment and beneficiary outreach across states. The lack of outpatient care coverage remains a significant gap, leading to continued high out-of-pocket spending. Cases of provider fraud, inflated claims, and unnecessary medical procedures pose risks to the scheme's financial sustainability. Enhancing monitoring mechanisms, improving transparency, and deploying AI-driven fraud detection systems will be crucial in the scheme's long-term sustainability.

Future advancements in PM-JAY should focus on integrating value-based care models to improve efficiency and quality while reducing unnecessary procedures. Strengthening healthcare provider empanelment and quality assurance mechanisms will be crucial to ensuring standardized, high-quality care across sectors. Leveraging digital health technologies, such as e-RUPI digital payment systems and artificial intelligence (AI)-driven claims processing and blockchain for secure data management, can enhance transparency and improve fraud detection.

India's experience with PM-JAY provides valuable lessons for other developing nations implementing large-scale, government-funded health insurance programs. A digital-first approach, such as India's *Ayushman Bharat Digital Mission*, can enhance data-driven policymaking and efficiency in claim processing. The country's blended model of public–private partnerships demonstrates how leveraging private sector capacity can expand healthcare access while ensuring financial sustainability. However, addressing supply-side challenges, such as healthcare workforce shortages and regional disparities, remains essential. Scaling PM-JAY equitably while transitioning toward a preventive, primary-care-focused model could serve as a global benchmark for achieving Universal Health Coverage in resource-limited settings.

References

1. Patnaik I, Shah A. The rise of government-funded health insurance in India. (231). Available from: https://www.nipfp.org.in/media/medialibrary/2018/05/WP_231.pdf.
2. GOI. Central Government Health Scheme [Internet]. [cited 2025 Jun 9]. Available from: https://www.cghs.mohfw.gov.in/AHIMSG5/hissso/Login.
3. GOI. ESIC Benefits | Employees' State Insurance Corporation [Internet]. [cited 2025 Jun 9]. Available from: https://www.esic.gov.in/information-benefits.
4. Hooda SK. Penetration and coverage of government-funded health insurance schemes in India. Clin Epidemiol Glob Health. 2020;8(4):1017–33.
5. Kumar S. Private sector in healthcare delivery market in india: structure, growth and implications. Inst Stud Ind Dev Work Paper. 2015;185:14–5.
6. Dubey S, Deshpande S, Krishna L, Zadey S. Evolution of Government-funded health insurance for universal health coverage in India. Lancet Reg Health Southeast Asia. 2023;13:100180.
7. Ministry of Labour and Employment. Unorganised worker. Annual report.
8. Malhi R, Goel D, Gambhir RS, Brar P, Behal D, Bhardwaj A. Rashtriya Swasthya Bima Yojana (RSBY) and outpatient coverage. J Family Med Prim Care. 2020;9(2):459–64.
9. Thakur H. Study of awareness, enrollment, and utilization of Rashtriya Swasthya Bima Yojana (National Health Insurance Scheme) in Maharashtra, India. Front Public Health. 2015;3:282.
10. Selvaraj S, Farooqui HH, Karan A. Quantifying the financial burden of households' out-of-pocket payments on medicines in India: a repeated cross-sectional analysis of National Sample Survey data, 1994–2014. BMJ Open. 2018;8(5):e018020.
11. Prinja S, Chauhan AS, Karan A, Kaur G, Kumar R. Impact of publicly financed health insurance schemes on healthcare utilization and financial risk protection in india: a systematic review. PLoS One. 2017;12(2):e0170996.
12. Virk AK, Atun R. Towards universal health coverage in India: a historical examination of the genesis of Rashtriya Swasthya Bima Yojana–The health insurance scheme for low-income groups. Public Health. 2015;129(6):810–7.
13. Shirisha P. What lessons should pradhan mantri jan arogya yojana learn from the shortfalls of rashtriya swasthya bima yojana: the case of rashtriya swasthya bima yojana in Chhattisgarh. Indian J Community Med. 2020;45(2):135–8.
14. National Health Authority. About NHA–National Health Authority | GOI [Internet]. [cited 2025 Mar 27]. Available from: https://nha.gov.in/NHA.
15. First meeting of NHA governing body on Mar 16; could finalise ceiling rate of premium for PMJAY [Internet]. The Indian Express. 2019 [cited 2025 Mar 25]. Available from: https://indianexpress.com/article/business/first-meeting-of-nha-governing-body-on-mar-16-could-finalise-ceiling-rate-of-premium-for-pmjay-5627108/.
16. Chauhan AS, Guinness L, Bahuguna P, Singh MP, Aggarwal V, Rajsekhar K, et al. Cost of hospital services in India: a multi-site study to inform provider payment rates and Health Technology Assessment. BMC Health Serv Res. 2022;22(1):1343.
17. National Health Authority. Health Benefit Package 2.2 [Internet]. 2022. Available from: https://nha.gov.in/img/resources/HBP-2.2-manual.pdf.
18. Chugh Y, Sharma S, Guinness L, Sharma D, Garg B, Mehndiratta A, et al. Establishing national hospital costing systems: insights from the qualitative assessment of cost surveillance pilot in Indian hospitals. BMJ Open. 2024;14(9):e082965.
19. National Health Authority. Volume based to Value Based Care_Policy Document [Internet]. National Health Authority; 2022. Available from: https://abdm.gov.in:8081/uploads/VBHC_Policy_Document_For_Upload_a20f871a55.pdf.
20. National Health Authority. Hospital empanelment module [Internet]. Available from: https://nha.gov.in/img/resources/SOP-NHA-Hospital-Empanelment-Module%20-Self-help-guide-new.pdf.

21. About Pradhan Mantri Jan Arogya Yojana (PM-JAY) | Official Website Ayushman Bharat Pradhan Mantri Jan Arogya Yojana | National Health Authority [Internet]. [cited 2025 Mar 27]. Available from: https://pmjay.gov.in/about/pmjay.
22. Quality Council of India. Guidebook for AB PM-JAY Quality Certification for Empanelled Hospitals [Internet]. 2020. Available from: https://pmjay.qcin.org/assets/img/nha-img/docs/Guidebook%20Empanelled%2008-09-2020.pdf.
23. Know all about e-RUPI, the new digital payment instrument [Internet]. [cited 2024 Aug 8]. Available from: https://pib.gov.in/PressReleasePage.aspx?PRID=1743056.
24. e-RUPI–Digital Payment Solution| National Portal of India. [cited 2024 Aug 8]. Available from: https://www.india.gov.in/spotlight/e-rupi-digital-payment-solution.
25. National Payments Corporation of India. E-RUPI product Booklet [Internet]. National Payments Corporation of India. Available from: https://www.npci.org.in/PDF/npci/e-rupi/Product-Booklet.pdf.
26. PGI Selected For Implementation of E-rupi Scheme | Chandigarh News – Times of India. [cited 2024 Aug 8]. Available from: https://timesofindia.indiatimes.com/city/chandigarh/pgi-selected-for-implementation-of-e-rupi-scheme/articleshow/92326358.cms.
27. ICD_11_and_ICHI_implementation_Report_Final_e668c70abd.pdf [Internet]. [cited 2025 Feb 3]. Available from: https://abdm.gov.in:8081/uploads/ICD_11_and_ICHI_implementation_Report_Final_e668c70abd.pdf.

Demand-Side Financing for Healthcare in India

10

Jyoti Dixit and Shankar Prinja

Abstract

Healthcare financing plays a critical role in shaping the accessibility, affordability, and quality of health services. Traditionally, health systems have relied on supply-side financing (SSF), wherein governments or other financing entities allocate funds directly to healthcare providers, such as hospitals and clinics, in the form of budgets, input-based payments, or infrastructure investments. While SSF ensures the availability of healthcare infrastructure and essential medical services, it has inherent limitations, including inefficiencies in resource allocation, limited responsiveness to patient needs, and potential provider-side inefficiencies such as absenteeism and lack of incentives for quality improvement. Growing evidence suggests that although healthcare supply improved, it did not necessarily bring the desired health outcomes. The glaring delays and obstacles in accessing healthcare were poor decision-making for seeking treatment, high out-of-pocket expenditure (OOPE), transportation and treatment costs, loss of wages, and subpar service quality. These impediments were especially true for the socio-economically vulnerable populations, who were primarily supposed to benefit the most from these services. In contrast, demand-side financing (DSF) represents an alternative approach that shifts the focus of financial flows from providers to patients. DSF was introduced as a tool to bridge the gap between healthcare supply and its utilization. The core features to develop successful DSF schemes include specific targeting of beneficiaries, transfer of funds or subsidies, and inclusion of essential services using selected criteria. Hence, DSF schemes aim to actively put the purchasing power in the hands of the user, ultimately delivering the desired results.

J. Dixit · S. Prinja (✉)
Department of Community Medicine and School of Public Health, Post Graduate Institute of Medical Education and Research, Chandigarh, India

S. Prinja (ed.), *Healthcare Financing and Insurance*,
https://doi.org/10.1007/978-981-95-3513-2_10

DSF has been established as a great concept in multiple countries to meet the healthcare needs of the population's most vulnerable and underserved groups. Each scheme varies in its strategic framework and mechanism. While vouchers and conditional transfers work best for achieving short-term goals, such as institutional deliveries and postnatal care, publicly-financed health insurance schemes ensure long-term financial protection while accessing inpatient services in secondary and tertiary healthcare facilities. In India, national- and state-led DSF schemes have been put in place to address the unmet health needs among the financially disadvantaged groups of society. Despite the observed advantages of DSF schemes, concerns regarding their long-term sustainability have been raised as the main challenge. The other important challenges stem from poor targeting, subpar service quality and non-availability of services, narrow focus of DSF scheme, inconsistent fund pooling and budget allocation, and adverse incentives. Therefore, a well-equipped supply-side service delivery, awareness among the targeted groups regarding the availability of services, timely provision of support in informed decision-making to understand healthcare needs, financial support to access healthcare services, and improving healthcare staff, and provider skills for a more favourable experience are crucial to achieving the desired objective of any DSF program. This chapter provides an overview of DSF mechanisms and challenges in its implementation in India.

Keywords

Demand-side financing · Mechanisms of Demand-side financing · Vouchers · Conditional cash transfers · Direct benefit transfer

Learning Objectives

After going through the chapter, you will be able to:

Understand the core features of demand-side healthcare financing in India.
Differentiate between the different mechanisms and underlying principles of demand-side healthcare financing.
Learn about the challenges faced in implementing the DSF schemes and programs in India.

Key Terms

Out-of-pocket expenditure: Payments made by an individual at the time of receiving healthcare services or goods.

Catastrophic health expenditure: Catastrophic heath expenditure occurs when a household's total out-of-pocket health payments equal or exceed 40% of household's capacity to pay or non-subsistence spending.

Merit goods: Healthcare goods or services that are considered to be beneficial to individuals and society as a whole, but are often under-consumed, and hence ought to be provided free or subsidized by the Government.

Positive Externality: Benefit of a given product or service gained by another person who has not directly received the same and paid for the same. A classical example includes the herd immunity benefit of immunization.

10.1 Introduction

Healthcare financing is the "function of a health system concerned with the mobilization, accumulation, and allocation of money to cover the health needs of the people, individually and collectively" [1]. In India, the majority of healthcare financing is through out-of-pocket (OOP) payments. Recent estimates by the National Health Accounts show that approximately 48% of the healthcare financing is OOP [2]. Healthcare financing plays a critical role in shaping the accessibility, affordability, and quality of health services. Traditionally, health systems have relied on supply-side financing (SSF), wherein governments or other financing entities allocate funds directly to healthcare providers, such as hospitals and clinics, in the form of budgets, input-based payments, or infrastructure investments [3]. For example, in India, financing of the entire public health system, from subcentres to tertiary care medical colleges, is a case of SSF. While SSF ensures the availability of healthcare infrastructure and essential medical services, it has inherent limitations, including inefficiencies in resource allocation, limited responsiveness to patient needs, and potential provider-side inefficiencies such as absenteeism and lack of incentives for quality improvement.

In contrast, demand-side financing (DSF) represents an alternative approach that shifts the focus of financial flows from providers to patients. DSF mechanisms include health vouchers, conditional cash transfers (CCTs), and insurance-based models, all designed to empower individuals by subsidizing the cost of accessing healthcare services [4]. A defining feature of DSF is that "money follows the patient", meaning that financial resources are directed towards providers based on the actual utilization of services by patients rather than predetermined budgets. This ensures a performance-driven system where providers are incentivized to deliver quality care and attract patients [5].

The potential advantages of DSF over SSF are manifold. By directly targeting individuals, DSF can improve healthcare utilization among underserved populations, particularly in low- and middle-income countries (LMICs), where financial barriers often deter service uptake [6, 7]. Furthermore, DSF mechanisms can enhance provider accountability, promote competition among healthcare facilities, and encourage efficiency in service delivery [8]. Hence, DSF was introduced as a tool to positively influence health-seeking behaviour and improve people's uptake of the available health services [9]. However, the effectiveness of DSF schemes depends on careful design, implementation, and regulatory oversight to prevent unintended consequences such as fraud, cost escalation, and inequitable service distribution [10].

This chapter discusses different mechanisms of demand-side healthcare financing and its core features. It critically reviews various DSF schemes in India. The chapter further discusses the potential advantages and challenges in implementation of DSF. By understanding the nuances of DSF, policymakers and health system stakeholders can better harness financial tools to enhance health outcomes and equity in healthcare delivery.

10.2 Overview of Demand-Side Financing

Globally published literature shows various ways of implementing DSF schemes that use diverse principles. However, a striking difference that makes DSF stand out from SSF is that DSF directly links the beneficiaries to the subsidy or benefit and its intended goal. The remuneration offered to beneficiaries and/or providers for health insurance or voucher schemes is dependent on the fulfilment of the desired action or output and hence holds promising value in improving the efficiency of healthcare service delivery [9]. DSF mechanisms can be consumer-led or provider-led and include vouchers, cash transfers, direct benefit transfers, and health insurance, where incentives or subsidies may be allocated before or after service utilization [9]. A typical DSF scheme consists of three core features—targeted beneficiaries, financial support, and set criteria for selecting services to be covered under each scheme (Fig. 10.1).

Each DSF scheme may differ in terms of its parent agency (central/union government or state government), choice (public, private, non government organization (NGOs), or mixed), and number of service providers tied to each service, performance-based incentives, and inclusion of third-party payers (insurance companies or NGOs), and autonomy of the scheme (stand-alone or integrated as part of an umbrella scheme).

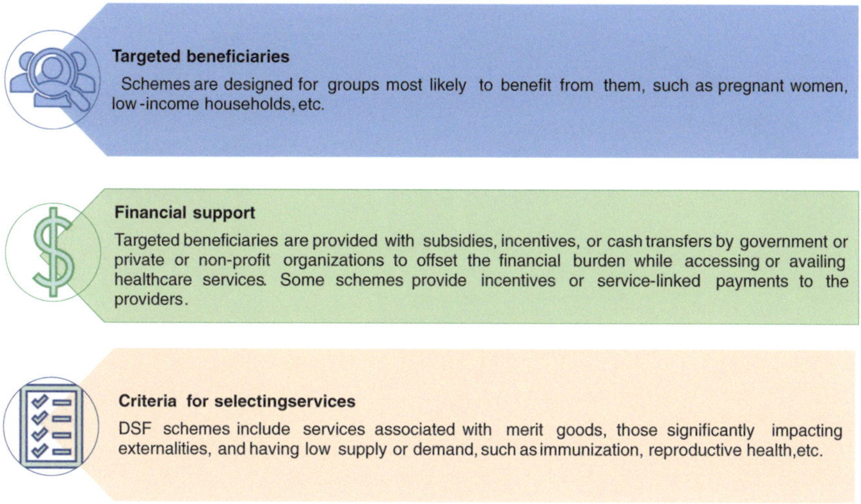

Fig. 10.1 Core features of a demand-side financing scheme

10.3 Mechanisms of Demand-Side Financing

DSF mechanisms have different principles and modes of delivery in terms of benefits received by individuals or families as shown in Fig. 10.2.

Some of the DSF mechanisms currently implemented in India are as follows:

- Vouchers
- Conditional cash transfers (CCTs)
- Direct benefit transfers (DBTs)
- Health insurance schemes

10.3.1 Vouchers

Vouchers are the most commonly adopted mechanisms for implementing DSF schemes. The World Bank defines a voucher as "a token that can be used in exchange for a restricted range of goods or services. Vouchers tie the receipt of cash to provision of particular goods, provided by particular vendors, at particular times. Health care vouchers are used in exchange for consumption or provision of health services (such as medical consultations or laboratory tests) or health care consumables (such as drugs)" [9]. They serve as tools to promote the utilization of underutilized

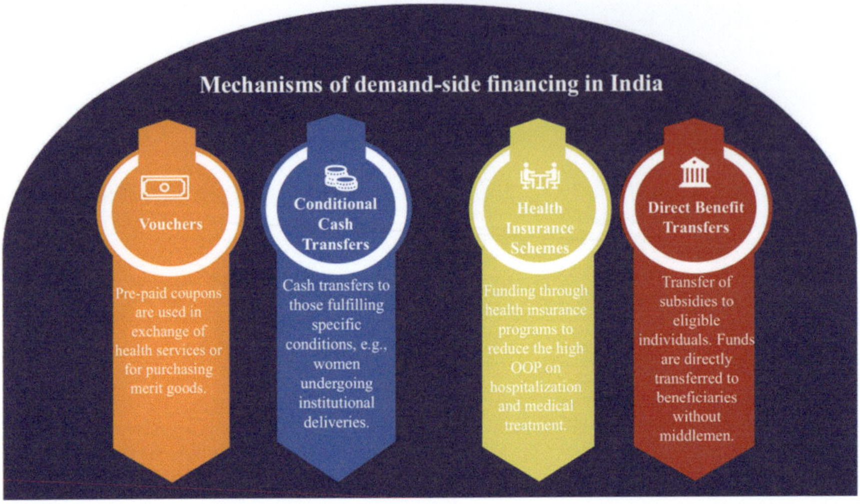

Fig. 10.2 Description of different mechanisms of demand-side financing in India

services, such as family planning, infectious disease treatment, immunizations, mental healthcare, and maternal and child health services, by fully or partially subsidizing healthcare costs. Their function is similar to that of a redeemable prepaid coupon that can be used to access certain healthcare services from accredited public or private partners. Therefore, they are considered highly efficient in targeting the selected population [11].

The government of Gujarat launched *"Chiranjeevi Yojana"* through a public-private partnership under which vouchers were given to help pregnant women from economically disadvantaged populations access maternal healthcare services with financial protection. The scheme was launched to encourage institutional deliveries, increase coverage of women from below poverty line (BPL) strata, and reduce transportation costs [12].

10.3.2 Conditional Cash Transfers

CCTs involve the transfer of incentives upon fulfilment of the desired output or action. Incentives are given as cash to eligible individuals seeking healthcare services or families who fulfil the conditions required to avail the incentives. This mechanism of demand-side financing is focused on encouraging behaviours that positively impact health outcomes, such as institutional deliveries, attending prenatal and antenatal check-ups, and immunization.

Janani Suraksha Yojana (JSY) is an example of CCT. It was introduced to lower maternal and neonatal mortality rates by promoting safer institutional deliveries, especially among pregnant women from BPL and underserved communities. Financial assistance of ₹1000/– and ₹1400/– was provided to women from urban and rural areas of low-performing states, respectively, and ₹600/– and ₹700/– in high-performing states based on the beneficiary's area of residence; rural beneficiaries received more amount than those from urban areas [13]. The rates, however, may vary by the State of residence.

10.3.3 Direct Benefit Transfers

Cash incentives or subsidies are transferred directly into the beneficiaries' accounts. This encourages a more transparent, leakproof, and corruption-free flow of funds from the government to eligible individuals. The mechanism also helps in accurately targeting eligible people, prevents duplicate transfers, and removes middlemen for a seamless cash transfer [14].

The Jharkhand government's *Mukhyamantri Maiya Samman Yojana* (MMSY, 2024) was launched to provide financial protection and welfare to women of lower- and middle-socio-economic sectors of the community. A total of ₹12,000/– is transferred annually, paid on a monthly basis (₹1000/– per month), to the bank accounts of all eligible women. DBT has been used by multiple financing schemes, such as Prime Minister's Matru Vandana Yojana (PMMVY), *Pradhan Mantri Kisan Samman Nidhi* (PM-KISAN), and Mahatma Gandhi National Rural Employment Guarantee Scheme (MGNREGS).

10.3.4 Health Insurance Schemes

Health insurance, which has been explained in Chapter 2 of Part I of this book, is also an example of DSF. These schemes are funded through premiums or contributions collected from individuals or governments. These funds are pooled to strategically purchase healthcare services from providers, which may be government agencies (such as health departments, state-run corporations, trusts, or societies) or private insurance companies. Claims are reimbursed to beneficiaries after services are rendered or paid directly to providers where patients receive services without paying anything or cashless. This mechanism requires verification to prevent fraud. Public subsidies can adopt this model if the healthcare system is well developed. When refunds are limited to partial reimbursements, they help control moral hazards but are less helpful for the poorest section of society [9, 15]. Among the most popular publicly funded health insurance schemes is *Ayushman Bharat Pradhan Mantri Jan Arogya Yojana* (AB PM-JAY), under which financial protection against catastrophic health expenditure is provided to beneficiaries for availing secondary and tertiary care services. Beneficiaries can avail healthcare services at empanelled public and private hospitals. The scheme was launched to move towards achieving universal health coverage [16].

Different countries adopt various mechanisms to implement DSF schemes depending on the target beneficiaries, feasibility, scalability, and desired health outcomes. In several regions and countries, such as Latin America, India, Nepal, and

Bangladesh, DSF initiatives were primarily implemented to improve maternal and child health (MCH) outcomes. In India, the purpose of focusing on MCH was to achieve Millennium Development Goals (MDGs) 4 and 5 as early as possible. Among the different DSF models, vouchers (tokens used for availing health services) and cash transfers are more commonly used for MCH than health insurance. This is because these models are more effective for achieving short-term health outcomes [17, 18]. At the national level, the first major demand-side financing scheme was JSY, launched in 2005, which provided financial incentives to encourage institutional deliveries in both public and private healthcare facilities. In 2006, the Gujarat government introduced *Chiranjeevi Yojana*, which engaged private healthcare providers to facilitate institutional deliveries, recognizing that public hospitals lacked the capacity and reach to adequately serve rural areas. The rationale behind these schemes was to leverage the existing private sector infrastructure to improve maternal and child health outcomes [11, 15]. These demand-side financing initiatives also started actively encouraging institutional deliveries rather than merely promoting safe deliveries—whether at home or in a facility.

The design, implementation, and monitoring of DSF schemes may vary across states. Other than vouchers and cash transfers, multiple DSF models are used in India depending on the targeted health outcome. After the evident success of cash transfers and vouchers, the DSF mechanisms proliferated and publicly financed health insurance programs gained popularity at the national and state levels. The Indian Regulatory and Development Authority of India (IRDAI) reported a massive increase in people with health insurance from 1% to 27% in over a decade (2005–2016) [11, 12]. With the ideation and development of newer and more efficient models, the DSF schemes were improved and adopted over time. India's healthcare financing is undergoing major reforms, with simultaneous strengthening of health systems while also expanding government-funded health insurance. Alongside the moderate efforts under the National Rural Health Mission (NRHM), central and state governments have systematically developed a government-funded health insurance system. The expansion of government-funded health insurance schemes at both national and state levels opened new opportunities for the private sector. For instance, the *Rajiv Aarogyasri Scheme* in Andhra Pradesh inspired similar programs in states like Tamil Nadu, Karnataka, Maharashtra, and Gujarat [11].

At the national level, the *Rashtriya Swasthya Bima Yojana* (RSBY) was introduced in 2008 in a phased manner. By 2015, it was estimated that 50% of India's population would be covered under government-funded health insurance schemes. The primary objective of these programs was to provide financial protection to below poverty line (BPL) households against financial catastrophe, particularly from requiring inpatient care. Many of these new schemes drew inspiration from community-based health insurance (CBHI) models such as *VimoSewa, Karuna, and Yeshasvini*, though on a much larger scale [11, 17]. The next section provides a description of mechanisms of DSF in India and how they were implemented in some of the popular schemes.

Activity Box 10.1

Match each DSF strategy in healthcare with its intended outcome.

DSF strategy	Intended outcome
A. CCTs	1. Encourages timely use of maternal and child health services
B. Health insurance subsidies	2. Reduces financial barriers to healthcare access for low-income families.
C. Vouchers for maternal health services	3. Provides access to specific services at accredited facilities.

10.4 DSF Schemes in India: A Review of Selected Cases

Multiple DSF schemes have been rolled out in India. Along with the typical features of a DSF scheme, Table 10.1 compares selected DSF schemes implemented in India across some other features to understand their strategic application in the Indian context. These features compare whether the scheme targets positive externalities, offer provider choice to beneficiaries, operates on a public–private partnership model, includes provider incentives, involves intermediate agencies to implement the scheme, and is integrated with other schemes. The scheme may be designed with a specific target, meaning it is limited to a well-defined population subgroup. It can involve financial transfers, where beneficiaries receive subsidies either in cash or through vouchers. The scheme may also allow for choice of providers, giving beneficiaries the option to select from available healthcare providers. A public–private mix may be present if both public and private entities are involved in service delivery. Additionally, provider incentives may be included to encourage better performance and service quality. The scheme might involve intermediaries, such as third-party administrators or insurers, in its implementation. Finally, it may be integrated with other schemes, enabling better coordination and coverage across different programs.

DSF initiatives in India utilize targeted groups, financial incentives and many of them predominantly focus on MCH outcomes, which are often considered merit goods or having positive externalities. Positive externalities or merit goods are healthcare goods or services considered beneficial to individuals and society as a whole but are often under-consumed. For example, JSY not only improves the health outcomes for a pregnant woman opting for institutional deliveries but also strengthens the health system by encouraging regular antenatal care (ANC) visits, timely referrals, and increased interaction with Accredited Social Health Activists (ASHAs), creating a culture of preventive health-seeking behaviour. This improved engagement with formal health systems leads to better vaccination coverage, birth registration, and health education, further benefiting the wider community. A key feature of DSF is the combination of financial targeting and earmarked grants,

Table 10.1 Demand Side Financing schemes in India

DSF Scheme	Specified targeted group	Financial transfer to beneficiaries	Provider choice	Public-private partnership	Provider incentives	Intermediate agencies	Integrated with other schemes
e-RUPI Voucher Scheme	Yes	Yes	Yes	Yes	Yes	Yes	No
Arogya Raksha	Yes	Yes	Yes	Yes	Yes	Yes	No
Chiranjeevi Yojana	Yes	Yes	Yes	Yes	Yes	Yes	No
CINI-ASHA)	Yes	Yes	Yes	Yes	Yes	Yes	No
Mamta	Yes	Yes	Yes	Yes	Yes	Yes	Yes
Muthulakshmi Reddy Memorial Scheme	Yes	Yes	No	No	No	No	No
Janani Suraksha Yojana	Yes	Yes	Yes	Yes	Yes	No	Yes
Pradhan Mantri Matru Vandana Yojana	Yes	Yes	No	No	No	No	Yes
Rashtriya Swasthya Bima Yojana	Yes	Yes	Yes	Yes	No	Yes	Yes
Ayushman Bharat-Pradhan Mantri Jan Arogya Yojana	Yes	Yes	Yes	Yes	Yes	Yes	Yes

Authors' adaptation based on World Health Report (2010), Background Paper 27 [9] CINI-ASHA: Child In Need Institute –Accredited Social Health Activist provided in the form of vouchers, health cards, or membership roll numbers. These initiatives, such as JSY, establish a connection between beneficiaries—pregnant women, new mothers and newborns—and the healthcare system through vouchers or similar tokens (e.g., Child In Need Institute–Accredited Social Health Activist (CINI-ASHA), Gujarat's *Chiranjeevi Yojana*). The tokens are accepted by empanelled service providers (both public and private) who get reimbursed by the project management authorities or funding agencies [2].

State-led DSF programs use means-testing criteria to identify eligible individuals, often focusing on women of reproductive age from economically disadvantaged backgrounds. Although defining BPL status is complex and changes over time, the identification process has been majorly streamlined by including local authorities to help assess household poverty levels in their administrative area. For instance, the Dr. Muthulakshmi Reddy Memorial Maternity Assistance Scheme, now integrated with the *Pradhan Mantri Matru Vandana Yojana* (PMMVY), utilizes village-level health workers and local officials to establish eligibility criteria before enrolling beneficiaries [2]. These criteria include socially and economically disadvantaged pregnant and lactating women belonging to scheduled castes and scheduled tribes, partially or fully disabled women, BPL women, women with net family income of less than ₹8,00,000 per annum. While these DSF programs share common features, they vary in terms of provider involvement, public-private partnerships, the role of intermediaries, and the level of integration with other schemes or services. There is a balanced mix of initiatives from government and non-government organizations, many of which rely on village-level health workers as intermediaries, such as ASHAs. In fact, most state-led programs emphasize collaboration with NGOs and private providers in their implementation [2].

Certain state-driven programs, such as the e-RUPI voucher Scheme in Uttar Pradesh, provide cash incentives in exchange for essential health service utilization defined in their strategic frameworks. The framework of these state-led schemes highlights financial incentives as a crucial element in improving maternal and child health outcomes. The scheme was introduced to prioritize pregnant women's health across the state by helping them access timely diagnostic services. The scheme is fully digital to guarantee direct benefits to the beneficiaries, thus reducing corruption. The *Aarogya Raksha Scheme* targets beneficiaries who are below the poverty line and have only one or two children. Financial transfers are facilitated through *Aarogya Raksha* certificates, which are issued by a medical officer. The scheme provides hospitalization and personal accident benefits to the individual and up to two of their children under 5 years of age. Beneficiaries are entitled to inpatient treatment in hospitals, with a maximum benefit of ₹2000 per hospitalization, subject to an annual limit of ₹4000 per certificate. Treatment is provided free of cost to the beneficiary, and the hospital claims reimbursement from the New India Insurance Company. In the event of death due to an accident, the maximum benefit payable is ₹10,000 under one certificate.

The scheme generates positive externalities, both in terms of improving health outcomes and encouraging limited family size. Beneficiaries have the choice of providers, and a public–private mix is employed in service delivery. Supply-side incentives are built into the scheme through performance-based reimbursement to ASHAs for facilitating institutional deliveries and ensuring the completion of ANC, postnatal care (PNC), and immunization under the Voucher Scheme. There is involvement of intermediaries, such as Self-Help Groups (SHGs) and Integrated Child Development Services (ICDS) workers, who play a key role in mobilizing communities to adopt terminal family planning methods after completing their families. The scheme is not standalone, as eligibility for free hospital treatment is conditional upon sterilization being performed in a government hospital. It is a provider-led initiative and is currently functional.

Another state-led scheme, the *Chiranjeevi Scheme*, targets pregnant women from BPL families in Gujarat, aiming to reduce maternal and infant mortality by improving access to institutional deliveries. Under this scheme, private providers deliver cashless maternity services to eligible women. Beneficiaries receive a *Chiranjeevi Yojana* (CY) card, issued by an *Anganwadi* Worker (AWW), Female Health Worker (FHW), or Auxiliary Nurse Midwife (ANM), which also entitles them to reimbursement for local travel expenses, including ambulance services. The scheme promotes positive externalities, as health workers track and support the expectant mother from pregnancy through the postnatal period, and also initiates child immunization services after delivery. Beneficiaries also have the freedom to choose from empanelled private providers, offering a public-private mix in service delivery. These providers are formally contracted through a Memorandum of Understanding (MoU) with the government. While there are no additional performance-based incentives, providers are compensated through a fixed capitation rate per delivery. There is limited involvement of intermediaries; however, NGOs may participate in areas lacking active *Panchayati Raj Institutions* (PRIs). The scheme functions as a standalone, provider-led intervention and is currently operational across all districts of Gujarat.

The CINI ASHA Scheme in West Bengal targets pregnant women, children under the age of two, and adolescents, addressing a broad spectrum of reproductive, maternal, child, and adolescent health needs. The scheme employs a voucher-based approach tied to user fees, where clients pay ₹ 5 per visit for a consultation voucher and ₹ 10 for a voucher that provides access to subsidized diagnostic services. The scheme generates positive externalities, particularly in maternal and child health, and also focuses on adolescent health, including reproductive tract infections (RTI)/ sexually transmitted infections (STI) and human immunodeficiency virus (HIV)/ acquired immunodeficiency syndrome (AIDS) prevention, due to CINI ASHA's engagement with street children and youth.

Beneficiaries also have the option to choose from a network of private medical practitioners, ensuring choice of providers and promoting a public–private mix. Women are registered for antenatal and postnatal check-ups at government health posts, while private providers handle routine consultations and refer complicated cases to tertiary-level government hospitals. Supply-side incentives are provided in the form of honoraria to community health volunteers, who play a critical role in mobilizing and motivating the target groups. These community health volunteers act as intermediaries, supporting the linkage between the community and service providers. The scheme is not stand-alone, as it works in coordination with existing government services. It is provider-led, with the use of referral vouchers to guide clients through the continuum of care.

The *Mamta* scheme is one of the provider-led initiatives, which was launched by the Delhi government in 2008. The scheme is designed to support pregnant women belonging to BPL households from scheduled caste and scheduled tribe communities, specifically those aged 19 years and above. It combines both demand- and supply-side financial incentives, offering ₹ 600 directly to the beneficiary under JSY and ₹ 4000 to the service providers involved in the delivery of care. These incentives aim to reduce financial barriers to institutional delivery and ensure continued engagement with health services. The scheme operates through a network of empanelled healthcare providers, giving women access to antenatal and postnatal care at government health posts, while also involving private practitioners who refer complicated cases to higher-level government facilities. The approach creates a public-private collaboration, strengthening service delivery across different tiers of the health system. To improve outreach and uptake, community health volunteers play a crucial role in identifying and supporting eligible women. Their efforts are recognized through honoraria, which serve as a form of supply-side motivation. Functioning as a stand-alone and provider-led intervention, the *Mamta Scheme* contributes to improving maternal and child health outcomes while reinforcing the importance of early registration, regular check-ups, and institutional care.

Dr. Muthulakshmi Reddy Memorial Maternity Assistance Scheme, a consumer-led initiative by the state of Tamil Nadu, was launched in 2009–10. The scheme offers maternity assistance to poor women, aiming to improve maternal health and nutritional outcomes during pregnancy. Unlike many other schemes, it is entirely consumer-focused, providing direct financial support of ₹ 6000 to expectant mothers. This amount is disbursed without the need for an income certificate, based solely on the recommendation of the village health nurse, making the scheme more accessible to marginalized women who may lack formal documentation. While the scheme does not involve provider networks, intermediaries, or a public-private mix, it promotes better nutrition and care during pregnancy, which in turn supports improved birth outcomes. The scheme continues to function as a vital source of support for economically disadvantaged pregnant women.

One of the most significant state-driven programs, *Janani Suraksha Yojana,* uses the conditional cash transfer mechanism to encourage reproductive and child healthcare service uptake. It is a flagship maternity benefit program aimed at BPL pregnant women, with a special focus on low-performing states, including the eight Empowered Action Group (EAG) states, Assam, Jammu & Kashmir, and the remaining Northeastern states. Under the scheme, expectant mothers receive a voucher and admission slip for delivery, which covers the mother's care package and transport assistance. The amount can be cashed directly at the hospital's counter at the time of discharge, ensuring immediate financial support. After childbirth, JSY encourages new mothers to visit healthcare facilities or Anganwadi centres for newborn immunization services. Women who avail these services are provided with additional financial benefits. Beneficiaries are also given a choice of providers, including accredited private healthcare facilities, with a norm of at least two accredited providers per block, selected as per defined protocols. On the supply side, ASHAs receive cash incentives to mobilize and support women for institutional deliveries. There are also proposals to introduce incentives for private providers to enhance participation. ASHAs play a pivotal role as intermediaries, guiding women through the process from registration to postnatal care. Under this initiative, cash assistance is linked to antenatal care during pregnancy, institutional delivery at healthcare facilities, and postnatal care, creating a structured system supported by field-level health workers.

Thus, JSY contributes to lower maternal and neonatal mortality by increasing the proportion of births attended by skilled professionals in healthcare facilities, which in turn reduces the burden on emergency care systems and improves long-term child development outcomes. These health gains extend beyond the immediate beneficiaries, enhancing public health at the community level, especially in regions where maternal and child health indicators have traditionally been poor. Moreover, the scheme strengthens the health system by encouraging regular ANC visits, timely referrals, and increased interaction with ASHAs, creating a culture of preventive health-seeking behaviour. This improved engagement with formal health systems leads to better vaccination coverage, birth registration, and health education, further benefiting the wider community. These systemic improvements and healthier mothers and children create positive societal and economic spillovers—a hallmark of positive externalities.

In 2011, the Government of India introduced the *Indira Gandhi Matritva Sahyog Yojana* (IGMSY), now implemented as PMMVY, to provide financial assistance of ₹4000 to pregnant women for their first two live births. The program aimed to offer partial wage compensation to pregnant women to ensure adequate rest before and after childbirth, support maternal health and nutrition, and improve health-seeking behaviour by directly depositing funds into the bank accounts of beneficiaries for using essential MCH services, including antenatal check-ups and immunizations. Women aged 19 and above were eligible to receive the benefit in three instalments upon meeting predefined conditions [11].

The *Rashtriya Swasthya Bima Yojana* (RSBY) was introduced to provide health insurance coverage to BPL families, with the aim of protecting them from catastrophic health expenditures. Under the scheme, each enrolled family received a smart card that entitled them to cashless hospitalization coverage of up to ₹ 30,000 per year at empanelled public and private hospitals. This card-based system allowed beneficiaries to access care without upfront payments, ensuring financial risk protection and increasing access to secondary healthcare services. The scheme was structured around a public-private partnership model, allowing beneficiaries a choice of providers across a wide network of accredited hospitals. It also generated positive externalities by encouraging the use of formal healthcare systems, which lead to early detection and treatment of illnesses, reducing the overall burden of disease in communities. While supply-side incentives for providers were embedded through fixed reimbursement packages, there were no direct payments to intermediaries. However, insurance companies acted as key players in implementation, and third-party administrators (TPAs) supported enrolment and claims processing. RSBY functioned as a stand-alone, consumer-led insurance initiative, empowering beneficiaries to make healthcare decisions while promoting competition and quality among providers.

Building on the foundation laid by RSBY and following the global call for Universal Health Coverage to ensure accessible, affordable, and equitable healthcare services for all, the Government of India launched the AB PM-JAY in 2018 as a tax-funded national health insurance program aimed at delivering accessible, affordable, and equitable healthcare to the most vulnerable populations.

Under the scheme, PM-JAY provides free and cashless secondary and tertiary inpatient care with an annual coverage limit of ₹500,000 per eligible family, targeting over 50 million low-income citizens. Beneficiaries have the freedom to choose between empanelled public and private hospitals, enhancing competition and responsiveness in service delivery. The scheme ensures provider reimbursement through a standardized case-based bundled payment system, which promotes efficiency and controls costs. The scheme has expanded the reach of health protection in India, reinforcing equity and financial risk protection as central pillars of national health policy [16]. Detailed information about the AB PM-JAY scheme can be found in Chap. 9.

10.5 Advantages of Demand-Side Financing

DSF has several advantages [15], such as:

- It positively impacts health outcomes by encouraging the utilization of specific healthcare goods and services.
- It offers choice to individuals to assess certified partners or service providers available to them and choose the facility based on service quality, lower transportation cost, and shorter distance.
- DSF allows multiple empanelled service providers to render services to the population in a specific geographical area. The option to choose from several facilities providing the same services increases competition among them, consequently improving service quality.
- It changes the health-seeking behaviour of individuals and families, especially those for whom the schemes are the most beneficial. Hence, DSF enhances targeting the right population efficiently.
- It reduces the financial burden of expenditure on specific healthcare services and non-medical costs associated with accessing them.

Activity Box 10.2

Case Reflection—Janani Suraksha Yojana (JSY), India

Scenario: The Indian government launched JSY, a conditional cash transfer scheme, to promote institutional deliveries among poor pregnant women. Eligible women receive cash incentives upon delivering at a public or accredited private facility.

Questions for Discussion:

1. What public health problem is JSY trying to solve?
2. How does a cash incentive change health-seeking behaviour?
3. What challenges might arise in ensuring equitable access under JSY?

10.6 Challenges of Demand-Side Financing

DSF schemes vary in their strategic framework and implementation, which makes it difficult to generalize the merits and demerits with certainty. Demand-side financing is mainly focused on breaking the barriers that prevent people from accessing healthcare facilities and utilizing services while also generating impactful and positive health outcomes. However, some concerns regarding DSF have been raised that need addressing for these schemes and programs to be effective among the target population [19]. The challenges of DSF are illustrated in Fig. 10.3.

10.6.1 Means-Test to Identify Target Groups Is a Key Challenge

A weak identification system to enrol eligible beneficiaries poses significant challenges, especially in densely populated regions. This creates scope for errors, mismanagement, and corruption. Without strict monitoring, there is a significant risk of mistargeting beneficiaries or fraudulent practices in benefit distribution [20]. For large-scale implementation, it is necessary to push the scope of these schemes beyond NGO-led initiatives. A professional infrastructure and skilled management personnel are required to deploy substantial financial and administrative operations successfully. This is particularly crucial in rural regions with limited human resources [17, 20]. Lack of awareness and difficulty in ascertaining eligibility for utilizing services to correctly identify the target groups can limit their enrolment in the programs.

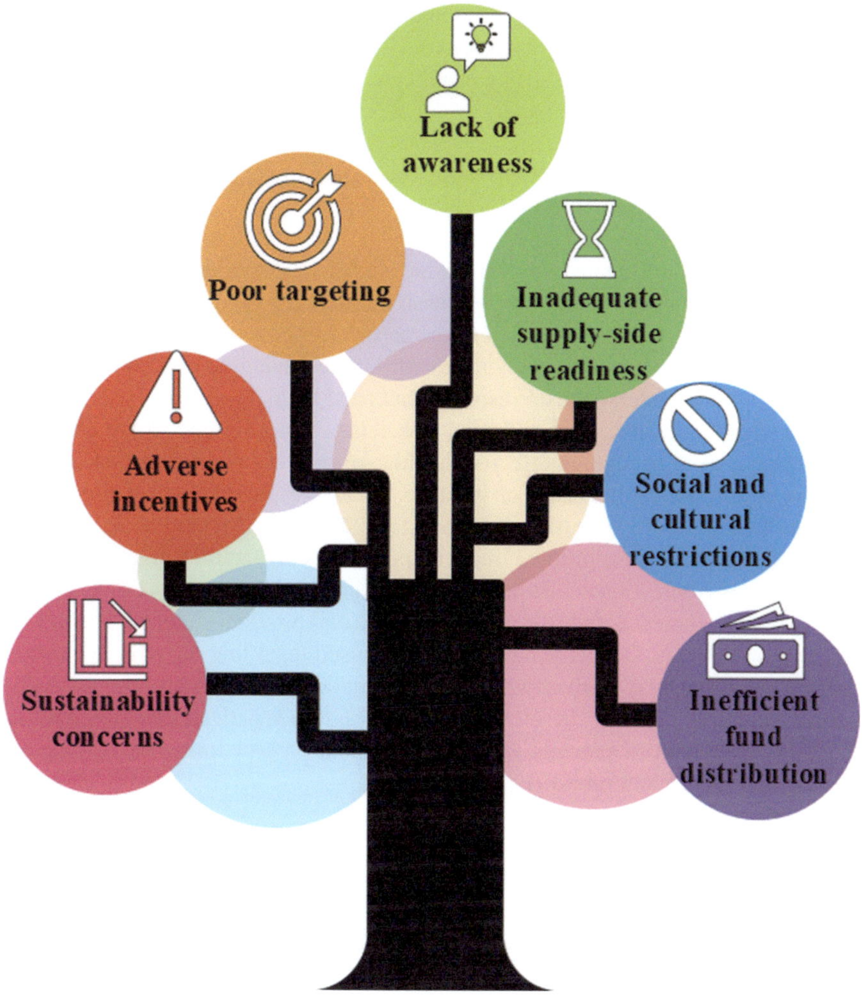

Fig. 10.3 Challenges of demand-side financing

10.6.2 Inadequate Readiness of Supply-Side Services

The most efficient way to run DSF schemes is to have a well-established service supply in place. Hence, supply-side infrastructure investments are crucial to have sufficient healthcare capacity to accommodate a surge in service utilization. For example, a sudden increase in voucher users can overwhelm healthcare facilities, while delays in provider reimbursements may lead some private participants to withdraw from the program. Additionally, a scarcity of trained medical personnel, especially obstetricians and gynaecologists, is still a major challenge in many regions [12]. A lack of quality services across both public and private healthcare sectors still persists [21]. If skilled healthcare providers are limited [22], especially in remote and rural locations, even competitive voucher-based schemes may not succeed in delivering high-quality services. Hence, it is important to recognize that even for the success of DSF, a strong healthcare infrastructure—usually built on the SSF— is an important prerequisite.

10.6.3 Adverse Incentives

DSF programs may create unintended incentives in provider payment models, which can lead to overutilization of services. Inefficient fund distribution, such as a surplus of allocated funds compared to the actual user costs of healthcare services, may encourage unnecessary expenditures while also having an opportunity cost in areas that have to underspend on resources but need them more. This is also known as an adverse incentive. Such financial imbalances not only encourage unethical practices but also discourage effective healthcare delivery and utilization in other regions with more challenges. For instance, excessive prescription of procedures like caesarean sections have often been pointed out as potential drawbacks [12]. For example, JSY includes additional financial provisions for facilities to cover caesarean deliveries where a specialist to manage emergency obstetric services is unavailable [23]. This increases the risk of moral hazard and provider-induced demand for a C-section delivery. Concerns have also been raised regarding the effectiveness of the scheme, which may inadvertently encourage undesired behaviours. Additionally, poorly structured provider-driven schemes can result in negative incentives, such as the mere enrolment of patients without subsequent care or follow-up, ultimately leading to high dropout rates [9].

10.6.4 Social and Cultural Attitudes

Being labelled as economically disadvantaged, cultural traditions surrounding childbirth, and deeply held beliefs about modesty and gender norms significantly influence participation in the schemes. In many communities, traditional family norms that require women to give birth in their maternal home challenge the possibility of institutional deliveries. Beyond financial constraints, personal attitudes and ingrained practices further restrict the utilization of healthcare services. The reluctance to seek institutional care is commonly observed in communities where traditional home births are the norm. As a result, even well-structured DSF schemes may prove less impactful given the failure to account for such socio-cultural factors.

In such areas where cultural beliefs significantly challenge positive healthcare-seeking behaviour, DSF programs alone may not be sufficient to improve health outcomes. In some regions, even when financial incentives are provided, women continue to prefer home deliveries due to traditional expectations, family pressures, and concerns about unfamiliar healthcare settings [11, 23]. To maximize the impact of DSF schemes, efforts must extend to include comprehensive community engagement, increased awareness programs, and proactive involvement of health workers and volunteers. By promoting health, educating families, addressing misconceptions, and ensuring that healthcare environments are welcoming and inclusive, demand generation for essential services can become a sustained and effective process [9].

10.6.5 Sustainability Concerns

DSF schemes require meticulous planning, a well-structured administrative and management framework, and diligent monitoring and evaluation of implementation to ensure the schemes function efficiently and meet their intended objectives. This necessitates a sustained investment in resources with a long-term commitment. A key challenge here is securing stable and uninterrupted financial support, which determines the long-term success or failure of these schemes. Therefore, aiming to implement or expand DSF models must comprise comprehensive financial planning to ensure that effective healthcare programs are not discontinued due to budgetary constraints or policy shifts [9].

10.6.6 Perceived Problems Related to Service Quality

Even when financial resources are available, the quality of healthcare services under DSF schemes is often questioned. Several factors contribute to dissatisfaction among beneficiaries, including long waiting times at healthcare facilities, inadequate service delivery, and instances of discrimination by healthcare staff [23]. In some cases, there is a social stigma associated with availing free or subsidized healthcare services, leading to hesitancy in utilizing them. Corruption at different levels of administration may further complicate access to benefits, with some beneficiaries facing bureaucratic hurdles while trying to claim their entitlements [10].

10.6.7 Delays in Provider Payments and Their Consequences

Another major challenge affecting DSF implementation is the delay in reimbursements to healthcare providers. Timely payments or reimbursements to hospitals and clinics is crucial to preventing compromised quality of services offered and from certified partners to withdraw from DSF programs altogether. This undermines the intended goal of increasing access to healthcare [9, 15].

10.6.8 Shortage of Competitive Service Providers

In regions where the healthcare service network is weak, the intended benefits of DSF models may not materialize as expected. While DSF aims to expand provider choices for beneficiaries, the effectiveness of this approach depends on the availability of multiple service providers.

10.6.9 Challenges of Narrowly Focused DSF Schemes

Some DSF schemes are designed to address specific health concerns, such as targeted programs for breast cancer screening or maternal health. While these focused interventions may successfully improve uptake in particular areas, they may not necessarily improve access to healthcare. A broader approach to DSF, integrating multiple services, may yield better long-term outcomes. For instance, if the ultimate goal is to reduce maternal and neonatal mortality, instead of focusing solely on institutional deliveries, a holistic approach that encompasses antenatal care, postnatal care, nutritional support, and broader maternal health interventions would be highly efficient [9].

10.7 Conclusion

In India, DSF was implemented to improve utilization and access to healthcare services, particularly for marginalized and vulnerable groups at risk of financial hardship. It strives to offset out-of-pocket OOP expenses, and provide financial protection, thus preventing poor families from sinking further into poverty while accessing healthcare. Although DSF schemes or programs demonstrate their effectiveness, their long-term sustainability remains a primary concern. For designed interventions to succeed, the key barriers to healthcare utilization need to be identified. Ensuring sustained financial investments, reasonable service quality from providers, and the existence of an adequate network of quality service providers are all crucial to a successful and efficient DSF scheme. Therefore, a thorough assessment necessitates technical outcome evaluation studies with properly designed controls to measure the effectiveness of DSF schemes with scenarios where it is not implemented yet. A strong health system with an efficient coverage framework, coupled with socio-economic progress such as improved education and employment rates, has a high potential to be the most cost-effective strategy for improving healthcare utilization rates among the poor in the long term.

References

1. World Health Organization. The world health report 2000: health systems: improving performance. World Health Organization; 2000. 244 p.
2. Ministry of Health and Family Welfare, Government of India. National Health Authority 2020–21 report [Internet]. [cited 2025 Feb 25]. Available from: https://mohfw.gov.in/sites/default/files/NHA%202020-21_up.pdf.
3. Koy S, Fuerst F, Tuot B, Starke M, Flessa S. The flipped break-even: re-balancing demand- and supply-side financing of health centers in Cambodia. Int J Environ Res Public Health. 2023;20(2):1228. https://doi.org/10.3390/ijerph20021228.
4. Ensor T, Cooper S. Overcoming barriers to health service access: influencing the demand side. Health Policy Plan. 2004;19(2):69–79.
5. Hunter BM, Murray SF. Demand-side financing for maternal and newborn health: what do we know about factors that affect implementation of cash transfers and voucher programmes? BMC Pregnancy Childbirth. 2017;17(1):262. https://doi.org/10.1186/s12884-017-1445-y.

6. Lagarde M, Palmer N. The impact of user fees on access to health services in low- and middle-income countries. Cochrane Database Syst Rev. 2011;2011(4):CD009094. https://doi.org/10.1002/14651858.CD009094.
7. Shamanna B, Murthy G, Ravilla T, Jones I. Demand-side financing: can it help deliver eye care for all? Community Eye Health. 2022;35(115):27–8.
8. Witter S, Fretheim A, Kessy FL, Lindahl AK. Paying for performance to improve the delivery of health interventions in low- and middle-income countries. Cochrane Database Syst Rev. 2021;5:CD007899. https://doi.org/10.1002/14651858.CD007899.
9. Gupta I, Joe W, Rudra S. Demand-side financing in health: how far can it address the issue of low utilization in developing countries? [Internet]. World Health Report (2010) Background Paper, No. 27. Geneva: World Health Organization; 2010. [cited 2025 Apr 10]. Available from: https://cdn.who.int/media/docs/default-source/health-financing/whr-2010-background-paper-27.pdf.
10. Gopalan SS, Das A, Mutasa R. What makes health demand-side financing schemes work in low-and middle-income countries? A realist review. J Public Health Res. 2014;3(3). https://doi.org/10.4081/jphr.2014.304.
11. Acharya A, McNamee P. Assessing Gujarat's "Chiranjeevi" scheme. Econ Polit Wkly. 2009;44(48):13–5.
12. Puri R. Three essays on demand-side health policies in India. 2020. Dissertations – ALL.1260. Available from: https://surface.syr.edu/etd/1260.
13. Kiplagat S, Coudray MS, Ravi K, Jayakrishna P, Krupp K, Arun A, et al. Evaluating a conditional cash transfer scheme in a maternal health care utilization program among rural pregnant women in Mysore District, India. Womens Health Rep [New Rochelle]. 2020;1(1):159–66.
14. Director DM. DBT | Direct Benefit Transfer. [cited 2025 Feb 24]. About Us | [DBT]. Direct benefit transfer. Available from: https://dbtbharat.gov.in/static-page-content/spagecont?id=1.
15. Ensor T, Tiwari S. Demand-side financing in health in low-resource settings. In: World Scientific Series in Global Health Economics and Public Policy [Internet]. World Scientific; 2020 [cited 2025 Feb 17]. p. 217–37. Available from: https://www.worldscientific.com/doi/abs/10.1142/9789813272378_0008.
16. National Health Authority. PM-JAY: Pradhan Mantri Jan Arogya Yojana (PM-JAY). 2021 [cited 2025 Feb 18]. Available from: https://pmjay.gov.in/.
17. Kurian OC. Financing healthcare for all in India: towards a common goal. Oxfam India; 2015. [cited 2025 Feb 18]. Available from: https://www.oxfamindia.org/sites/default/files/WP-Financing-Healthcare-for-All-In-India-29-05-2015-EN_0.pdf.
18. Ensor T. Consumer-led demand side financing in health and education and its relevance for low and middle income countries. Int J Health Plann Manag. 2004;19(3):267–85.
19. Powell-Jackson T, Morrison J, Tiwari S, Neupane BD, Costello AM. The experiences of districts in implementing a national incentive programme to promote safe delivery in Nepal. BMC Health Serv Res. 2009;9(1):97.
20. Government of India. Managing human resources for health in India: a case study of Madhya Pradesh and Gujarat. New Delhi: Central Bureau of Health Intelligence, Directorate General of Health services, Ministry of Health & Family Welfare, Nirman Bhawan; 2007.
21. Government of India. Jharkhand Mukhyamantri Maiya Samman Yojana. [Internet]. [cited 2025 Feb 25]. Available from: https://www.myscheme.gov.in/hi/schemes/jmmsy.
22. Gujarat Government. Chiranjeevi Yojana. [Internet]. [cited 2025 Feb 25]. Available from: https://gujhealth.gujarat.gov.in/images/pdf/chiranjeevi-yojana-details.pdf.
23. Carvalho N, Rokicki S. The impact of India's Janani Suraksha Yojana conditional cash transfer programme: a replication study. J Dev Stud. 2019;55(5):989–1006.

Value-Based Care in Health Insurance: Concepts, Need, and Application

11

Gaurav Jyani and Shankar Prinja

Abstract

This chapter explores the paradigm shift from volume-based to value-based healthcare delivery, emphasizing its significance within the Indian health insurance sector. It delineates the core principles of value-based care (VBC), which aims to enhance health outcomes while optimizing healthcare costs. By shifting the emphasis toward patient-centric care, VBC seeks to enhance efficiency, quality, and responsiveness in healthcare delivery. A key aspect of VBC is the alignment of incentives among healthcare providers, payers, and policymakers to encourage high-quality care. This requires robust performance metrics and outcome-based reimbursement mechanisms. The adoption of health technology also plays an important role in enabling VBC. Digital health interventions, including telemedicine and electronic health records (EHRs), facilitate real-time monitoring and enhance care coordination. The integration of such technologies is essential for tracking patient outcomes and ensuring accountability in healthcare delivery.

Despite its potential benefits, the implementation of VBC in India faces several challenges. These include infrastructural gaps, limited data interoperability, provider resistance, and the need for standardized quality metrics. Addressing these challenges requires policy interventions, capacity building, and stakeholder collaboration to create a conducive environment for VBC adoption. Recent policy initiatives, such as Ayushman Bharat Pradhan Mantri Jan Arogya Yojana, provide an opportunity to incorporate value-based principles into India's health insurance framework.

G. Jyani · S. Prinja (✉)
Department of Community Medicine and School of Public Health, Post Graduate Institute of Medical Education and Research (PGIMER), Chandigarh, India

S. Prinja (ed.), *Healthcare Financing and Insurance*,
https://doi.org/10.1007/978-981-95-3513-2_11

Keywords

Value-based care · Patient responsiveness · Outcome-based indicators · Value-based healthcare · Performance-based indicators

Learning Objectives

After reading this chapter, you will be able to:

- Understand the concept of value-based care (VBC) and its significance in the Indian health insurance sector.
- Analyze the limitations of traditional provider payment models and the need for a shift toward outcome-driven healthcare financing.
- Examine the role of health technology, including telemedicine and electronic health records (EHRs) in facilitating VBC implementation.
- Identify key challenges in adopting VBC in India.
- Understand the impact of recent policy initiatives of the government of India on promoting value-based reimbursement mechanisms.
- Assess the role of stakeholder collaboration, including insurers, providers, and policymakers, in driving the transition toward a VBC model.
- Develop recommendations for integrating VBC principles into India's health insurance framework to improve healthcare quality and cost efficiency.

Key Terms

1. *Ambulatory Care Sensitive Hospitalizations:* Hospital admissions that could be avoided with effective primary and community care. These are used as an indicator of care quality and system efficiency within value-based care models.
2. *Ayushman Bharat Health Account (ABHA) ID:* A unique digital identifier linking a beneficiary's health records across providers, improving continuity of care and supporting data-driven outcome tracking.
3. *Beneficiary Satisfaction Rate:* An indicator capturing patients' satisfaction with the healthcare experience and system responsiveness. In value-based care, it is used as a patient-centered measure for assessing healthcare provider performance.
4. *Catastrophic Health Expenditure (CHE):* Health spending that is so high relative to a household's income that it pushes the family into financial distress. Reducing CHE is a key goal of value-based and universal coverage reforms.

5. *Complaint/Grievance Rate:* The number of confirmed complaints raised by insurance beneficiaries against healthcare providers. It reflects problems with service quality, communication, or rights, and is used as a negative performance indicator in value-based care linked incentives.
6. *Continuum of Care:* An approach that covers the entire healthcare pathway, from prevention and diagnosis to treatment, rehabilitation, and palliation. Value-based care emphasizes that the focus should be on continuum rather than isolated episodes, as total value depends on outcomes across this full cycle.
7. *Convergence of Risk Pools:* The integration or coordination of multiple health financing schemes into a unified or harmonized system. This supports value-based care by enabling more consistent benefits, stronger bargaining power, and more equitable resource allocation.
8. *Volume-Based Care:* A payment approach that reimburses providers on the basis of number of services delivered or number of patients treated. It tends to incentivize higher volume rather than focusing on improved health outcomes.
9. *Health Benefit Package (HBP):* The defined set of services covered under a scheme like PM-JAY, with inclusion based on population needs, value, and financial protection goals.
10. *Health Financing and Technology Assessment (HeFTA) Unit:* A specialized unit in the National Health Authority that applies economic evidence to pricing, benefit design, and valuc-based purchasing decisions.
11. *Hospital Readmission Rate:* The proportion of patients readmitted within a specified period (e.g., 30 days) after discharge for related conditions for which the patient had received treatment. It serves as a proxy for quality of care and is frequently used as a performance indicator in value-based care.
12. *Outcome-Based Indicators:* Metrics that reflect the results of healthcare/treatment, such as reduced mortality, improved health-related quality of life, or fewer complications, rather than just processes (e.g., guideline adherence). They form the backbone of outcome-linked payments in value-based care models.
13. *Patient-Reported Outcome Measures (PROMs):* PROMs are standardized tools through which patients directly report their health status, symptoms, functional ability, and health-related quality of life without interpretation by lab tests or clinicians. They capture outcomes that matter most to patients, such as pain, mobility, daily functioning, and emotional well-being, and are essential in value-based care because they enable evaluation of the real-world impact of healthcare on patient's lives.

14. *Performance-Based Incentives / Outcome-Based Incentives:* Financial rewards provided to healthcare providers based on their performance relative to predefined quality or outcome indicators, such as lower readmission rates, reduced out-of-pocket expenditure for patients, higher patient satisfaction, or improved health-related quality of life. These incentives align provider behavior with the goals of value-based care by directly linking payment to the delivery of high-value results.
15. *Value-Based Care (VBC):* A healthcare delivery and financing approach where providers are rewarded based on the value of care delivered, measured in terms of health outcomes relative to costs rather than the sheer volume of services provided. It aims to improve quality, efficiency, and patient-centeredness.

11.1 What Is Value-Based Care?

India has pledged to attain universal health coverage (UHC) by 2030, viewing it as a cornerstone for achieving broader sustainable development goals (SDGs) objectives [1–3]. In a significant move toward this goal, India introduced Ayushman Bharat Pradhan Mantri Jan Arogya Yojana (AB PM-JAY) in 2018, the world's largest government-financed health insurance initiative [4]. As an important component of the Ayushman Bharat program, this scheme was designed to accelerate India's progress toward UHC. The broader vision behind these efforts is to ensure universal access to affordable, high-quality, and equitable healthcare that is both responsive and accountable to the needs of the population. Ayushman Bharat adopts a comprehensive approach by integrating preventive healthcare through Health and Wellness Centers (HWCs) with curative services under PM-JAY, thereby laying the groundwork for a "value-based care" model.

Historically, from a payer's standpoint, healthcare financing has largely been centered on the volume of services rendered, with providers receiving payments according to service quantity. However, across the globe, there is a gradual transition evident toward value-based care, wherein provider reimbursements are linked to treatment outcomes rather than only the service volume [5]. To align with this evolving paradigm, the payment structure of Indian health insurance must also adapt to a system that prioritizes value over volume. By fostering cost-effective care delivery, value-based healthcare ultimately serves the most important stakeholder in the Indian healthcare landscape—the patient.

Value-based care represents a proactive approach to enhancing care quality and patient outcomes by implementing standardized healthcare practices. Under this model, healthcare providers—including hospitals and physicians—are compensated based on the improvements in health among patients treated, rather than the number of services provided (Fig. 11.1). By incentivizing providers to enhance patient health, this approach contributes to long-term reductions in disease burden across the population. The value-based care model rewards providers based on the "value" of care delivered, measured in terms of health benefits generated. Consequently, this model encourages healthcare professionals to prioritize service quality over quantity. In a broader sense, "value" in healthcare can be conceptualized as the overall contribution of the health system to societal well-being.

In addition to the commonly recognized dimensions of value-based care, such as incentivizing outcomes over volume, enhancing patient-centeredness, and improving system efficiency, there are two important dimensions that also hold particular relevance for health insurance systems: the convergence of risk pools to reduce fragmentation and the application of value-based pricing for drugs and medical devices. **First**, the consolidation of risk pools refers to integrating multiple fragmented insurance schemes into a unified or better-coordinated system. Fragmentation of risk pools, whether across public and private schemes, central and state programs, or among different occupational groups, often leads to inefficiencies, inequities in access, and suboptimal purchasing power. By converging risk pools, the system can enhance financial protection, reduce administrative redundancies, and promote more strategic purchasing by leveraging economies of scale. This convergence supports the core principles of value-based care by enabling more equitable and efficient resource allocation across population groups.

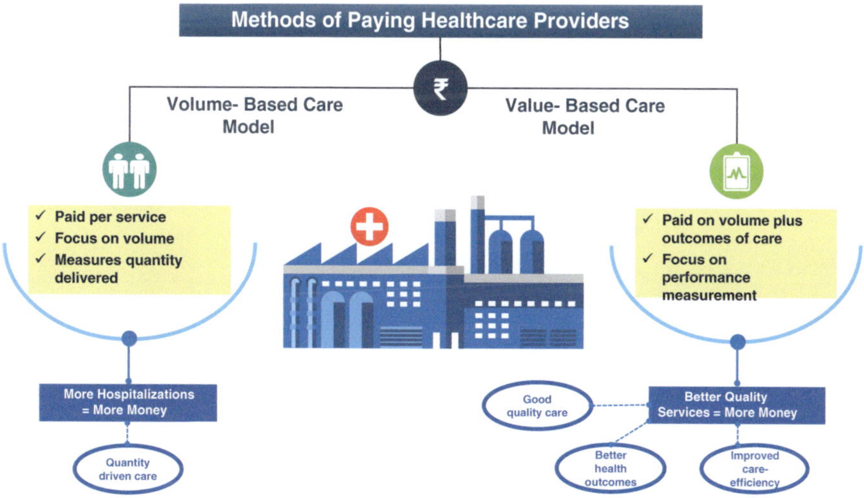

Fig. 11.1 Volume-based and Value-based models for paying healthcare providers

Second, value-based pricing of health technologies, particularly pharmaceuticals and medical devices, ensures that prices reflect the actual health outcomes or therapeutic benefits these products deliver, rather than being solely based on production costs or market dynamics [6]. By linking the price of a drug or device to its clinical effectiveness and impact on quality of life, value-based pricing promotes affordability, cost-effectiveness, and innovation that truly aligns with patient needs. Together, these two dimensions extend the scope of value-based care beyond service delivery, embedding it more deeply into the structural and financial design of health insurance systems.

The advantages of value-based care extend across multiple stakeholders, including patients, healthcare providers, payers, suppliers, and society as a whole (Fig. 11.12). **Patients** experience improved health outcomes and higher satisfaction with the care they receive, while providers benefit from enhanced care efficiencies [7]. **Payers**, in turn, achieve greater value for their healthcare expenditures and gain stronger mechanisms for cost control. A healthier population with reduced healthcare utilization results in lower financial strain on insurance premium reserves and investments. Meanwhile, **suppliers** can align their products and services with positive patient outcomes and cost-efficiency by reducing complications and keeping the population healthy. Ultimately, from a societal perspective, value-based healthcare holds the potential to drive substantial overall health gains.

The pursuit of value-based care (VBC) in health insurance can be operationalized at two stages of any health program or health technology: ***the design stage*** and ***the implementation stage***. At the design stage, value can be embedded by applying the principles of *health technology assessment (HTA)* and *value-based pricing*, which enables evidence-informed decisions about the inclusion of interventions based on their cost-effectiveness, equity implications, and budgetary impact (details

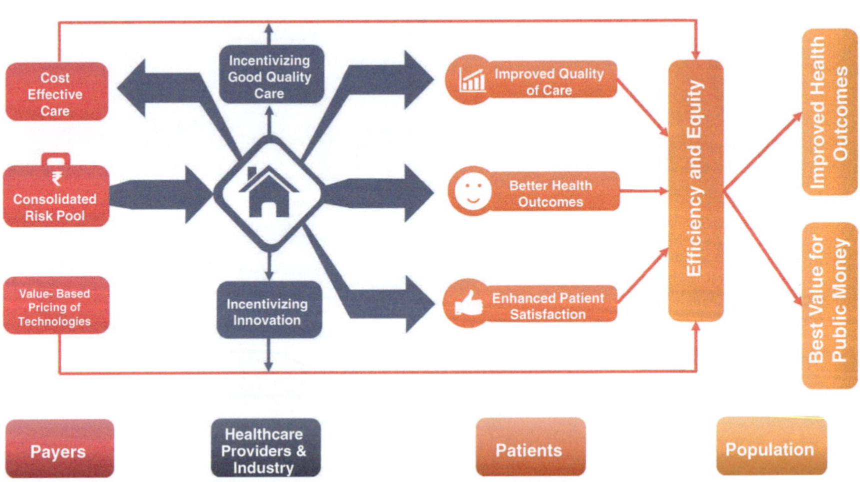

Fig. 11.2 Advantages of value-based care model to different stakeholders

are discussed in Chap. 6 on the use of HTA for strategic purchasing of healthcare services) [8]. Additionally, incorporating a *continuum of care* approach ensures that services are designed to address patient needs across the entire care pathway, from prevention and diagnosis to treatment, rehabilitation, and palliation, thereby improving outcomes and reducing unnecessary costs. *Strategic purchasing*, another key design principle, allows payers to actively decide what services to buy, from whom, and at what price, aligning financial flows with desired health outcomes and system priorities (details are discussed in Chap. 4 on strategic purchasing). At the implementation stage, the realization of value-based care depends on the adoption of appropriate *provider payment mechanisms*. The details of these different methods are provided in the chapter on setting provider payment methods and pricing (Chap. 5). This chapter describes how embedding value-based principles in payment structures helps incentivize providers to deliver care that improves patient outcomes, enhances satisfaction, and ensures efficient use of resources. Together, these design and implementation strategies create a cohesive framework that aligns policy intent with frontline practice, thereby advancing the goals of value-based care within health insurance systems.

11.2 Interpreting the "Value" in Value-Based Care

The concept of value in a healthcare system is multifaceted and can be interpreted from various perspectives, including those of payers (such as governments, insurers, and individuals), clinicians, the healthcare industry, caregivers, and, most importantly, patients. Definitions of value differ, with some emphasizing ethical and moral principles, while others focus on economic dimensions [9]. For instance, Porter conceptualizes value as the difference between the health outcomes achieved and the financial resources expended [10]. Similarly, Gray defines healthcare value as the net benefit derived by weighing the positive effects of a service against potential harms, considering the resources invested [11].

The growing recognition that healthcare should focus on value, rather than merely the effectiveness of interventions, underscores the need to assess improvements in health outcomes in relation to the cost incurred to achieve them. It is essential to emphasize that value-based healthcare integrates multiple elements, including enhancements in care quality, patient satisfaction, and cost-efficiency. To truly maximize healthcare value, these components must be considered collectively, as no single metric fully encapsulates the comprehensive notion of value in healthcare.

In the framework of value-based care, value extends beyond the quality of healthcare services alone. Quality is often assessed based on adherence to clinical guidelines and process compliance, which, while important, may not always translate into better patient outcomes. Whereas the healthcare sector acknowledges that quality care is important for patient well-being and financial sustainability, nonetheless, studies indicate that improvements in quality processes do not always lead to superior health outcomes [12]. Even when clinical protocols are consistently followed, patient outcomes may vary across different healthcare teams. Additionally, the administrative burden of tracking and reporting compliance metrics can sometimes divert providers' focus from the ultimate goal—enhancing patient health. For instance, an analysis of diabetes care in Italy revealed that while process compliance was higher in northern regions, better health outcomes were observed in southern Italy [12]. This underscores the need for providers to not only adhere to evidence-based guidelines but also prioritize the health outcomes that are most meaningful to patients.

In the context of PM-JAY also, the primary objective of the scheme is to enhance population health, with a core focus on improving patient outcomes. The improvement in patient outcomes can be measured through reduced mortality and enhanced health-related quality of life (HRQoL) [13]. In recent years, the shift toward patient-centered medical care has led to the growing adoption of patient-reported outcome measures (PROMs) to assess HRQoL [14]. However, while designing a value-based care model, we must understand that short-term HRQoL improvements alone may not provide a complete representation of value, as temporary symptomatic relief may not indicate long-term health benefits. Similarly, defining value solely through patient satisfaction may be inadequate. While patient satisfaction initiatives have rightly emphasized the importance of treating individuals with dignity and respect, the fundamental aim of healthcare is to improve health outcomes.

Furthermore, since value is realized only when a patient's health improves, any characterization of value-based care that focuses exclusively on cost containment is incomplete. The true essence of value-based care lies in improving health outcomes relative to the cost of care, a goal shared by stakeholders across the healthcare system. Critics who argue that value-based care reduces healthcare to an industrial model centered on cost-cutting, misinterpret its core intent [15]. Rather than prioritizing financial efficiency at the expense of care quality, value-based care aligns clinical practices with patient-centered goals. By systematically measuring health outcomes, this model fosters continuous improvements in patient care while also reducing unnecessary healthcare expenditures. Improved health outcomes also contribute to cost savings by mitigating disease progression and reducing the need for extensive medical interventions. For example, a diabetes patient who avoids complications such as kidney failure, blindness, or neuropathy due to effective disease management will require significantly less healthcare expenditure over time compared to a patient whose condition deteriorates.

It is also worth emphasizing here that healthcare systems create value by delivering both health-related benefits (such as improved HRQoL) and nonhealth benefits (such as financial protection and cost-efficiency). While these benefits contribute to overall societal well-being, they must be assessed in relation to the resources utilized [16]. Consequently, most frameworks for evaluating healthcare value consider the ratio of achieved health outcomes to the corresponding costs. It is important to adopt a comprehensive perspective on value and ensure precise identification and measurement of its components. A transparent and holistic approach to value-based care will enable healthcare systems to allocate resources efficiently and maximize patient benefits.

Insights from global healthcare systems indicate that competition among providers should shift toward value-driven competition, where healthcare institutions strive to achieve the best patient outcomes relative to costs [5, 17]. Rather than focusing solely on discrete treatments, providers must consider the entire continuum of care, as the cumulative health outcomes of a complete care cycle ultimately define the value delivered to patients. This strategic shift, referred to as the "value agenda"—as conceptualized by Michael Porter and Elizabeth Teisberg—aims to transform fragmented, supply-driven healthcare systems into outcome-focused models [5, 18, 19]. Porter and Teisberg's "value agenda" outlines six key components, which insurers, such as PM-JAY in the Indian context should implement. These six components include the following:

1. Organizing healthcare services around medical conditions rather than provider expertise or facility types.
2. Systematic assessment of patient-level outcomes and associated costs.
3. Implementing performance-based payment models for complete care cycles, replacing conventional volume-driven reimbursement systems.
4. Establishing integrated care delivery networks with clearly defined service scopes.
5. Expanding geographic accessibility, particularly for specialized providers, and fostering collaborations with satellite facilities for broader service delivery.
6. Developing robust information technology platforms to facilitate multidisciplinary, coordinated care across various locations and healthcare services.

11.3 Potential Avenues for Infusing "Value" in the Provision of Healthcare: Framework for India's Health Insurance Paradigm

This section of the chapter will explore in detail how various components of value-based care can be integrated into the structure and operation of a health insurance scheme, and we will try to understand it from the perspective of an insurer within the context of India's national health insurance program. We know that the National Health Authority (NHA), implementing agency of the PM-JAY, as the principal custodian of patient welfare, plays a pivotal role in defining the concept of value within its policies. The interpretation of value within PM-JAY should be anchored in the ultimate health outcomes achieved at the population level, rather than only being confined to intermediate markers such as procedural adherence or operational benchmarks. For an insurer, a significant challenge in defining value lies in the process through which consensus is reached. While the perspectives of citizens and patients should be central in determining how healthcare contributes to overall well-being, incorporating these viewpoints into a concrete value framework necessitates extensive stakeholder engagement. Once a consensus on value is achieved, the insurer must undertake a comprehensive set of actions to align the health system with these defined principles. PM-JAY has taken various steps in embedding value into healthcare delivery. These efforts can be analyzed through the lens of the value agenda outlined in the preceding discussion:

1. *Reorienting Healthcare Delivery Around Medical Conditions Rather than Infrastructure and Skills*: To operationalize Porter and Teisberg's first element of the value agenda, PM-JAY seeks to shift the focus of healthcare delivery from isolated facilities and provider-driven services toward organizing care around patient needs and specific medical conditions. In the Indian context, this reorientation can be advanced through multiple strategies including strengthening comprehensive primary health care (CPHC), adopting bundled payment models, prioritizing services for the most vulnerable populations, and covering high-burden conditions that often lead to catastrophic spending. Together, these elements reflect PM-JAY's intent to move beyond traditional infrastructure-centric care toward a value-driven, integrated continuum of services. PM-JAY adopts a continuum-of-care approach that comprises two interconnected components: first, the establishment of Health and Wellness Centres (HWCs) to bring healthcare closer to communities by offering CPHC, covering maternal and child health services as well as noncommunicable diseases, inclusive of free essential medications and diagnostic services; and second, the provision of financial protection through PM-JAY for economically disadvantaged families requiring secondary and tertiary care [20]. In terms of provider payment mechanisms, PM-JAY employs a case-based bundled pricing model, wherein healthcare providers receive a predetermined rate for a set of services included within specific health benefit packages (HBP) [21]. Case-based bundled payment system is a form of payment method that is considered an effective way to increase both technical and allocative efficiency, as well as create more accountable systems in the purchaser-provider relationship [22]. Further details of all the provider payment methods are provided in the chapter on Setting Provider Payment and Pricing (Chap. 5) and in the chapter on Government- Funded Health Insurance Schemes in India (Chap. 9).

   Additionally, PM-JAY is designed to target the most socioeconomically vulnerable 40% of India's population, thereby promoting equity in healthcare access. By covering diseases with the highest potential to drive catastrophic out-of-pocket (OOP) expenditures, PM-JAY seeks to fulfill its dual mandate of financial risk protection and improved health outcomes for the population, aspiring to accommodate the principles of "value" in the delivery of healthcare.

2. *Comprehensive Measurement of Health Outcomes and Costs at the Patient Level*: To ensure optimal utilization of financial resources, the NHA has established the Health Financing and Technology Assessment (HeFTA) unit, which applies health technology assessment (HTA) principles to evaluate interventions in terms of costs and health benefits [23]. The details of the application of principles of HTA in PM-JAY have been described in the chapter on Use of HTA for Strategic Purchasing of Healthcare Services (Chap. 6). The HeFTA unit aims to enhance healthcare accessibility, strengthen financial protection, and reduce

health disparities by facilitating evidence-based priority setting at both national and state levels. Specifically, this unit guides the inclusion and exclusion of interventions in the HBP by leveraging cost-effectiveness data, determines appropriate pricing for new technologies proposed for inclusion, and employs threshold price analysis to set value-based ceiling prices [21, 23]. Recognizing the indispensable role of cost evidence in pricing decisions, HeFTA is establishing a dynamic price discovery mechanism for HBPs, complemented by market price assessments of HBP components [24].

HBP pricing in PM-JAY is determined through a combination of existing package rates in other publicly funded insurance schemes, cost evidence from healthcare studies in India (such as the Cost of Health Services in India- CHSI study), and consultations with key stakeholders—including professional associations, specialist societies, hospital representatives, the Association of Healthcare Providers, and industry bodies like FICCI [25]. Furthermore, economic evidence generated by HeFTA helps inform the development of standard treatment guidelines (STGs), ensuring that clinical protocols are aligned with cost-effectiveness and health outcome considerations. By incentivizing adherence to STGs and quality assurance indicators, PM-JAY aims to enhance the quality of care and promote value-driven healthcare delivery [8]. Additionally, the program is instituting quality cells and checklists to provide both supervisory and supportive roles, helping providers elevate their care standards.

3. *Transitioning Towards Performance-Based Payments for Care Cycles*: Under PM-JAY, reimbursement structures are progressively evolving from broad uniform rates to more nuanced, value-based pricing mechanisms. The HBP 2022 introduced differential pricing, which accounts for hospital location (urban vs. rural) and level of specialization (secondary vs. tertiary), recognizing their impact on resource consumption and cost [26].

   Additionally, PM-JAY envisions the introduction of value-based incentives for providers, ensuring that payments are aligned not only with service provision but also with tangible health improvements [27]. This shift represents a fundamental transformation in the reimbursement model, moving beyond mere service delivery to rewarding demonstrable health gains. The NHA has introduced a value-based care policy under the PM-JAY [27]. This policy seeks to facilitate the integration of a value-based care framework within PM-JAY by establishing mechanisms that link provider incentives to the quality of services delivered. The proposed incentive structure is designed to reward healthcare providers based on specific, patient-centered performance metrics. These measurable indicators encompass factors such as beneficiary satisfaction rate, hospital readmission rates, out-of-pocket (OOP) expenditures borne by patients, the volume of validated grievances against empaneled healthcare providers (EHCPs), and improvements in the beneficiaries' health-related quality of life because of the treatment. As global health systems continue to shift toward value-oriented care models, this initiative reflects an effort to create a more patient-centric and outcomes-driven healthcare environment for PM-JAY beneficiaries.

4. *Integrating Care Delivery Systems by Defining Service Scope*: The NHA should implement a continuum of care approach, which is structured around two interrelated components. First, the establishment and strengthening of HWCs should be there as it aims to bring healthcare services closer to communities by providing CPHC, encompassing maternal and child health services, management of noncommunicable diseases, and access to essential medications and diagnostic services. Second, PM-JAY should further extend financial protection to economically disadvantaged families, covering a greater number of households and an increased number of secondary and tertiary healthcare services.

   At the community level, this initiative seeks to enhance beneficiary support by utilizing HWCs for patient identification, telemedicine consultations with specialists, referrals to higher-level care facilities, transportation facilitation, and posthospitalization follow-ups. For instance, postdischarge care can be delivered through HWCs or home-based settings. The integration of these services is facilitated through digital health linkages, streamlined care pathways, and the implementation of Ayushman Bharat Health Account (ABHA) IDs to ensure portability of health records. Additionally, training and sensitization of healthcare personnel at various system levels will empower patients with greater autonomy in selecting their healthcare providers. Furthermore, the design of HBPs has been refined to include follow-up and day-care service packages, thereby improving continuity of care. The availability of follow-up services enhances treatment adherence, mitigates complications, and reduces the likelihood of hospital readmissions. Such provisions have been incorporated into specialties including cardiology, cardiothoracic and vascular surgery, and urology. In addition to it, there should be avoidance of ambulatory care-sensitive hospitalizations, which increase the efficiency of the health system and contribute to VBC.

5. *Expanding the Geographic Reach of Healthcare Providers*: PM-JAY's pricing structure is designed to account for regional cost variations while simultaneously incentivizing healthcare service provision in underserved areas. It has been done with the aim of channeling investments into public health infrastructure, offering financial incentives to private providers willing to operate in underserved regions, and adopting differential pricing strategies based on city tiers and levels of care. For example, healthcare facilities empaneled under PM-JAY in aspirational districts are eligible for a 10% bonus on the standard package rates, helping to ensure equitable remuneration for providers working in these challenging contexts [28, 29]. Additionally, the Government of India has introduced a viability gap funding (VGF) scheme to support public-private partnerships in healthcare infrastructure development [7, 13, 30]. Through this initiative, the government offers subsidies to make socially important projects financially feasible. The scheme prioritizes investment in Aspirational Districts and encourages private sector participation in Tier 2 and Tier 3 cities to broaden access to healthcare services. By promoting the establishment of hospitals in areas with limited or no PM-JAY empanelment, the initiative aims to expand the network of service providers. This enables insurers to engage a wider range of healthcare facilities and thereby ensure that services reach marginalized and remote populations.

6. *Developing a Robust Digital Health Infrastructure for Integrated, Multidisciplinary Care*: A fundamental component of India's healthcare digitization strategy is the Ayushman Bharat Digital Mission (ABDM), which aims to create an integrated digital health ecosystem [31]. This initiative seeks to bridge existing gaps among healthcare stakeholders by leveraging digital infrastructure to enhance accessibility, ensure continuity of care, and empower citizens as primary custodians of their health data. ABDM is designed to support a holistic, IT-enabled approach to healthcare delivery, aligning with India's broader efforts to establish a citizen-centric, technology-driven health system.

   ABDM intends to develop a cutting-edge digital health system for managing core healthcare data and facilitating its seamless exchange. India's existing digital infrastructure—including Aadhaar, Unified Payments Interface (UPI), and extensive mobile and internet penetration—serves as a strong foundation for ABDM's implementation. The initiative leverages digital identification for individuals, healthcare professionals, and facilities; facilitates electronic transactions and signatures; and enables secure storage of medical records, thereby enhancing efficiency in healthcare management. The implementation of ABDM is expected to enhance efficiency, transparency, and effectiveness in healthcare service delivery. Patients will benefit from secure access to their medical records, including prescriptions, diagnostic reports, and discharge summaries, which can be shared with providers to ensure continuity of care. Additionally, ABDM will empower individuals with reliable information regarding healthcare facilities and providers, facilitate remote healthcare services such as telemedicine and e-pharmacy, and enable informed decision-making.

   Healthcare professionals will gain improved access to patient medical histories—contingent on informed consent—allowing for more precise and effective treatment planning. The integrated digital ecosystem will enhance coordination between healthcare providers, fostering a seamless continuum of care. Furthermore, ABDM will streamline the claims process, enabling faster reimbursements and reducing administrative burdens for healthcare providers. From a policymaking perspective, ABDM will facilitate data-driven decision-making, offering access to high-quality micro- and macro-level healthcare data. Advanced analytics, population health monitoring, and predictive modeling will support the development and refinement of health programs and policies. Additionally, researchers will have access to aggregated datasets, allowing for in-depth evaluations of healthcare interventions and enabling an evidence-based feedback loop between researchers, policymakers, and healthcare providers.

11.4 Need for Enhancing Value-Based Care in India's Publicly Funded Health Insurance Schemes

Healthcare systems worldwide have long sought to maximize value within their available resources. The urgency of this pursuit has been amplified by various factors, including population aging, the rising prevalence of complex morbidities, rapid advancements in health technology, increasing public expectations, and escalating healthcare expenditures. India is no exception, facing a "triple burden" of disease—comprising a growing incidence of noncommunicable diseases (NCDs), the unfinished agenda of communicable disease control, and emerging health challenges linked to climate change [32–34]. In 2017 alone, NCDs accounted for approximately 4.7 million deaths (49% of all-cause mortality) in India [35]. Communicable diseases contributed to 27.5% of total deaths, as per the Global Burden of Disease Study [32].

Compounding this health burden is the significant reliance on out-of-pocket expenditure (OOPE), which comprises nearly half of the total health spending in India [36]. This combination of high disease burden, limited public health investment, and inadequate protection against catastrophic health expenditure (CHE) presents significant risks. Annually, an estimated 32–39 million individuals in India are pushed into poverty due to healthcare expenses [37]. Against this backdrop, integrating concepts such as value-based healthcare, cost-effectiveness, patient-reported outcomes, and patient-centered responsiveness has become imperative to ensure a more efficient, structured, and responsive health system that effectively meets population health needs.

It is worth noting that for decades, healthcare systems in low- and middle-income countries (LMICs) have focused primarily on expanding access to care. However, the emphasis on service volume is no longer sufficient to address the most pressing public health challenges. A pivotal study by The Lancet Global Health Commission in 2018 revealed that of the healthcare-amenable mortality, 60% was attributable to poor quality care, compared to 40% resulting from lack of access [38]. Globally, an estimated eight million deaths were deemed preventable through effective healthcare interventions, leading to economic losses estimated at US$6 trillion in the LMICs in 2015. In India, approximately 2.4 million deaths are considered treatable, while 1.6 million deaths occur annually due to deficiencies in healthcare quality [39]. This underscores the urgent need for a shift toward prioritizing quality of care.

Under the AB-PMJAY, several key objectives have been set to enhance healthcare quality. These include ensuring the provision of high-quality healthcare to beneficiaries, promoting transparency in patient care and mitigating fraudulent activities, establishing a network of empaneled providers committed to delivering evidence-based clinical and support services, raising awareness about quality standards and fostering the adoption of structured quality systems in all empaneled hospitals, and quality Certification and Incentives. The details regarding different quality assurance mechanisms are elaborated in Chap. 9, which focuses on Government-Funded Health Insurance Schemes in India. To promote quality assurance, the NHA has collaborated with the Quality Council of India (QCI) to establish the AB-PMJAY Quality Certification Program [29]. This initiative provides certification to empaneled healthcare providers (EHCPs) at three levels—Bronze, Silver, and Gold. Additionally, financial incentives are linked to accreditation and certification. The National Accreditation Board for Hospitals & Healthcare Providers (NABH), an autonomous body under QCI, is responsible for granting accreditation to healthcare organizations [29]. The accreditation process is supported by key stakeholders, including industry representatives, consumer groups, and government agencies, ensuring an independent and standardized assessment. For public sector hospitals, accreditation under the National Quality Assurance Standards (NQAS) is encouraged, with a 15% incentive aligned with NABH accreditation standards. The current incentive-based quality certification framework presents both advantages and challenges. The advantages include independent third-party assessment and certification, adoption of standards that are internationally recognized and rigorously approved, comprehensive evaluation of structural and procedural quality, and a robust documentation mechanism. However, there are certain challenges also. For instance, there is a heavy reliance on documentation, increasing the administrative burden on healthcare facilities. There is a failure to account for critical aspects of quality under PM-JAY, such as improved patient health outcomes, instances of fraud, patient grievances, and the extent of OOPE incurred despite scheme enrolment.

The adoption of value-based care in India's publicly funded health insurance schemes is increasingly essential in the context of ongoing challenges related to fraud and abuse. Instances of upcoding, unnecessary procedures, ghost beneficiaries, and other fraudulent practices not only compromise the integrity of the system but also result in significant financial losses and misallocation of resources. Such abuse contributes to systemic inefficiencies by diverting funds away from genuine patient needs and undermining trust in the healthcare delivery system. Transitioning to a value-based care model—where payments are linked to patient outcomes rather than service volume—can serve as a powerful mechanism to mitigate these issues. By tying provider incentives to measurable quality indicators and patient satisfaction, the system discourages exploitative practices and promotes responsible, patient-centered care. Strengthening fraud prevention through value-based approaches is thus critical to ensuring efficient use of public resources and enhancing the overall impact of health insurance programs.

11.4.1 Value-Based Care Policy in PM-JAY

Addressing this call to action, the NHA has announced the policy of value-based care in PM-JAY [27]. This policy document aims to establish effective ways to adopt a value-based care model in PM-JAY. The mechanism of value-based incentives proposes to reward the healthcare providers with incentives for the quality of care they give to the beneficiaries of PM-JAY. This value-based policy presents a choice of patient-centric measurable indicators that can be used to assess the performance of healthcare providers. These indicators include beneficiary satisfaction rate, hospital readmission rate, extent of OOP expenditure incurred by the patients, number of confirmed grievances against an EHCP, and improvement in health-related quality of life of the PM-JAY beneficiary [40, 41].

The selection of these indicators is guided by three key considerations. First, they must embody the core principles of universal health coverage and value-based care, while also aligning with the broader goals of the health system. Second, the data required to calculate financial incentives based on these indicators should be readily available and feasible to collect as part of routine administrative processes, without placing an excessive burden on the system. Lastly, the data should be internally valid, meaning the indicators must reliably and accurately capture the specific aspects of performance they are intended to assess, and they are less amenable to alteration or "gaming" by the healthcare providers.

The first outcome-based indicator, the beneficiary satisfaction rate, reflects how satisfied patients are with the healthcare services received during a hospitalization episode or outpatient visit. It serves as a direct measure of the health system's responsiveness—one of the three core objectives outlined by the World Health Organization for assessing health system performance [42]. The second indicator, hospital readmission rate, measures the proportion of patients who are readmitted within 30 days of discharge due to similar symptoms or complications for which they were previously treated. Since readmission can vary depending on the clinical condition, disease-specific thresholds should be applied in its calculation. It is widely recognized as a proxy for evaluating the quality and effectiveness of care delivery. The third indicator, OOP expenditure, captures the direct medical expenses borne by beneficiaries or their families while receiving treatment under PM-JAY. As a core element of the UHC agenda, this indicator aligns with the health system's goal of ensuring financial protection for patients. The fourth indicator measures grievances, which refer to patient complaints or dissatisfaction arising from actions, omissions, decisions, or services rendered. The volume of confirmed grievances serves as a crucial performance indicator, offering insight into patient experience and perceived quality of care. The final outcome-based indicator is change in health-related quality of life, which measures the improvement in a patient's health status before and after receiving treatment, using validated tools such as the EQ-5D-5L. This standardized, generic instrument provides utility values for various health states, with a specific Indian value set available to capture preferences unique to the Indian population [40, 41]. As a comprehensive measure of treatment outcomes, this indicator plays a pivotal role in evaluating the effectiveness of care.

As health systems across the world are increasingly embracing the value-based care agenda, this policy strives for a more patient-focused, value-based care delivery environment for PM-JAY beneficiaries.

11.5 Application of Value-Based Care in Different Settings: Lessons for the Indian Health Insurance Landscape

Healthcare systems worldwide are increasingly adopting value-based care models. This part of the chapter examines the experiences of selected health systems that have integrated value-based care, offering insights for India. The four health systems analyzed—those of the United States, the Netherlands, Norway, and England (the United Kingdom)—represent a spectrum ranging from predominantly public models to those with significant private-sector involvement. These experiences suggest that certain elements of value-based care function more effectively in some systems than others. Key lessons include the role of government intervention in setting the conditions for systemic change (such as regional integration) and the importance of continuous IT advancements to ensure outcome data availability throughout the care cycle.

The selected healthcare systems differ not only in scale but also in the extent of government and private payer involvement in service delivery and funding [43]. While the United States has primarily used value-based care as a mechanism to shift away from fee-for-service models, European systems have focused on improving care coordination and using outcome-driven platforms to enhance the quality and appropriateness of care [44]. First, let us try to very briefly understand the broad characteristics of the health system of these countries. In the United States, the healthcare system is largely privatized, with multiple payers and some government oversight as both regulator and payer. It is also where value-based care originated as a theoretical framework. While private insurers play a dominant role, public programs such as Medicaid and Medicare set spending caps and provide coverage for low-income populations as well as certain disadvantaged population subgroups like disabled individuals.

The Netherlands operates on a hybrid healthcare system, transitioning from a predominantly public model pre-2006 to one that integrates both public and private elements. Government regulation remains strong, with mandatory insurance coverage ensuring all citizens receive a basic benefits package [45]. Norway features a largely public health system based on the National Health Service (NHS) model [46]. Healthcare is funded through taxes, and a single national insurance body provides coverage for all citizens. Specialty care is managed through four government-run regional health trusts, which may contract private providers for additional services. Lastly, the United Kingdom represents the most publicly funded healthcare system among the four. The NHS provides universal coverage funded by taxation, with oversight from the Department for Health. While private providers exist, they operate in parallel with the NHS, serving a small segment of the population (around 10%) who purchase supplemental private insurance [47].

Now we will try to understand the implementation of outcome-based measurements in the provision of healthcare in these countries. We know that value-based care relies on standardized outcome data to guide informed decision-making and drive quality improvements through benchmarking. To be effective, outcome data should be comprehensive, relevant to both clinicians and patients, and span the full continuum of care. In the Netherlands, hospitals and the government are actively expanding outcome measurement systems. The government has committed to making outcome data available for 50% of the disease burden in specialty care by 2022. In 2020, an outcome-driven healthcare program was launched to support this goal [45, 46]. A network of 28 general hospitals collaborates on implementing outcome measurement sets for conditions such as colon cancer, hip fractures, and heart failure. The data collected are benchmarked across hospitals and integrated into clinical discussions for quality improvement. Hospitals also use a scorecard incorporating outcome, cost, and process metrics. In the United States, providers lead the implementation of outcome measurement, with a strong focus on patient-reported outcome measures (PROMs) to guide clinical decision-making [44, 46]. Some hospitals have integrated electronic dashboards tracking PROM trends over multiple years, and certain contracts now mandate PROM data collection.

In the United Kingdom, the NHS hospitals have begun gathering PROMs and are working toward incorporating patient experience data to support shared decision-making. One prominent initiative involves collecting PROMs for total hip and knee arthroplasty across all hospitals as part of a national registry [46]. However, challenges such as weak IT infrastructure, lack of benchmarking, and stringent cost containment policies have hindered the integration of outcomes into clinical workflows, which offer important policy lessons for Indian health insurers aspiring to adopt an outcome-based approach in their system. The Norwegian health system has long maintained high-quality disease-specific registries for national outcome tracking. Public hospitals (which comprise 90% of the system) are evaluated using publicly available quality metrics, including infection and mortality rates [46]. Strengths of Norway's system include high compliance and data coverage—such as the Norwegian Spine Registry, which covers 80% of spinal surgeries and maintains a 70–80% follow-up rate. However, access to this data remains largely restricted to researchers, with limited availability for physicians and patients in clinical settings. A recent government initiative in Norway aims to centralize all datasets into a single national platform [46].

The experiences of these countries underscore that no single health system has perfected the value-based care model. Furthermore, the implementation of value-based principles varies significantly both between and within countries. India's approach must consider local enablers and barriers while selectively adopting elements that align with its healthcare priorities. Instead of a one-size-fits-all model, India should focus on phased implementation, leveraging successful international strategies while tailoring them to the country's unique healthcare landscape.

One of the key lessons is that government involvement is important in facilitating systemic change, whether through regulatory oversight, outcome measurement mandates, or financial incentives that drive quality improvements. In countries like the Netherlands and Norway, strong government regulation has enabled the integration of PROMs and quality benchmarking into routine care, ensuring that reimbursements are aligned with the value delivered rather than the volume of services provided. For India, this highlights the need for a more structured approach where government policies actively incentivize quality-based reimbursement. The recently launched value-based care policy of the NHA is a welcome step in this regard [27].

Another important lesson is the role of robust health information technology in ensuring seamless data sharing and transparency across the care continuum. Countries like the United States and England have attempted to implement outcome-driven healthcare models; however, challenges related to IT infrastructure and benchmarking have hampered their progress. This suggests that India must prioritize the development of interoperable digital health records and a centralized data-sharing platform to track patient outcomes across public and private healthcare facilities. Therefore, the role of Ayushman Bharat Digital Mission will be instrumental in realizing the success of value-based care in India. Thirdly, the evidence from other countries underscores the significance of patient engagement in value-based care. By incorporating PROMs, patients can actively participate in treatment decisions, leading to better adherence and satisfaction. This aligns with India's goal of enhancing patient-centered care within Ayushman Bharat and other insurance schemes, emphasizing the importance of integrating quality and outcome-based reimbursement mechanisms into the existing framework.

11.6 Conclusion

The path to embedding value-based care within India's health insurance landscape necessitates a fundamental shift from volume-driven reimbursements to outcome-based models that prioritize quality, efficiency, and patient well-being. Moving forward, a multipronged strategy must be adopted, focusing on policy reforms, technological advancements, and financial realignment. First, policy frameworks

Check Your Learning by Answering These Questions

1. Compare the traditional fee-for-service model with value-based care (VBC). How does the shift from volume-based to value-based reimbursement impact healthcare providers and patients in India?
2. What are the key challenges in implementing VBC in India's health insurance sector? How can policymakers and stakeholders address these challenges?
3. Discuss the role of health technology assessment in enabling VBC. How can digital health interventions improve patient outcomes and ensure cost efficiency in Indian healthcare?
4. Ayushman Bharat has been a major policy initiative in India's health sector. How can value-based principles be integrated into existing public health insurance programs to maximize their effectiveness?
5. The success of VBC depends on stakeholder collaboration. What incentives could be designed to align the interests of insurers, providers, and policymakers toward delivering high-quality care?
6. How does VBC impact health equity in India? Can this model help reduce disparities in healthcare access and outcomes across different socioeconomic groups?
7. In the context of rising healthcare costs, what strategies can be employed to ensure that VBC remains financially sustainable for both insurers and providers without compromising patient care?

should mandate outcome-based reimbursement models where hospitals and healthcare providers are incentivized for delivering high-quality care, reducing complications, and improving long-term patient outcomes. Second, leveraging digital health technologies, such as the Ayushman Bharat Digital Mission, can enable real-time tracking of patient data, allowing insurers and policymakers to monitor treatment effectiveness and identify areas for improvement. Third, financial incentives under schemes like PM-JAY should be restructured to reward healthcare providers based on quality metrics rather than solely on service volume. A hybrid approach that combines performance-based payments with traditional reimbursements can encourage hospitals to focus on preventive care, reduce avoidable hospitalizations, and enhance patient experience. Furthermore, India must establish independent auditing and monitoring mechanisms to prevent fraudulent activities and ensure compliance with quality benchmarks. The importance of value-based care for Indian health insurance cannot be overstated—it holds the potential to improve healthcare access, affordability, and outcomes while safeguarding millions of citizens from financial distress due to medical expenses. By aligning financial incentives with patient-centered outcomes and strengthening regulatory oversight, India can create a more sustainable, efficient, and equitable healthcare system that truly delivers value to its people.

References

1. Chalkidou K, Glassman A, Marten R, Vega J, Teerawattananon Y, Tritasavit N, et al. Priority-setting for achieving universal health coverage. Bull World Health Organ. 2016;94(6):462–7. https://doi.org/10.2471/BLT.15.155721.
2. Prinja S, Kanavos P, Kumar R. Health care inequities in North India: role of public sector in universalizing health care. Indian J Med Res. 2012;136:145–55.
3. Sharma A, Prinja S. Universal health coverage: current status and future roadmap for India. Int J Noncommun Dis. 2018;3(3):78.
4. National Health Authority. Ayushman Bharat Pradhan Mantri Jan Arogya Yojana [Internet]. 2018 [cited 2024 Nov 11]. Available from: https://pmjay.gov.in/about/pmjay.
5. Porter ME, Teisberg EO. Redefining health care: creating value-based competition on results. Boston: Harvard Business School Press; 2006.
6. Prinja S, Jyani G, Gupta N, Rajsekar K. Adapting health technology assessment for drugs, medical devices, and health programs: methodological considerations from the Indian experience. Expert Rev Pharmacoecon Outcomes Res. 2021;21(5):859–68. https://doi.org/10.1080/14737167.2021.1921575.
7. Jyani G, Gedam P, Sharma S, Dixit J, Prinja S. Financial viability of private hospitals operating under India's National Health Insurance Scheme Ayushman Bharat Pradhan Mantri Jan Arogya Yojana (AB PM-JAY). Appl Health Econ Health Policy. 23(5):841–53. https://doi.org/10.1007/s40258-025-00966-9.
8. Gupta N, Jyani G, Rajsekar K, Gupta R, Nagar A, Gedam P, et al. Application of health technology assessment for oncology Care in India: implications for Ayushman Bharat Pradhan Mantri Jan Aarogya Yojana. Indian J Med Paediatr Oncol. 2021;42(05):479–83.
9. Gentry S, Badrinath P. Defining health in the era of value-based care: lessons from England of relevance to other health systems. Cureus. 2017;9(3):e1079.
10. Porter M. Value-based health care delivery. Harvard Business School; 2012.

11. Gray M. The 'triple value agenda' must be our focus this century. NHS Confederation 2015. Available at: https://www.nhsconfed.org/articles/triple-value-agenda-must-be-our-focus-century.
12. Cimino A, Giroda C, Meloncelli I, et al. Quality indicators in diabetes care in Italy: The AMD Annals. Rome, Italy: AMD Associazione Medici Diabetologi; 2006.
13. Prinja S, Jyani G, Goyal A, Sharma S, Kaur T, Sundararaman T. Framework for responsive financing of district hospitals of India. Front Public Health. 2024;12:1398227.
14. Jyani G, Yang Z, Sharma A, Goyal A, Stolk E, Purba FD, Grover S, Kaur M, Prinja S. Evaluation of EuroQol valuation technology (EQ-VT) designs to generate national value sets: learnings from the development of an EQ-5D value set for India using an extended design (DEVINE) study. Med Decis Mak. 2023;43(6):692–703.
15. Montori VM. Turning away from industrial health care toward careful and kind care. Acad Med. 2019;94:768–70.
16. Jyani G, Prinja S, Goyal A, Garg B, Kaur M, Grover S. Do people with different sociodemographic backgrounds value their health differently? Evaluating the role of positional objectivity. Front Public Health. 2023;11:1234320.
17. Groenewoud AS, Westert GP, Kremer JAM. Value based competition in health care's ethical drawbacks and the need for a values-driven approach. BMC Health Serv Res. 2019;19(1):256.
18. Teisberg E, Wallace S, O'Hara S. Defining and implementing value-based health care: a strategic framework. Acad Med. 2020;95(5):682–5.
19. Porter ME, Lee TH. The strategy that will fix health care. Harv Bus Rev. 2013;91:50–70.
20. National Health Authority. Ayushman Bharat Pradhan Mantri –Jan Arogya Yojana Operation Manual [Internet]. 2022 [cited 2024 Nov 11]. Available from: https://nha.gov.in/img/resources/Operation%20Manual%20for%20AB%20PM-JAY.pdf.
21. Provider payments and price setting under PMJAY: improving efficiency, acceptability, quality and sustainability. [Internet]. National Health Authority, Government of India. Official website of Ayushman Bharat Digital Mission. [cited 30 Oct 2024]. Available from: https://abdm.gov.in/sites/default/files/2022-03/AB%20PM-JAY%20Price%20Consultation%20Paper.pdf.
22. World Health Organization. Case-based payment systems for Hospital Funding in Asia an investigation of current status and future directions: an investigation of current status and future directions. OECD Publishing; 2015.
23. Prinja S, Chugh Y, Gupta N, Aggarwal V. Establishing a health technology assessment evidence ecosystem in India's Pradhan Mantri Jan Arogya Yojana. Health Syst Reform. 2023;9(3):2327097.
24. Prinja S, Chugh Y, Garg B, Guinness L. National hospital costing systems matter for universal healthcare: the India PM-JAY experience. BMJ Glob Health. 2023;8(11):e012987.
25. Prinja S, Singh MP, Guinness L, Rajsekar K, Bhargava B. Establishing reference costs for the health benefit packages under universal health coverage in India: cost of health services in India (CHSI) protocol. BMJ Open. 2020;10(7):e035170.
26. Government of India. Ayushman Bharat- Pradhan Mantri Jan Arogya Yojana. Health benefit packages packages & empanelment criteria for AB PMJAY. [Cited on 31 Dec 2023]. Available from: https://www.pmjay.gov.in/sites/default/files/2018–07/HBP.pdf.
27. Volume-based to value-based care: ensuring better health outcomes and quality healthcare under AB PM-JAY. [Internet]. National Health Authority, Government of India. Official website of Ayushman Bharat Digital Mission. [cited 30 Oct 2024]. Available from: https://abdm.gov.in:8081/uploads/VBHC_Policy_Document_For_Upload_a20f871a55.pdf.
28. Health Benefit Package 2.2 [Internet]. National Health Authority. Pmjaygovin 2021 [Cited 27 Oct 2020]. Available from: https://nha.gov.in/img/resources/HBP-2.2-manual.pdf.
29. Government of India. Ayushman Bharat- Pradhan Mantri Jan Arogya Yojana. Guidelines on Hospital Empanelment and De- Empanelment (Version – 3.0). [Cited on 19 Mar 2025]. Available from: https://nha.gov.in/img/resources/Revised-Empanelment-and-De-empanelment-Guideline.pdf.
30. Cabinet approves continuation and revamping of the scheme for financial support to public private partnerships in infrastructure viability gap funding VGF scheme [internet].

Pibgovin 2020 [cited 19 Mar 2025]. Available from: https://pib.gov.in/PressReleasePage.aspx?PRID=1671914.
31. Mishra US, Yadav S, Joe W. The Ayushman Bharat digital Mission of India: an assessment. Health Syst Reform. 2024;10(2):2392290.
32. India State-Level Disease Burden Initiative Collaboration. Nations within a nation: variations in epidemiological transition across the states of India, 1990–2016 in the global burden of disease study. Lancet. 2017;390(10111):2437–60.
33. Dhara VR, Schramm PJ, Luber G. Climate change and infectious diseases in India: implications for healthcare providers. Indian J Med Res. 2013;138(6):847–52.
34. Jyani G, Prinja S, Ambekar A, Bahuguna P, Kumar R. Health impact and economic burden of alcohol consumption in India. Int J Drug Policy. 2019;69:34–42. https://doi.org/10.1016/j.drugpo.2019.04.005.
35. Menon GRM, Singh L, Sharma P, Yadav P, Sharma S, Kalaskar S, et al. National burden estimates of healthy lives lost in India, 2017: an analysis using direct mortality data and indirect disability data. Lancet Glob Health. 2019;7(12):E1675–84.
36. National Health Systems Resource Centre (NHSRC). Ministry of Health and Family Welfare. National Health Accounts Estimates for India 2021–22 [Internet]. New Delhi: National Health Systems Resource Centre; 2024. [Cited 5 Nov 2024]. Available from: https://nhsrcindia.org/sites/default/files/2024-09/NHA%202021-22.pdf.
37. Berman P, Ahuja R, Bhandari L. The impoverishing effect of healthcare payments in India: new methodology and findings. Econ Political Wkly. 2010;45:65–71.
38. Kruk M. The Lancet Global Health Commission on high-quality health systems in the SDG era. In: 2017 Interest groups meeting. AcademyHealth; 2017.
39. Kruk ME, Gage AD, Joseph NT, Danaei G, García-Saisó S, Salomon JA. Mortality due to low-quality health systems in the universal health coverage era: a systematic analysis of amenable deaths in 137 countries. Lancet. 2018;392:2203.
40. Jyani G, Sharma A, Prinja S, Kar SS, Trivedi M, Patro BK, et al. Development of an EQ-5D value set for India using an extended design (DEVINE) study: the Indian 5-level version EQ-5D value set. Value Health. 2022;25(7):1218–26.
41. Jyani G, Prinja S, Garg B, Kaur M, Grover S, Sharma A, Goyal A. Health-related quality of life among Indian population: the EQ-5D population norms for India. J Glob Health. 2023;13:04018.
42. World Health Organization. The world health report 2000. Health systems: improving performance. Geneva: World Health Organozation; 2000. [Cited on 10 Apr 2025]. Available at: https://apps.who.int/iris/handle/10665/42281.
43. The Economist Intelligence Unit. Value-based healthcare: a global assessment. London: Feb 26, 2018. Available at: https://impact.economist.com/perspectives/sites/default/files/EIU_Medtronic_Findings-and-Methodology_1.pdf.
44. Tikkanen R, Osborn R, Mossialos E, Djordjevic A, Wharton GA. International health care system profiles – United States. The Commonwealth Fund. June 5, 2020. Available at: https://www.commonwealthfund.org/international-health-policycenter/countries/united-states.
45. Wammes J, Stadhouders N, Westert G. International health care system profiles – Netherlands. The Commonwealth Fund June 5, 2020. Available at: https://www.commonwealthfund.org/international-health-policy-center/countries/netherlands.
46. Mjåset C, Ikram U, Nagra N, et al. Value-based health care in four different health care systems. NEJM Catalyst 2020 Nov. Available at: https://www.hbs.edu/ris/Publication%20Files/CAT.20.0530%20feeley_df30263f-9b78-4cc9-ac14-4728c0dda92e.pdf.
47. Thorlby R. International Health Care System Profiles – England. The Commonwealth Fund. June 5, 2020. Available at: https://www.commonwealthfund.org/international-health-policy-center/countries/england.

Suggested Readings for Further Learning

Gentry S, Badrinath P. Defining health in the era of value-based care: lessons from England of relevance to other health systems. Cureus. 2017;9(3):e1079.

Porter M. Value-based health care delivery. Harvard Business School; 2012.

Smith PC, Sagan A, Siciliani L, Figueras J. Building on value-based health care: towards a health system perspective. Health Policy. 2023;138:104918.

Teisberg E, Wallace S, O'Hara S. Defining and implementing value-based health care: a strategic framework. Acad Med. 2020;95(5):682–5.

Volume-based to value-based care: ensuring better health outcomes and quality healthcare under AB PM-JAY. [Internet]. National Health Authority, Government of India. Official website of Ayushman Bharat Digital Mission. [cited 30 Mar 2025]. Available from: https://abdm.gov.in:8081/uploads/VBHC_Policy_Document_For_Upload_a20f871a55.pdf.

Part III

Strategic Application for Health Insurers and Policymakers

Fraud Management

12

Kameshwar Rao and Arvind Agrawal

Abstract

Health insurance fraud presents a multidimensional problem impacting many stakeholders that include patients, businesses, taxpayers, premium payers and public and private health insurance providers. With specific reference to health insurance providers, health insurance frauds not only lower earnings in the insurance business, leading to substantial losses, but also impact their pricing strategy and socio-economic contributions of the insurance sector. Health insurance is highly vulnerable to frauds due to the high volume of claims, largely manual verification of claims and potential collusion among beneficiaries, hospitals, as well as employees of insurance companies. Health insurance frauds not only result in depletion of financial resources making them unavailable when needed, but also increases health insurance costs. It is therefore imperative that health insurance frauds ought to be fought using specialized fraud management systems.

In this chapter, we attempt to present a holistic approach, beginning with basics of frauds; finer shades of difference between fraud, abuse and waste; voluntary and mandatory health insurance and the nature and challenges associated with frauds in both segments; identification of fraud and its mitigation with focus on prevention, detection, and deterrence strategies; and finally use of modern techniques of fraud detection using artificial intelligence.

As India has taken steps towards Universal Health Coverage in line with Sustainable Development Goals through publicly financed health insurance, its implementation policy across India's diverse states has paved the way for a piv-

K. Rao
Formerly, National Anti Fraud Unit, National Health Authority, New Delhi, India

A. Agrawal (✉)
National Anti-Fraud Unit, National Health Authority, New Delhi, India

S. Prinja (ed.), *Healthcare Financing and Insurance*,
https://doi.org/10.1007/978-981-95-3513-2_12

otal role of private insurers as well. However, frauds in the system and leakages will invariably influence actuarial strategies. Frauds also cause a dent in the allocative and technical efficiencies in the health system, thus impacting progress towards Universal Health Coverage.

Keywords

Health insurance · Health insurance frauds · Anti-fraud framework · Artificial Intelligence · Machine Learning

Learning Objectives

After going through the chapter, you will be able to understand:

- What is a health insurance fraud, its meaning, different types, and mitigation strategies.
- Insurance industry, voluntary private insurance, and mandatory government insurance.
- Impact of health insurance frauds.
- Emerging trends, prevention, and detection techniques using advanced tools to detect frauds in large volume of health claims.
- Global practices in managing health insurance frauds.
- A case study of fraud management in the world's largest publicly financed health assurance program, the *Ayushman Bharat Pradhan Mantri Jan Arogya Yojana (AB PM-JAY)* in India.

Key Terms

- *Government-sponsored public health insurance:* Insurance or assurance programs offered to a defined group of citizens as social protection, where central or state governments spend huge sums, usually tax-funded.
- *Insurer:* A private sector or public sector organization (including government), which insures the health of individuals for a premium amount received from them or in the case of government, which assures health and financial protection under social responsibility towards its citizens.
- *Insured:* An individual who is covered against unforeseen health conditions for financial risk protection. The health conditions for which a person is insured and the extent of financial risk protection depend on the terms and conditions of the policy agreement between the insured and the insurer.
- *Policy:* In general, refers to a health insurance policy, but in this chapter may also mean organizational protocol or procedure, depending on the context.

- *Member/beneficiary:* An individual who purchases a health insurance policy or enrolled in a public insurance scheme of the government. (used interchangeably in this chapter.)
- *Pre-existing diseases (PED)*: Diseases that exist in an individual prior to signing up for the health insurance policy. The act of hiding these diseases by the insured at the time of signing up and subsequent discovery by the insurer may lead to the repudiation of claims.
- *Network hospitals:* Facilities registered with any private sector insurance organization for providing health insurance services to its members, often through cashless methods. The term is interchangeably used (particularly in public sector/government schemes) as empanelled hospitals.
- *Incurred claims:* The amount the insurers incur against the claims.
- *Incurred claims ratio (ICR):* The ratio between premiums collected and incurred claims (e.g. ICR of 90% indicates that for every 100 rupees earned in premium the insurer is spending 90 rupees in claims). A reasonable ICR ranges from 50% to 80%. Too high an ICR means the insurer is paying too much amount in claims, thus impacting the company's financial health and too low an ICR indicates that the insurers may not be honouring genuine claims.
- *Third-party administrator (TPA)*: An independent (usually private) organization that is appointed by an insurer company or by a government entity to process health claims on its behalf.
- *IRDAI*: Insurance regulatory and development Authority of India, a statutory and autonomous body that is set up to protect the interests of the insurance policy holders and ensure fair practices in the insurance industry.
- *Desk audit:* Internal audit mechanism of claims (paid or unpaid) by reviewing claim documents to identify the anomalies or validate the claim as per policy terms and conditions without validating the same in the field.
- *Field audit and investigation:* Suspicious cases found through desk audits or other technology-aided alerts referred for on-field investigation to validate genuineness or otherwise and collect on-ground evidence. Conducted either through the organization's own resources or outsourced to a third party. In case of the latter, strict monitoring and controls are warranted.
- *Turnaround time (TAT):* Timelines stipulated for services rendered by insurance companies. IRDAI mandates that the timelines for services of every insurance company be published in the public domain for the awareness of members. Of particular interest from a beneficiary perspective is claim settlement and grievance resolution timelines.
- *Bharatiya Nyaya Sanhita* (BNS): The official criminal code in India that came into force from July 2024, which replaced the erstwhile Indian Penal Code (IPC 1860). Several sections (popularly known to the general public in India, such as "420" for cheating) have now been moved under different sections in BNS with renewed definitions and provisions.

- *Artificial intelligence (AI):* Technological advancement wherein machines (computers) can perform tasks that usually require human intelligence, but have the capacity to perform in a multidimensional sphere.
- *Machine learning:* A subset of AI, in the form of computer programs and algorithms that give machines (computers) the power to learn from large labelled or unlabelled datasets and basing on the learnings can perform future tasks on unseen datasets.
- *Deep learning:* A subset of machine learning that uses artificial neural networks similar to human neural networks and is mostly used for processing image data.
- *Generative AI:* A subset of AI that leverages natural language processing and other machine learning technologies to create new content, text, images, audio, or video.

12.1 Introduction

"Fraud" by definition means an intentional deception or misrepresentation made by any individual or entity with the knowledge that such deception would result in financial benefits to self or others. With specific reference to the insurance sector in India, such misrepresentation includes manipulation of facts and/or documents as well as any activity that may constitute fraud under any applicable law in India. However, human errors or wastages in the system are not included under the definition of fraud. From here on, the word fraud(s) and related terms exclusively refer to health insurance frauds, more specifically in insurance.

It leads us to understand some important terms associated with fraud, i.e. *errors*, *waste*, and *abuse*, as it is important to distinguish them in relation to the definition of fraud. Any mistake due to misunderstanding during the process of health insurance delivery (e.g. prescribing incorrect medications to a patient), which is unintentional, constitutes *errors*. Unintentional or inadvertent use of resources (e.g. high-cost services or drugs where low-cost efficient alternatives are available) is *waste* that results in needless cost to insurance providers. *Abuse,* on the other hand, refers to those provider practices that are inconsistent with sound fiscal, business, or medical practices; or in reimbursement for services that are not medically necessary; or services that fail to meet professionally recognized standards for healthcare, all of which result in unnecessary cost to the insurers. A few examples of common health insurance abuse would be—excessive diagnostic tests, extended length of stay, and conversion of a day procedure to overnight admission. The main intention of both fraud and abuse is financial and non-financial gain. In essence, awareness, and intent are the keywords that distinguish fraud from other practices.

What Is a Fraudulent Insurance Claim?

An insurance claim prepared with the intention to deceive, conceal, or distort relevant information that eventually accounts for healthcare benefits for an individual or a particular group is defined as a fraudulent health insurance claim [1].

12.2 What Are the Different Types of Frauds?

In insurance, frauds can be categorized both based on the nature of fraud as well as the stakeholder involved.

Hard fraud is a planned activity to get money from insurance companies. Cases where patients (members of insurance) are not admitted for treatment, or a non-eligible member taking treatment on behalf of an eligible member can be classified as hard frauds.

Soft fraud happens when there is an incidence of treatment or hospitalization, but the claim amounts are exaggerated. This is generally in the form of abuse. Examples include claiming a higher health benefits package and procedures unnecessary for the given health condition.

Frauds can also be classified based on the stakeholder(s) involved; it can be initiated by the insured, by the provider, by both insured and provider, or by the insured-provider-insurer nexus. Examples of all these types are described in Table 12.1.

Finally, frauds take place both in the public and private health insurance space. There are multiple process- and policy-related leakages in public health insurance, which is exploited by multiple stakeholders and converted into frauds. Private insurers and standalone health insurers in general have robust systems and processes to

Table 12.1 Types of frauds

Fraud type	Description
Insured-initiated fraud	When the member of the insurance prefers a claim through reimbursement mode by using some fake stationary of any hospital.
Provider-initiated fraud	When providers use the health card of members without their consent for a claim, which is commonly seen in publicly financed health insurance schemes. It amounts to identity theft.
Insured- and provider-initiated fraud	When the members and providers complicitly join together to claim financial gains through false claims.
Insured-, provider-, and insurer-initiated fraud	When employees of an insurance company or third-party administrator (TPA) join the party in nexus with the member and provider. Usually, claims tend to be processed at odd hours in an effort to remain unnoticed.

handle the claims and identification of anomalies based on policy exclusion and previous claim track record; however, a white-collar crime with professionally managed claim documents becomes hard to detect and poses challenges even to private insurers.

Activity Box 1
Discuss differences of fraud, abuse, waste, and error with suitable example?
Do you think there are minor differences or *grey areas* that make it hard to distinguish fraud from abuse or errors or waste?
Where do you think soft fraud can be commonly seen?

12.3 Common Fraudulent Practices of Providers

Several fraudulent practices of providers have been identified that are routinely found in health claims as listed below:

(i) *Upcoding* refers to the practice of billing for services or diagnoses that are more complex in nature than those rendered or diagnosed. Public health insurers mostly use health benefits packages with a bundled payment method (package rate); whereas most private insurers have an open billing system or fee-for-service method. "*Setting provider payment methods and pricing*" has been more clearly explained in Chap. 7. The challenges of lower reimbursement rates coupled with increased patient volumes and delayed payments in publicly funded schemes may put financial pressure on providers leading to upcoding. Overuse of diagnostic tests; prescribing higher antibiotics without justification; minor procedures converted to major procedures; and upcoding diagnoses like simple essential hypertension into accelerated hypertension are some of the examples.

(ii) *Unbundling* is a method where providers fragment a single procedure into multiple items and bill separately for each. This type of fraud is mostly seen in public health insurance schemes where providers are supposed to bill for a single incidence of treatment rather than the fee-for-service method. For example, given a case of a 55-year-old mother of two children complaining of menorrhagia and evidence of uterine fibroids on ultrasound sonography needs an abdominal hysterectomy; however, the provider chooses to perform a dilatation and curettage first, followed by hysterectomy after 2 days; whereas such dual procedures could have been easily avoided.

(iii) *Double billing* is done by providers by billing for the same service more than once.

(iv) *Phantom or "ghost" billing* is done by providers for billing for services that were never rendered and the patient never received.
(v) *Misrepresentation* billing happens when an ineligible procedure (as per the terms of insurance) is claimed in an attempt to get away. Sometimes, such instances can get missed in volumes of claims processed manually.

Case Study 1

In September 2017, the case of a 7-year-old girl who died in a private hospital in India shocked the country. It was much talked about in the media and required intervention of Minister of health and other government authorities, not for medical reasons but issues related to treatment costs. The girl's father had to incur a hospitalization bill of ₹18 lakh ($27,595) for 15 days of treatment. This was posted in social media by the father's friend and instantly it became much talked about issue.

Study this case and track its journey end-to-end from information available in public domain and discuss various elements of fraud and actions taken. {Read the case here https://www.ndtv.com/gurgaon-news/billed-18-lakhs-by-gurgaons-fortis-hospital-alleges-family-of-7-year-old-who-died-1778010}.

12.4 The Health Insurance in India

It is important to understand the essentials of health insurance in India and the different insurance products that are available, since the type of frauds committed and the mechanism of discovery tend to differ across different products. Health insurance in India has evolved over time with very low penetrations due to socio-economic and cultural barriers as well as awareness and reach [2]. While generally private sector participates in individual (retail insurance) or corporate group insurance, government-sponsored public health insurance schemes form part of the social protection for citizens (mass insurance). Private insurers may also take part in government-funded programs, where they are run in insurance mode. Although government schemes are *assurance schemes* in nature, the term *insurance* is used interchangeably in this chapter; however, the larger objective of government-sponsored public health insurance schemes is to provide financial risk protection, equity in health access, and preventive and promotive healthcare to safeguard public health rather than a transactional insurance product, as in private sector health insurance.

12.5 The Business of Health Insurance

It is important to consider the business of health insurance to understand the impact of health insurance frauds on the industry directly. The impact will also be felt by the insured indirectly in the way of enhanced premiums due in part to losses incurred by insurers from frauds.

As per National Health Accounts Estimates for India [3], the combined health insurance expenditure of government and private sector in 2021–22 was 1.15 lakh crore, of which government expenditure constitutes ~42% for various social health insurance schemes, whereas private sector health insurance including individual and group insurance constitutes ~58%, highlighting the role of private health insurance in India in terms of expenditure.

As shown in Fig. 12.1, among various segments under non-life insurance business, the health insurance business is the largest segment with a contribution of 38.02% (36.48% in 2021–22) in terms of the total premium in 2022–23 [4]. Segment-wise share of premium of general and health insurers is shown below to get an idea of the business of health insurance in the private sector.

The revenue collection of private insurers comes through premium and reinvestment. The IRDAI Annual Report 2022–23 [4] states that a total of 89,492 crore was collected as health insurance premium. About 44% of health insurance premium collected through public sector general insurance companies (Fig. 12.2). In the last 5 years, from 2018–19 to 2022–23 the health insurance premium registered a two-fold jump.

During 2022–23, general and health insurers have settled 2.36 crore number of health insurance claims and paid 70,930 crore towards the settlement of health insurance claims. The average amount paid per claim (ACS) ₹30,087. The net incurred claim amount was 64,631 crore and the reported incurred claim ratio (ICR) by insurers is 88.89% with public sector insurance companies reporting a very high ICR of 104.91% and private sector at 86.82%.

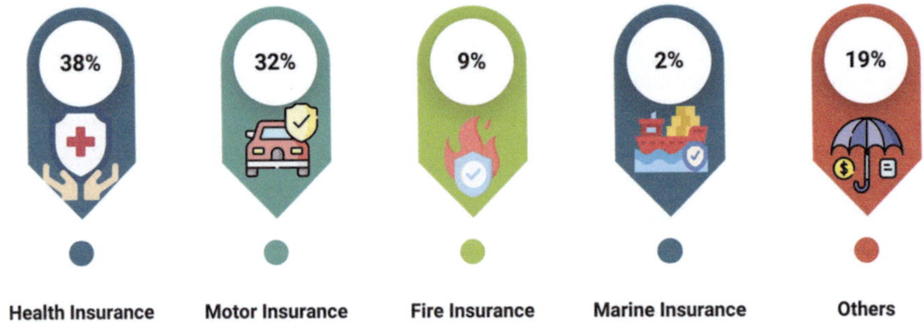

Fig. 12.1 Segment-wise share of general and health insurance premium in private sector

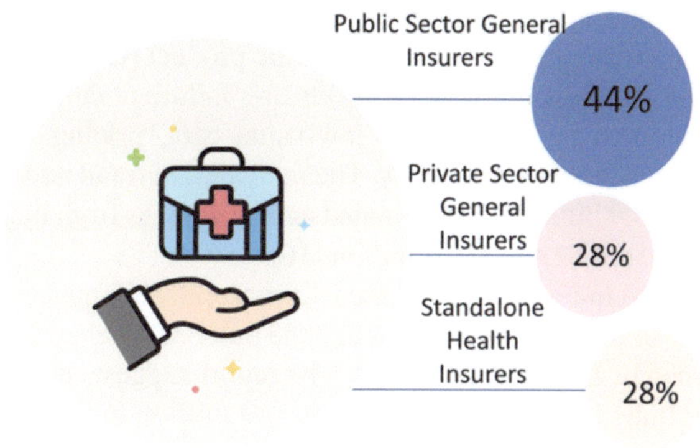

Fig. 12.2 Sector-wise share of health insurance premium

12.6 The Impact of Frauds

Health insurance fraud significantly burdens various aspects of global and national health insurance systems—affecting finances, patient trust, legal structures, and resource allocation. To give an idea of its impact, global and national scenarios are discussed from available literature and research, not only in the insurance industry but also on health systems overall as it has ramification for health financing.

12.6.1 Financial Consequences of Fraud and Abuse

Globally, approximately $455 billion of the $7.35 trillion spent on healthcare worldwide is lost yearly to fraud and corruption. Furthermore, the Organization for Economic Co-operation and Development (OECD) estimates that 45% of global citizens believe the health sector is corrupt. An estimated 1.6% of annual deaths in children under 5 (more than 140,000 deaths) can be explained in part by corruption [5]. According to global research institutions such as the National Health Care Antifraud Association, USA (NHCAA) [6] and National Health Service Counter Fraud Authority, UK (NHSCFA) [7], health insurance frauds present immense challenges in the health insurance industry and are responsible for loss of substantial amounts of money reaching up to several millions of dollars annually. In a conservative estimate by NHCAA, frauds amount to 3% of total healthcare expenditure, while some government and law enforcement agencies place the loss as high as 10% of our annual health outlay, which could mean more than $300 billion. What it essentially means is it is difficult to estimate exact number of frauds in the system due to multiple reasons such as using legacy systems in claims processing; processing systems that are siloed due to involvement of multiple entities (e.g. enrolment, approvals, authorizations, claims adjudications); having sensitivity related to health insurance data privacy and difficulty in proving intent of fraud in litigation settings [8].

The United States spends more on healthcare than any other country, with costs approaching 18% of gross domestic product (GDP) [9]. A systematic review identified six waste domains in healthcare; failure of care delivery, failure of care coordination, over-treatment or low-value care, pricing failure, fraud and abuse, and administrative complexity. The total annual fraud and abuse cost ranges from $58.5 to $83.9 billion. The estimated annual savings from measures to eliminate fraud and abuse are $22.8–$30.8 billion [10].

The Indian insurance industry is similarly impacted. According to a recent survey in India, it is estimated that the number of false claims in the industry is approximately 15% of total claims. The report suggests that the health insurance industry in India is losing approximately $69 million to $92 million incurred on fraudulent claims annually [11].

12.6.2 Effects on Patient Care and Trust in the Health Insurance System

Frauds can lead to unnecessary medical procedures and misdiagnosis that adversely impact patients' health. Such compromised patient care erodes public trust in the health insurance system. This lack of trust can lead to many negative consequences. Patients might feel that the provider's interest lies in commercial gains rather than a genuine interest in patient care. Such patients are less inclined to follow care plans and exhibit suboptimal response to the treatment. Patients may also be reluctant to seek care if they do not trust their providers or the system. Increased costs make it more difficult for patients to afford care. Fraud and abuse can damage the public's confidence in the health insurance system, making it more difficult for policymakers to enact reforms that are needed to improve the system [12].

In India, health insurance fraud has led to mistrust among patients, particularly in private health insurance settings where "kickback culture" (payments given to doctors for referrals) is sometimes practiced. This results in unnecessary treatments or referrals, increasing costs without improving patient outcomes. This creates an environment where patients may begin to distrust medical professionals and institutions, which can discourage them from seeking timely health insurance.

12.6.3 Broader Implications for Public Health Funding and Resource Allocation

The impact of fraud extends beyond individual patients and institutions, affecting public health funding and resource allocation.

Diversion of Limited Resources Fraud and abuse in health insurance results in the misallocation of already scarce public health funds. When funds are misused or directed towards fraudulent claims, fewer resources are available for essential services, such as primary care, preventive medicine, and emergency preparedness. This misallocation can hinder the ability of health insurance systems to serve vulnerable populations effectively [13]. Studies on fraudulent claims and misuse of funds in public health insurance schemes showed a reduction of impact and sustainability of these programs, which rely on limited budgets to provide health insurance to millions of underprivileged citizens [14].

Increased Health Insurance Costs Fraudulent activities drive up health insurance costs significantly. This increase in costs is often transferred to governments and public health programs, leading to higher taxes or premiums for the public. The funds lost to fraud could have otherwise been used to subsidize health insurance for low-income individuals, invest in medical infrastructure, or improve health services [15]. A report by the National Health Authority in India revealed that several hospitals were involved in billing for services not provided and inflating charges under the AB PM-JAY scheme, ultimately leading to stricter regulations and monitoring systems [16].

Reduction in Quality of Care Fraud and abuse can lead to a reduction in the quality of care due to over-medicalization and unwarranted care leading to side effects and poor quality of life. A report on health insurance fraud in OECD countries showed that practices like unnecessary surgeries and excessive testing due to financial incentives compromise the quality of care, harming patients, and increasing public mistrust in healthcare systems [17].

In India, misallocation of health insurance funds due to fraud hinders progress towards universal health coverage and strains public health initiatives. The diversion of funds limits the government's ability to invest in essential services such as maternal and child health, vaccination programs, and primary care. For instance, fraud-related losses in government insurance schemes would mean fewer resources are available for scaling health insurance access in rural and underserved areas.

Strain on Health Systems and Resources Fraudulent practices can overload health systems by diverting resources towards unnecessary treatments and procedures, creating inefficiencies and reducing the availability of services for genuine cases. This burden strains health systems, particularly in low- and middle-income countries, where resources are already limited. By consuming a large share of funds, frauds and corrupt practices also hamper health system resilience and preparedness for public health emergencies [18].

Negative Impact on Public Health Goals Health insurance fraud has a direct impact on achieving India's public health goals, including universal health coverage (UHC). Fraudulent practices divert funds away from essential services, making it harder to reach vulnerable populations and undermining initiatives aimed at improving public health. For instance, fraud in maternal and child health programs, such as focusing on high revenue services at the cost of simple preventive services to detect problems early on during pregnancy, fraudulent procurements leaving health centres without basic equipment and drugs, deploying low-skilled and non-qualified workforce in empanelled hospitals could delay progress in improving maternal mortality and child health outcomes.

12.7 The Fraud Control

Fraud control is more complex and difficult than is usually appreciated in health insurance. Officials of insurance responsible for payment safeguards generally receive no formal training in fraud control [19]. Certain factors make fraud control particularly difficult in the health insurance industry, such as neutral behaviour of government policies and social acceptability, as per the degree of fraud committed.

> Fraud control in any profession is a miserable business. Failure to detect fraud is bad news, and finding fraud is bad news too. Senior managers seldom want to hear news about fraud, because such news is never good. *(License to Steal, Malcolm K Sparrow)*

It is difficult for most insurers, public or private, to assess the problem of fraud in the system or the problem they face in their daily operation business. Traditional routine-focused manual audits may be useful up to a certain extent, but ineffective in detecting criminal fraud, especially with the volume of claims increasing manifold. The lack of robust systems makes it difficult to quickly identify and prevent health insurance fraud. This leads to funds leakage, long claims cycle time and an increase in rejected claims owing to a conservative approach adopted by insurance providers. This creates a vicious cycle of disillusioned service provider who refuses to participate in such schemes, which in turn pushes up the out-of-pocket expenditure (OOPE) [20].

Fraud perpetrators can easily and intelligently navigate existing controls by preparing bills that appear foolproof and staying within the boundaries of policy coverage. The advent of conditional automated claims processing mechanisms, with electronic submission and electronic payment presents new dangers for fraud control in the absence of mechanisms to quickly detect frauds. Fraudsters tend to be one step ahead making fraud control is a cat and mouse game, and organizations must constantly work towards building strong checks and balances to minimize frauds.

12.8 Anti-fraud Framework

The organizational approach towards fraud control begins with having a robust anti-fraud framework (Fig. 12.3) backed by well-documented policies and strict enforcement methods. It is not just important to have fraud control measures and policies, but critical to update them in line with changing scenario, communicate, and educate the employees of the organization periodically.

The health insurance industry should cover the entire gamut of activities of fraud under prevention, detection, and deterrence mechanisms, often called a three-legged stool.

While most organizations focus on detection techniques, it is equally or more important to focus on prevention strategies as they are often the components of a larger risk management approach. It makes sense because prevention methods are cost-effective and interventions in fraud management can become early rather than late. Detection strategies although important are more time-consuming and expensive because it follows a whole gamut of exercise to recover monies lost in fraud or may end up in write-offs. Prevention, on the other hand, is cost saving and makes revenues available when needed. The other pillar of the anti-fraud framework, deterrence strategies, helps in reducing the likelihood of future frauds by examining root causes and addressing them, eliminating favourable ground for committing frauds and attempt to modify the behaviour of fraudsters.

The prevention–detection–deterrence framework is detailed in Table 12.2, which is equally applicable in the public as well as private sector insurance. Some best practices that should be followed by organizations at different stages are enlisted below. Again, the list is not exhaustive, and every organization must invent its own strategies while remaining updated about the latest developments in the fraud control area, both nationally and globally.

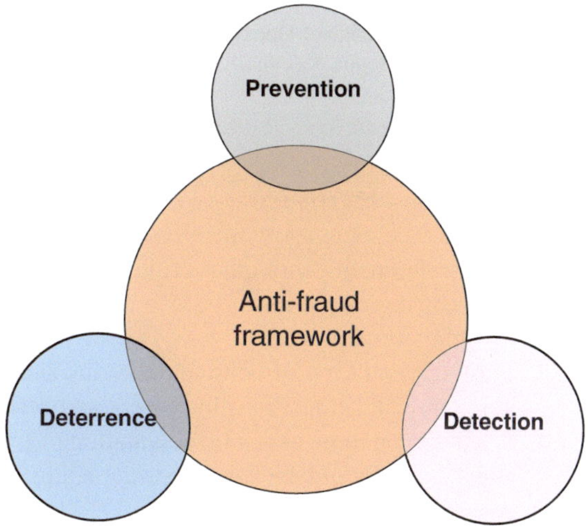

Fig. 12.3 Anti-fraud framework

Table 12.2 Anti-fraud framework

Activities	Preventive approach	Detection approach	Deterrence approach
Applicable stage	Enrolment/onboarding	Claim submission	Documentation of policies
Action	Development of internal guidelines and SOPs. Strict underwriting guidelines Strong KYC mechanism Careful policy wording Exclusion period for certain fraud–/abuse-prone packages. Strict guidelines for the mode of payment of the premium Verification of corporates/ members in group policies Use of the latest technologies to scan the applicant(s) Employee engagement for a balanced and well-coordinated approach by sales and underwriting teams Careful selection of network providers/empanelment with a well-drafted memorandum of association outlining monetary penalties for non-conformance and fraudulent/corrupt practices Performance bank guarantees and forfeiture clauses	A dedicated claims investigation department and field teams. Regular proactive desk audits and field investigations Strict monitoring and evaluation of outsourced agencies in case the audits and investigations are outsourced. Random hospital visits/inspections Deploy robust claims data analytics using updated technologies for anomaly detection	Well-defined punitive actions against errant entities. Strong claim repudiation and red-flagging entities/ members Penalties and legal action against errant entities. Defamation of providers/facilities on social media Blacklisting and public notification of providers/facilities through IRDAI. Strong internal policies against collusive practices and punitive actions against errant employees Periodical internal communication through newsletters about new discoveries and initiatives
Results	Appropriate risk evaluation for incidence management	Effective risk mitigation plans	Maximize risk avoidance

Abbreviations: *SOP* Standard Operating Protocol, *KYC* Know Your Customer, *IRDAI* Insurance Regulatory and Development Authority of India

Activity Box 2

1. Reflect on what criteria should be applied for hospital empanelment? Is the pre-empanelment assessment process adequate? (e.g. background checks, cross-referencing with other programs, on-site verification, etc.).
2. How can digital platforms be leveraged to improve member/provider/facility onboarding process.
3. Explore what kind of contractual terms should be documented with network/empaneled facilities to prevent and deter frauds.
4. What do you think of public defamation of fraudulent providers/facilities? What care should be taken before doing so? Explore legal or ethical considerations.

12.9 The Role of Technology in Fraud Detection

Fraud detection in health insurance claims has evolved over time. One of the most common approaches to identify fraud is to use domain or expert knowledge to identify anomalies in billing practices [7]. This is an intensive process and much time and effort are lost before the identification of frauds. As the volume of health claims has grown and electronic databases of claims have been created, insurers have increasingly started to rely on technology to aid them in fraud detection.

Initial detection methods using technology revolved around creating certain rules and running queries on the databases to detect anomalies in individual claims. The rules hardcoded as a software program are run periodically on claims databases and suspicious claims are flagged for further manual review. This practice of deploying rules on claims data, also called *alerts* or *triggers*, is still in vogue in many organizations and often also used in conjunction with the latest technologies. While providing a complete set of rules is beyond the scope of this chapter, some of the rules generally defined in the industry are given below with examples for understanding. These are not mutually exclusive, but some overlap can occur among them. Many of these alerts are common across public and private insurers.

1. *Rules based on claim history*: Frequent claims for acute medical conditions, claims from multiple hospitals with the same ownership.
2. *Rules based on claim geography*: Claims for frequent hospitalization in geographies distant from the original location of the member; frequent admissions in multiple locations; and same beneficiary admitted in multiple locations around the same time.
3. *Rules based on hospitalization pattern*: Multiple members of the same family admitted and discharged around the same time, regular claims with no claim-free years, prolonged intensive care unit (ICU) stays, extended length of stay (LoS) for trivial conditions.
4. *Rules based on diagnostic conditions*: Mismatch between age, gender, and diagnosis; once in lifetime procedures performed many times (cholecystectomy, prostatectomy, etc.), conservative treatment for surgical conditions or vice versa, missing documents/reports.
5. *Rules based on providers*: Mismatch between procedures/specialty and qualifications of provider, specialty unavailable in hospital,
6. *Rules based on billing patterns*: Multiple specialties and consultations in a single bill, abnormally high cost of treatment for a given disease condition, high-value claim from small hospitals.

It is further emphasized that some of the above rules are intended only as red flags for auditors to be alert about, but do not necessarily constitute a fraudulent claim. Every insurer or organization may have a different set of rules or alerts depending on internal intelligence and experience. Further, the above rules can be applied on claims either at the pre-authorization stage (in case of cashless claims) or before claim processing in reimbursement claims. However, the feasibility of investigation at the pre-authorization stage is minimal due to turnaround time (TAT) and other procedural challenges. An example set of rules for pre-authorization and reimbursement claims is provided below for reference of the reader.

Some rules run at the pre-authorization stage are as follows:

- Members of the same proposer family getting admitted and discharged together, along with the proposer.
- High number of admissions in the previous 1 month.
- High number of admissions on weekends/holidays.
- Admission beyond the capacity of the hospital.
- Excessive ICU admission.
- Diagnosis and gender mismatch.
- Once in a lifetime procedure reported many times.

Some rules run at the claim submission stage:

- Claims for medical management admission for exactly 24 h as a coverup for outpatient treatment and expensive investigations.
- Claims with LoS which is in a significant variance with the average LoS for a particular ailment.
- Claims where the clinical findings do not correlate with the chief complaints or diagnosis or line of treatment; exaggeration of classical clinical findings to portray severity in acute medical illness/minor surgical conditions.

12.9.1 Artificial Intelligence

Until the advent of artificial intelligence (AI), insurers have been relying largely on manual auditing and rule-based alerts or triggers that flag suspicious claims. However, as artificial intelligence technologies unfolded and being increasingly deployed in almost every domain, it presents a great opportunity not only in the detection of frauds but also towards potential prevention.

With the ubiquitous presence of AI in our everyday life, it is important to understand basic concepts associated with it (Fig. 12.4). The term *artificial intelligence* involves a broad definition that includes the ability of computer devices to perform tasks and problem-solving abilities associated with human intelligence. The concept of AI has been there since the 1950s, but it only took off when high-powered, high-memory computing systems were introduced in the 1990s–2000s. At the core of the AI techniques is the mathematical foundation of statistics and probability.

Machine learning is a subset of AI that includes usage of data and algorithms and attempts to learn from the data and patterns through artificial neural networks that mimic the human neural networks. The learnings from past data are then applied to future unseen data to find patterns and discoveries. There are two ways that machine learning is used. One is called *unsupervised learning,* where the algorithms learn

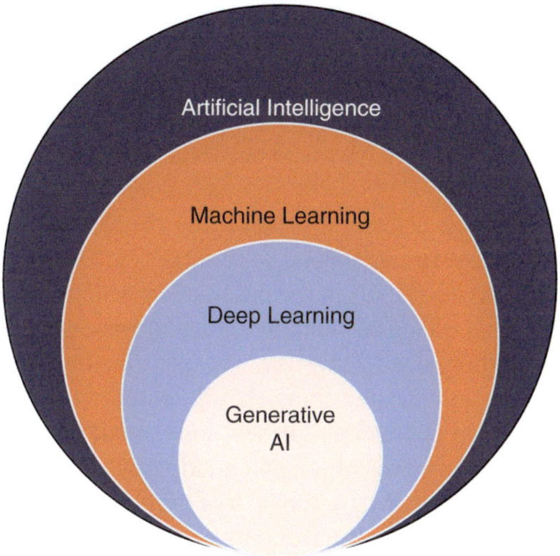

Fig. 12.4 The hierarchy of artificial intelligence (AI)

from the patterns and cluster the historical data and discover anomalous patterns. Future data are then classified into one of these clusters or groups by detecting anomalies. The second method is *supervised learning,* where domain experts label the data into one or more categories (e.g. each claim record labelled as fraud or not fraud). The algorithms then learn the patterns in the claims data as per the classification labels, then these learnings are applied to new unseen data. Although this explanation appears more simplistic, the actual learning relies on complex mathematical and statistical modelling techniques, including various types of regression techniques. It is important to understand that no model is perfect; therefore, it is critical that the models perform in an accurate manner so that misclassification of fraud as not fraud and vice versa is minimized. Using the ML techniques, various prediction and risk scores can be developed for a facility or provider or member as well as an overall risk score of the claim being fraudulent. One caveat is that AI algorithms learn and perform better only when they see large data sets often spanning millions of records, therefore, the importance of volumes of historical data.

Deep learning is again a subset of machine learning which uses more advanced algorithms and more complex neural networks. These algorithms can process and learn from image data, such as photographs or radiographic images and videos, and apply the learnings to new image data for classification, which is also known as computer vision. The medical data that exist in the claims contain mostly *unstructured data*, which means the data are in the form of digitized clinical notes, medical histories, discharge summaries, images from laboratory, radiographic and other investigation data. This contrasts with *structured data,* which are largely in the form of fixed-length structured databases, such as patient demographic data, disease names, diagnostic codes, etc.

Generative AI (Gen AI) is a more recent form of deep learning technologies which applies natural language processing (NLP) techniques to large volumes of text data to identify patterns and extract complex information. This ability of Gen AI can be used to detect frauds in real time and hence more as a prevention technique than a detection technique. Using Gen AI in fraud detection is also critical because fraudsters may also take advantage of the very same Gen AI to create foolproof claim documents to outwit any archaic fraud detection techniques deployed in organizations.

Having discussed the exciting capabilities of AI in fraud detection, it is also important to understand its limitations. Given that the AI systems learn from the patterns and labels in the past data as well as require large amounts of data to learn, the importance of "number of actual frauds" in the historical claims data cannot be overemphasized. However, it is seen that the detection rate of frauds in health claims is very low despite frauds being present in high numbers. Therefore, the available historical claims data present only small numbers of fraudulent claims for the AI systems to learn, which potentially impacts the model performance and accuracy to detect frauds. Many times, this presents a situation where the dataset has ratio of fraud claims to normal claims as low as 10–90 or 5–95 or even lower. (For every 100 claims, there may be only 10 or 5 or even lower fraud claims.) This challenge is known as *imbalanced data* and presents problems with failure to detect frauds (sensitivity) and is often overcome by special techniques and algorithms as well as creating synthetic datasets to enable better fraud predictions by the AI systems [21]. However, AI algorithms are prone to classification problems (Table 12.3) in correctly flagging true fraud and true genuine claims.

12.9.2 What Kind of Information Is Used by AI Algorithms in Fraud Detection?

Typically, any medical claim data consist of certain attributes that can be described as below:

1. *Patient demographics and characteristics* such as Identification (ID), location, age, gender, diagnosis, other medical information, etc.
2. *Insurer information* such as private or public, policy/product information, type, coverage and sum insured, co-payment or voluntary deductibles, exclusions, waiting period, pre- and post-hospitalization expenses and limits, entitlements, other benefits, etc.
3. *Provider/facility information* such as hospital ID, name, doctor's name and ID, geographic location, number of claims and claims history, type and size of facility, bed strength, specialties available, doctors and qualifications, history of frauds, risk score, etc.
4. *Claim-specific data* such as claim ID, admission and discharge information, diagnosis, investigation reports, images, claim amount, approved, rejected, flagged/confirmed fraud.

Table 12.3 Classification problems in AI algorithms

Sensitivity and specificity—Algorithm challenges
Two performance metrics are used during model development to evaluate how well AI models perform in classifying fraud and non-fraud cases.
Sensitivity (true positive rate): Ability of the AI model to correctly identify the number of fraudulent claims out of actual fraudulent transactions. Supposing there are 100 fraud claims in the data, and if the AI model flags only 90 of them as fraud and passes 10 fraud cases as genuine, then sensitivity is calculated as 90%.
Specificity (true negative rate): Ability of the AI model to correctly identify the number of legitimate claims out of all genuine claims in the data. Supposing if that there are 100 legitimate claims and the AI algorithm identifies 95 of them as legitimate but wrongly identifies five of them as frauds, then the specificity of the algorithm is 95%.
Given this, a 2 × 2 matrix called a confusion matrix can be shown as below to map model performance vs. actual ground truth.

Model Prediction

Actual		Fraud	Not Fraud
	Fraud	True Positive	False Positive
	Not Fraud	False Negative	True Negative

Sensitivity is calculated as: $\frac{\text{True Positive}}{\text{True Positive} + \text{False Negative}}$

Specificity is calculated as: $\frac{\text{True Negative}}{\text{True Negative} + \text{Fase Positive}}$

If the model is trained with a focus on high sensitivity and low on specificity, it may flag more genuine transactions as fraud. On the contrary, if the model is trained for high specificity, there is a danger of missing out on actual fraud cases. Therefore, a trade-off or a balance between sensitivity and specificity becomes crucial in deciding the best possible model. Towards this, several techniques are deployed such as data augmentation (for imbalanced data), fine-tuning models with regulation and penalties, ensemble methods (combination of different models), and continuous model adaptation with new data and ground truth.

5. *Additional information*, such as inputs provided by field investigators during field audits.
6. In addition, during the process of modelling, the coders create additional information from the given features on the basis of their experience and add fields of data, which are termed as *feature engineering*.

Each of the above characteristics or information is available in the data as a field (also called variable or feature or dimension) and is used by the AI algorithms to learn the patterns, detect frauds and make predictions in future claims. Human intelligence can decode information at most up to three dimensions. The ability to process multiple dimensions (sometimes even up to 100 or more), huge volumes of information and at high speeds is the crux of AI systems that allow for flagging suspicious claims and prevention of potential frauds.

Activity Box 3

What do you think are the prerequisites for AI systems to be efficient in fraud detection. What is the corner stone?

Discuss how computer vision techniques can be deployed to analyse digitized documents and detect frauds.

Discuss difference between structured and unstructured data and which type of AI algorithms works better with each of them.

What dangers can AI-based fraud detection pose? What care should be taken from an ethical perspective?

Discuss on sensitivity and specificity and trade-off. What do you think is more important? (Hint: There is a cost associated with processing flagged and unflagged claims).

From the section on "*information used by AI algorithms*" discuss what makes data as labelled data and what is the importance of it.

12.10 Financial Considerations for Setting Up Fraud Control Systems

Having understood the anti-fraud framework and role of technologies in fraud detection, we turn our focus to cost considerations for identifying frauds in the system. Efficient fraud control mechanisms need accurate data collection, which comes from relevant sources such as policyholder applications, historical data of claims, payments, interaction logs, including public databases and social media. This also means efficient integration across several departments of the organization, such as underwriting, claims, payments, etc. Dedicated fraud departments manned by human expertise and well-trained resources must be set up within organizations that have cost implications. An alternative approach is to outsource fraud investigations to external agencies, which could be either part of a third-party administrator (TPA) or exclusive fraud investigative agencies.

In the absence of openly available data, from the industry experience of authors, an attempt has been made to capture the cost of fraud investigation setups. Most insurance companies tend to investigate 7–10% of total claims, with an average claim size of ₹~50,000 and aim to achieve a success rate (finding a confirmed fraud claim) of about 40%. For every 100 claims, this amounts to an investigation of about 10 claims and finding 4 claims of fraud amounting to ₹2,00,000.

In case of an external fraud investigative agency, the per claim investigation charges could range from ₹700 to 1000 for a cashless claim and from ₹2500 to 3000 for a reimbursement claim. On an assumption of 40 investigated claims per month, the cost of investigation could range from ₹28,000 to 1,20,000 for a saving of ₹8,00,000 at a 40% success rate of finding fraudulent claims (40 × 40% × 50,000).

As against this, if an insurance company establishes an in-house fraud department with a target of 40 claims per month per employee on a cost-to-company (salary plus other travel incidentals, etc.) of ₹50,000 per month, the average cost of investigation per claim works out to be ₹1250. Organizations can also set up fraud investigation departments on a self-sustainable basis, where the cost savings accrued from repudiated claims are used for running the departments. These departments also have complete control over their operational and other activities with minimal dependency on the organization for separate funding and bear all the risks associated with running the department.

Use of AI/ML technologies can be deployed to flag suspicious fraudulent claims and since the algorithms are more sensitive in flagging fraudulent claims, the success rate of finding a fraudulent claim among the flagged cases likely goes up from 40% to 70%, even at a conservative estimate. Cost implications of setting up AI units, such as computers, servers, cloud architecture, and the cost of software is beyond the scope of this chapter, but it is estimated that in the long run, the per-claim cost of flagging a fraudulent claim works out to be as low as ₹10 even after considering all capital expenditure. All the above considerations are outlined below (Table 12.4) showing a high-level cost savings that can accrue from setting up anti-fraud units.

As a final note, the true realization of the benefits of setting up anti-fraud units can only be achieved when the suspicious claims are flagged before the payments are made, as recoveries from paid-up fraudulent claims are extremely challenging and may incur higher costs. It is exactly for this reason, use of AI/ML technologies is increasingly finding favour among both public and private payers. The technologies also come to the aid of investigating the most significant cases and improve turnaround times of genuine claims, as well as making funds available for payments to providers.

12.11 Legal Perspectives in Health Insurance Frauds

Globally, several governments have recognized the serious nature of health insurance frauds not only from a financial perspective but also the impact on patient care as well. Therefore, several laws have been enacted that allow for the implementation of strict regulations and penalties, including heavy fines, criminal charges, and imprisonment of fraudsters involved in health insurance frauds. Global and Indian Acts and Laws under which health insurance frauds are covered and legal ramifications for individuals and organizations involved in fraud are discussed.

In the United States, the False Claims Act, Anti-Kickback, and the Health Care Fraud Statute impose stringent penalties for health insurance fraud. Penalties may include jail time, monetary fines, and restitution requirements [14]. Under the US False Claims Act, whistleblowers can file qui tam lawsuits, which may lead to

Table 12.4 Cost savings from setting up fraud investigation departments (per 100 claims)

Attributes	Inhouse model	Outsourced model
A. Total claims received	100	100
B. Claims flagged for investigation (@10%) A × 10%	10	10
C. Cost of investigation per claim	₹1250	₹3000
D. Total cost of investigation (B × C)	₹12,500	₹30,000
E. Success rate @40% (B × 0.4)	4	4
F. Average claim size	₹50,000	₹50,000
G. Savings from repudiated fraud claims (E × F)	₹2,00,000	₹2,00,000
H. Operational expenses	₹10,000	–
I. Total investment (D + H)	₹22,500	₹30,000
J. Net savings (G-I)	₹1,67,500	₹1,70,000
K. Return on investment (J / I)	~7.4 times	~5.7 times
With use of technology (AI/ML)		
L. Cost of flagging claims (@ ₹10 per claim) (A × 10)	₹1000	₹1000
M. Success rate of finding frauds @70% (B × 0.7)	7	7
N. Total savings (F × M)	₹3,50,000	₹3,50,000
O. Total investment (I + L)	₹23,500	₹31,000
P. Net savings (N - O)	₹3,27,500	₹3,20,000
Q. Return on investment (P / O)	~13.9 times	~10.3 times

Note: All costs shown above are based on the experience of authors and only reimbursement claims are considered. Legal costs, if any, for challenged repudiated claims are not envisaged in the above scenario

significant financial recoveries and damages. Many countries impose additional sanctions on health insurance providers, including the revocation of licenses, exclusion from participation in public health insurance programs (e.g. Medicare or Medicaid), and other professional disciplinary actions.

Several laws and acts in India cover health insurance frauds directly or indirectly, where fraudsters can be penalized. Fraud in health insurance in India may be prosecuted under *Bharatiya Nyaya Sanhita* (BNS) [22]. Section 316 (IPC 420) deals with cheating and dishonesty. Section 336 (IPC 468) deals with forgery, Section 335 (IPC 464) for creating falsified documents, and Section 340 (IPC 471) deals with the use of forged documents or electronic records as genuine. Provisions under these sections can lead to imprisonment and fines.

For public officials involved in health insurance fraud, the Prevention of Corruption Act, 1988, Sections 13 and 7 are applicable. This act outlines penalties, including jail terms and fines, for corrupt practices.

Health insurance providers may also face liabilities under the Consumer Protection Act 2019 [23], particularly if fraudulent activities result in harm to patients.

Information Technology Act 2000 [24] under sections 43 and 63D provides for penalizing unauthorized access to computers and cheating by personation using computer resources, respectively. These may be particularly invoked for dealing with employee-committed frauds in an organization.

The National Health Authority (NHA) has taken several steps through well-documented policies to identify and penalize hospitals involved in frauds under the AB PM-JAY scheme, including recoveries and penalties, reporting and blacklisting facilities, displaying a list of such facilities in the public domain, etc.

Despite these efforts, enforcement remains a challenge, with many cases going unreported or unresolved due to resource constraints and the complex nature of health insurance frauds.

12.12 Global Practices in Fraud Management

Besides approaching health insurance frauds through legal means, several nations have established separate fraud control agencies and/or independent statutory authorities as strategies to mitigate frauds in the system. Strategies adopted by selected countries are discussed below and the practitioner of fraud management is encouraged to explore such global strategies in depth.

In the United States, the Centers for Medicare and Medicaid Services (CMS) identifies suspicious claims through data analytics. Similarly, the US Department of Health and Human Services (HHS) deploys Medical Fraud Strike Force teams in various areas that also use data analytics methods to target suspicious claims. These teams have a proven record of success in analysing data and investigative intelligence to quickly identify fraud and bring prosecutions [25]. The are inter-agency collaborations where HHS communicates credible allegations of frauds to CMS and payments are immediately stopped, which facilitates a preventive approach. Reportedly, the strike force teams have stopped operations of fraudulent schemes, arrested more than a thousand individuals and recovered millions in taxpayer money.

The National Health Service Counter Fraud Agency (NHSCFA) [5] in the United Kingdom is a special health authority to lead the fight against fraud, bribery, and corruption in the NHS. It is authorized to conduct audits, investigations, and public awareness campaigns. It encourages whistleblowers and the general public to reports frauds. It also appoints local counter fraud specialists (LCFS) who actively report frauds and work with chief financial officers and directors of finance. A separate digital forensics unit (DFU) under NHSCFA specializes in digital, computer, and mobile forensic investigations.

Australia manages health insurance frauds through Medicare Compliance Integrity Programs [26] run by Services Australia. Here again, data analytics and artificial intelligence technologies are used to flag suspicious cases. In collaboration with the Australian Federal Police, high-value frauds and organized frauds are handled. Australian Health Practitioner Regulation Agency (AHPRA) is an overseeing agency and has the power to investigate into malpractices and fraudulent billing practices.

In the European Union, cross-border collaborations are established through the European Health Insurance Fraud and Corruption Network (EHFCN) [27] to tackle frauds across the European Union. Best practices, research, fraud analytics, and shared intelligence across member states are some of the ways frauds are managed. Some countries in the European Union, such as France and the Netherlands have established dedicated investigative agencies within their health systems.

In South Africa, the Council for Medical Schemes is the overseeing department for the regulation of the medical schemes industry.

Singapore has established the Agency for Care Effectiveness [28] to evaluate care delivery practices and promote cost-effective solutions and reduce medical frauds. The Ministry of Health also oversees directly through regular audits and ensuring strict standards for billing practices.

In India, IRDAI stipulates that every private sector insurance company should have anti-fraud policies in place that are approved by the respective boards [29]. The anti-fraud policies shall focus on identification potential areas of fraud, fraud prevention mechanism, monitoring, coordination with law enforcement agencies for reporting and follow-up, a framework for fraud information sharing across insurers and due diligence procedures for background checks of employees, agents, intermediaries, and TPAs. The National Health Authority, which administers the world's largest publicly financed health assurance program, the AB PM-JAY, has established a national anti-fraud unit (NAFU) for monitoring frauds [30]. It recognized the importance of focus on technology to contain frauds in the scheme that is implemented in a completely paperless electronic format through its claims' transaction platform. The scheme implemented in 33 states and union territories across India established regional fraud control units in the form of state anti-fraud unit (SAFU). NHA utilizes advanced data analytics, artificial intelligence, and machine learning technologies for prevention, detection, and monitoring of frauds in the system as well as regular communication to the implementing states. NHA also has well-documented prevention, detection, and deterrence policies since the inception of the scheme in 2018, which are updated from time to time. It encourages public awareness, whistleblower activism, and issues public advisories.

In essence, most of the global and national fraud management strategies include establishing dedicated statutory authorities, use of data analytics, AI and ML technologies, well-documented policies, partnerships and collaborations, information sharing, public advisories, and whistleblower encouragement.

Activity Box 4

Explore anti-fraud measures adopted by other countries especially digital health focused countries like Estonia and South Korea. Enlist best practices.

Deep dive into fraud control measures in India and discuss how they can be further improved.

Review various initiatives, anti-fraud measures, and policy framework of NAFU. Classify the activities as per fraud control framework under prevention, detection and deterrence. Do you find any gaps, discuss.

Consider the structure of NAFU/SAFU by going through references provided. What do you think the institutional framework and governance structures adopted by NHA as fraud control measures? Are they in line with your thoughts in the previous activity?

Review the outcomes of NAFU activities. Gather information on the claims submitted in the PM-JAY system from the public dashboard (https://dashboard.pmjay.gov.in/publicdashboard/). Compare the volume of claims and expenditure incurred in the scheme. Consider the volume of fraudulent claims detected as of August 2022 referred in this section. What thoughts cross your mind. Discuss.

If you were to be the CEO of an organization such as NHA, what anti-fraud measures would you take. Discuss.

12.13 Case Study: India's Flagship Public Health Assurance Scheme AB PM-JAY

The *Ayushman Bharat Pradhan Mantri Jan Arogya Yojana* (AB PM-JAY) [31] is the world's largest publicly financed health assurance scheme launched in September 2018 as a step towards achieving Universal Health Coverage in India. The scheme is discussed at length as a case study covering its design, implementation, and initiative taken for fraud control.

12.13.1 Design of the Scheme

The scheme intends to ensure financial risk protection to India's population in the bottom 40% of the socio-economic pyramid on the basis of deprivation and occupation criteria using the socio-economic and caste census (SECC) 2011 database. This comprises ~55 crore population (~12 million families) across different states of India [29]. More recently, the scheme has been extended to cover senior citizens of 70+ years [32] regardless of their income criteria, thus adding an additional 4.5 crore families.

The scheme offers a sum insured of 5 lakh per year on a family floater basis for treatment of secondary and tertiary illnesses. There is no restriction on the family size, age, or gender. All pre-existing diseases (PEDs) are covered from day 1. The scheme provides for cashless services across a network of empanelled hospitals. It covers up to 3 days of pre-hospitalization and 15 days post-hospitalization expenses, such as diagnostics and medicines. Services include approximately 1929 procedures covering all the costs related to treatment, including but not limited to drugs, supplies, diagnostic services, physicians' fees, room charges, surgeon charges, OT, ICU charges, etc.

The scheme has been implemented in 34 Indian states and Union Territories. (Odisha is the latest state to implement the scheme. West Bengal and Delhi have not implemented the scheme.) The scheme is implemented in states either in conjunction with existing state health schemes or as a standalone scheme. The premium per family has been worked out at ₹1062 (in some cases up to ₹1500), with the central government contributing 60% and the state government 40%. (In select states/ Union Territories, the central Government contributes 100% premium.)

12.13.2 Scheme Implementation

National Health Authority (NHA) under the Ministry of Health is the implementing and policy-making body of the scheme. The State Health Authority (SHA) in respective states has the responsibility to oversee the scheme's implementation and progress in each state.

The states have been given flexibility to implement the scheme in three modes [33]. In a *Trust mode*, the SHA acts as a trustee and oversees the payment to the hospitals for their services; however, the states engage a TPA to process the claims and recommend claim approvals and payments. In an *insurance mode*, the states transfer the premium to a selected insurance provider, who then processes the claims and makes payments to the hospitals. In a *mixed mode*, claims up to a certain limit are processed and paid by insurance providers and claims beyond the limit by the SHA.

The scheme has been implemented in a completely paperless mode with a strong technology platform as the backbone. The identified eligible beneficiaries are issued a PM-JAY health card from a beneficiary identification system (BIS) platform. States, where existing health schemes have been merged with PM-JAY, are given flexibility to issue a co-branded health card.

A network of more than 31,809 public and private health insurance facilities has been empanelled to provide treatment to the scheme's beneficiaries. The scheme also has a portability feature where beneficiaries can take treatment across the country in any of the empanelled health insurance facility. Public hospitals are reimbursed for the health insurance services at par with the private hospitals.

The hospitals are onboarded through the hospital empanelment system platform. After rendering treatment to beneficiaries, the health insurance facilities submit claims through a transaction management system (TMS). Thus, the BIS, HEM, and TMS form the technology backbone for operationalizing the scheme.

NHA has developed 1900+ health benefits packages (HBP) to provide treatment to beneficiaries through this scheme. Standard treatment guidelines (STGs) have been documented for the HBPs that serve as a standard of care expected from the health facilities.

Activity Box 5

Carefully consider the entire design of the scheme. Discuss possible areas where and at what stages potential frauds can occur.

Discuss what fraud control measures should be ideally taken in the scheme [*Hint: Refer to section on anti-fraud framework*].

Given public empanelled hospitals also receive reimbursements at par with private facilities, do you think frauds are possible in public health facilities?

12.13.3 Fraud Control Measures

The National Health Authority recognized the importance of fraud control and has adopted a zero-tolerance approach [34] to frauds right from the inception of the Scheme. A dedicated National Anti-Fraud Unit has been established at NHA with a mandate to design policies, develop tools and technologies to detect frauds in the system with a focus on a preventive approach, and provide guidance and alerts to SHAs. State anti-fraud units (SAFU) have been established at each of the implementing States and Union Territories to support the initiatives of NAFU. Carefully drafted policy documents have been prepared and disseminated across the SHAs. Capacity building sessions are regularly conducted to sensitize and educate the implementing officials on frauds management [35].

As part of policy documents, NHA has designed prevention, detection and deterrence strategies, and developed anti-fraud guidelines [28] since the inception of the scheme. Separate guidelines for actions against confirmed fraud cases have also been provided. Whistleblower policies and public advisories have been developed and disseminated. In addition, a framework for field investigation and verification of suspicious cases has been developed.

12.13.4 Functioning of NAFU

The anti-fraud unit at NHA maintains a close watch of the utilization patterns and monitors on a daily basis through real-time dashboards, through continuous claims data pouring in from TMS. Risk assessment detection and analytical reporting (RADAR), fraud analytics control tracking system (FACTS), case level analysis dashboard, state performance analysis dashboard, and trigger performance dashboard are some of the analytical dashboards developed for closely tracking claim patterns, suspicious cases, and SHA activities [36]. These dashboards help in analysing outlier cases of claims based on hospitals, procedures, health benefit packages, length of stay, etc. These patterns are further used to develop triggers, select cases for desk audits, and audit of audits. Additionally, multiple third-party vendors have been engaged by NHA to develop triggers based on industry best practices, latest technologies, and on-ground intelligence.

Using data analytics and AI/ML technologies, different fraud control triggers have been deployed in the system and suspicious cases and alerts generated by these triggers are forwarded to the SHA of implementing states for further investigations and actions as per policy guidelines. Proactive measures are taken for fraud control by developing risk scores of hospitals and claims. Aadhar-based biometric verification of beneficiaries is done at the time of admission and discharge at the hospital. On-bed photographs of beneficiaries availing treatment in the hospitals are made mandatory while submitting claims along with other specified mandatory documents. Random joint medical audits and field investigations are carried out in association with SAFU [33, 37, 38].

12.13.5 Outcome of Initiatives of NAFU

Various measures taken by the NAFU at NHA have resulted in fraud discoveries in the scheme, penalties, recoveries of monies, de-empanelment of hospitals, and institution of criminal actions/FIRs against erring entities. As per publicly available information and from replies to various parliament questions and press releases, the following outcomes are seen:

March 2020:

(i) A total of 205 hospitals de-empanelled.
(ii) Show cause notices/suspensions/penalties have been imposed against 442 hospitals.
(iii) FIRs have been registered in six cases.

August 2022:

Around 0.18% of the total authorized hospital admissions under the scheme are confirmed as fraud since its inception [32].

July–August 2023:

(i) Actions taken against 1.6 lakh claims worth 287 crore and penalties amounting to 20.71 crore have been levied against errant entities.
(ii) 9.5 crore penalty amounts have been recovered [39].
(iii) 5.3 lakh fraudulent beneficiary AB PM-JAY health cards have been blocked in the system with the help of AI technologies [40].

March 2025:

Suitable actions taken by NAFU include the following [41]:

(i) Rejection of 3.56 lakh claims worth 643 crore.
(ii) Levy of penalties worth 122 crore against 1504 errant hospitals.
(iii) De-empanelment of 1114 hospitals.
(iv) Suspension of 549 hospitals.

Activity Box 6
Review various initiatives, anti-fraud measures, and policy framework of NAFU. Classify the activities as per fraud control framework under prevention, detection, and deterrence. Do you find any gaps, discuss.

Consider the structure of NAFU/SAFU by going through references provided. What do you think of the institutional framework and governance structures adopted by NHA as fraud control measures? Are they in line with your thoughts in the previous activity?

Review the outcomes of NAFU activities. Gather information on the claims submitted in the PM-JAY system from the public dashboard (https://dashboard.pmjay.gov.in/publicdashboard/). Compare the volume of claims and expenditure incurred in the scheme. Consider the volume of fraudulent claims detected as of August 2022 referred in this section. What thoughts cross your mind. Discuss.

If you were to be the CEO of an organization such as NHA, what anti-fraud measures would you take. Discuss.

12.14 Summary

In conclusion, frauds in health insurance are inevitable. Public and private health insurance equally suffers due to frauds in the system with multifarious outcomes such as impact on budgets and finances, loss of reputation and trust deficit, and quality of care endangering health of people, weakening health systems as well as negative impact on achieving sustainable development goals and financing for Universal Health Coverage.

It is imperative that organizations responsible for administering public and private insurance schemes are perpetually vigilant, develop and strengthen systems for the best possible fraud control, control frauds arising both within and outside the organization and try to be one step ahead of the fraudsters in the constant pursuit of catching frauds and fraudsters. Dedicated and trained teams that can read criminal minds are the best resources in this regard. Fraud detection can also be considered as a profession and programs similar to Certified Fraud Examiners should be designed towards the development of human resources. Senior leadership awareness programs should be introduced in both public and private organizations to orient and sensitize top management.

Organizations must also invest in emerging technologies and constantly update fraud detection methods as they tend to quickly become obsolete and fraudsters up their game to be one step ahead. Such investments pay rich dividends in the long run. Focus and emphasis on "prevention" is pivotal to save critical finances and budgets, especially in resource-constrained economies. Collaborations and partnerships play a significant role in knowledge sharing and cross-learning. Just as frauds impact multiple stakeholders, fraud control should also be a multi-stakeholder engagement; coming togetherness, interactions of organization leaders, public authorities, statutory bodies, vigilante civil societies, law enforcement agencies would make everyone alert, and stay focused towards controlling frauds.

References

1. Sippy DS. Fraudulent health insurance claims [Internet]. Medindia. 2012; [cited 2025 Feb 5]. Available from: https://www.medindia.net/health/insurance/fraudulent-health-insurance-claims.htm
2. Bhatia M. Evolution of the Indian health insurance sector: a review. J Manag Res Anal. 2018;5(2):107–12. https://doi.org/10.18231/2394-2770.2018.0017.
3. National Health Accounts Estimates for India (2021–22) [Internet]. National Health Systems Resource Centre (NHSRC), Ministry of Health and Family Welfare; 2024 p. 30. Available from: www.nhsrcindia.org
4. Annual Reports [Internet]. IRDAI. Available from: https://irdai.gov.in/document-detail?documentId=4273788
5. The Critical Health Impacts of Corruption. In: Crossing the global quality chasm: improving health care worldwide [Internet]. National Academies Press (US); 2018 [cited 2024 Nov 7]. Available from: https://www.ncbi.nlm.nih.gov/books/NBK535646/
6. National Health Care Anti-Fraud Association Headquarters. NHCAA—A private-public partnership against health care fraud [Internet]. Available from: http://www.nhcaa.org
7. Counter fraud services | National Services Scotland [Internet]. National Services Scotland 2021 [cited 2025 Mar 20]. Available from: http://www.cfs.scot.nhs.uk
8. Kumaraswamy N, Markey MK, Ekin T, Barner JC, Rascati K. Healthcare fraud data mining methods: a look back and look ahead. Perspect Health Inf Manag. 2022;19(1):1i. PMID: 35440932; PMCID: PMC9013219
9. Gunja MZ, Gumas ED, Williams II RD. U.S. Health care from a global perspective, 2022: accelerating spending, worsening outcomes [Internet]. The Commonwealth Fund 2023. Available from: https://www.commonwealthfund.org/publications/issue-briefs/2023/jan/us-health-care-global-perspective-2022
10. Shrank WH, Rogstad TL, Parekh N. Waste in the US health care system. JAMA [Internet]. 2019;322(15) https://doi.org/10.1001/jama.2019.13978.
11. Speaking notes on health insurance frauds [Internet]. [cited 2025 Feb 20]. Available from: https://www.insuranceinstituteofindia.com/c/document_library/get_file?uuid=e4632c21-da80-494c-9264-395283e3e4c0&groupId=16940
12. Cylus J, Papanicolas I, Smith PC. Health system efficiency: how to make measurement matter for policy and management [Internet]. Nihgov European Observatory on Health Systems and Policies; 2016 [cited 2025 Feb 12]. Available from: https://www.ncbi.nlm.nih.gov/books/NBK436883/

13. Gee J, Button M, Brooks G. The financial cost of healthcare fraud: what data from around the world shows. Milton Keynes: MacIntyre Hudson, 2010. 15.
14. Reddy KS, Selvaraj S, Rao K, Chokshi M, Kumar P, Arora V, et al. A critical assessment of the existing health insurance models in India [Internet]. Yumpu. New Delhi: Public Health Foundation of India; 2011 Jan [cited 2025 Feb 14] p 66–79. Available from: https://www.yumpu.com/en/document/view/40071121/a-critical-assessment-of-the-existing-health-insurance-models-in-india
15. Sparrow MK. Fraud in the U.S. Health-Care System: Exposing the vulnerabilities of automated payments systems. Soc Res. 2008 Dec;75(4):1151–80. https://doi.org/10.1353/sor.2008.0015.
16. National Health Authority. Measures to curb fraud under Ayushman Bharat. Available from: https://www.pmjay.gov.in.
17. Tackling Wasteful Spending on Health [Internet]. OECD 2017. Available from: https://www.oecd.org/en/publications/tackling-wasteful-spending-on-health_9789264266414-en.html
18. Hausenkamph DS, Cuadrado DC, Kirya M. Logistics in health emergencies: dealing with fraud and corruption risks across supply chains (Part 3 of 3) [Internet]. U4 Anti-Corruption Resource Centre; 2023. [cited 2025 Feb 12]. Available from: https://www.u4.no/blog/logistics-in-emergencies-dealing-with-fraud-and-corruption-risks-across-supply-chains
19. Sparrow MK, Fraud control in the health care industry: assessing the state of the art, research in brief, National Institute of Justice, NCJ Number 172841. Available from: https://www.ojp.gov/library/publications/fraud-control-health-care-industry-assessing-state-art-research-brief
20. Niti Aayog. National health stack strategy and approach [internet]. 2018. Available from: https://abdm.gov.in:8081/uploads/NHS_Strategy_and_Approach_1_89e2dd8f87.pdf
21. Hasanin T, Khoshgoftaar TM, Leevy JL, Bauder RA. Severely imbalanced big data challenges: investigating data sampling approaches. J Big Data. 2019;6(1) https://doi.org/10.1186/s40537-019-0274-4.
22. Ministry of Law and Justice, Government of India, Bharatiya Nyaya Sanhita, 2023, The Gazette of India [Internet]. 2023 [cited 20s25 Feb 12]. Available from: https://www.mha.gov.in/sites/default/files/250883_english_01042024.pdf
23. Ministry of Law and Justice, Government of India, The Consumer Protection Act 2019, The Gazette of India [Internet]. 2019 [cited 2025 Feb 12]. Available from: https://ncdrc.nic.in/bare_acts/CPA2019.pdf
24. Information Technology Act 2000 | Ministry of Electronics and Information Technology, Government of India [Internet]. www.meity.gov.in. Available from: https://www.meity.gov.in/content/information-technology-act-2000-0
25. Medicare Fraud Strike Force | Medicare and Medicaid Fraud | HHS-OIG Office of Inspector General | U.S. Department of Health and Human Services [Internet]. oig.hhs.gov. Available from: https://oig.hhs.gov/fraud/strike-force/
26. Our Medicare compliance approach [Internet]. Australian Government Department of Health and Aged Care. 2024. Available from: https://www.health.gov.au/topics/medicare/compliance/our-approach
27. European Health Insurance Fraud and Corruption Network (EHFCN),2024. Available from: https://www.ehfcn.org/
28. Government of Singapore. Agency for Care Effectiveness [Internet]. ACE. Available from: https://www.ace-hta.gov.sg/
29. Insurance regulatory and development Authority of India (IRDAI). Insurance fraud monitoring Framework 2013. Available from: https://irdai.gov.in/web/guest/document-detail?documentId=371824
30. National Health Authority. National Anti-Fraud Unit, Anti-Fraud guidelines [Internet]. Pmjaygovin 2018. [cited 2025 Feb 21]. Available from: https://pmjay.gov.in/resources/documents
31. Official Website Ayushman Bharat PM-JAY | National Health Authority [Internet]. Available from: https://pmjay.gov.in/
32. Cabinet approves health coverage to all senior citizens of the age 70 years and above irrespective of income under Ayushman Bharat Pradhan Mantri Jan Arogya Yojana (AB PM-JAY) |

Ministry of Health and Family Welfare | GOI [Internet]. Mohfw.gov.in. 2024. Available from: https://mohfw.gov.in/?q=pressrelease-64
33. National Health Authority. States at a Glance [Internet]. pmjay.gov.in. 2018 [cited 2023 Apr]. Available from: https://pmjay.gov.in/states/states-glance
34. Anti-fraud system for India's National Health Insurance Scheme (AB-PMJAY) [Internet]. pib.gov.in. 2022 [cited 2025 Feb 21]. Available from: https://pib.gov.in/PressReleasePage.aspx?PRID=1847423
35. Cost of Treatment Under Ayushman Bharat PMJAY [Internet]. pib.gov.in. 2019 [cited 2025 Feb 21]. Available from: https://pib.gov.in/PressReleasePage.aspx?PRID=1594170
36. National Health Authority. Annual Report 2022–23 [Internet]. 2023 [cited 2025 Feb 21] p. 80–84. Available from: https://abdm.gov.in:8081/uploads/NHA_Annual_Report_2022_2023_4f3bc6e2a5.pdf
37. Government of India Ministry of Health and Family Welfare, Department of Health and Family Welfare, Lok Sabha Unstarred Question No. 3292 [Internet]. 2022 [cited 2025 Feb 15]. Available from: https://sansad.in/getFile/loksabhaquestions/annex/179/AU3292.pdf?source=pqals
38. Government of India Ministry of Health and Family Welfare, Department of Health and Family Welfare, Lok Sabha Unstarred Question No. 3292 [Internet]. 2022 [cited 2025 Feb 15]. Available from: https://sansad.in/getFile/loksabhaquestions/annex/173/AU3448.pdf?source=pqals
39. Government of India Ministry of Health and Family Welfare, Department of Health and Family Welfare, Lok Sabha Unstarred Question No. 325 [Internet]. 2022 [cited 2025 Feb 15]. Available from: https://sansad.in/getFile/loksabhaquestions/annex/1712/AS325.pdf?source=pqals
40. Perappadan BS. AB PM-JAY employs AI anti-fraud initiative, collects ₹9.5 crore in penalty [Internet]. The Hindu. 2023; [cited 2025 Mar 21]. Available from: https://www.thehindu.com/news/national/ab-pmjay-employs-ai-anti-fraud-initiative-collects-95-crore-in-penalty/article67083426.ece
41. Government of India Ministry of Health and Family Welfare, Department of Health and Family Welfare Rajya Sabha Unstarred Question No. 1403 To be answered on 11th March 2025 [Internet]. [cited 2025 Mar 18]. Available from: https://sansad.in/getFile/annex/267/AU1403_AyF1hc.pdf?source=pqars

Governance, Monitoring and Evaluation, and Capacity Building

13

Kameshwar Rao, Ruchira Agrawal, Rituparna Sengupta, and Babita Dhankhar

Abstract

While health financing is a core function of health systems, there are several structural determinants for the implementation of successful health financing strategies. Strong governance establishes institutional structures, policies, accountability principles, and regulations; capacity building ensures the strengthening human resources to implement policies and enforce regulations; monitoring and evaluation provides data and insights to assess policy effectiveness. Thus, governance, capacity building, and monitoring and evaluation provide three closely interrelated elements of health financing. This chapter introduces the basic concepts of these three elements, their respective roles, challenges, and best practices. It attempts to provide insights into how they can be integrated to enhance accountability, sustainability, and efficiency in health financing.

With financial resources always being finite, it becomes critical to ensure that financial flows are well aligned with the goals of health systems. Without good governance, health financing systems run the risk of leakages, inefficiencies, and inequitable distribution, leading to suboptimal health systems. Monitoring and evaluation systems provide critical feedback mechanisms by tracking financial flows, progress made by measuring performance and achievements in line with

K. Rao
Formerly, Monitoring Evaluation & Research, National Health Authority, CGHS, Pune, India

R. Agrawal (✉)
Capacity Building, National Health Authority, AB PM-JAY, New Delhi, India
e-mail: lead.mel@nha.gov.in

R. Sengupta
National Health Authority, New Delhi, India

B. Dhankhar
Capacity Building, National Health Authority, New Delhi, India

S. Prinja (ed.), *Healthcare Financing and Insurance*,
https://doi.org/10.1007/978-981-95-3513-2_13

the objectives, and enabling policymakers to make adjustments and midcourse corrections as needed. For effective implementation of governance and monitoring and evaluation frameworks, capacity building provides strong human, institutional, and technological capabilities. Investments in technical expertise, digital innovations, and management skills enhance the efficiency of policymakers and administrators in managing health financing systems in an optimal way.

This chapter highlights the intricate relationships and interdependencies between governance, monitoring and evaluation, and capacity building, and their importance for building resilient systems and driving better health system outcomes.

Keywords

Governance structures · Tracer indicators · Monitoring and evaluation (M&E) framework · LogFrame

Learning Objectives

After going through the chapter, you will be able to understand:

- Basic concepts of Governance, Capacity Building, and Monitoring and Evaluation (M&E)
- Interdependencies of these three elements and the importance of each of them for efficient health financing systems and institutional challenges
- Governance structures for health financing
- Prerequisites for implementation of M&E systems including technology considerations
- Approach for setting up Capacity Building processes for health financing

Key Terms

- *Accountability:* Means by which individuals and organizations report to a recognized authority and are held responsible for their actions. It involves the responsibility of the individual or organization to remain answerable for the activities and accept the consequences of one's actions—both positive and negative.
- *Financial sustainability*: In the context of public institutions or government—the ability to continue, now and in future, current policies without creating excessive debt burden, dependency on external funding resources, or compromising quality of essential public services.

- *Corporate social responsibility (CSR)*: Voluntary commitment of private sector organizations to contribute to public health goals by financing or supporting health initiatives beyond their statutory obligations.
- *Open-source software (OSS)*: Software programs whose source code is publicly available allowing users to view, modify, distribute, and enhance the code freely. The products are often developed by collaborative contributions from individuals, organizations, and communities promoting transparency, innovation, and accessibility.
- *Commercial off-the-shelf (COTS) software*: Ready-made, commercially available software products that are developed, marketed, and sold by vendors to meet general or specific business needs.
- *Key performance indicators (KPIs):* Quantifiable metrics used to assess and measure the effectiveness, efficiency, and success of an organization, program, or initiative in achieving its strategic objectives. Often represented on the dashboard for institutional decision-makers or public information purposes.
- *Tracer indicators:* Selected set of key indicators, which act as representative of a broader health system. Multiple KPIs together form an index, for example, UHC coverage index.
- *Digital Personal Data Protection (DPDP) Act*: A law in India promulgated in August 2023 that protects the rights of individuals with respect to their digital personal data, including health data. The act also provides guidelines for processing such data, enforcement, penalties, and other provisions.
- *General Data Protection Regulation (GDPR)*: The European Union regulation on information privacy, which is a component of privacy law and human rights law in the European Union and the European Economic Area. It provides for rights of individuals over their personal information.
- *Learning management system (LMS)*: A software platform designed to *create, deliver, manage, and track educational content and training programs.* It is widely used in *corporate training, educational institutions, and government organizations* to facilitate learning and development.
- *iGOT Karmayogi:* Integrated Government Online Training (iGOT) *Karmayogi* platform is the digital learning platform that provides e-learning courses, assessment, and certifications to India's civil servants.
- *Capacity Building Commission (CBC)*: An institution constituted in April 2021 by the Government of India. CBC has been mandated to drive standardization and harmonization across the Indian civil services landscape. As the custodian of civil services capacity building reforms, the Commission's role is central to the overall institutional framework of iGOT *Karmayogi.*

13.1 Introduction

Effective health financing is the backbone of a well-functioning healthcare system. It determines how resources are mobilized, allocated, and utilized to ensure equitable and affordable access to quality healthcare. However, financial resources alone do not guarantee better health outcomes. The three important pillars for the success of any health financing system are governance, monitoring and evaluation (M&E), and capacity building. These elements work together to enhance efficiency, transparency, and accountability, ensuring that finite financial resources are used optimally to achieve the desired health goals.

Governance in health financing refers to the structures, policies, and decision-making processes that guide financial management in the healthcare sector. Strong governance ensures that resources are allocated efficiently, fraud and corruption are minimized, and financial policies align with national health priorities. Good governance establishes clear rules, accountability mechanisms, and strategic oversight, fostering trust and sustainability in health financing.

M&E plays a crucial role in assessing the effectiveness, efficiency, and impact of health financing policies and programs. It involves tracking health expenditures, program efficiencies, tracking metrics of performance, and analyzing service delivery outcomes. Through M&E, governments and stakeholders can identify gaps, prevent fund mismanagement, and adjust policies to improve resource allocation. Key mechanisms include financial tracking systems, impact assessments, real-time data analytics and dashboards, as well as periodical audits. A robust M&E framework ensures that health financing achieves its intended results, contributing to evidence-based policy decisions.

Capacity building strengthens the ability of health institutions, financial managers, and policymakers to efficiently manage health financing systems. It includes training, technical support, and institutional development by providing learning resources to enhance skills. Capacity building also extends to health workers, local governments, and community organizations, ensuring that all stakeholders understand and engage effectively in program implementation. Without adequate capacity, even the best-designed financing models may fail due to inefficiencies and lack of expertise.

13.1.1 Interdependence of Governance, M&E, and Capacity Building

These three critical elements of health financing are interconnected and mutually reinforcing. While good governance sets the rules and accountability structures for financial management, M&E provides the evidence to assess whether financial resources are being used effectively. Capacity building ensures that institutions and individuals have the skills to implement institutional policies successfully. Together, they create a transparent, accountable, and efficient health financing system, ensuring that limited resources are utilized optimally to improve healthcare access and outcomes. The next section of this chapter examines these three closely with examples to enhance the concepts.

13.2 Governance in Health Financing

Governance is a broad term that encompasses of the many ways in which human beings, as individuals and groups, organize themselves to achieve agreed goals. Governance, described in [1] as a broad concept, captures the organization of individuals and groups in pursuit of collective aims across public, private, or combined spheres. Health systems governance refers to the processes, structures, and institutions that are in place to oversee and manage a country's healthcare system [2]. However, a World Bank research paper [3] notes that agreeing on a single definition of governance in the health sector is challenging because governance functions across multiple levels. After examining different interpretations, it proposes that governance can be understood as the interaction of political, social, economic, and institutional factors that shape how organizations and individuals act, thereby influencing performance. Perhaps such a definition also supports broader aspects of *nudge theory*, which, in the context of governance framework, brings positive behavioral changes in people and guides or nudges them to make decisions that effectively work in the long term.

It is important also to understand that governance is not the same as government in that the rule systems of the latter are rooted in formal and legal procedures, while those of the former are also marked by informal rule systems [4]. While health service delivery and financing can involve public, private, or voluntary actors, strong governance is necessary to ensure that fundamental functions operate efficiently [5]. Thus, multi-stakeholder engagement from the public and private sectors becomes critical in the formation of governance structures based on certain key principles.

13.2.1 Foundational Principles of Governance in Health Financing

In order to ensure that health financing is well regulated, equitable, and capable of delivering quality healthcare services to its citizens, countries should form governance structures on certain key principles:

- *Accountability*: Well-defined roles and legal frameworks to prevent corruption and inefficiencies
- *Transparency*: Clear and open data on health expenditures and financial reporting
- *Efficiency*: Performance- and needs-based resource allocation
- *Equity and Inclusivity*: Health financing structures should promote fair, universal, and equitable access to healthcare services
- *Sustainability*: Health financing should be aligned with long-term economic and health priorities

13.2.2 Components of Governance Structures for Health Financing

Health financing has been elaborately discussed in previous chapters. The three core components of health financing such as revenue collection, resource pooling, and purchasing services come with a specific requirement of governance at each level, but a common thematic area that emerges is a broader role of *stewardship* as defined by the World Health Organization that includes oversight, regulation, and accountability of all actors involved in health system functioning including financing and all aspects of resource generation [6]. The key actors involved in health financing and related governance areas are depicted in Fig. 13.1.

Each of the elements of the governance structure is discussed below for a better understanding of the role of various players and actors in health financing.

1. *Ministry of Health—Role in Policy Leadership and Oversight*

The Ministry of Health (MoH) plays a critical role in providing *policy leadership and oversight* in health financing. As the central authority in the health sector, the MoH is responsible for developing *national health financing policies*, setting strategic priorities, and ensuring that financial resources are effectively allocated to improve health outcomes. To achieve these goals, it works in collaboration with the Ministry of Finance and other stakeholders to secure adequate funding, design sustainable financing mechanisms, and oversee the implementation of health budgets.

To enhance *oversight*, the MoH establishes regulatory frameworks, monitors financial flows, and enforces accountability mechanisms to prevent inefficiencies and financial mismanagement (Box 1). It also ensures that financing decisions align with broader health system goals, such as achieving *Universal Health Coverage (UHC)* and promoting equitable access to healthcare. Additionally, the MoH plays a key role in evaluating the impact of health financing policies through M&E systems, enabling data-driven policy adjustments for better financial sustainability and service delivery.

Box 1 Policy and Oversight Initiatives of the MoH

1. *National Health Policy 2017: This policy outlines strategic directions for health financing, aiming to achieve universal health coverage and ensure equitable access to quality healthcare services.*
2. Financial resource allocation and monitoring: The MoH collaborates with central and state governments for allocation of financial resources effectively across various health programs. It monitors public health expenditure to ensure funds are utilized efficiently and align with policy objectives. Detailed reports such as health sector financing by Centre and states/union territories in India and other annual and budget reports [7–10] provide

Fig. 13.1 Governance structures for health financing. CAG Comptroller and Auditor General of India, IRDAI Insurance Regulatory and Development Authority of India

insights into expenditure patterns and support informed decision-making. National Health Accounts Estimates [11] give clear insights into government and private expenditure on health and details of out-of-pocket-expenditure (OOPE) incurred by citizens.
3. Strategic health initiatives: The MoH leads the execution of major health financing schemes such as the National Health Mission and *Ayushman Arogya Mandirs* (Health & Wellness Centers for primary health) and the *Ayushman Bharat Pradhan Mantri Jan Arogya Yojana* (AB PM-JAY for secondary and tertiary health) toward attainment of UHC and sustainable development goals of health.

Through these mechanisms, the MoH demonstrates its commitment to strengthening health financing governance, ensuring that financial resources are mobilized, allocated, and utilized to improve health outcomes for the Indian population.

2. *Ministry of Finance—Budgeting and Financial Management*

The Ministry of Finance (MoF) of India plays a pivotal role in health financing, primarily through the following mechanisms:

The MoF is responsible for allocating financial resources to the health sector during the national budgeting process. It collaborates with the MoH to determine annual funding requirements for various health programs and initiatives through budget estimates and revised estimates. This collaboration ensures that adequate funds are earmarked to meet the country's healthcare objectives. The MoF also publishes annual economic surveys, which includes analyses of health sector financing. These analyses provide insights into public health expenditure trends and inform policy decisions. For instance, the economic survey often references data from the National Health Accounts to assess the efficiency and effectiveness of health expenditure. The MoF also influences health financing through taxation policies. For example, the Goods and Services Tax (GST) Council, chaired by the Finance Minister, deliberates on tax rates applicable to health-related goods and services, which reflects the role of MoF in shaping policies that affect healthcare costs.

3. *Institutional Arrangements for Health Coverage and Risk Pooling*

The National Health Authority (NHA) in India serves as an apex body to implement the flagship public health assurance program, the *Ayushman Bharat Pradhan Mantri Jan Arogya Yojana* (AB PM-JAY), currently implemented in 35 states and union territories and covering over 600 million population as of March 2025 [12, 13]. The NHA coordinates various State Health Authorities and manages the scheme administration including premium-related budget allocation to states, beneficiary enrolment, provider empanelment and claim settlement processes. It is also responsible for designing and fine-tuning policies for scheme implementation, fraud prevention, monitoring and evaluation, and capacity building processes. The NHA has also been additionally tasked with convergence of various public health insurance schemes operating in India to improve operational efficiency and financial sustainability. The NHA also implements India's digital health mission—the *Ayushman Bharat* Digital Mission (ABDM) and responsible for development of technology building blocks and structures, implementation policies and designing incentive programs among various other tasks associated with ABDM. While the NHA implements these two pillars of India's health system envisioned in National Health Policy 2017, the other two pillars—the National Health Mission and the *Ayushman Bharat* Health and Infrastructure Mission (ABHIM) are being implemented by the MoH directly.

Through these roles, the National Health Authority plays a crucial part in strengthening India's health financing framework, ensuring that financial resources are effectively utilized to provide accessible, affordable, and quality healthcare to the intended beneficiaries.

4. *Donors, Development Partners, and External funding*

Contributions from various international organizations, philanthropic foundations, bilateral agencies, and multilateral institutions support different facets of India's health system. These efforts supplement domestic resources and enhance health delivery. World Bank, Asian Development Bank, United States Agency for International Development (USAID), Gates Foundation, Rockefeller foundation, are some of these organizations. Besides, contributions from corporate social responsibility (CSR) initiatives and high-net-worth individuals (HNIs) are playing a growing role in funding health programs. While the Indian donor base is broadening, CSR and HNI/affluent donations are growing moderately. Private philanthropy grew 10% in FY 2023 to ₹1.2 lakh crore ($15 billion). This faster growth (vs. 5% annual growth between 2018 and 2023) was driven by growth in family philanthropy (15%) and retail (12%) [14].

The external funding is not just limited to public sector, but investments are also seen in private sector such as investments from sovereign wealth fund of Singapore in efforts to further strengthen India's private sector healthcare.

5. *Public-Private Partnership (PPP)*

PPPs are one of the important strategies in India's healthcare sector, aiming to leverage the strengths of both public and private entities to enhance healthcare delivery, accessibility, and quality. These collaborations address various challenges, including infrastructure deficits, resource limitations, and the need for advanced medical technologies.

The National Health Mission has implemented PPP models to establish diagnostic centers and upgrade facilities in public hospitals. Reports from National Health Systems and Resource Centre (NHSRC) provide guidelines [15] and highlight successful models to encourage such collaborations. "10 Bed Intensive Care Unit (ICU)" project [16] established intensive care units in rural hospitals, utilizing telemedicine to connect with urban specialists. PPPs in India's healthcare sector represent a dynamic approach to bridging gaps in service delivery and infrastructure. By fostering collaboration between the public and private sectors, these partnerships aim to create a more resilient and inclusive healthcare system.

6. *Independent Regulatory and Oversight Authorities*

Independent regulatory and oversight bodies are essential in India's healthcare sector to ensure adherence to transparency, accountability, and standards. These institutions operate autonomously from the executive branch, providing checks and balances that uphold the integrity of healthcare delivery and financing. Comptroller and Auditor General of India (CAG) performance audits of major health schemes such as the AB PM-JAY, NHM, and other national health programs, PPP models, utilization of donor funds, to assess whether allocated funds are used appropriately. The audit reports published in public domain highlight inefficiencies, fund mismanagement, or underutilization of health budgets thus helping in corrective measures, improving fund management and better efficiencies.

Some other examples are National Medical Commission (NMC) for medical education and practice; Central Drugs Standard Control Organization (CDSCO), the national regulatory authority for pharmaceuticals and medical devices; Insurance Regulatory and Development Authority of India (IRDAI) for Overseeing the insurance sector, including health insurance. These bodies establish clear standards and guidelines for healthcare practices, products, and services. They conduct regular inspections and audits to ensure compliance, taking corrective actions when necessary. Many regulatory authorities make their observations and actions available for public consumption.

7. *Local Government Authorities*

In Indian health systems, financial management is often decentralized, enabling and empowering local government authorities to take financial decisions. This reduces bureaucratic delays, enhances accountability and better management by contextualizing resource utilization to the local community needs. State and District Health Agencies/Societies, Panchayat Raj Institutions (PRI), Urban Local Bodies like municipal corporations are some examples where healthcare financial needs of local community are tackled independently by authorities heading these organizations.

Fund flows are also decentralized and controlled through direct benefit transfer (DBT) into beneficiary accounts directly without intermediary interventions. Government grants and patient-service generated revenues flow directly into hospital accounts like *Rogi Kalyan Samiti* [17] accounts for direct use by the hospitals for improved service delivery.

8. *Legislative Oversight*

Role of elected representatives plays a crucial role in health financing. Parliament and state legislatures take on monitoring and ensuring accountability in health financing policies, budget and expenditures. CAG reports attract the attention of Parliamentary Committees—the Public Accounts Committee (PAC) reviews and recommendations and their implementation. The Standing Finance Committee on the MoH reviews policies, performance, and expenditures. The Estimates Committee evaluates the effectiveness of government spending on healthcare programs. Question hour debates and discussions on health expenditure, shortages, quality of program implementation ensure improved policies and corrective actions.

Laws with reference to the health sector such as the Clinical Establishment Act 2010, National Medical Commission Act 2019, Ayushman Bharat schemes are discussed, debated, and passed by the legislature. Thus, legislative oversight is crucial for ensuring transparency, accountability, and efficiency in health financing to drive health sector improvements.

Besides the governance structures discussed above, the National Institution for Transforming India (the NITI Aayog) is a key policy think tank that plays a strategic role in advising the union government on shaping health financing policies and reforms. Unlike the ministry of health and the ministry of finance, it functions as a policy driver and reform catalyst to ensure health financing remains in alignment with long-term sustainable development goals.

Establishing efficient governance structures is not without challenges. Overlapping roles and responsibilities between ministries can lead to suboptimal implementation and policy conflicts and poor execution. Weak monitoring and auditing can potentially lead to inefficiencies, leakages, and corruption. Political influence and priorities may influence budget allocations rather than public health needs. Inadequate, unreliable data and poor tracking systems can hinder evidence-based decision-making. Disparities and inequalities in resource allocation can result in imbalances and unequal healthcare access. Policies may be unduly influenced by vested interests of external agencies. Policymakers should therefore be well aware of these governance challenges and guard against them for creating efficient health financing systems.

Toward the end of this chapter, a case study is presented on the National Health Authority (NHA) on the implementation of two critical pillars of India's health system, i.e., the *Ayushman Bharat Pradhan Mantri Jan Arogya Yojana* (AB PM-JAY) and the *Ayushman Bharat* Digital Mission (ABDM). Readers are advised to review the theoretical aspects of Governance, M&E, and Capacity Building and study their practical implementation at the NHA.

13.3 Monitoring and Evaluation

Monitoring and Evaluation (M&E) is a systematic process used to assess the performance of programs, projects, and policies to ensure they achieve their intended outcomes effectively and efficiently. While monitoring involves the continuous collection and analysis of data to track progress and identify challenges, evaluation focuses on assessing the value or significance of a policy or program by determining the relevance of objectives, effectiveness of design and implementation, efficiency of resource utilization, and the sustainability of outcomes [18]. Both the processes are synergistic, providing evidence-based inputs to enhance decision-making, improve accountability, and optimize resource allocation. Monitoring provides real-time data for management, while evaluation offers in-depth assessment. Further, evaluation relies heavily on monitoring data, including baseline information, implementation insights, and result measurements, to answer key questions. A well-structured M&E system is crucial for efficiently overseeing and guiding the execution of various health schemes.

Key Components of M&E Include the Following

- Assessing whether a policy is being implemented as intended on the ground
- Creating and defining key performance indicators (KPIs) to measure progress
- Monitoring KPIs through data collection and management
- Identifying and addressing challenges in implementing new mandates
- Setting goals and expected outcomes
- Creating an evaluation framework to assess the impact of the scheme, program, or policy
- Engagement of Stakeholders
- Identifying and addressing challenges through analysis and interpretation of data

13.3.1 Relevance of M&E to Health Financing

M&E in health financing is essential for ensuring that financial resources are used efficiently, equitably, and effectively to improve health outcomes. Monitoring involves the continuous tracking of financial flows, expenditures, and health system performance to ensure that health financing mechanisms are functioning as intended. Some of the essentials of M&E in health finance include tracking budgets and health expenditures, evaluating fund allocations and efficiency, monitoring service coverage whether target beneficiaries are covered sufficiently, and assessing financial protection through out-of-pocket-expenditure of beneficiaries. It also includes conducting impact assessments of financing reforms, cost-effectiveness analysis, financial and health equity analysis and performance evaluations. All these metrics can be monitored as Key performance indicators (KPIs) to serve as program efficiency and effectiveness measures. With specific reference to health financing and Universal Health Coverage, tracer indicators are often used, which act as a proxy or representative markers to gauge overall health system performance.

13.3.2 Principles of M&E

The principles of effective monitoring and evaluation are crucial to ensure accuracy, efficiency, and implementation of the programs and intervention. In the absence of these guiding principles, there may be a decline in time optimization, increasing unnecessary workload without adding value to the system. Establishing these standards ensures consistency across all levels and enhances clarity in the process [19]. The following are the key principles to uphold:

- *Comprehensive:* A monitoring system should align with the overarching objectives of the scheme with key indicators providing a comprehensive measure of the scheme's progress.
- *Relevance:* By aligning programs with stakeholder priorities and focusing on the outcome and impact, M&E ensures that interventions remain meaningful, effective, and sustainable.
- *Stakeholder engagement:* By engaging stakeholders in planning, implementation, and evaluation, M&E enhances the relevance, effectiveness, and sustainability of programs and ensures stakeholder priorities are taken care of.
- *Efficiency:* By leveraging technology, use of proper sampling techniques, collaborating with other organizations, and streamlining reporting processes M&E processes help minimize costs, reduce time burdens, and ensure efficiency.
- *Effectiveness:* M&E focuses on outcome-based monitoring, impact evaluations, and process evaluations to measure the effectiveness of programs and make data-driven recommendations
- *Well-defined timelines:* M&E activities follow clear timelines to help track progress against set milestones, optimize resource use, and enable real-time learning and adaptation. Such activities contribute meaningfully to achieving program objectives.
- *Sustainability:* By evaluating factors like organizational capacity, resource availability, stakeholder support, and potential risks, M&E processes ensure continued success of the programs.
- *Ethical considerations:* Ethical M&E practices should include informed consents, confidentiality and respect cultural diversity to build trust, enhance participation, and uphold accountability.

13.3.3 Frameworks for Monitoring and Evaluation

There are several types of frameworks for M&E, each serving a different purpose, depending on the context. In this chapter, we attempt to cover generic frameworks that are applicable in the M&E of any domain, whereas specific frameworks are applicable particularly to health systems. One of the frameworks is explained below as an example.

13.3.3.1 Logical Framework (LogFrame)

Leon Rosenberg in 1969 developed LogFrame for USAID to improve project planning, monitoring and evaluation [20]. It is a structured tool used in M&E to plan, track, and evaluate programs and policies effectively. It provides a clear framework linking project objectives to measurable output, means of verification, and underlying assumptions. The framework discusses a result chain that requires to be fulfilled to achieve the goals set for a development program and makes monitoring systematic, ensuring that activities align with objectives. Table 13.1 lists the key components and terms used in the logical framework.

Table 13.1 The logical framework

Questions	Terminologies	What's included	Elements
What are we trying to achieve? Why are we working on this problem? What is our overall goal?	*Vision, goal, objective, longer term outcome, long-term results*	Ultimate benefits for target population	Impact
Where do we want to be in 5 years? What are the most immediate things we are trying to change? What are the things that must be in place first before we can achieve our goals and have an impact?	*First, positive result (or) immediate result, prerequisites, short- and medium-term results*	Short- to medium-term change in the development situation. Normally more than one outcome will be needed to attain the impact.	Outcome
What are the things that need to be produced or provided through projects or programmes for us to achieve our short-to medium-term results? What are the things that different stakeholders must provide?	*Interventions programmes*	Products and services (tangible/ intangible) delivered or provided. Normally more than one output will be needed to achieve the outcome	Outputs
What needs to be done to produce these outputs?	*Actions*	Tasks undertaken in order to produce research outputs Each output normally has a number of activities	Activities
How will we know if we are on track to achieve what we have planned?	*Measure Performance measurement Performance standard*		Inputs
What precise information do we need to measure our performance? How will we obtain this information? How much will it cost? Can the information be monitored?	*Data sources, evidence*		Means of verification

13.3.4 Technological Considerations of Implementation of M&E Systems

Implementation of M&E systems should be a well-thought-out process and requires deliberations and discussions with multiple stakeholders before making choices. Some of the considerations that are critical before implementation are discussed below.

- *Data flows and integration*: Since much of the M&E systems focus on dashboards for monitoring the KPIs, it is important to ensure that the systems are ready to consume data coming from disparate sources such as spreadsheets, Structured Query Language (SQL) databases, Application Program Interfaces (APIs) for a comprehensive view. Data capture and data integrity should also be accorded top priority since major policy decisions are taken in consideration of the information and KPIs presented to the policymakers.
- *Scalability*: The systems should be ready to handle increasing volumes of data flow as time progresses as well as number of users that use the M&E systems.
- *User interface (UI) and user experience (UX)*: The dashboards should be reflective of intuitive and interactive visualizations that cater to diverse stakeholders.
- *Security*: Since much of the data is confidential in nature, robust security measures should be implemented to protect sensitive information, user authentication, data encryption, and compliance with applicable laws such as Digital Personal Data Protection (DPDP) Act 2023.
- *Customization*: There should be flexibility for customization as M&E systems and user requirements evolve over time.
- *Maintenance and Support*: Consideration should be given to ease of maintenance of dashboards including updates and troubleshooting with minimal support.
- *Decision regarding business intelligence (BI) tools:* Careful consideration should be given prior to implementing the M&E systems on the kind of business intelligence software tools used. Choices to be made for selection of open source versus Commercial Off The Shelf (COTS) products as this will have ramifications on the costs and maintenance in the long run.

13.3.4.1 Available Tools for Business Intelligence Dashboards

Various open source and COTS products are available for implementation of dashboarding solutions. Both come with their own pros and cons which are briefly outlined below:

Open-Source Products Apache Superset, Metabase, Grafana, Redash, and Kibana are some of the open-source products. These products being open source need no licensing fee and offer a great deal of flexibility in designing visualizations. However, they incur initial setup and maintenance costs and qualified technical resources. No Service Level Agreements (SLAs) exist and the users have to depend on community support, which, however, is abundantly available.

Commercial Products PowerBI, Tableau, Qlick are some of the commonly known COTS products. The pros include easy-to-use tools, quick development, and vendor support in maintenance. However, the cost of licensing or subscription is often prohibitive depending on the number of users and length of licensing period. There is little scope for customization as the built-in features can only be used for developing visualizations. There is also a high degree of vendor lock-in once a particular software has been implemented.

13.3.5 Financial Considerations

Setting up M&E systems within organizations comes at a cost that includes human resource cost, development, licensing, and maintenance costs of dashboards. Since the cost is a factor of the size of the institution, number of users, and the type of product chosen, it is difficult to put up a cost associated with it. According to some studies, in smaller institutions the commercial tools can cost twice as much as using open-source products. In larger organizations up to 500 users, it can go as high as 5 times [21].

Therefore, institutional leadership must carefully weigh the options and make an informed choice to use a particular product considering the total cost of ownership for implementing the M&E systems.

13.3.6 Ethical and Privacy Considerations

Ethical and privacy considerations in M&E are essential to protecting participants' rights, ensuring data integrity, and maintaining trust. Informed consent must be obtained, allowing individuals to understand the purpose, risks, and benefits of participation while ensuring their right to withdraw. Health financing in India, like in many other countries, relies on large-scale data collection and analysis for effective M&E. However, the use of sensitive patient information raises critical ethical and privacy concerns that insurance practitioners must address. Adhering to data protection laws, such as India's DPDP and international standards like General Data Protection Regulations (GDPR), is essential to prevent misuse of health data. Key ethical principles such as informed consent, data anonymization, and secure storage should be strictly followed to protect patient confidentiality. Additionally, insurers must ensure that premium calculations and claim approvals remain unbiased, avoiding any discriminatory underwriting practices that may disadvantage vulnerable populations. Ethical M&E frameworks must also consider transparency in policy exclusions, grievance redressal mechanisms, and fairness in pricing models, ensuring that health financing remains equitable and accessible to all segments of society.

13.3.7 M&E for Research Purposes

Robust research methodologies under M&E help insurers, policymakers, and healthcare providers refine health financing mechanisms. Through longitudinal studies, actuarial analyses, and impact evaluations, researchers can identify trends in healthcare utilization, financial risk protection, and out-of-pocket-expenditure. This research plays a pivotal role in evidence-based policymaking, ensuring that insurance coverage remains responsive to the evolving healthcare needs of the population. Additionally, research findings can help insurers design customized health plans that aligned with disease prevalence, demographic risks, and socioeconomic factors. Collaborations between academia, industry, and government agencies further enhance the quality of research, driving continuous improvements in health financing models.

13.3.8 Future Trends in M&E

13.3.8.1 Claims Data Analytics

With the growing adoption of digital claims processing, insurers have access to large datasets that can be leveraged for fraud detection, cost control, and predictive analytics. By applying machine learning algorithms and statistical models, insurers can identify patterns of overutilization, unnecessary hospitalizations, and fraudulent claims. Claims data analytics also helps in benchmarking provider performance, ensuring that hospitals and healthcare providers adhere to evidence-based treatment protocols. Real-time analytics can further streamline claim adjudication, reducing processing times and improving the efficiency of health insurance operations.

13.3.8.2 Disease Burden Analysis

Effective M&E in health financing must focus on disease burden analysis, which involves assessing the prevalence and economic impact of diseases across different regions and population groups. Insurers can use epidemiological data as well as claims data analysis to design tailored insurance packages for high-risk groups, ensuring better financial protection for individuals with chronic or critical illnesses. Moreover, disease burden analysis helps in identifying emerging health threats and enables insurers to adjust their premium structures, underwriting criteria, and risk pools accordingly. By integrating real-world evidence and healthcare utilization patterns, insurance companies can optimize their coverage models, making them more sustainable and responsive to public health needs.

13.3.8.3 Continuum of Care

Traditional insurance models have primarily focused on hospitalization and acute care, but the future of health financing lies in integrated, holistic care models. M&E frameworks should track patient journeys beyond hospitalization, incorporating preventive, primary, and post-discharge care. The continuum of care approach ensures better patient outcomes by promoting early interventions, disease management programs, and long-term wellness strategies. Insurers can incentivize preventive screenings, telemedicine consultations, and lifestyle modification programs, reducing overall healthcare costs and improving policyholder health outcomes. Additionally, linking insurance benefits with electronic health records (EHRs) can enhance seamless care coordination among different healthcare providers.

13.3.8.4 Artificial Intelligence and Machine Learning (AI/ML)

AI and ML technologies are transforming health insurance M&E by enabling predictive modeling, risk assessment, and personalized policy pricing. AI-driven underwriting can analyze genetic predisposition, lifestyle habits, and historical claims data to customize insurance plans for individuals. Machine learning models can also identify high-risk individuals and provide early intervention strategies to prevent disease progression. Furthermore, AI-powered chatbots and virtual assistants can enhance customer engagement, claims processing efficiency, and fraud detection capabilities. In the future, AI-driven M&E frameworks can potentially drive real-time decision-making, policy innovation, and cost efficiency, making health financing more adaptive and responsive to the evolving healthcare landscape.

In conclusion, effective M&E in health financing is important to ensure financial resources are efficiently allocated, transparently managed to bring about improved health outcomes. A well-designed M&E framework enables evidence-based decision-making, accountability and leads to continuous improvement in financing mechanisms. However, to enhance credibility and utility of M&E processes, challenges such as data accuracies and real-time data collection, weak reporting, and governance systems should be taken care of.

Activity Box 1

1. *Discuss the Key Performance Indicators for health financing.*
2. How many KPIs are combined to form a tracer indicator in relation to achieving Universal Health Coverage? Where does India stand in terms of UHC coverage index? [Hint: Search indicators listed at https://www.who.int/data/gho/data/indicators]
3. Explore a few health & family welfare public datasets that are of interest to you. [https://www.data.gov.in/]. What thoughts cross your mind while exploring the datasets?

13.4 Capacity Building

Capacity building is commonly understood as the development of skills, systems, and resources that allow organizations and communities to thrive despite external change. Its most important element is an internally sustained transformation that influences not only actions but also the values and attitudes that guide them [22].

However, with changes in time and need, capacity building is not limited to individuals but expands to the development of institutions and complex systems. Recent definitions highlight capacity building as a sustained process through which organizations improve their capacity to perform fundamental tasks, solve problems, pursue objectives, and manage development demands [23].

The further extension of capacity building while targeting the masses is considered as awareness wherein the approach and methodologies are adopted as per the large target audience. It is well thought out as part of information, education, and communication (IEC) wherein different mediums are utilized to disseminate crucial information.

13.4.1 Relevance of Capacity Building in Healthcare Financing

Capacity-building interventions can significantly boost knowledge, skills, and individual efficacy, which includes confidence. They can also drive changes in practices or policies, lead to behavior change, promote the application of new techniques, and enhance system-level capacity.

It has been a mandate of various development organizations. For instance, the World Health Organization (WHO) has emphasized giving the right training to the right people to create an effective workforce for the delivery of healthcare [24]. Similarly, the World Bank is helping countries build capacity of public health managers through various complementary means, including training, technical assistance, studies, and equipment. Besides, USAID also mandates building the capacity of global health workforce to strengthen the health system through various programs. A few academic organizations and institutes are also involved in the capacity building of public health managers, focusing on their country's current health scenario. Joint Learning Initiative (JLI), a consortium of over 100 global public health leaders, has also emphasized strengthening the health workforce through training in public health management [25]. The Global Learning Collaborative for Health Systems Resilience (GLC4HSR) argues that health systems ought to be designed to deliver care and financial protection consistently, whether under normal conditions or during emergencies [26]. Capacity development is part of sustainable development goals (SDGs) 17 and is being considered an internal part of implementing any of the SDGs, including universal health coverage.

With respect to healthcare financing, capacity building along with awareness generation plays a crucial role in understanding the concept, managing resources, implementing publicly funded insurance schemes, strategic purchasing, and improving service delivery leading to universal health coverage. The challenges faced toward governance and learnings and shortfalls analyzed under monitoring and evaluation can be overcome through an appropriate capacity-building activity.

It has been noted that the target audience or beneficiaries of public-funded schemes are unaware about the existence of the schemes. Further, health being the state subject, all such schemes are being implemented at the state, district, and block levels by the officials who are not well versed with the schemes, which may lead to distrust among beneficiaries. Thus, the training of such officials becomes crucial to provide complete information about the scheme, technical complexities of the scheme, and hands-on experience of information technology (IT) platforms. In the context of public health institutions, change management and transition management of public authorities become crucial for continuity of the pace of progress in the programs and schemes. The Government of India has recognized the importance of capacity building and established the Capacity Building Commission. The initiatives under the commission led to the development of Mission *Karmayogi* Integrated Government Online Training (iGoT) platform [27], a learning management system that is domain agnostic, for all government officials. Guidelines have been issued to all the ministries to establish separate capacity-building teams to ensure continuous learning and knowledge dissemination in an effective and efficient manner.

The trainings will not just provide them with information but also the confidence to brief the beneficiaries and bring about behavioral change. The workshops and trainings on soft skills like verbal and nonverbal communication, body language, teamwork, etc. would further enhance the morale of the officials, leading to higher productivity. Many studies support the fact that training enhances productivity; however, the quality of training must be ensured for the real benefits to accrue. Notably, many countries have prioritized the capacity building of healthcare human resources to address primary care needs and achieve Universal Health Coverage.

While talking about the quality of capacity building, the stepping stone is to have a dedicated team for capacity building, which is separate from the human resource department. The capacity building team/ department should encompass the qualifications and expertise in identifying the gaps based on outcomes of governance studies and monitoring and evaluation and designing the trainings accordingly.

As discussed under governance structures, the stakeholders of healthcare financing are multiple, multi-departmental and multi-organizational. It includes central and state government officials, field-level functionaries, healthcare providers, and insurance companies. The citizens, who are the ultimate beneficiaries of health financing programs, cannot be trained but need to be reached through extensive IEC and awareness activities, whereas all other stakeholders must be trained based on their roles and responsibilities, work profiles, and skill levels. For example, the senior public authorities require policy-level knowledge, whereas the field functionaries and healthcare providers need to understand the nuances of health financing schemes and their functional aspect.

Accordingly, capacity building is required at individual and institutional levels followed by the knowledge management for sustainable upskilling in order to achieve health financing objectives.

13.4.2 Principles and Models of Capacity Building

Capacity building is a continuous process and must have a participatory approach to enhance effectiveness. It comprises a variety of approaches and processes such as organizational strengthening, institutional learning, exposure, horizontal sharing, and solidarity, which provide for practical, hands-on, and experiential learning processes to capacity building [28].

Capacity building in the public health context construes the development of sustainable skills, organizational structures, resources, and commitment to health improvement in health and other sectors, to prolong and proliferate health gains many times over. Based on the concept of Systemic Capacity Building [29], it is designed over three pillars as shown in Fig. 13.2:

(1) Institutional Structure, (2) Human Resource and Institutional and Individual Capacity, and (3) Sustaining Knowledge and Skills [30].

The institutional structure indicates the organizational setup at different levels to disseminate knowledge to each of the stakeholders. A robust institutional structure

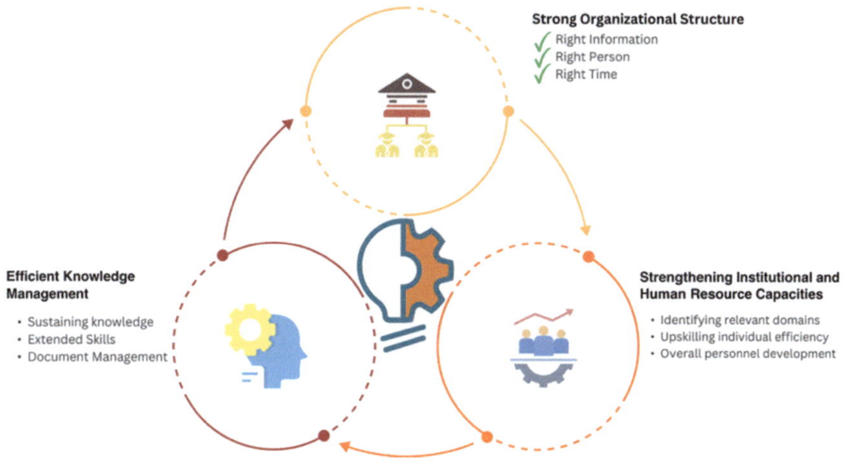

Fig. 13.2 The three dimensions of capacity building

would help in extending the right information to the right person at the right time. It will include the availability of necessary content and facilitators for strengthening the skills of individuals.

The strengthened institutional structure is followed by the *upskilling of individual efficiency* and knowledge of the relevant domain. It also includes the overall development of the personnel working under the healthcare ecosystem.

The most important aspect of capacity building is *sustaining the knowledge and skills* extended through different modes. The lack of sustainability may lead to adverse results of waste of money and time and may lead to poor management and implementation. Accordingly, apart from robust institutional structure and upskilling of individual capacity, a mechanism of knowledge management must be incorporated. It includes the storage, retrieval, and dissemination of relevant information as per the requirement, leading to a sustainable structure.

13.4.3 Training Stakeholders on Healthcare Financing

Capacity building involves four steps:

1. *Stakeholder Mapping and Need Assessment*

Stakeholder mapping and assessment refers to the process of identifying and analyzing all relevant individuals or groups (stakeholders) who are required to be targeted in a capacity-building initiative, evaluating their level of interest, influence, and current knowledge/capabilities to effectively participate, and then tailoring the capacity-building activities to meet their specific needs and facilitate their engagement in the project. It is also considered as gap analysis with respect to the knowledge required against the knowledge that exists, leading to the development of an effective training plan.

The monitoring and evaluation reports and assessment of governance structures play an important role in analyzing the knowledge gaps among stakeholders.

Activity Box 2

1. What are the key elements of effective capacity building in health financing? Discuss.
2. What do you think about the influence of capacity building in the sustainability of health financing?
3. In the context of low-resource settings, what are the challenges of building institutional capacities for health financing? Discuss.

2. *Design Training Structure*

The training structure can be designed based on the target stakeholders and the level of knowledge to be disseminated. It can include a mix of activities such as training sessions, workshops, seminars, mentorship, cross-learning activities, hands-on experiences, and resource provision. The content and delivery methods may be tailored according to the audience's needs and preferences, ensuring a diverse and inclusive approach.

3. *Training Facilitation and Knowledge Dissemination*

Training facilitation and knowledge dissemination include selection of facilitators and the methodology of knowledge repository and continuous dissemination at the right time. The most common model of knowledge dissemination is the cascade model wherein the knowledge is passed down from a central source to multiple levels of recipients. It can cater to a large stakeholder base in a cost-effective and scalable manner; however, it can sometimes lead to a dilution of information if appropriate quality measures are not undertaken. Apart from this, the Knowledge-to-Action (KTA) Cycle, Knowledge Brokering, Socio-Ecological Model, Community-Based Participatory Research (CBPR), Social Network Model, or Collaborative Model may be explored by the specific organization.

4. *Feedback and Assessment*

Another important aspect of training design is to receive feedback and assess the learnings of the participants through assessments. It helps in quick analysis of the quality of training and the level of understanding among the participants.

13.4.4 Leveraging Technology for Capacity Building

The technology has supported capacity building by providing different means of knowledge dissemination in a faster and effective manner. Digital platforms capture engagement data that can be used to personalize content for intended audiences. In healthcare, where user diversity and learning needs are wide-ranging, technology must be applied effectively to support this personalization.

Virtual conference sessions, self-paced learning modules through learning management systems, digital learning material, and social media are some of the common technological tools for capacity building. Technology helps in overcoming the challenges of time and schedules of the individuals by allowing them to undergo the trainings as per their convenient choice of time and place. It also helps in upskilling the masses at a faster rate and extending the knowledge at the right time.

Hybrid modes by clubbing physical activities with digital learning materials are leading to more interactive and effective capacity building. It further supports in analyzing the feedbacks and undertaking impact assessment.

13.4.5 Challenges

While capacity building is an integral part of an effective and efficient management and implementation of schemes, it has not obtained the due recognition and importance in an institutional structure. Capacity building is a straightforward yet complex activity in terms of quality and effectiveness and requires professional knowledge and skill sets; however, the same is lacking in the overall ecosystem of healthcare.

Apart from lacking a prominent and robust institutional structure for capacity building, designing an effective training strategy and plan is becoming a challenge considering the less attention span of participants and lack of motivation toward learning among them. In the fast-growing world, the workforce is more inclined toward learning by doing rather than accumulating the relevant knowledge beforehand. People generally face difficulty in adopting the practices discussed during trainings because of the distrust of such methods.

Various papers had highlighted the results and importance of capacity building; the same is not yet welcomed considering the evaluation being qualitative rather than quantitative. It is a slow-growing process that takes time to show results over a period of time and thus becomes less important than routine activities.

Technology interventions have helped to disseminate knowledge as per the requirement of the audience; however, they still need momentum for achieving the objectives of capacity building.

Case Study

Governance, M&E, and Capacity Building at the National Health Authority—the implementing body of the *Ayushman Bharat Pradhan Mantri Jan Arogya Yojana (AB PM-JAY)*

13.4.6 Background

The National Health Authority (NHA) [31] has been set up as an attached office with full functional autonomy under the Ministry of Health and Family Welfare, to implement the world's largest publicly funded health assurance program, popularly known as AB PM-JAY. The program covers over 600 million individuals comprising the (i) economically vulnerable population forming the bottom 40% of the socioeconomic pyramid in India as per the Socio-Economic Caste Census 2011 database, (ii) Frontline health workers such as the accredited social health activists (ASHAs), Anganwadi workers and helpers, (iii) Senior citizens aged over 70 years, (iv) Any member of the transgender community registered on the National Portal for Transgender Persons, (v) Building and other construction workers (BoCW) registered as members of the building and other construction workers welfare board (BoCWWB). AB PM-JAY provides for an annual cover of ₹5 lakh per family on a floater basis for cashless treatment of secondary and tertiary illnesses at over 31,809 empaneled public and private hospitals. As part of the convergence of other government health schemes, the NHA also provides a technical support platform for processing the claims of Central Government Health Scheme (CGHS), Central Armed Police Forces (CAPF), Employees' State Insurance Corporation (ESIC). As of March 2025, AB PM-JAY has been implemented in 35 of the 36 states/union territories in India. The financing of the scheme is shared between the Central and State governments generally in a 60:40 ratio, but 90:10 in Northeastern and Himalayan States and up to 100% in certain cases such as union territories without legislatures [32].

As explained in Chap. 9, states have been given the flexibility to implement the AB PM-JAY scheme in three different modes [33]. In the *trust mode,* the state establishes a government-owned trust or society, which acts as the insurer. In the *insurance mode,* the state selects a private insurance company to manage the claims and payouts. The state pays a fixed premium per beneficiary to the insurance company. In the *hybrid or mixed mode,* the state implements the scheme in both the trust and insurance modes.

13.4.7 Governance Structures

The NHA is governed by a *Governing Board* [34] chaired by the Union Minister for Health and Family Welfare. It is headed by a chief executive officer (CEO), an officer of the rank of Secretary to the Government of India, who manages its affairs, supported by an additional chief executive officer (ACEO) of the rank of Joint Secretary.

The CEO is the Ex-Office Member Secretary of the Governing Board, which comprises a chairperson and 11 other members.

- Chairperson: Union Minister for Health and Family Welfare, Government of India
- Member: Chief Executive Officer, NITI Aayog, Govt. of India (ex officio)
- Member: Secretary (Expenditure), Ministry of Finance, Govt. of India (Ex Officio)
- Member: Secretary (Health and Family Welfare), Ministry of Health and Family Welfare, Govt. of India (ex officio)

- Members 4 and 5: Two domain experts from the fields such as Administrative, Insurance, Public and Private Healthcare providers, Economics, Public Health, Management, etc.
- Members 6–10: Five principal secretaries (Health) of the state government (one representing each of the five zones of the country viz. North, East, South, West, and Northeast) on a rotational basis, and
- Member: Chief Executive Officer (CEO) of the National Health Authority (ex officio)

A brief list of the powers and functions of the governing board (GB) is provided below:

1. *It is the supreme decision-making authority of the NHA and is responsible for all policy-related matters of AB PM-JAY.*
2. The GB shall frame the rules, regulations, guidelines, and procedures for the human resources of the NHA as well as lay down the rules, procedures and guidelines for procurement of goods and services for the NHA.
3. All major regulations need the approval of the GB and follow a public consultation process.
4. GB may delegate certain powers to the CEO, NHA. Subcommittees may be formed for the smooth functioning of AB PM-JAY.
5. The GB shall periodically review the performance of the NHA on parameters considered expedient by the board, including expenditures and budget.
6. The NHA through the GB shall be responsible for developing strategic partnerships and collaborations with the Central and State governments, other public and private institutions including not-for-profit institutions, insurance companies, academic institutions, universities, missions, think tanks, and other national and international bodies of repute in areas relevant to the objectives of AB PM-JAY.
7. Proposals are made by the CEO, NHA and the GB shall meet once in 3 months to decide on them.

For the complete list of powers of the GB and functions of the NHA, the reader is advised to refer to Notification [35] issued by Niti Aayog.

13.4.8 Three-Tier Scheme Implementation

AB PM-JAY is implemented in a three-tier structure (Fig. 13.3) with well-defined roles and responsibilities.

The *National Health Authority (NHA)* is responsible for the formulation of various operational guidelines, policies, model documents, and contracts to ensure standardization and interoperability. It also determines the central share of premium based on field evidence and actuarial analysis and releases funds to states from time to time. NHA oversees development and enforcement of Standard Treatment Guidelines, quality standards and documentation protocols, data privacy and data sharing protocols, fraud control, prevention and detection measures. Strategic

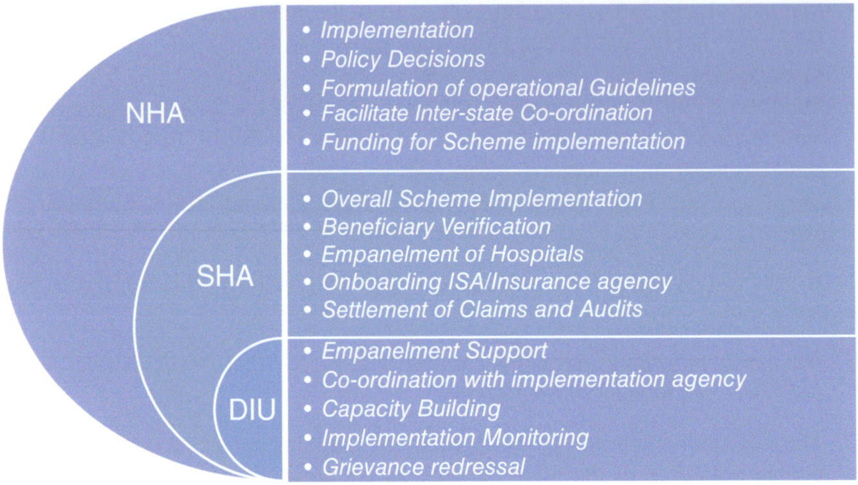

Fig. 13.3 Three-tier implementation of the AB PM-JAY scheme

purchasing of health services by preparing a list of health benefits packages and their rates and payment mechanisms to providers also is governed by the NHA. Other functions include the state-of-the-art health technology assessment ecosystem, process for convergence of other central and state government health schemes, working closely with IRDAI on the development and implementation of health insurance regulations targeting insurance companies, ensuring effective implementation of the scheme through regular monitoring, capacity building of state health agencies and other stakeholders, periodical beneficiary awareness programs, setting up grievance redressal mechanisms. The complete list of responsibilities is available from the Gazette publication referred to above [31]. The NHA has also established a robust hierarchical organizational structure [36] with well-defined functional departments and roles and responsibilities for various organizational activities and operationalizing the Scheme. The detailed organogram is available at https://pmjay.gov.in/about/organization-chart.

State Health Agencies (SHA) are nodal agencies responsible for implementation of AB PM-JAY in the respective states. Every SHA has a Governing Council. SHA is headed by a CEO appointed by the respective state government, who is also the ex-officio member of the Governing Council at SHA.

SHA has several roles and responsibilities that include policy-related issues and linkages of state schemes with AB PM-JAY, selection of insurance company in the insurance mode of implementation or Implementation Support Agency (ISA) in the trust mode of implementation. Beneficiary identification and issuance of PM-JAY cards to valid beneficiaries, empanelment of network hospitals, monitoring services provided by healthcare providers, fraud and abuse control, monitoring pre-authorizations and claims, payments and management of funds, setting up and overseeing functions of district level offices, adoption and implementation of guidelines and protocols are the various responsibilities handled by SHAs.

The *district implementation unit (DIU)* is established by SHA to support the implementation at the district level. The DIU is chaired by the Deputy Commissioner/ District Magistrate/ Collector of the district. The DIU coordinates with the implementing agency (ISA/insurer) and the network hospitals to ensure effective implementation and also sends review reports periodically. The DIU has to work closely and coordinate with the office of the District Chief Medical officer. The DIU also plays a key role in beneficiary identification and enrolment, hospital empanelment and monitoring, awareness and grievance redressal, documentation and reporting.

13.4.9 Policies and Processes

Right at the inception of the scheme, the NHA worked on various processes and functions of the scheme and released guidelines for implementation and published them in the public domain. These functions include Human resources and recruitment, Health benefits packages, standard treatment guidelines and Claim adjudication, Procurement processes and model tender documents for uniformity across SHAs, Hospital network Policy and Quality Assurance, IEC, Capacity building, Information technology and security policies, beneficiary grievance and call center, etc. These have helped standardize processes across the implementing states.

AB PM-JAY has been conceptualized as a technology-driven scheme in completely digital (paperless) mode, with a strong IT infrastructure forming the backbone for operationalizing various processes. The NHA has developed dedicated web portals for beneficiary identification system (BIS), hospital empanelment module (HEM), transaction management system (TMS) for claim adjudication, and a Grievance portal.

Activity Box 3

1. *Examine the governance structures at NHA. Go through the references provided. Discuss the current governance structure with reference to the Governance in health financing described in this chapter. Are there any gaps or improvements needed?*
2. What do you think of the three modes of scheme implementation? Think about the challenges with each of them.

13.4.10 Monitoring and Evaluation at the NHA

Given the scale of the AB PM-JAY scheme, ensuring effective implementation necessitated a robust monitoring and evaluation framework to identify implementation status, trends, strengths, and areas for improvement as the scheme progresses. Accordingly, the NHA established a dedicated Monitoring and Research (M&R) division from the outset of the scheme's implementation. The division emphasises on systematically monitoring progress, assessing impact, and enabling decisions based on evidence. Some of the key activities for monitoring and evaluation of the scheme are as follows:

Dashboards

The NHA employs a comprehensive real-time management information system (MIS) that supports monitoring KPIs at both the state and national levels. These advanced dashboards offer insights into various aspects, including beneficiary management, transaction management, and provider management.

The NHA maintains three key dashboards [37].

(a) *A dashboard utilizing open-source tools is made available in the public domain that captures and displays key metrics of the AB PM-JAY scheme for public consumption that include the number of beneficiary cards created, hospital admissions and expenditure, number of public and private hospitals empaneled, among other parameters. The trends since the inception of the scheme are captured through dynamic charts that are updated on a daily basis.*

(b) Seven different internal dashboards for internal consumption of the NHA leadership and policymakers. The KPIs captured include performance metrics of the users and agencies, progress of empanelment and beneficiary card making and their disbursement status to the state, district, and village levels, utilization metrics of hospitalization and procedures, etc. Daily, weekly, monthly, and yearly trends are also captured and displayed. Dashboards are also updated and developed to track the progress of various initiatives and special drives introduced by the NHA from time to time.

(c) An IMPACT dashboard has also been developed which monitors specific metrics like claim adjudication and service provider engagement, ensuring transparency and accountability.

Over the years, these dashboards have expanded to include specialized ones according to the need, providing granular insights for policymakers and administrators for making evidence-based decisions and policy refinement.

Reports The M&R division generates regular reports presenting performance summaries and identifying areas requiring intervention. While the "Score Cards" which track the progress of the scheme in key areas are shared individually with the States every month, the "State Factsheet" and "State at a Glance" provide detailed overviews of the implementation status, enrollment data, challenges and information of KPIs and are available in the public domain [38]. Apart from these, daily and monthly reports on KPIs are also shared with the leadership as well as ministry. Besides these, the best practices followed by different states are also captured and documented from time to time. The division also takes responsibility to publish various other reports such as Annual Reports, Best Practices and Innovations, Lessons Learned documents, etc.

Research and Partnerships Building and promoting a research-driven culture is a key objective at the NHA. The M&R division actively engages in high-quality research, producing working papers and policy briefs that analyze PM-JAY package utilization and state-specific disease patterns, to identify priority areas for the scheme and generate evidence to inform policy decisions. Apart from the in-house research, the NHA has also actively fostered a culture of research through collaborations with global organizations such as the German Development Agency Gesellschaft für Internationale Zusammenarbeit (GIZ), the World Bank, and the WHO, which further strengthened the evidence generation efforts. The NHA has also formed associations with nonprofit organizations such as the Bill & Melinda Gates Foundation (BMGF), Clinton Health Access Initiative (CHAI), ACCESS Health International; Universities such as the Indian Institute of Health Management Research (IIHMR), Heidelberg University, Indian Institute of Technology (IIT) Madras, National Institute of Mental Health and Neurosciences (NIMHANS), and the Goa Institute of Management. To streamline research efforts, a Technical Advisory Committee (TAC) was formed, approving various evaluation studies and ensuring quality research outcomes. In a span of 5 years, the division has published 18 policy briefs, 20 working papers, and 6 reports.

The commitment to transparency, continuous learning, and data-driven decision-making has positioned the NHA as a leader in health scheme implementation and management in India.

Activity Box 4

1. *Examine the activities of the M&R division at the NHA. To what extent are the principles of monitoring and evaluation followed? Are there any gaps? Discuss.*
2. Study the references provided and read through various reports for a better understanding of the functioning of the M&R division and the performance of the AB PM-JAY scheme.

13.4.11 Capacity Building at the NHA

The NHA shoulders the critical responsibility of implementing two flagship health programs: AB PM-JAY and ABDM. Recognizing the pivotal role of capacity building in achieving the program objectives, the NHA has established a dedicated unit to build the requisite skills of all stakeholders and ensure effective dissemination of knowledge and information. Similarly, SHAs and District Implementation Units are mandated to conduct capacity-building initiatives systematically at the state and district levels.

To streamline these efforts, the NHA has issued comprehensive capacity-building guidelines. These guidelines not only provide a roadmap for states and master trainers to conduct training efficiently but also outline methodologies for assessing the impact of such activities.

Considering that both AB PM-JAY and ABDM are implemented nationally and include a variety of stakeholders at all levels, the NHA has adopted the *cascade model of training*. Under this model, the NHA trains master trainers at the state and district levels, who in turn conduct further training for a variety of stakeholders. Separate groups of master trainers are developed for different thematic areas and trained annually. This model enables the NHA to reach grassroots levels effectively, facilitating the successful implementation of its schemes. Beyond training master trainers, the NHA extends its training efforts to SHAs, empaneled hospitals, insurance companies, and stakeholders from non-PM-JAY states.

The NHA employs a blended training approach, combining virtual and physical sessions, which helped during the COVID-19 pandemic to ensure uninterrupted learning for stakeholders. This dual mode enhances outreach, fosters continuous engagement with stakeholders, and facilitates cross-learning among different states, while strengthening trust in the NHA's efforts. Continuous interactions with master trainers and other stakeholders allow the NHA to provide timely updates and clarifications, ensuring sustained program success.

The NHA releases an Annual Training Calendar outlining all planned activities for the year in advance. To plan Annual activities, a Capacity Gap Analysis is undertaken by the NHA on a yearly basis. It helps in identifying the stakeholders and thematic areas where the capacity-building activities need to be focused during the year.

Besides building capacities in the thematic areas of the schemes, the NHA also launched a virtual lecture series titled '*Nirantar Shiksha*,' inviting experts to cover key topics like insurance and health financing, thereby enriching stakeholders' understanding of foundational health concepts.

Internally, the NHA prioritizes the upskilling of its own workforce. Orientation programs and specialized sessions are conducted in collaboration with esteemed institutions such as the Institute of Government Accounts and Finance (INGAF), the National Institute of Health and Family Welfare (NIHFW), Indian Institutes of Technology, Kanpur and Mumbai, Institute of Secretariat Training and Management (ISTM), Indian Institute of Management (IIM), Indian School of Business (ISB). These special sessions focus on public health, finance, government rules and regulations, and communications and soft skills. To further support its training initiatives, the NHA has developed its own learning management system wherein the stakeholders can learn at their own pace.

Activity Box 5

1. *What do you think of the capacity-building approach undertaken by the NHA? Discuss.*
2. Given the nature of schemes run by the NHA, what other approaches can be considered? Discuss.

13.5 Summary

This chapter explored the interrelation and role of governance, M&E, and capacity building in health financing, emphasizing their collective impact on health system efficiency, financial sustainability, and service delivery outcomes. Various governance structures and their role in health financing have been discussed. Tracking the performance of institutions and programs through key performance indicators and the theoretical application of appropriate evaluation models. Finally, the importance of capacity building to strengthen institutional structures and various modes of delivering capacity building and their impact evaluation strategies have been discussed. To sum up, governance, M&E, and capacity building are integral to strengthening health financing systems to deliver services with transparency and accountability, data-driven decision-making and create a skilled workforce to manage financial resources effectively. A well-structured approach integrating these elements leads to sustainable, equitable, and efficient health financing, ultimately improving health outcomes.

References

1. Dodgson R, Lee K, Drager N. Global health governance a conceptual Review [Internet]. 2002 [cited 2023 Mar 9]. Available from: https://researchonline.lshtm.ac.uk/id/eprint/18031/1/a85727_eng.pdf
2. World Health Organization. Health systems governance [Internet]. www.who.int. 2021. Available from: https://www.who.int/health-topics/health-systems-governance
3. Savedoff WD. Governance in the health sector: a strategy for measuring determinants and performance [Internet]. Ssrn.com. 2011 [cited 2025 Mar 16]. Available from: https://papers.ssrn.com/sol3/Delivery.cfm/5655.pdf?abstractid=1837205&mirid=1
4. Rosenau JN, Czempiel EO. Governance without government: order and change in world politics [Internet]. Cambridge UK/New York: Cambridge University Press; 2009. Available from:. https://doi.org/10.1017/CBO9780511521775.
5. Kai Hong Phua. Governance Issues in Health Financing. Int Encyclopedia Public Health, 2nd edn. 2018 ;330–341.
6. World Health Organization, Travis P, Egger D, Davies P, Mechbal A. Towards better stewardship: concepts and critical issues. World Health Organization; 2002. https://iris.who.int/handle/10665/339291
7. National Health Accounts Cell, Ministry of Health and Family Welfare, Government of India. Health Sector Financing by Centre and States/UTs in India [Internet]. mohfw.gov.in. 2016. Available from: https://mohfw.gov.in/sites/default/files/88269152501453973989_0.pdf
8. Ministry of Health & Family Welfare, Government of India, Department of Health & Family Welfare. Annual Report 2024–25 [Internet]. Ministry of Health and Family Welfare. 2025 [cited 2025 Mar 15] p. 493–7. Available from: https://mohfw.gov.in
9. Ministry of Health and Family Welfare, Government of India, Department of Health and Family Welfare. Health and Family Welfare Statistics in India 2019–20 [Internet]. Ministry of Health and Family Welfare. 2020 [cited 2025 Mar 15] p. 210–9. Available from: https://mohfw.gov.in/sites/default/files/HealthandFamilyWelfarestatisticsinIndia201920.pdf
10. Ministry of Health and Family Welfare, Government of India, Department of Health and Family Welfare. Detailed demands for grants of Ministry of Health and Family Welfare 2025–26. [Internet]. Ministry of Health and Family Welfare Available from: https://mohfw.gov.in/sites/default/files/DDG%202025-26%20Final.pdf

11. National Health Systems Resource Centre, Ministry of Health & Family Welfare, Government of India. National Health Accounts Estimates for India 2021–22 [Internet]. National Health Systems Resource Centre. 2024. Available from: https://nhsrcindia.org/sites/default/files/2024-09/NHA%202021-22.pdf
12. Government of India, Ministry of Health and Family Welfare, Department of Health and Family Welfare Rajya Sabha Unstarred Question No. 2057 [Internet]. [cited 2025 Mar 23]. Available from: https://sansad.in/getFile/annex/267/AU2057_Ljieyk.pdf?source=pqars
13. Press Information Bureau. Update on Ayushman Bharat Cards [Internet]. pib.gov.in. 2024. Available from: https://pib.gov.in/PressReleaseIframePage.aspx?PRID=2040860
14. Seth A, Sridharan R, Nundy N, Mira A, Pal P. Philanthropy as the bridge for impact in India's growth [Internet]. https://www.bain.com. Bain & Company; 2024 [cited 2025 Feb 21]. Available from: https://www.bain.com/globalassets/noindex/2024/bain_report_india_philanthropy_report_2024.pdf
15. Nundy M, Sharma S, Anjaney, Jain M, Kotwal A. Public-private partnerships in health care under the national health mission in India: A Review [Internet]. https://nhsrcindia.org/. New Delhi, India: National Health Systems Resource Centre (NHSRC); 2021 [cited 2021 Feb 20]. Available from: https://nhsrcindia.org/sites/default/files/2022-09/PPP%20BOOK%20 27.05.2022_0.pdf
16. 10 Bed ICU. Introduction to the 10BedICU Program [Internet]. 10 Bed ICU. 2023 [cited 2025 Feb 21]. Available from: https://10bedicu.org/
17. Guidelines for Rogi Kalyan Samitis in Public Health Facilities [Internet]. National Health Mission. Ministry of Health & Family Welfare, Government of India; 2015 [cited 2023 Feb 21]. Available from: https://nhm.gov.in/New_Updates_2018/communization/RKS/Guidelines_for_Rogi_Kalyan_Samities_in_Public_Health_Facilities.pdf
18. Handbook on Planning, Monitoring qnd Evaluating for Development Results [Internet]. https://mandeguidelines.iom.int. New York: United Nations Development Programme (UNDP); [cited 2009]. Available from: https://mandeguidelines.iom.int/sites/g/files/tmzbdl2306/files/2023-03/pme-handbook.pdf
19. What are the principles of monitoring and evaluation? – EvalCommunity [Internet]. https://www.evalcommunity.com. Available from: https://www.evalcommunity.com/career-center/principles-of-monitoring-and-evaluation/
20. Wayback Machine [Internet]. Archive.org. 2025 [cited 2025 Sep 1]. Available from: https://web.archive.org/web/20131004220343/http://pdf.usaid.gov/pdf_docs/PNADW881.pdf
21. Madsen M. Lowering the Cost of Business Intelligence With Open Source [Internet]. dataprix.com. Third Nature. 2010; Available from: https://www.dataprix.com/files/bi-comparison-of-open-source-and-traditional-vendor.pdf
22. United Nations. Capacity-building [Internet]. United Nations. Available from: https://www.un.org/en/academic-impact/capacity-building
23. Milèn A. An overview of existing knowledge and good practice [Internet]. WHO; 2001. [cited 2025 Feb 26]. Available from: https://iris.who.int/bitstream/handle/10665/67394/a76996.pdf?form=MG0AV3
24. Heller R. Capacity-building for public health: http://peoples-uni.org. Bull World Health Organ [Internet]. 2007;85(12):930–4. [cited 2019 Mar 22]; Available from: https://pmc.ncbi.nlm.nih.gov/articles/PMC2636296/
25. Upadhyay K, Goel S, John P. Developing a capacity building training model for public health managers of low and middle income countries. Plos One. 2023;18(4):e0272793–3.
26. Context [Internet]. Glc4hsr.org. 2025 [cited 2025 Mar 15]. Available from: https://glc4hsr.org/context
27. iGot [Internet]. igotkarmayogi.gov.in. 2025 [cited 2025 Feb 27]. Available from: https://igotkarmayogi.gov.in/#/
28. Empowerment of Local Bodies Unit 2 Capacity Building Structure [Internet]. [cited 2025 Mar 20]. Available from: https://www.egyankosh.ac.in/bitstream/123456789/59200/1/Unit2.pdf
29. Potter C. Systemic capacity building: a hierarchy of needs. Health Policy Plan. 2004;19(5):336–45. https://doi.org/10.1093/heapol/czh038.

30. National Health Authority. Capacity Building Guidelines [Internet]. pmjay.gov.in. 2019 [cited 2025 Mar 16]. Available from: https://pmjay.gov.in/sites/default/files/2019-02/Capacity%20Building%20Document,%2022.01.2019_Approved.pdf
31. About NHA. National Health Authority | GOI [Internet]. nha.gov.in. Available from: https://nha.gov.in/NHA
32. Amalgamation of Ayushman Bharat Yojana with State Health Schemes [Internet]. pib.gov.in. 2021 [cited 2025 Mar 15]. Available from: https://pib.gov.in/PressReleasePage.aspx?PRID=1694437
33. National Health Authority. States/UTs at a Glance [Internet]. pmjay.gov.in. 2023 [cited 2025 Mar 16]. Available from: https://pmjay.gov.in/states/states-glance
34. Ministry of Health & Family Welfare, Government of India. The National Health Authority (Governing Board) Conduct of Business Rules, 2019 [Internet]. pmjay.gov.in. 2019 [cited 2025 Mar 15]. Available from: https://pmjay.gov.in/sites/default/files/2020-01/e-Gazette_Governing_Board_Conduct_of_business_Rules.pdf
35. Gazette Notification, Niti Aayog [Internet]. Pmjay.gov.in. 2019 [cited 2025 Mar 16]. Available from: https://pmjay.gov.in/sites/default/files/2020-01/E-Gazette_of_NITI_creating_NHA.pdf
36. https://pmjay.gov.in/about/organization-chart
37. National Health Authority. Annual Report 2021–22 [Internet]. 2022 p. 63. Available from: https://nha.gov.in/img/resources/Annual-Report-2021-22.pdf
38. National Health Authority. Status of Implementation of PM-JAY across States [Internet]. pmjay.gov.in. Available from: https://pmjay.gov.in/states/status-implementation

Applications of Digital Technologies for Healthcare Financing

14

Mukund Kulkarni, Prafful Kalla, Krishan Dev Nidumolu, Yasaswini Ganti, and Mridini Kulkarni

Abstract

Digital transformation is fundamentally reshaping healthcare financing globally. This chapter comprehensively examines this evolution, focusing on opportunities within the Indian landscape while drawing upon key global trends. It analyses the confluence of innovative digital technologies—including artificial intelligence (AI) and machine learning (ML) for predictive analytics and risk scoring, sophisticated data analytics, health data exchange platforms, centralized data repositories, blockchain for secure data transactions, and telemedicine platforms—and their strategic application in optimizing insurance processes, enhancing risk assessment, fortifying fraud detection, and improving patient engagement.

This chapter explores the foundational role of health data, dissecting its diverse types and forms, elucidating data flow, and emphasizing data security measures. It details how these technologies leverage health data across various functions, ranging from claims processing and fraud prevention to personalized care and value-based contracting.

Through diverse case studies and national initiatives, this chapter provides a nuanced understanding of the transformative potential and inherent challenges of digitizing healthcare financing ecosystems. It underscores the neces-

M. Kulkarni (✉) · K. D. Nidumolu · Y. Ganti
Insurance Information Bureau of India, Hyderabad, Telangana, India
e-mail: mukundkulkarni@iib.gov.in

P. Kalla
Ernst & Young India, Gurugram, Haryana, India

M. Kulkarni
OP Jindal Global Law University, Sonipat, Haryana, India

S. Prinja (ed.), *Healthcare Financing and Insurance*,
https://doi.org/10.1007/978-981-95-3513-2_14

sity of balancing technological innovation, ethical considerations, and infrastructural development to advance efficient, secure, and equitable healthcare financing in India.

Keywords

Digital transformation · Data security · Interoperability · Artificial intelligence (AI) · Algorithmic modelling

Learning Objectives

- *Understanding the landscape of health data*—Learn to identify diverse types and forms of health data, and analyse their crucial role in driving efficiency, personalization, and equity within digital healthcare financing.
- *Understanding health data regulations and security*—Examine regulatory frameworks like India's Digital Personal Data Protection (DPDP) Act 2023 and global standards e.g. General Data Protection Regulation (GDPR), Health Insurance Portability and Accountability Act (HIPAA) to comprehend data security, privacy obligations, and their influence on healthcare financing systems.
- *Exploring key digital technologies*—Investigate health data exchange technologies, smart algorithms, AI-driven predictions, registries, and advanced data analytics, and their applications in transforming healthcare financing.
- *Identifying key challenges and policy solutions*—Recognize infrastructural, cultural, and ethical challenges, and policy gaps hindering digital healthcare financing advancements, and propose solutions for effective implementation.
- *Envisioning the future of technology in healthcare financing*—Explore futuristic applications of emerging technologies in healthcare financing, including automation, atypical data integration, and advancements in data management, and their potential impact.

14.1 Introduction

The global healthcare financing landscape is undergoing a fundamental transformation, driven by digital technologies that enhance efficiency, accessibility, and quality. From the United Kingdom's National Health Service (NHS) digital initiatives to the US emphasis on interoperability via the twenty-first Century Cures Act [1], nations leverage technology to optimize resource allocation and improve patient outcomes. In India, the Ayushman Bharat Digital Mission (ABDM) is building a national digital health ecosystem, fostering interoperability and seamless data exchange [2]. The Unified Payments Interface (UPI) enhances affordability and reduces administrative burdens through real-time, secure payment solutions. Telemedicine, legalized in 2020, expands healthcare access, while electronic health records (EHRs) and personal health records (PHRs) empower patients with personalized care. Artificial intelligence (AI) and machine learning (ML) are poised to revolutionize risk assessment and personalized care, optimizing resource allocation. However, data privacy, interoperability, and the digital divide pose challenges.

This chapter explores the digital transformation of healthcare financing, beginning with the role of health data in strategic decision-making and resource optimization. We address data security, referencing India's Digital Personal Data Protection Act, 2023 ("DPDP Act") and an overview of governing policies and standards [3]. We then examine health information exchange (HIE), repositories like the Registry of Hospitals in the Network of Insurance (ROHINI), AI/ML algorithms, and patient-facing technologies, such as telemedicine, to build a resilient, efficient, and equitable healthcare financing system.

14.2 Health Data, Standards, and Real-World Evidence

India's national development is deeply intertwined with the health of its growing population. Achieving "*Health for All*" demands effective healthcare systems, reliant on comprehensive data about health conditions, facilities, and socio-economic factors. Digital technologies are revolutionizing healthcare, emphasizing the need for ethical data usage. Historically, health data resided in physical, traditional paper records; now, it is progressively transitioning to digital formats, transforming how information is stored and utilized. This shift is crucial; digital health data is no longer merely archival but a dynamic engine driving efficiency, personalization, and accessibility. For India, with its rapidly expanding digital health infrastructure, responsible data deployment is vital. This data empowers informed decisions, enhances patient care, and ensures equitable healthcare access, propelling advancements across the healthcare landscape.

Health data, a multifaceted collection of information pertaining to individual and population health, is undergoing a profound transformation with the advent of digital technologies. This data, increasingly captured, stored, and analysed electronically, serve as the bedrock for personalized healthcare, evidence-based policy formulation, and groundbreaking medical research.

Structurally, health data bifurcates into structured and unstructured forms. *Structured data*, characterized by its high degree of organization, is typically presented in tabular formats, using standardized medical codes such as the *International Classification of Diseases, 11th Revision* (ICD-11) for diagnoses and *Systematized Nomenclature of Medicine—Clinical Terms* (SNOMED CT) for clinical terminologies, etc. This organization helps with efficient data analysis, automated reporting, and seamless system interoperability. Conversely, *unstructured data*, encompassing clinical narratives, medical images, audio recordings, and handwritten notes, lacks a predefined format, posing challenges for analysis but has rich, nuanced insights.

The *diverse types of health data* include clinical data (patient medical histories, diagnoses, treatments), administrative data (patient demographics, insurance details, billing records), financial data (healthcare expenditure, budget allocations), public health data (disease surveillance, epidemiological statistics), wearable data (heart rate, activity levels, sleep patterns), genomic data (genetic information), and some others.

Data generation occurs at multiple levels: patient-level, capturing individual medical records and wearable device data; institution-level, encompassing hospital and clinic records; and regional/national-level, involving public health surveillance and aggregated insurance data.

The frequency of data generation varies from real time, as seen in wearable device monitoring, to periodic, such as scheduled check-ups, and episodic, like hospital admissions. The granularity of data ranges from detailed patient-level records to aggregated regional trends, each serving distinct purposes in healthcare management and research. Ownership of health data is a complex issue, with patients, healthcare providers, insurance companies, and government agencies each holding specific rights and responsibilities.

Data utilization spans a wide range of applications, including diagnosis and treatment by healthcare providers, risk assessment by insurance companies, policy development by government agencies, personal health management by patients, clinical research, and administrative efficiency by third-party administrators.

Data standards: In the Indian healthcare context, data standardization is paramount for ensuring interoperability and seamless data exchange. The Ministry of Health and Family Welfare (MoHFW) is spearheading this effort through the ABDM, which promotes the adoption of standardized data formats, terminologies, and protocols.

Recognizing the critical need for interoperability—the capacity of diverse health information systems to exchange, interpret, and utilize data effectively—the government is prioritizing the adoption and implementation of globally recognized standards. This is essential to facilitate seamless data exchange between disparate systems employed by healthcare providers, payers, and other stakeholders within the healthcare ecosystem.

Central to this initiative is the adoption of key standards, including the following:

- *HL7 FHIR (Fast Healthcare Interoperability Resources)* [4]: This is a next-generation standard designed to enable the electronic exchange of healthcare information. Leveraging web-based Application Programming Interfaces (APIs), HL7 FHIR offers a modular and extensible framework, facilitating interoperability across diverse platforms, including mobile applications, and emerging technologies. This approach promotes a more dynamic and adaptable data exchange paradigm.
- *SNOMED CT (Systematized Nomenclature of Medicine—Clinical Terms)*: This is a comprehensive and highly structured clinical health terminology. SNOMED CT provides a standardized vocabulary for representing clinical concepts with precision and consistency, encompassing diagnoses, proce-

dures, findings, and other clinical entities. The establishment of an interim National Release Centre (NRC) for SNOMED CT in India signifies a commitment to supporting its adoption and ensuring its effective utilization within the Indian healthcare context.

- *ICD-11 (International Classification of Diseases, 11th Revision)*: This is the globally recognized standard for classifying diseases, injuries, and health-related conditions. ICD-11 provides a standardized coding system that enables international comparability of health data, supports epidemiological surveillance, and informs public health policy development.

India's strategy for *data standardization* involves the judicious adoption and adaptation of these global standards to align with the specific requirements and context of the Indian healthcare system. This process is characterized by collaboration among experts, clinicians, policymakers, and industry representatives, ensuring the practicality and relevance of the implemented standards. The emphasis on *open standards* is consistent with India's broader digital health initiatives, fostering wider adoption, promoting innovation, and enabling the development of a robust and interconnected digital health ecosystem.

Activity Box 14.1. Exploring Interoperability Standards in Action
The chapter discusses the importance of data standards like HL7 FHIR, SNOMED CT, and ICD-11 for interoperability. Choose one of these standards and research a real-world implementation of it in a healthcare system (e.g., a hospital, a national health program, or a health information exchange). Draft a brief report (200–300 words) summarizing:

- The standard's role in the implementation
- The benefits of using the standard
- Any challenges encountered in its adoption

Real-world evidence (RWE) derived from health claims data offers a powerful tool for assessing treatment effectiveness and safety in diverse populations (Fig. 14.1). Unlike traditional clinical trials, which often involve highly selected patient groups, claims data reflects real-world usage of medical interventions, offering valuable insights into treatment patterns, outcomes, and costs. Analysis of claims data can inform clinical guidelines, drug formularies, and healthcare policy decisions, enabling evidence-based decision-making. Furthermore, RWE from claims data facilitates post-market surveillance, allowing for rapid assessment of the safety and effectiveness of medical procedures after approval. This approach offers a cost-effective and efficient alternative to traditional clinical trials, providing prompt and relevant information for improving healthcare delivery.

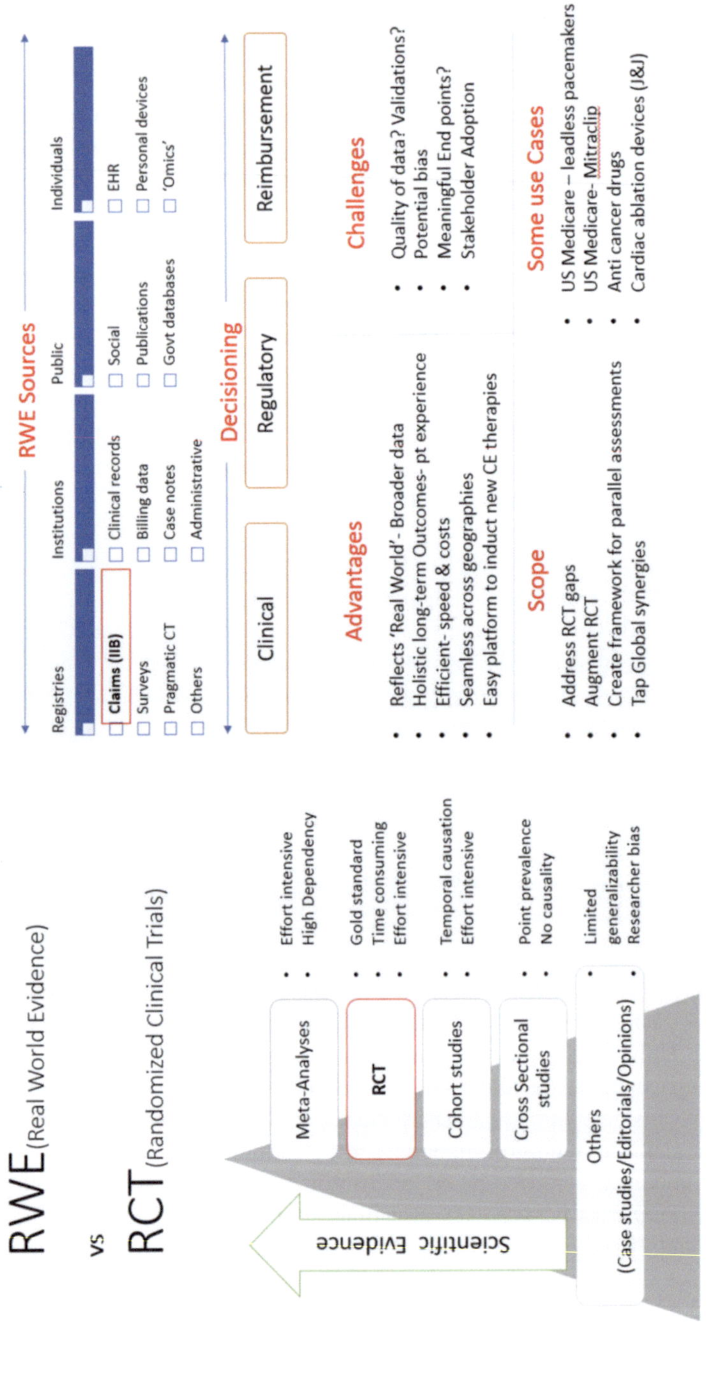

Fig. 14.1 Health claims data as a source of real-world evidence (RWE)

Going ahead, India's digital health revolution demands AI-powered automation, streamlining data from diverse sources like social media and environmental sensors. Integrating genomic data into EHRs will personalize medicine, while incorporating Social Determinants of Health data addresses health disparities. Quantum computing holds long-term potential for complex data analysis. Scaling mobile telemedicine and empowering community health workers are crucial for widespread access. Equitable financing, linked to financial inclusion, ensures affordability. Prioritizing automation, diverse data utilization, and robust infrastructure will unlock India's vast health data potential, driving personalized, accessible healthcare for all. Standardization of provider documents like discharge summary, claim form and bills by a central agency like the Bureau of Indian Standards (BIS) [5] will be a great step fostering efficiency in the healthcare financing ecosystem.

14.3 Securing Health Financing Data

Within the digitized healthcare financing landscape, the imperative of safeguarding sensitive information is paramount for maintaining trust and ensuring regulatory compliance. Global regulatory frameworks, such as the European Union's *General Data Protection Regulation (GDPR)*, emphasize the principles of *explicit consent*—requiring unambiguous authorization for data processing—and *data minimization*—limiting the collection of personal data to what is strictly necessary—thereby exerting considerable influence on global entities [6].

In the United States, the *Health Insurance Portability and Accountability Act (HIPAA)* mandates the implementation of robust safeguards to protect patient health information and stipulates requirements for breach notification in the event of unauthorized data disclosure [7]. Furthermore, the *ISO/IEC 27001* standard provides a framework for establishing, implementing, maintaining, and continually improving an information security management system (ISMS) to ensure the confidentiality, integrity, and availability of healthcare data repositories.

These regulatory standards align with the fundamental health financing principles of *equity* and *efficiency*, thereby supporting the core functions of health system financing.

India's *Digital Personal Data Protection Act (DPDP Act)* underscores the importance of consent, transparency in data processing practices, and accountability for data protection. While the *Information Technology Act, 2000*, provides a foundational legal framework, sector-specific guidelines from regulatory bodies such as the *Insurance Regulatory and Development Authority of India (IRDAI)* are essential for its effective application within the healthcare financing sector.

Despite advancements in digital technologies, several challenges persist, including infrastructural limitations, insufficient data literacy among stakeholders, and fragmented regulatory approaches. To mitigate these challenges, the implementation of robust security controls is indispensable.

- *Encryption*, employing algorithms such as *AES-256*, serves to render data unintelligible to unauthorized parties, while *multi-factor authentication (MFA)* enhances security by requiring users to provide multiple forms of verification before gaining access to systems or data.
- *Blockchain* technology, characterized by its immutability, offers a secure and transparent ledger for recording transactions, thereby aiding in fraud detection within claims processing ecosystems and supporting the purchasing and provision of services.
- A *zero-trust architecture* represents a security paradigm that eliminates implicit trust, requiring rigorous identity verification and authorization for every user and device attempting to access resources within a network, thus bolstering the security of health record databases.

These security measures, coupled with comprehensive education initiatives and the harmonization of regulatory frameworks, are crucial for establishing a secure and trusted digital healthcare financing ecosystem, which in turn supports the strategic purchasing function. The implementation of robust data integrity and security measures directly enhances the efficiency and equity of health financing.

Activity Box 14.2. Debating Data Privacy in Healthcare

The chapter discusses the importance of data privacy and security in healthcare financing, referencing regulations like GDPR and India's DPDP Act, the standard's role in the implementation.

Organize a class/group debate on '*Balancing the need for data sharing to improve healthcare with the need to protect individual patient privacy is achievable*'.

Divide the class/group into two teams: one to argue for the proposition and the other to argue against it. Each team should research and present arguments supported by evidence and relevant examples.

Case Study: Health Data Across Various Healthcare Financing Schemes

1. *Ayushman Bharat Pradhan Mantri Jan Arogya Yojana (AB PM-JAY), India*: AB PM-JAY aims to provide free access to secondary and tertiary care hospitalization for vulnerable populations by utilizing a wide array of health data. This includes demographic details like name, age, gender, and address, alongside socioeconomic data to determine eligibility. Biometric data from Aadhaar, such as fingerprints and iris scans, is crucial for beneficiary authentication. Furthermore, the scheme relies on comprehensive health records encompassing hospitalization details, diagnoses, treat-

ments, and medical history, as well as transaction data documenting claims and payments. *Key Data Fields*: Aadhaar number, ration card number, patient ID, hospital ID, diagnosis codes (ICD codes), treatment codes, medication details, and discharge summary.

2. *Medicare and Medicaid, United States (US)*: Medicare provides health insurance for individuals aged 65 and older, and some younger individuals with disabilities, while Medicaid offers coverage to low-income individuals and families. Both programs rely on the processing of various forms of health data. This includes demographic information like name, age, address, and Social Security number, along with enrollment data specific to each program's plans. Claims data detailing medical services, including diagnoses, procedures, and costs, is essential for both Medicare and Medicaid. Additionally, both schemes use prescription drug data and provider data, which have information on healthcare providers and facilities. *Key Data Fields*: Medicare/Medicaid beneficiary ID, Social Security number, provider National Provider Identifier (NPI), diagnosis codes (ICD codes), procedure codes (CPT codes), and medication NDC codes.
3. *The National Health Service (NHS), United Kingdom (UK)*: The NHS provides comprehensive healthcare services to UK residents, utilizing extensive health data. This includes demographic details such as name, age, address, and NHS number, alongside comprehensive electronic health records (EHRs) that encompass medical history, diagnoses, treatments, and medications. Prescription data from the Electronic Prescription Service (EPS), Hospital Episode Statistics (HES) detailing hospital admissions and treatments, and public health data on disease prevalence and health outcomes are crucial components of the NHS's data management. *Key Data Fields*: NHS number, patient identifier, General Practitioner (GP) practice code, diagnosis codes (ICD-10 codes), procedure codes (OPCS-4 codes), and medication details.

14.4 Digital Technologies in Health Financing

In the realm of health financing, data and digital technologies serve as cornerstones for achieving strategic objectives and delivering tangible value. To begin, insurers aim to bolster underwriting profitability by employing granular risk assessments that align precisely with assumed pricing boundaries. This precision, in turn, fuels operational efficiency through the automation of customer-facing processes, such as underwriting and claims, while empowering customers with self-service options. By harnessing data-driven insights, insurers gain a deeper understanding of the market, enabling them to scale their business and uncover untapped opportunities. Furthermore, accurate capital and reserve assessments, facilitated by these technologies, ensure long-term sustainability. Customer experience is significantly enhanced through empowerment, self-service tools, and real-time status updates, fostering transparency and convenience. Crucially, technologies that improve provider-payer alignment streamline transactional processes, enabling evidence-based provider classification for better contracting and informed patient choices. Real-time data analytics and visibility empower multiple stakeholders, aiding governance in scientific scheme monitoring and optimal budget allocation, optimizing provider service delivery and quality, and empowering patients to make informed choices that reduce out-of-pocket expenses and increase preventative care demand. Finally, data and technologies deployed in health technology assessment promote value-based, cost-effective services at a national level, while social platforms foster information exchange among patients with chronic conditions, enhancing self-accountability and shared learning.

1. *Interoperable Digital Technologies: Enhancing Ecosystem by Seamless Data Exchange*

Secure and seamless data exchange is fundamental to the efficiency and effectiveness of modern health financing systems. In a landscape of rising healthcare costs and complex service delivery, the ability to share information fluidly among providers, payers, and patients is essential. Data underpin critical processes, from analysing historical trends and adjudicating claims to proactively managing data discrepancies and non-disclosures. Historically, fragmented manual processes have caused inefficiencies across the sector; however, interoperable digital technologies offer a transformative solution.

Interoperability is key to this transformation, enabling the fluid exchange of data across diverse systems. This approach supports in-depth analysis of healthcare utilization for personalized care and improved outcomes. Leveraging vast datasets, advanced analytics facilitates predictive modelling for risk stratification and resource allocation. Furthermore, pattern and anomaly identification enhances fraud detection, protecting against financial losses. Standardized evaluations using performance measurement tools ensure accountability and drive continuous improvement. Health Information Exchange (HIE) platforms provide real-time access to critical patient data, empowering population health management and enabling timely interventions.

In India, the push for interoperability is exemplified by initiatives like the Insurance Information Bureau of India's *(IIB) portability platform*, which enables seamless movement of policy credits across insurers benefiting the customers and meeting their respective insurance cover requirements. This mandates the need for a unique patient identifier (e.g. ABHA—Ayushman Bharat Health Account initiative [8]), facilitating the accurate and consistent identification of individuals across multiple databases and systems, enabling seamless data linkage and enhancing the precision of health financing data exchange.

Case Study: IIB's Health Insurance (HI) Portability

IIB, India's sole health insurance data repository, introduces HI Portability, a smart data exchange platform revolutionizing policy transition. This tool simplifies customer portability across insurers by providing instant access to longitudinal policy and claims data using basic member details. Insurers gain accurate risk assessments without extensive customer inquiries, accelerating underwriting. HI Portability enables real-time data exchange, eliminating customer reliance on recalling complex medical histories and preventing misrepresentations or non-disclosures of key underwriting information. This quick, efficient, and cost-effective solution is regulatorily mandated, standardizing portability across the industry. It reduces administrative burdens for insurers and streamlines transitions for policyholders. By fostering transparency and minimizing information asymmetry, HI Portability empowers informed customer decisions. This platform exemplifies the transformative potential of data exchange technologies, enhancing operational efficiency, customer experience, and regulatory compliance in healthcare financing.

Benefits Across the Health Financing Ecosystem

- *Patients/customers*: Improved care coordination, enhanced patient safety, increased efficiency, better patient engagement, and proactive population health management.
- *Payers/third-party administrators (TPAs)*: Reduced administrative costs through automated claims processing, improved risk assessment and fraud detection, enhanced customer satisfaction through faster service, and data-driven product development.
- *Hospitals/providers*: Streamlined workflows, reduced administrative burden, improved clinical decision-making through access to comprehensive patient data, enhanced revenue cycle management, and improved patient outcomes.
- *Government*: Enhanced public health surveillance, improved policy formulation through data-driven insights, reduced healthcare fraud and abuse, and improved efficiency of public health programs.

ABDM architecture: The Ayushman Bharat Digital Mission (ABDM) is a significant digital health platform implementation in India, designed to foster integrated care delivery and transform the healthcare ecosystem by prioritizing accessibility, equity, and patient empowerment. Rather than a centralized repository, ABDM uses a federated architecture, enabling secure interconnection of existing digital health systems, thus empowering individuals to control their health information while facilitating seamless data sharing across providers. A core strength of ABDM is its interoperability framework, enabling communication between disparate systems via standardized Application Programming Interfaces (APIs). This promotes connectivity by leveraging key components: registries of individuals (ABHA Registry), professionals (Healthcare Professionals Registry), and facilities (Health Facility Registry), each with unique identifiers. To ensure privacy and consent, ABDM incorporates the Health Information Exchange and Consent Manager (HIE-CM), enabling identity verification, consent management, and secure data sharing between Health Information Providers (HIPs) and Users (HIUs). Patients authorize record access via their ABHA, supporting continuity of care, and health locker providers can integrate with ABHA to centralize records.

The National Health Claim Exchange (NHCX) is designed to revolutionize health insurance claims processing by facilitating secure, standardized exchange of claim data between payers and providers. By automating and streamlining this process, NHCX aims to reduce processing times, errors, and enhance transparency, expediting reimbursements and improving the efficiency of the healthcare financing system.

The Unified Health Interface (UHI) functions as a digital marketplace, like the Unified Payments Interface (UPI), enabling patients to access various health services. Leveraging open technology and the JAM trinity (Jan Dhan, Aadhaar, Mobile), ABDM fosters innovation and seamless integration of digital health tools. The mission's focus on patient privacy, control, and interoperability aligns with the National Health Policy 2017s goal of a patient-centric healthcare system, enhancing healthcare delivery and financing in India.

Despite the transformative potential, the implementation of interoperable data exchange presents significant *challenges*. Data integrity issues, stemming from the need to maintain accuracy and consistency, require robust data governance frameworks and rigorous quality control measures. System compatibility, particularly with legacy systems, necessitates meticulous data mapping and integration strategies. Data security and privacy, threatened by evolving cybersecurity threats, demand stringent compliance measures and robust security protocols. The sheer volume and complexity of data necessitate sophisticated data management strategies and advanced analytics capabilities. Interoperability itself, involving multiple systems and the need for standardization, requires collaborative efforts and the adoption of common data standards. Downtime and service disruption, with their operational impact, require a phased approach, meticulous planning, and robust contingency measures. Finally, effective stakeholder communication and engagement are crucial for successful implementation, requiring clear communication strategies and collaborative partnerships.

For initiatives focused on interoperability to achieve their full potential, a strategic and phased approach is essential. This includes prioritizing data standardization, implementing robust security measures, and fostering collaboration among stakeholders. The establishment of unique patient identifiers, like ABHA, is instrumental in ensuring accurate data linkage and patient identification across the health financing ecosystem. By addressing these challenges proactively, policymakers and practitioners can unlock the full potential of interoperable digital technologies, creating a more efficient, secure, and patient-centric health financing ecosystem. This transformation will not only improve operational efficiency but also contribute to better health outcomes and enhanced stakeholder value.

2. *Centralized Registries: Empowering Data-Driven Decisions in Health Financing*

The efficiency and effectiveness of modern health financing systems are increasingly dependent on robust data management. Centralized repositories, or registries, serve as authoritative sources of information, enabling stakeholders to make informed decisions, improve efficiency, and enhance patient care. By acting as standardized data repositories, registries capture information on various aspects of healthcare, including hospitals, diseases, and suspicious entities. This comprehensive and accessible data source supports effective health financing management and policy development, facilitating data-driven strategies for risk assessment, fraud detection, and performance evaluation.

In India, the development of several key registries contributes significantly to health financing. Beyond hospital and fraud-related repositories, disease-specific registries, such as those tracking cancer, tuberculosis, or organ transplants, provide critical insights into disease prevalence, treatment patterns, and patient outcomes. These registries enable payers to assess risk, develop targeted interventions, and allocate resources effectively. For example, registries tracking medical devices or adverse events contribute by providing data for cost-effectiveness analyses and quality improvement initiatives. The Registry of Hospitals in Insurance Network of India (ROHINI), managed by the Insurance Information Bureau of India (IIB), serves as a comprehensive database of hospitals, facilitating efficient claims processing and network management for insurers. Similarly, the Caution Repository, also maintained by IIB, acts as a database of suspicious entities, aiding in fraud detection and prevention within the health insurance sector. Globally, similar initiatives like Global Burden of Disease Study (GBD) from IHME, The Surveillance, Epidemiology, and End Results (SEER) program in the United States [9], European Network of Cancer Registries (ENCR) [10, 11], United Nation Sanction security council list for anti-money laundering (AML) activities, and the National Joint Registry in the United Kingdom [12], tracking joint replacement procedures, illustrate the effectiveness of such registries. ICD from the World Health Organization is leveraged widely for billing and utilization analysis purposes.

Case Study: IIB's ROHINI

ROHINI (Registry of Hospitals in Insurance Network of India) stands as the nation's definitive repository, housing over 75,000 hospitals participating in the health insurance ecosystem. Hospitals register online, providing essential data on ownership, services, location, and capacity, for a nominal fee. A unique feature of ROHINI is its real-time validation process. Existing health insurers or TPAs verify hospital applications, ensuring accuracy and reliability. Upon successful validation, each hospital receives a unique registration number (ROHINI ID) serving as its universal identifier across all datasets. ROHINI plays a pivotal role in curbing fraud by offering insurers a validated hospital database. It also serves as a critical tool for analytics, enabling the monitoring of hospital performance and utilization. This data-driven approach is instrumental in controlling healthcare costs and improving outcomes. By standardizing hospital information and providing a reliable registry, ROHINI enhances transparency and efficiency in India's health insurance landscape.

These registries are instrumental in driving the adoption and effectiveness of digital technologies within healthcare financing. By enabling data-driven decision-making, they provide the necessary analytics to understand healthcare trends, identify gaps in service delivery, and make informed choices regarding resource allocation. Furthermore, the rich datasets within these registries support predictive modelling, allowing for the forecasting of healthcare costs and the development of proactive budgeting and planning strategies. In the critical area of fraud detection, registries play a vital role by identifying discrepancies and patterns indicative of fraudulent claims or transactions, particularly through the cross-referencing of claims data with registry information. For instance, the standardized data from registries like ROHINI significantly streamlines claims processing by providing accurate and readily accessible information about hospitals and their services. This standardization reduces administrative overhead and accelerates reimbursement cycles. Program monitoring and evaluation are also greatly enhanced, as registries enable the tracking of healthcare program effectiveness and the assessment of their impact on health outcomes, ensuring that healthcare funds are utilized efficiently. The data within these registries are also invaluable for research and development, fostering innovation in healthcare delivery, the development of new treatments, and the formulation of evidence-based policies. Crucially, ongoing efforts to enhance interoperability, particularly through linking registries with platforms like the ABDM, aim to create a seamless flow of information [13]. This interconnectedness empowers comprehensive data analysis and facilitates a more integrated and efficient healthcare financing ecosystem, improving patient outcomes and optimizing resource utilization.

The hosting and operation of health registries require collaboration among various stakeholders, including government agencies, healthcare providers, insurance companies, and research institutions. Registries should operate on principles of data standardization, interoperability, and security, ensuring data sharing while protecting patient privacy and ensuring data integrity. However, several *challenges* exist in leveraging registries for health financing. Data quality and completeness are crucial, but data collection and validation can be resource-intensive. Interoperability between different registries and healthcare systems is essential for seamless data exchange, but achieving this requires standardization and collaboration. Data security and privacy concerns necessitate robust security measures and compliance with regulations. Stakeholder engagement and buy-in are also critical for successful implementation and utilization. The sustainability of registries requires long-term funding and governance mechanisms. Addressing these challenges through collaborative efforts and robust governance frameworks is essential to unlock the full potential of health registries in enhancing health financing efficiency and patient care.

Activity Box 14.3. Designing a Health Data Repository

The chapter discusses the importance of data repositories like the Registry of Hospitals in the Network of Insurance (ROHINI) and Health Information Exchanges (HIEs).

Activity: Imagine you are tasked with designing a data repository for a regional health system. Outline the key considerations for your design, including the following:

- What are the key purposes of using the repository?
- What types of data would you include?
- Who will be the users and what values will they derive?
- What security measures would you implement?
- How would you ensure data quality and accuracy?
- How would the repository facilitate data sharing with other healthcare providers and HIEs?

3. *Algorithmic Modelling: Transforming Risk Intelligence in Health Financing Ecosystems*

The financial stability and long-term viability of voluntary private health insurance hinge on the precision of risk assessment and quantification for the insurers. Contrarily, in compulsory health schemes, the value of such risk models rests more on demand analyses, budgeting, and utilization analyses. Robust predictive capabilities enable insurers to optimize pricing strategies, manage portfolio exposure, and ensure sustainable operations. The inherent complexity of health risk assessment (Fig. 14.2) poses formidable challenges. Unlike traditional risk

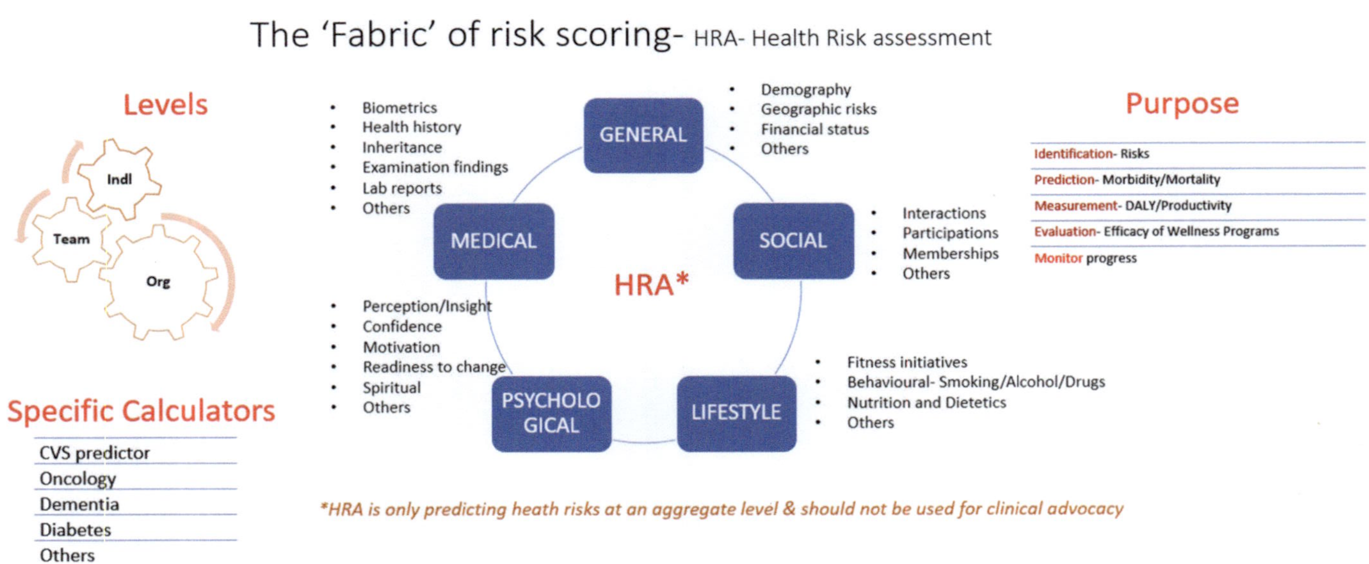

Fig. 14.2 Health risk assessment (HRA). DALY: Disability adjusted life years

paradigms, health risks are influenced by a confluence of variables, including heterogeneous data sources (e.g. electronic health records, wearable sensor data), dynamic environmental factors (e.g. pandemic outbreaks), personalized genetic predispositions, lifestyles, and the ever-present threat of fraudulent activities, such as non-disclosure or misrepresentation during policy underwriting. Furthermore, disparities in diagnostic infrastructure, including accessibility, affordability, and quality, can obfuscate accurate risk profiling. The issue of applicant misrepresentation is significant; studies, such as those published by the Coalition Against Insurance Fraud, indicate a substantial prevalence of misstatements in health insurance applications, leading to escalated costs and potential claim disputes [14]. The principle of *uberrimae fidei* (utmost good faith) is crucial as it underscores the necessity for both the insurer and the insured to provide complete and honest disclosures. Without this foundational principle, algorithms relying on applicant-provided data will be inherently flawed, undermining accurate risk prediction and the equitable distribution of insurance benefits.

Digital technologies, particularly algorithmic models and machine learning (ML) paradigms, offer a transformative approach to these challenges. By assimilating and synthesizing data from diverse sources, insurers can transcend the limitations of self-reported disclosures and underestimated healthcare demand. ML algorithms, leveraging techniques such as deep learning and gradient boosting, excel at identifying intricate patterns within health financing data, enabling scalable and adaptive risk modelling. Real-time analytics and anomaly detection provide proactive insights into evolving risk landscapes, facilitating timely interventions. Moreover, these technologies offer cost-effective solutions for population-level risk monitoring and the identification of potentially fraudulent activities. Globally, advanced risk scoring solutions, exemplified by Optum and Milliman [15, 16], employ sophisticated analytics to provide predictive insights for health insurers, demonstrating the value derived from implementing data-driven algorithms. Complementing these, AI-driven fraud detection systems like AiDA Technologies' SMART-FRAUD in Singapore [17], and the machine learning-based system used by South Korea's NHIS, showcase the tangible benefits of technology in combating fraud and waste. Government initiatives such as the US False Claims Act and Medicare Fraud Strike Force, the UK's NHS Counter Fraud Authority, Australia's Medicare compliance programs, and Canada's provincial systems further highlight the international focus on data analytics and collaborative models to derive value and ensure healthcare financing integrity [18–21]. In India, both government health schemes and private insurers are increasingly adopting similar algorithmic approaches. The Insurance Information Bureau of India (IIB) enhances this landscape with "BIMA SATARK", a system providing real-time risk triggers during customer inquiries.

Case Study: BIMA SATARK

The Indian health insurance sector grapples with pervasive fraud, waste, and abuse (FWA), resulting in significant financial losses and operational inefficiencies. Traditional manual detection methods prove inadequate, often slow, reactive, and incapable of identifying subtle fraud indicators. Manual claims processing is time-consuming, error-prone, and hinders timely reviews. Insurers face limitations in analysing complex data patterns, leading to delayed fraud detection and revenue recovery. The absence of real-time alerts allows suspicious activities to persist unchecked. A proactive, real-time tool capable of generating instant FWA alerts is crucial.

IIB's BIMA SATARK addresses these challenges with a sophisticated algorithm designed to analyse extensive datasets, identifying anomalies and patterns indicative of FWA. By employing customizable, complex, real-time trigger rules, BIMA SATARK integrates with insurers' claims processing systems, generating immediate alerts. The tool identifies high-risk hospitals, doctors, locations, claimants, intermediaries, insured individuals, multiple claims, exaggerated lengths of stay, high-risk products, distribution channels, and their complex associations.

BIMA SATARK has demonstrated remarkable effectiveness, achieving a 40% reduction in fraud and a 50% decrease in investigation costs in 2024–25. This proactive, data-driven approach strengthens the integrity of India's health insurance ecosystem, safeguarding against financial losses and enhancing operational efficiency.

The architecture of these algorithms typically involves the generation of risk scores based on a constellation of predictive factors. Smart rule-based systems, for instance, employ pre-defined heuristics derived from historical claims data, clinical guidelines, and epidemiological studies. These rules might incorporate metrics such as average claim size for specific medical conditions, hospital performance indicators (e.g. length of stay, complication rates), and reported fraud patterns. Social network analysis (SNA) algorithms can further enhance risk assessment by detecting covert collusive networks among stakeholders. Risk algorithms have the potential to generate triggers based on anomalies in claims, provider behaviour, patient activity, and system operations. These include unusual billing patterns, credentialing issues, diagnostic inconsistencies, and data entry errors. Additionally, algorithms can detect suspicious connections between hospitals and distribution channels, demographic-based fraud hotspots, and billing irregularities, such as sudden increases or duplicate billings. Moving beyond static rule-based systems, ML techniques, such as neural networks and support vector machines, enable the discovery of subtle, non-linear relationships within the data. Continuous model retraining, informed by new data and feedback loops, ensures the adaptability and accuracy of risk predictions. By incorporating real-world claims data, market trends, and emerging risks, models can adapt to evolving patterns and maintain their predictive power. In the context of government-sponsored health schemes like Pradhan Mantri Jan Arogya Yojana (PM-JAY) [22], which aim to provide Universal Health Coverage (UHC), these algorithms are not only used for underwriting selection but also for the development of targeted care programs, budget forecasting, and the identification of high-risk populations. Back testing, using techniques like cross-validation and sensitivity analysis, is crucial for validating model performance against real-world claims experience.

The implementation of these advanced risk scoring tools is not without *challenges*. Data quality is paramount for the effectiveness of risk prediction algorithms because inaccurate or inconsistent data lead to flawed models. For instance, errors in medical coding, such as misclassifying a claim, can skew risk assessments, leading to incorrect predictions of patient health and claim costs. Similarly, incomplete or outdated patient demographic information can lead to biased risk profiles, impacting the fairness and accuracy of the algorithm's outputs. The protection of sensitive personal information necessitates stringent data security measures and compliance with regulations like the DPDP Act. The integration of disparate data systems poses significant technical hurdles. Ensuring algorithmic transparency and explainability, especially in the context of equitable access to insurance, is crucial. Other challenges include addressing algorithmic bias, ensuring model robustness against adversarial attacks, and building stakeholder trust in technology. The deployment of these technologies must be accompanied by robust ethical frameworks and governance mechanisms to ensure responsible and equitable use.

Activity Box 14.4. Algorithmic Bias in Healthcare

The chapter mentions the use of algorithms for risk assessment and other purposes in healthcare financing.

Activity: Research the potential for bias in algorithms used in healthcare. Draft a short essay (400–500 words) discussing:

- How can bias enter these algorithms?
- What are the potential consequences of biased algorithms (e.g., in risk assessment, claims processing)?
- What strategies can be used to mitigate bias and ensure fairness?
- How would you ensure data quality and accuracy?
- How would the repository facilitate data sharing with other healthcare providers and HIEs?

4. *Leveraging Data Analytics—Transforming Health Financing Through Actionable Insights*

Data analytics is rapidly transforming health financing by converting raw data into actionable insights, driving efficiency, and improving patient access and outcomes. In India, where health insurance penetration remains low, 37% [23], as highlighted by indicating significant coverage gaps, data analytics becomes particularly vital for expanding access and enhancing healthcare delivery.

The "power of payer data" (Fig. 14.3) offers crucial insights for health financing, offering substantial opportunities to enhance business value across three key dimensions: strategic business growth, operational excellence, and enhanced quality of care. It is important to note that the specific analytic parameters discussed are not mutually exclusive; they often provide benefits across multiple categories, showing the holistic value of data analysis in healthcare financing.

For *strategic business growth*, payer data analysis empowers payers to connect effectively with customers. By using business analytics, payers gain essential performance and financial insights for market expansion. Touchpoint analytics enables a deeper understanding of customer interactions, revealing needs and pain points. Customer profiling then uses this understanding to identify and target high-potential customers, predicting their behaviour and needs. Simultaneously, product analytics assesses insurance product performance, guiding development and pricing for maximum market impact. Ultimately, this data-driven approach allows payers to refine their communication, personalize customer experiences, and build lasting relationships, which are essential for sustainable growth in the insurance sector.

In the realm of *operational excellence*, payer data analysis drives efficiency and service improvement. Claims maturity models objectively evaluate claims processing, balancing cost control with compliance and customer satisfaction. Operational analytics provides key metrics to monitor performance and streamline processes. Intermediary profiling optimizes distribution channels and intermediary relationships by assessing their performance. These are supported by operational excellence frameworks that employ data-driven methodologies to enhance effectiveness, ensure compliance, and minimize risks. By using these analyses, payers can streamline operations and deliver superior customer service, fostering loyalty.

Finally, regarding *enhanced quality of care*, payer data analysis is vital for improving healthcare delivery and financing. Care outcome analytics evaluates healthcare service quality and patient outcomes, identifying areas for improvement. Fraud triggers detect patterns indicative of fraud, waste, and abuse, enabling proactive prevention. Provider classification uses data to categorize providers based on capacity, utilization, and outcomes, facilitating informed patient choice. Value-based contracting leverages performance data to create payment models that incentivize quality care and cost-effectiveness. Furthermore, real-world evidence (RWE) from claims data complements traditional trials, accelerating the adoption of valuable medical innovations. In essence, these analyses enable payers to promote high-quality care within available resources.

By effectively analysing payer data across these three dimensions, healthcare financers can achieve strategic objectives, enhance customer satisfaction, optimize operations, and ensure financial sustainability. The applications of advanced analytic tools are extending across the health financing spectrum. Beyond basic reporting, natural language processing (NLP) is increasingly vital for extracting

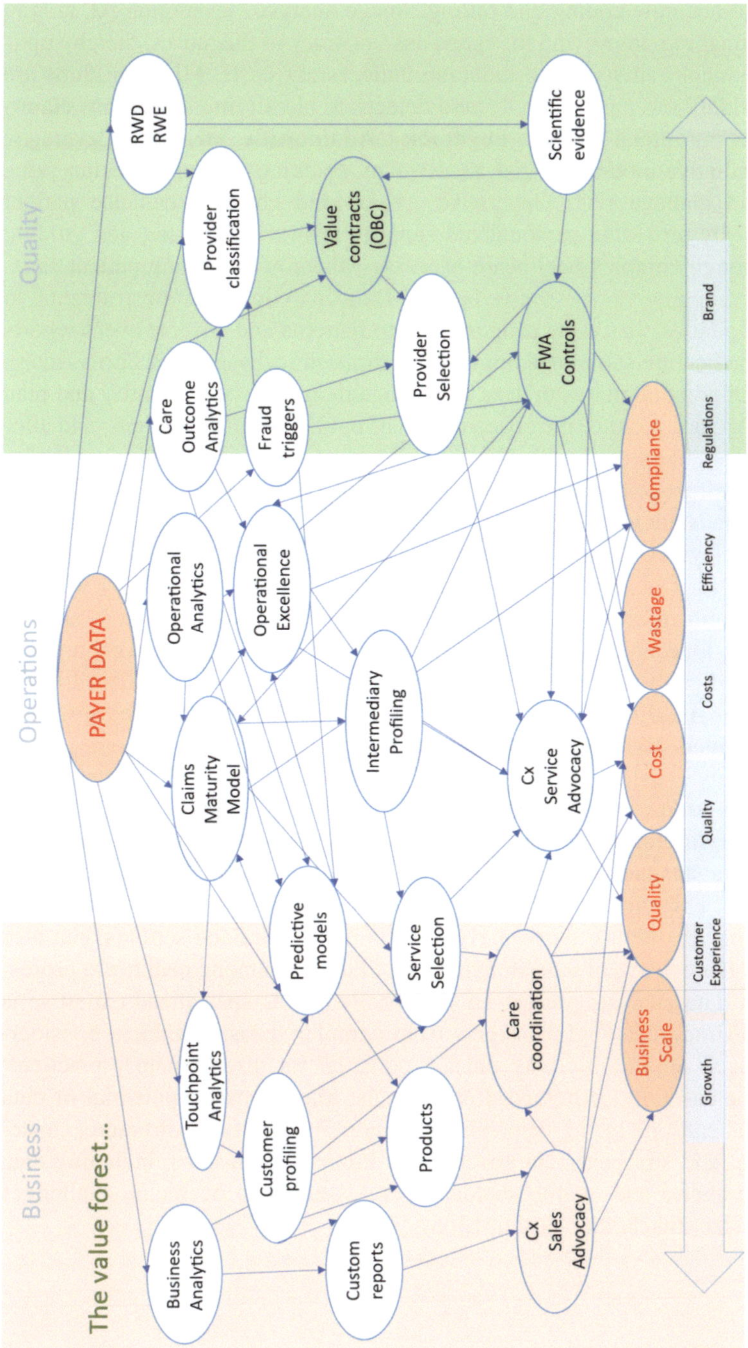

Fig. 14.3 Power of payer data

actionable information from electronic clinical documentation, enabling more efficient and accurate coding and billing. Image analysis, leveraging AI, aids in diagnostic imaging, improving the speed and accuracy of diagnoses, thereby optimizing treatment pathways and reducing unnecessary costs. ML algorithms are deployed widely for sophisticated fraud detection, identifying anomalous claims patterns that traditional methods might miss. Additionally, ML is also leveraged to build predictive models for risk assessment, enabling insurers to better price policies and manage risk. Generative AI-powered chatbots enhance patient engagement by providing personalized support, answering queries, and guiding patients through complex healthcare processes, thereby improving patient satisfaction and reducing administrative burden. Data analytics is also instrumental in pharmacovigilance, analysing drug utilization patterns and adverse event reports to ensure medication safety and optimize pharmaceutical spending. Furthermore, by analysing population health data, public health agencies can identify and plan disease outbreaks, monitor the effectiveness of public health campaigns, and allocate resources to address health disparities. Finally, the use of analytics to evaluate the cost-effectiveness of various medical interventions is crucial to ensure healthcare funds are used optimally.

However, leveraging data analytics in health financing is not without significant *challenges*. Data privacy and security are paramount, particularly with the increasing digitization of health records. Data quality at the source is another major hurdle. Inaccurate or incomplete data, such as errors in medical coding, can lead to flawed analyses and incorrect decision-making. Studies published in the *Journal of the American Medical Informatics Association* (JAMIA) have repeatedly highlighted the impact of data quality on healthcare outcomes [24]. Interoperability in data flow is also a challenge, as healthcare data are often stored in disparate systems with varying formats. This lack of seamless data exchange hinders the ability to create comprehensive patient profiles and impedes real-time analysis. Data standards, such as the Fast Healthcare Interoperability Resources (FHIR), are essential for ensuring data consistency and interoperability. Infrastructure limitations, particularly in resource-constrained settings, can also hinder the effective use of data analytics [4]. Skill gaps among healthcare professionals and data analysts present another challenge, as specialized expertise is needed to extract meaningful insights from complex datasets. Ethical considerations, such as algorithmic bias and the potential for discriminatory practices, must also be carefully addressed. Realizing the transformative potential of data analytics in health financing demands investment in robust infrastructure, capacity building, and stringent data governance. Proactive measures, including data protection policies and quality standards, are essential to overcome challenges and incentivize stakeholder participation.

Activity Box 14.5. Data Analytics in Fraud Detection

The chapter discusses the role of data analytics in fortifying fraud detection mechanisms.

Activity: Investigate how data analytics and AI are used to detect fraud, waste, and abuse in healthcare claims.

Prepare a presentation outlining:

- Common types of healthcare fraud
- Specific technological tools and techniques used for detection (e.g. anomaly detection, pattern recognition)
- The effectiveness of these technologies
- Any ethical concerns (e.g. use of personal data for profiling)

5. *Patient-centric Innovation: Digital Technologies Redefining Health Financing*

The narrative of health financing is being rewritten by the advent of patient-centric digital technologies, ushering in an era of unprecedented engagement and empowerment. Patients, once passive recipients, are now active navigators of their healthcare journey, armed with tools that foster transparency, accessibility, and informed decision-making. These technologies extend beyond mere convenience, embodying a paradigm shift towards a more equitable and efficient healthcare ecosystem.

At the forefront of this transformation are technologies that streamline administrative and financial interactions. *Electronic payment systems*, exemplified by India's revolutionary Unified Payments Interface (UPI), have democratized financial transactions within healthcare [25]. UPI's seamless, real-time payment capabilities have significantly reduced the friction associated with healthcare payments, enhancing affordability and accessibility, particularly in a nation where digital literacy is rapidly expanding. For insurers, UPI reduces administrative overhead by automating premium collection and claim disbursements, minimizing the risk of payment errors and fraud. For patients, UPI offers instant payment confirmations, eliminates the need for physical cash or cards, and provides a secure, transparent transaction history. This digital payment revolution complements other patient-facing technologies, such as online appointment scheduling, which grants individuals the autonomy to manage their healthcare appointments with unparalleled ease. Claims submissions and tracking via digital platforms further simplify the often-cumbersome insurance process, allowing patients to monitor their claims in real-time [26]. Secure *document management systems*, encompassing EHRs and personal health records (PHRs), provide patients with secure access to their medical histories, empowering them to actively participate in their care. The National Digital Health Mission (NDHM) in India stands as a testament to the growing global emphasis on digital health records.

Case Study: National Health Claims Exchange (NHCX)

NHCX is a pivotal digital platform in India, designed to revolutionize health insurance claims processing. By leveraging FHIR standards, it sets up a seamless and secure data exchange ecosystem connecting payers, providers, and beneficiaries. This platform streamlines critical processes, including identity verification and record sharing, and is evolving to incorporate a personal health record (PHR) component. Addressing long-standing challenges in the patient journey, NHCX and the broader Ayushman Bharat Digital Mission (ABDM) expedite eligibility verification, pre-authorization, and claim approvals, while facilitating digital claim submissions and a unified query handling system, significantly improving efficiency and patient experience. NHCX offers core capabilities such as real-time coverage eligibility checks, status tracking, and registry integration, alongside insurance plan verification and secure participant access. This comprehensive approach enhances transparency and efficiency by providing a real-time list of providers and payers. Functionally, NHCX streamlines claims exchange through features like payment notices, pre-authorization requests, and claim reprocessing, fostering efficient communication and operational effectiveness. NHCX aims to transform the health insurance landscape by providing a robust, interconnected platform that benefits all stakeholders.

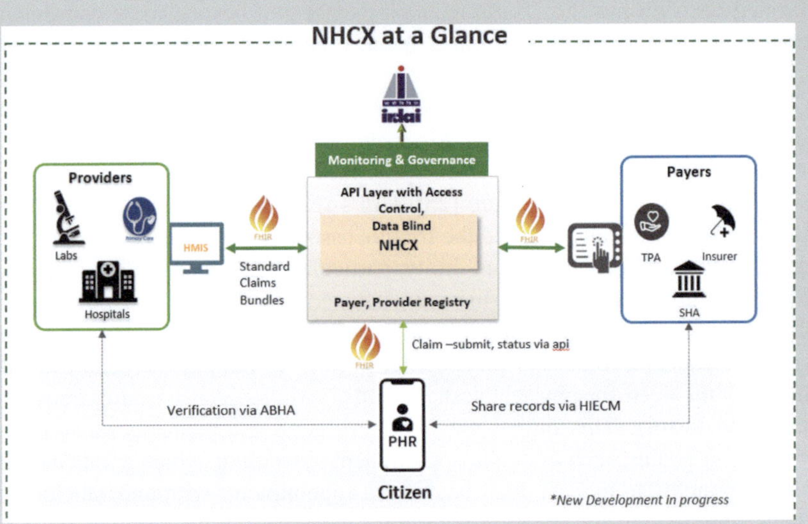

Beyond administrative efficiencies, these technologies facilitate informed decision-making. *Price transparency tools* provide patients with crucial insights into the costs of healthcare services, enabling them to make judicious choices [27]. *Health education and information resources* delivered through digital platforms empower individuals with knowledge, fostering proactive health management. *Telemedicine* and remote consultations bridge geographical barriers, ensuring access to care for even the most remote populations. Telemedicine in India gained significant momentum after being legalized in March 2020 through the "Telemedicine Practice Guidelines", issued by the Ministry of Health and Family Welfare, in response to the COVID-19 pandemic [28]. Its utilization has since surged, with millions of consultations conducted annually, particularly in rural and underserved areas, demonstrating its crucial role in expanding healthcare access. In a similar vein, patient feedback systems provide a platform for patients to voice their experiences, driving continuous improvement in healthcare delivery.

Furthermore, digital technologies enable personalized support and care management. *AI-powered chatbots* and *virtual assistants* offer instant support, while medication management apps promote adherence and reduce the risk of adverse events. Remote patient monitoring (RPM) systems provide continuous oversight for patients with chronic conditions, enabling timely interventions. *Wearable technology*, such as smartwatches and fitness trackers, provides continuous monitoring of vital health metrics like heart rate, activity levels, and sleep patterns [29]. These data enable personalized health insights and proactive care, potentially reducing healthcare costs by promoting preventative measures and early detection of health issues. In health financing, insurers can leverage wearable data for personalized risk assessment and incentive programs, promoting healthier lifestyles and potentially reducing claims.

Digital therapeutics (DTx) in India are emerging, offering software-based interventions for various health conditions. Companies like Pharmeasy and Tricog are exploring DTx applications, focusing on areas like chronic disease management and remote diagnostics [30, 31]. These technologies aim to improve patient adherence, reduce healthcare costs, and enhance accessibility, creating value by optimizing health financing through more efficient care delivery.

While the benefits are undeniable, challenges remain. The digital divide necessitates strategies to ensure equitable access, while data privacy and security demand robust safeguards. Interoperability between systems is essential for seamless data flow, and user adoption requires education and support. Clear regulatory frameworks are also imperative to ensure patient safety and ethical use. By addressing these challenges, we can fully harness the transformative power of patient-facing digital technologies, creating a healthcare ecosystem that is truly patient-centred, efficient, and equitable.

14.5 Conclusions

In synthesizing the explorations within this chapter, digital technologies are fundamental drivers of transformation in healthcare financing. This chapter has explored the multifaceted impact of these technologies, from AI and machine learning, which are refining risk assessment, enabling predictive analytics, and bolstering fraud detection, to blockchain's potential in securing transactions and ensuring data integrity. Telemedicine platforms have been examined for their role in expanding access to care and delivering patient-centric solutions. The critical role of health data, its secure management, and the diverse technologies that leverage it, including health information exchanges, centralized registries like IIB's ROHINI, and algorithmic modelling exemplified by IIB's BIMA SATARK, have been central to the analysis. Furthermore, this chapter has highlighted how health financing claims data can be leveraged as real-world evidence to facilitate the swift adoption of cost-effective healthcare solutions.

However, this digital evolution demands more than just technological adoption. As has been shown, *challenges* related to data security, interoperability, and equitable access persist. India, with its unique healthcare landscape, stands at a crucial juncture. The path forward requires a concerted effort from all stakeholders—policymakers, healthcare providers, technology developers, and regulators—to collaboratively shape the future of healthcare financing.

This is a *call to action*. Priority must be given to the development and enforcement of robust data governance frameworks, exemplified by India's DPDP Act and international standards, which protect sensitive information and foster trust. Investment is needed in infrastructure that supports seamless data exchange, promotes interoperability through standards like FHIR, and ensures that the benefits of digital technologies reach every segment of the population. Furthermore, initiatives that promote interoperability, enabling diverse systems to work together harmoniously, must be championed.

The potential is immense: a healthcare financing ecosystem that is transparent, efficient, and responsive to the needs of all. Progress should be made with purpose and collaboration, leveraging the power of digital technologies to build a healthier and more equitable future for India.

References

1. FDA. 21st Century Cures Act [Internet]. U.S. Food and Drug Administration; 2020. Available from: https://www.fda.gov/regulatory-information/selected-amendments-fdc-act/21st-century-cures-act.
2. About ABDM – National Health Authority. GOI [Internet]. nha.gov.in. Available from: https://nha.gov.in/NDHM.
3. Digital Personal Data Protection Act 2023. Ministry of Electronics and Information Technology, Government of India [Internet]. www.meity.gov.in. Available from: https://www.meity.gov.in/content/digital-personal-data-protection-act-2023.

4. Overview – FHIR v4.0.1 [Internet]. www.hl7.org. 2023. Available from: https://www.hl7.org/fhir/overview.html.
5. Standardization [Internet]. www.bis.gov.in. Available from: https://www.bis.gov.in/standardization-in-the-field-of-service-sector.
6. GDPR. General Data Protection Regulation (GDPR) [Internet]. General Data Protection Regulation (GDPR); 2018. Available from: https://gdpr-info.eu.
7. Digital Communications Division (DCD), Assistant Secretary for Public Affairs (ASPA). HIPAA [Internet]. HHS.gov. 2015. Available from: https://www.hhs.gov/programs/hipaa/index.html.
8. NHA. Ayshman Bharat Health Account [Internet]. Available from: https://abha.abdm.gov.in/abha/v3/.
9. National Cancer Institute. Surveillance, epidemiology, and end results program [Internet]. SEER. 2018. Available from: https://seer.cancer.gov/.
10. ENCR. European Network of Cancer Registries [Internet]. Encr.eu. 2025. Available from: https://encr.eu/.
11. Kölker S, Gleich F, Mütze U, Opladen T. Rare disease registries are key to evidence-based personalized medicine: highlighting the European experience. Front Endocrinol. 2022;13:832063.
12. National Joint Registry Home Page [Internet]. The National Joint Registry. 2025 [cited 2025 Mar 31]. Available from: https://www.njrcentre.org.uk/njrcentre/About-the-NJR.
13. NHA. Official website Ayushman Bharat Digital Mission [Internet]. abdm.gov.in. Available from: https://abdm.gov.in/.
14. Utilization Review 101 [Internet]. InsuranceFraud.org. 2020. Available from: https://www.insurancefraud.org/.
15. Natural language processing (NLP) methods for real-world data (RWD) insights [Internet]. Optum.com. 2025 [cited 2025 Mar 31]. Available from: https://business.optum.com/en/insights/natural-language-processing-methods-clinical-data.html.
16. Risk Score. Mortality – Milliman IntelliScript [Internet]. Milliman IntelliScript. 2025 [cited 2025 Mar 31]. Available from: https://www.rxhistories.com/irix/risk-score/.
17. gov.sg. Home [Internet]. www.gov.sg. 2019. Available from: https://www.gov.sg/.
18. Medicare Fraud Strike Force. Medicare and Medicaid Fraud. HHS-OIG Office of Inspector General. U.S. Department of Health and Human Services [Internet]. oig.hhs.gov. Available from: https://oig.hhs.gov/fraud/strike-force/.
19. About the NHS Counter Fraud Authority [Internet]. Cfa.nhs.uk. 2019. Available from: https://cfa.nhs.uk/about-nhscfa.
20. Health. Medicare compliance [Internet]. Australian Government Department of Health and Aged Care; 2022. Available from: https://www.health.gov.au/topics/medicare/compliance.
21. Ruff NJ. Provincial Government. The Canadian Encyclopedia [Internet]. Thecanadianencyclopedia.ca. 2006. Available from: https://www.thecanadianencyclopedia.ca/en/article/provincial-government.
22. PMJAY Dashboard [Internet]. Available from: https://dashboard.pmjay.gov.in/pmj/#/.
23. Maheshwari R. Top health insurance statistics of 2023 [Internet]. Forbes Advisor INDIA; 2023. Available from: https://www.forbes.com/advisor/in/health-insurance/health-insurance-statistics/.
24. J Am Med Inform Assoc [Internet]. OUP Academic. 2017. Available from: https://academic.oup.com/jamia.
25. NPCI. UPI: Unified Payments Interface – instant mobile payments. NPCI [Internet]. www.npci.org.in. 2023. Available from: https://www.npci.org.in/what-we-do/upi/product-overview.
26. NHCX Brochure [Internet]. Available from: https://abdm.gov.in:8081/uploads/NHCX_Brochure_ffdb63d9bc.pdf.
27. Healthcare Price Transparency Solution – Healthcare Bluebook [Internet]. Healthcare Bluebook; 2025 [cited 2025 Mar 31]. Available from: https://healthcarebluebook.com.

28. BOARD OF GOVERNORS In supersession of the Medical Council of India telemedicine practice guidelines enabling registered medical practitioners to provide healthcare using telemedicine [Internet]. 2020. Available from: https://www.mohfw.gov.in/pdf/Telemedicine.pdf.
29. Lu L, Zhang J, Xie Y, Gao F, Xu S, Wu X, et al. Wearable health devices in health care: narrative systematic review [Internet]. U.S. National Library of Medicine; 2020 [cited 2025 Mar 31]. Available from: https://pmc.ncbi.nlm.nih.gov/articles/PMC7683248/.
30. Kapani P. Revolutionizing the healthcare space – PharmEasy's vision for e-healthcare [Internet]. Entrepreneur. Entrepreneur Media India; 2021 [cited 2025 Mar 31]. Available from: https://www.entrepreneur.com/en-in/entrepreneurs/revolutionizing-the-healthcare-space-pharmeasys-vision/380538.
31. Why choose Tricog's AI-powered ECHO solutions for your cardiac care facility? Tricog Health [Internet]. Tricog Health; 2024 [cited 2025 Mar 31]. Available from: https://www.tricog.com/why-choose-tricogs-ai-powered-echo-solutions-for-your-cardiac-care-facility/.

15 Evaluating Equity in Healthcare Financing: Benefit Incidence Analysis

Indranil Mukhopadhyay and Sayantani Manna

Abstract

Benefit incidence analysis (BIA) is a method used to assess how government spending and subsidies are distributed among different socio-economic and demographic groups, not only in the context of healthcare but also in other social sectors like education. This chapter explores the rationale and development of BIA, outlining various approaches to conducting the analysis and demonstrating the essential steps involved. It highlights the implications of BIA findings for health financing policy development and includes case studies from different contexts to illustrate its practical applications. In the context of government-funded health insurance (GFHI) schemes, BIA can be used as an exercise to evaluate the equity implications of such programs.

Keywords

Benefit incidence analysis · Marginal benefit incidence analysis · Equity · Concentration curve · Lorenz curve

I. Mukhopadhyay (✉) · S. Manna
School of Government and Public Policy, OP Jindal Global University, Sonipat, Haryana, India
e-mail: imukhopadhyay@jgu.edu.in; smanna@jgu.edu.in

S. Prinja (ed.), *Healthcare Financing and Insurance*,
https://doi.org/10.1007/978-981-95-3513-2_15

Learning Objectives
After going through the chapter, the reader would be able to:

- Understand various concepts related to BIA methods and equity analysis.
- Understand various steps involved in the application of BIA methods in the evaluation of health insurance schemes.
- Understand the policy implications of BIA methods.

15.1 Introduction

BIA has gained widespread acceptance as a tool for evaluating the distributional effects of government spending and subsidies on health. In terms of the assessment of the equity implications of health insurance schemes, BIA methods are particularly important. BIA measures the extent to which different socio-economic groups benefit from government health spending through their use of health services [1]. It attempts to assign a monetary value to health service utilisation to assess the benefits from public healthcare spending accrued to different socio-economic groups. Given its ability to demonstrate equity implications of public healthcare spending, BIA studies have been instrumental in proposing radical policy reforms such as introducing user charges for the non-poor to ensure better redistribution of public resources through efficient targeting of the vulnerable and economically disadvantaged sections of the population [2, 3]. Some of these reforms had disastrous consequences for the health and financial protection by exacerbating inequities in access and undermining the quality of care [4]. More recently, this methodology has been used to assess progress towards universal health coverage (UHC) and the evaluation of insurance schemes [5, 6]. In the context of government-funded health insurance (GFHI) schemes which are often targeted towards the poor and vulnerable sections of society, it becomes quite critical to assess whether these schemes are able to bring in much-needed progressiveness in the distribution of resources under these schemes. BIA works here as an important tool for monitoring the progress of these programs.

Box 15.1: Key Concepts Associated with Benefit Incidence Analysis

Equity: The fair distribution of public resources. (Note that equity is context-dependent and can be defined differently by different people.)

Public spending: The money spent by the government to provide public goods and services, including healthcare services and infrastructure.

Healthcare benefits: The value of health services received by different socio-economic groups, estimated in monetary terms.

Public subsidy: The amount of financial support provided by the government to help cover the costs of healthcare.

Concentration curve: A curve that plots the cumulative percentage of the (health) variable of interest against the cumulative percentage of the population ranked by living standards, from the poorest to the richest.

Concentration index: A statistical measure used to assess the level and direction of inequality in the distribution of the variable of interest across different income groups within a population.

Lorenz curve: A graphical representation that illustrates the relationship between the cumulative proportion of income units and the cumulative proportion of income received when those units are arranged in ascending order of their income.

Numerous research indicate that government health spending in many low- and middle-income countries (LMICs) tends to disproportionately favour the affluent classes, particularly from urban areas [7–9]. Such inequity in the distribution of public funds exacerbates disparities in access to crucial health services, especially among economically marginalised groups [10]. The persistent challenge of unequal access to health services and the lack of financial protection against the risk of impoverishment from catastrophic health expenditures partly reflect the poor allocation of public spending in LMICs. Both theoretical frameworks and empirical evidence highlight the impact of income inequality on health outcomes and the importance of publicly provided subsidised or free healthcare to reduce inequalities in access [11, 12].

15.2 Evolution of BIA

BIA as a methodology for evaluating the incidence of public spending has evolved over time, incorporating several refinements in the analysis to better estimate the distributional impact of public expenditure. The BIA techniques can be classified into two main categories: expenditure incidence and benefit incidence. These categories offer a structured approach to understanding the impact of public spending on diverse segments of the population, while also highlighting the complexities involved.

Expenditure incidence focuses on changes in relative factor and product prices, along with real incomes, that emerge from government input purchases and the production of public output [13]. This approach primarily concerns itself with the financial outlays of the government and how these expenditures impact economic variables such as prices and incomes, without directly considering the actual benefits derived from the consumption of health services.

Benefit incidence, on the other hand, shifts the focus towards the actual consumption of government health services by different income groups or other subgroups within the population [14]. This method attempts to account for how the benefits of public spending are distributed across various segments of society. It considers the shifting of government benefits, along with the relative price and real income changes that occur due to adjustments in the demand for private goods such as curative health services [14]. The goal of benefit incidence analysis is to measure the extent to which individuals or groups benefit from public goods and services, ideally by comparing the distribution of these benefits in the actual world with a hypothetical scenario without government intervention ("post-fisc" vs. "pre-fisc" equilibrium).

15.3 Different Approaches to Conducting BIA

The initial studies measuring the benefits of public spending emerged in the 1970s in Canada and the United States [15, 16]. Benefits were allocated per capita or proportionately to household income. Arone and McGuire (1970) used a utility function to measure allocation of pure public good benefits to households [17]. Their findings showed a strong distributional benefit favouring the rich in developed countries. In health research, BIA emerged in the late 1970s, with notable studies by Seldon and Wasylenko (1992) [16] in Panama and Lim (1980) [15] in Malaysia.

In their paper, Seldon and Wasylenko (1992) outlined three distinct periods based on the literature on benefit incidence. The first period refers to the early literature, prior to 1975 [16]. The second wave of benefit incidence studies began after DeWulf's critique in 1975. The post-1989 period is considered the third wave of benefit incidence studies. In 1975, De Wulf criticised Arone and McGuire's approach for failing to consider the variable income elasticities associated with different public services, among many other concerns. Following De Wulf's critique, a second wave of benefit incidence studies emerged in both developed and developing countries. For instance, Reynolds and Smolensky [18] conducted a study in the United States, Meerman [19] in Malaysia and Selowsky (1979) [20, 21] in Colombia. In their 1977 paper, Reynolds and Smolensky found that despite significant increases in government expenditure and taxes from 1950 to 1970, the post-fiscal income distribution remained largely unchanged, showing no significant trend towards greater equality during this period. These studies aimed to allocate public expenditure on goods and services to households based on their use of public services [16].

The key difference between the first and second phases is the use of microdata to determine government spending on social benefits for households, to accurately measure income and to categorise households based on both total income and household size. Additionally, services related to social functions were further divided into segments [16].

The third wave of BIA studies was triggered by the need for better targeting of public subsidies. Numerous studies were conducted to assess the benefits of the incidence of different social services. For example, Gertler and Glewwe (1990) [23], Gertler and van der Gaag [23], Gertler et al. [24] and Seldon and Wasylenko (1992) [16] used the demand curve for specific population subgroups to estimate changes in welfare-based measures of social service benefits [16].

Marginal Benefit Incidence Analysis (MBIA) BIA studies conducted in the last two decades have also attempted to estimate the probable distribution of additional public spending, with the understanding that the distribution of benefits of additional public spending on health and health services may not be the same as distribution of benefits of existing spending [25, 26]. For instance, if the rich benefit more compared to the poor from existing public spending, and if there is some level of saturation in the services that can be provided to the rich, then the poor may benefit more from an increase in spending than from existing levels of spending. This approach is broadly called MBIA. Lanjouw and Ravallion introduced an innovative methodology using a single cross section of data to apply MBIA. Ajwad and Wodon provided an alternative to their approach for estimating the "timing of program capture" using a single cross section. They segregated households into income/consumption quintiles by dividing national data into various departments. This approach essentially uses the relative level of welfare along with traditional absolute welfare levels.

15.4 BIA Methods

Benefit incidence analysis has evolved significantly since its initial studies in the 1970s in Canada and the United States. Today, the analytical technique is extensively employed in LMICs, with enhancements and extensions that consider variations in unit costs based on factors such as region, gender, ethnicity and income [3, 14, 27]. These improvements have notably boosted the precision and practicality of BIA in assessing the equitable distribution of benefits from public expenditure on health and education [3]. BIA methodology involves the allocation of unit costs according to individual service utilisation rates and the application of concentration curves for estimating the distributive impact of public finances [28]. This approach provides critical insights into the fairness of public spending, particularly the provision of essential services like health and education [7].

The process of conducting BIA entails several key steps, including ranking the study population by a living standard measure, assessing the rate of utilisation of diverse types of health services, estimating the unit cost of each type of service and multiplying the utilisation rates and unit costs to determine the subsidy amount. Net government subsidies are calculated after direct user fees are deducted from the total amount [29]. The methodology has been refined to allocate unit cost according to individual utilisation rates of public services, allowing for the identification of how well public services are targeted at specific population groups [30].

Researchers have used various methods, like concentration curves and concentration index, to study how economic inequality affects health outcomes [31]. Concentration curves help compare the distribution of benefits, which shows whether public spending is regressive or progressive. In BIA, this involves examining the concentration curve, which illustrates the cumulative share of benefits in relation to the population's income ranking. A concentration curve positioned above the line of equality indicates a pro-poor distribution. This signifies that the less affluent population segments receive a larger portion of the benefits. Conversely, a concentration curve passing below the line of equality suggests a bias towards the rich.

BIA specifically evaluates the targeting efficiency of public services and health insurance interventions towards various determinants which are based on gender, social status, income levels and geographical location. These approaches provide critical insights into the efficiency and fairness of public spending, especially in health service provision [7].

The steps in BIA can be implemented using a simple spreadsheet:

1. Establish the rate of utilisation of health services and insurance schemes by the public: Define the scope of work
2. Assess the socio-economic characteristics of the population using the service: Define the targeted beneficiaries and data collection
3. Estimate the unit cost of services being used: Measure benefit incidence
4. Estimate the amount of healthcare benefit obtained by different socio-economic groups: Analyse the equity implications
5. Compare the resulting distribution of benefits with an ideal equity benchmark:
6. Interpret the results
7. Provide policy recommendations.

These steps provide a systematic approach to analysing the benefit incidence of public spending [3, 32].

15.5 Data Requirements, Analysis and Interpretation

As discussed in Table 15.1, we need three kinds of information to conduct BIA: how resources are mobilised and who contributes; how resources are allocated and who benefits from public spending or health insurance schemes. Data on contributions to various financing schemes, such as social health insurance (SHI), voluntary private health insurance (VPHI) and GFHIs) help answer the first set of questions. Government budget and national health accounts data provide information on the allocation of public spending. National health accounts estimates (in

Table 15.1 Key steps in BIA

Steps	Description
Defining the scope of work	Traditionally, BIA is applied to government spending in general; however, the same principles could be used for specific programs.
Define the targeted beneficiaries.	Defining the beneficiaries, such as individuals, households, or specific demographic groups.
Data collection	BIA needs three kinds of information: how resources are mobilised and who contributes; how resources are allocated, and who benefits from public spending. Data on the contributions to various financing schemes, such as Social Health Insurance (SHI), Voluntary Private Health Insurance (VPHI) helps answer first set of questions. Government budget and National Health Accounts data provide information on the allocation of public spending. Utilisation data should be obtained either from government sources or large health and demographic surveys. In LMICs, utilisation data available with government sources are often unavailable, with serious quality concerns, and generally do not possess information on socio-economic characteristics of beneficiaries and the non-beneficiaries (e.g. income or consumption expenditure) which are crucial in developing BIA estimates. In the absence of such data, large sample surveys become crucial.
Measuring benefit incidence	To determine the degree to which various socio-economic groups benefit from government spending, several key steps need to be taken:
	(a) Incidence: Calculate the progressivity of various sources of resource mobilisation.
	(b) Benefit allocation: Firstly, determine the monetary valuation or quantity of benefits received by each beneficiary group through their use of health services. The adult equivalence scale is used to adjust household consumption to the personal level.
	(c) Benefit concentration: Calculate benefit concentration indices, such as the concentration curve or Gini coefficient, to measure the degree of inequality in benefit distribution among different socio-economic groups.
	(d) Benefit incidence matrix: Establish a benefit incidence matrix to display how benefits are distributed across different demographic or income groups. This matrix shows how much each group benefits relative to their program expenditure.
Analysis of the equity Implications	In this step, the progressivity of incidence, the distribution of the benefits, and the overall distribution of the socio-economic status are compared. Evaluating the effectiveness of public spending in accurately targeting individuals in need and mitigating disparities between diverse groups is assessed, considering both vertical and horizontal equity.
Interpretation of the results	After the analysis, interpretation of the analysis to understand the benefits being gained by the targeted individuals. Identify any disparities or inequities in benefit distribution and consider the underlying factors driving these outcomes. Explore potential policy implications and trade-offs.
Policy recommendations	In the final step, they provide some recommendation for the policy based on the BIA analysis.

the absence of detailed budget data) help disaggregate public spending data into various functions, such as outpatient care, hospitalisation, and various types of preventive care.

Socio-economic characteristics of beneficiaries and non-beneficiaries (e.g. income or consumption expenditure) are crucial for developing BIA estimates.

Estimation of benefits accruing to various socio-economic groups requires data on health service utilisation, the socio-economic status of the target population and the costs of accessing healthcare (typically out-of-pocket expenditure (OOPE)). Ideally, the utilisation data should record every instance of health service use, including multiple visits and hospitalisations for the same illness episode. The data should be disaggregated by levels of care, such as facility type and service type. Many BIA studies rely on existing national datasets, often derived from cross-sectional household surveys such as the Living Standards Measurement Survey (LSMS) and the Demographic and Health Survey (DHS). However, these surveys usually do not provide detailed information on the rate of health service utilisation necessary for robust estimation of benefits. Some studies have collected primary data on health service utilisation, OOPE and the socio-economic characteristics of households. Primary data is sometimes necessary, especially in the context of LMICs, due to the limitations of secondary datasets [29].

BIA also requires the collection and analysis of cost data to estimate the unit cost of different types of health services, particularly when the constant unit cost approach is used. The unit cost approach estimates the value of healthcare benefits received by households based on the cost of providing the service [33]. NHA estimates could also be used to derive unit costs per hospitalisation case for insurance schemes. A separate costing study can be undertaken to estimate the unit cost of health services. However, due to time and resource constraints, many BIA studies estimate the unit cost of health services using secondary data on total expenditure and total utilisation of different types of services [30] (Fig. 15.1).

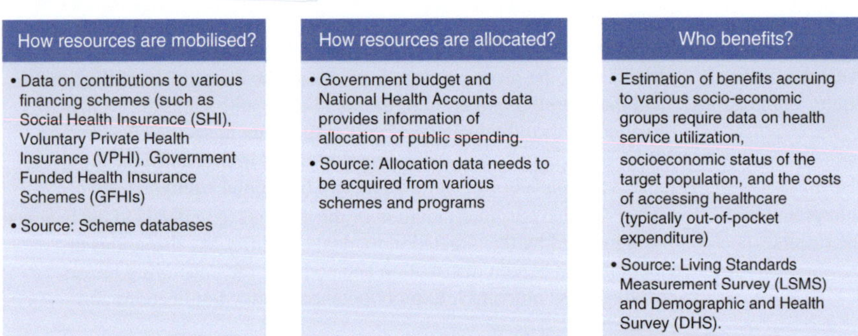

Fig. 15.1 Data requirements and sources for BIA for health insurance schemes

Activity Box 15.1

Suppose you have been asked to compare Social Health Insurance Schemes, Private Voluntary Insurance Schemes and Government-Funded Insurance Schemes operating in India in terms of their benefits, with particular focus on marginalised sections. Indicate the steps and data sources required to undertake the exercise.

Cues for answer: You need to explore important nationally representative data sets and also explore websites for various schemes.

Limitations of BIA

Please remember the following points:

1. BIA does not provide a complete picture of who benefits from public spending on healthcare, as it focuses mainly only on service users and neglects those who seldom use formal health services, especially in low- and middle-income countries.
2. BIA interprets how benefits are distributed among different income groups, whose socio-economic status may not always be accurately reflected by their income. In addition, it provides a snapshot of direct public spending, excluding indirect benefits such as improved economic conditions and other social outcomes.
3. In its traditional sense, BIA assesses the distribution of benefits from government health spending by examining the rate of service utilisation (quantity) and the unit cost of these services. It overlooks the quality of the services being utilised. It is important to note that poor-quality services can be harmful to users.
4. The commonly practiced methodology of BIA takes general government spending on health rather than specific programs or functions, which include levels of care such as outpatients (OP), inpatients (IP) and preventive care. This approach has its limitations. The government allocates resources to various functions, including OP, IP and preventive care, as well as for various levels of care. For each of these services and levels of care, utilisation pattern varies. In this regard, it is better to use NHA estimates, wherever possible, to distribute public spending in major types of care and link utilisation data with those specific components of spending to estimate the distribution of benefits.

15.6 Country Case Studies

BIA has been used to assess the distribution of benefits from government health spending in several countries. This section presents four case studies of BIA from chosen diverse LMIC contexts from different continents and discusses the policy implications highlighted by the authors. We have also used case studies which are specific to health financing policies and different types of insurance schemes.

15.6.1 Case Study 1: India

Context: In India, BIA has been used periodically by researchers to assess distributional implications of public subsidies. One of the first studies that linked a large nationally representative household survey conducted by the National Sample Survey Office (NSSO) and budgetary information was conducted by Mahal et al. [2, 34]. In their respective studies, Chakraborty (2011) [35], Acharya (2011) [36] and Ngangbam (2015) [37] utilised BIA to examine the level of equity in the allocation of public subsidies within the healthcare sector [35–37]. However, there has been limited use of BIA in the assessment of health insurance schemes in India. A study by Bose and Banerjee [38] applied BIA to estimate the utilisation, out-of-pocket expenditure and distribution of public subsidy among economic classes for non-communicable diseases (NCDs) among the elderly [38].

Data sources and methods: The study used unit records from the 71st round of the National Sample Survey (NSS) household survey. The study applied BIA to estimate the utilisation, out-of-pocket expenditure and distribution of public subsidy among economic classes.

In order to bring in household size and age composition in the construction of the monthly per capita expenditure (MPCE) classes from the household expenditure, the authors applied an equivalence scale. Specifically, they divided the total monthly expenditure of a household (T) by the square root of the household size (N) to get the MPCE ($= T/\sqrt{N}$). To accommodate state-wise differences in the cost of living, they constructed MPCE classes for each state and sector. In the absence of relevant cost data, the authors considered the modal OOPE of private hospitals as a proxy for the actual cost of providing services in public hospitals.

The authors also applied concentration curves and indices as measures of inequality. To derive the concentration curve for health inequality, the authors used: (a) public subsidy as the health variable, the distribution of which is subject of interest and (b) MPCE class as the socio-economic variable against which the distribution is to be assessed. Concentration curves were drawn for both urban and rural areas and for both outpatient and inpatient care (Fig. 15.2).

Results: The results of the paper are represented under three subsections—utilisation of healthcare services, OOPE for the treatment of NCDs and the benefit incidence of public subsidy. The results showed that public-sector hospitalisation for NCDs among the elderly had a pro-rich trend in rural India. However, in the urban sector, for both inpatient and outpatient care, the poorest class had a substantial share in utilisation of public facilities. BIA shows that the public subsidies has a pro-rich distribution for inpatient care treatment in both sectors. In case of outpatient care, the subsidy share is the maximum among the richest in urban sector, and in the rural region, the poorest class gets the maximum subsidy benefit.

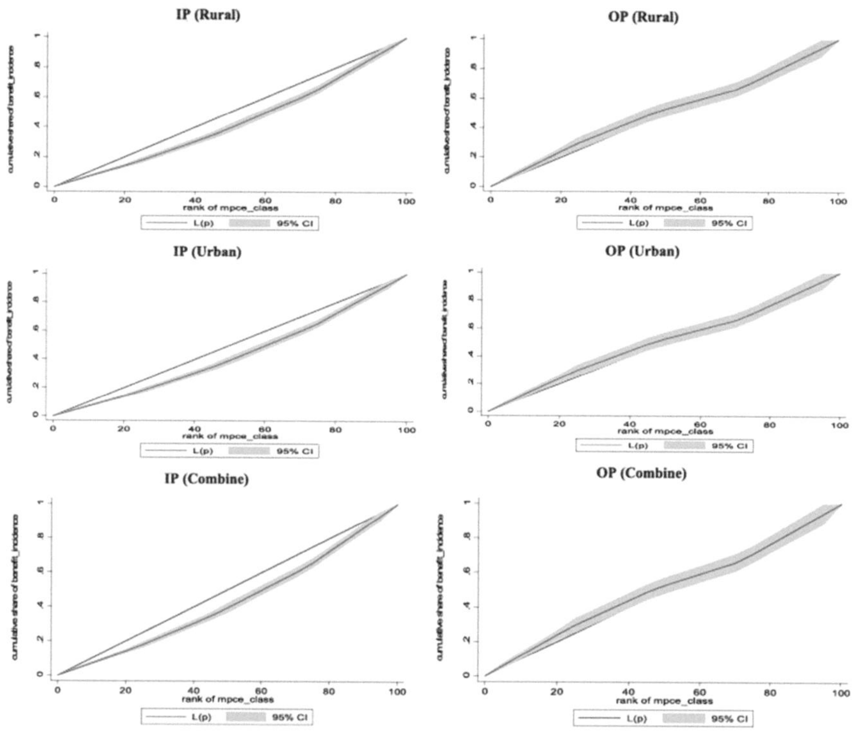

Fig. 15.2 Concentration curves of the BIA of Public Subsidies for IP and OP care. (Source: Bose and Banerjee (2018))

Activity Box 15.2
Refer to Fig. 15.2 from the India case study. Interpret the concentration curves (CCs) for inpatient and outpatient care. Compare the results for inpatient and outpatient care. Draw policy implications for health insurance schemes.

Cues for answer: Try to assess whether the CCs lie above or below the diagonal line. CCs above the diagonal represent a pro-poor distribution and those below pro-rich distribution.

15.6.2 Case Study 2: Fiji

Context: Fiji, a small upper-middle-income country in the Pacific Islands, has a population of nearly 940,000, with about 28% under the age of 15. Health service delivery is organised at primary, secondary and tertiary levels. Primary healthcare is provided through a network of nursing stations, health centres and subdivisional hospitals. Nursing stations, the lowest-level health facility, are mainly located in rural areas. Health spending in Fiji is predominantly government-funded, with the Ministry of Health and Medical Services (MHMS) receiving about 56% of current health expenditure. Out-of-pocket health spending was 23.1% of current health expenditure in 2020/2021 [39, 40].

Methods: BIA was conducted by Asante and colleagues [40] to assess the equity of health financing in Fiji. They examined how different socio-economic groups benefit from public health spending through their use of health services. Cross-sectional data from a household survey, conducted by the authors in collaboration with the Fiji Bureau of Statistics, were used. The survey collected information on health service utilisation, payments and living standards measures to assess the socio-economic status (SES) of households. Unit costs of different health services were calculated using data on total health expenditure and utilisation from the Ministry of Health.

Key findings: The study found that more than 70% of public healthcare spending in Fiji was allocated to hospital services, while nursing stations accounted for less than 1% of total spending. The distribution of healthcare benefits mildly favoured the poor across all public facilities. The most progressive distribution of benefits was at the nursing station level, where 61% of the benefits went to the poorest 20% of the population, compared to only 2.4% going to the richest quintile (Fig. 15.3). The resultant concentration index (CI) was −0.563, reflecting high progressivity.

The distribution of benefits across health centres and public hospital outpatient and inpatient care had negative concentration indices, indicating a measure of progressivity, though not as progressive as nursing stations. In contrast, benefits in the private sector (general practitioners/clinics and private hospital outpatient and inpatient care) were significantly pro-rich, with high positive concentration indices. However, this did not alter the overall distribution of benefits, which remained slightly progressive. The study assessed the distribution of healthcare benefits in the public sector as a whole relative to the level of need for healthcare and found that the distribution was neither strongly pro-poor nor pro-rich.

Conclusion: The study concluded that the distribution of benefits from public spending on health in Fiji is neither clearly pro-poor nor pro-rich, especially when the need for healthcare is considered.

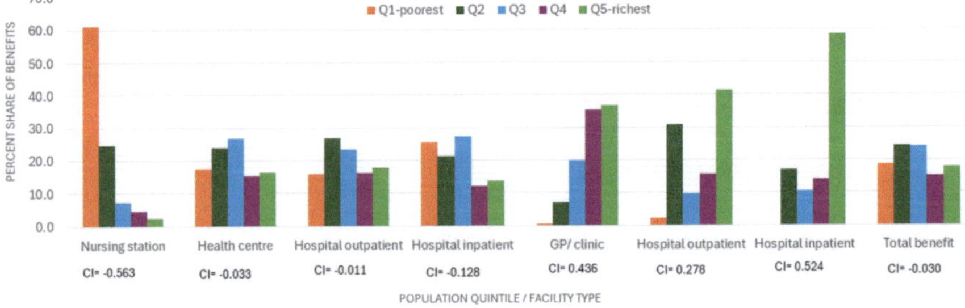

Fig. 15.3 Distribution of healthcare benefits by type of facility. (Source: Adapted from Asante et al. [40])

15.6.3 Case Study 3: National Health Insurance Scheme (NHIS) in Ghana

Context: In 2003, to improve the access to healthcare and reduce financial burden on citizens, Ghana introduced a National Health Insurance Scheme (NHIS). This scheme is funded through a combination of social security contributions, indirect taxes (a levy on VAT), insurance premiums and donor funding. The NHIS gained considerable popularity and attention. Mensah [41] conducted a BIA to understand the equity implications of the scheme [41].

Methodology: The authors used Ghana Living Standard Survey (GLSS) to conduct a BIA of the National Health Insurance Scheme. The GLSS is a nationally representative survey of 12,000 households which collected data on household income, expenditure and access to healthcare.

Key findings: In the study, it has been found that the benefits of the health insurance scheme were more concentrated among the richer segments of the population. Significantly, the richest 20% of the population received 40% of the benefits, whereas the poorest 20% received only 10% of the benefits. The benefits of the scheme were found to be more concentrated in rural areas than in urban areas. The study also found that the scheme had a positive impact on healthcare utilisation in the sense that insured households reported higher rates of healthcare utilisation compared to the uninsured.

Conclusion: The study concluded that the NHIS in Ghana is not equitable, with the benefits of the scheme concentrated among the richer segments of the population. It suggested that policymakers should consider reforms to make the scheme more progressive and equitable. One of the measures suggested was to increase premium contributions from the richer households and provide greater subsidies to poorer households.

15.6.4 Case Study 4: Community-Based Health Insurance (CBHI) in Rwanda

Context: Rwanda's community-based health insurance (CBHI) scheme, also known as "Mutuelle de Santé", was introduced in 1999 to improve healthcare access and reduce the out-of-pocket payments for the poor. This scheme is mainly based on the prepaid payment system, where members pay a premium to access a range of healthcare services. A benefit insurance analysis of the CGHS scheme in Rwanda was conducted by Schneider and Diop [42] to assess the distribution of healthcare benefits and understand the financial contribution across the different social income groups [42].

Methodology: Rwanda Demographic and Health Survey (RDHS) 2014–2015 was used, which included information on household characteristics, healthcare utilisation and health insurance coverage. The BIA framework was used to calculate the concentration index (CI) for healthcare benefits and financial contributions. The CI measures the distribution of healthcare benefits and financial contributions across different socio-economic groups, ranging from −1 to 1, where a value of 0 indicates perfect equality and values closer to −1 or 1 indicate greater inequality.

Key Findings: In this study, it was found that the poorer segments of the population received a slightly higher share of healthcare benefits than the population proportion. It was also noticed that higher-income households contributed a larger proportion of their income towards healthcare compared to the lower-income households. The higher-income households were less likely to experience financial hardship due to healthcare expenses compared to lower-income households.

Conclusions: The study concludes that the CBHIs in Rwanda is equitable, with the benefits of the scheme distributed progressively among the population. It recommends that policymakers consider maintaining the current financing structure of the scheme, which is based on a combination of premiums and subsidies for poorer households.

15.7 Policy Implications of BIA Studies

BIA holds substantial implications for health financing policymaking, particularly in developing nations. It enables policymakers to assess the benefits from publicly funded health financing interventions and the distribution of these benefits across diverse population groups. Some BIA studies have proposed radical policy reforms, such as introducing user charges for the non-poor, to ensure better redistribution of public resources through efficient targeting of vulnerable and economically disadvantaged sections of the population [2, 3].

In the 1980s, many developing countries faced considerable fiscal constraints in delivering quality healthcare to all segments of their populations. The question of efficient allocation of resources gained prominence during this time [43]. BIA studies were cited to argue that public services had a pro-rich distribution in LMICs. Given the low levels of budgetary allocations for socially productive spending such as healthcare, it was proposed that introducing user fees for the non-poor. The idea was to use these locally mobilised resources to cross-subsidise the health needs of the poor would improve efficiency and address equity concerns. Consequently, there was a widespread introduction of user charges in public facilities across developing countries, often under the guidance of the World Bank and the International Monetary Fund (IMF).

However, these user fees exacerbated inequities in access and had an adverse impact on the quality of care and efficiency [4]. Experience from LMICs suggests that any attempt to introduce user charges in health facilities must proceed with abundant caution. The widespread introduction of user charges in public facilities in the 1980s had disastrous consequences, exacerbating inequities in access and undermining the quality of care (Gilson [4], op cit.). A global campaign to remove user fees gained momentum in the 1990s following the decision by South Africa to provide health services free of charge to parts of its population in 1994 [44]. Eventually, user charges were withdrawn in many health systems [45].

However, recent BIA studies have highlighted the need for an expansion of public services. These studies have provided evidence that publicly financed and provided healthcare services have a pro-poor distribution [1, 10–17, 20, 22, 25–29]. It is therefore recommended that more resources be directed towards these services in line with the goal of UHC.

The following are some of the important policy implications of BIA:

1. Redistribute public subsidies: A pro-rich distribution of public subsidies has been cited as a reason for redesigning public subsidies to ensure a more equitable distribution.
2. Implement progressive user charges: Introduce or increase user charges for the non-poor to subsidise care for poorer segments of the population, ensuring that it does not deter necessary healthcare utilisation. Existing evidence, however, highlights considerable errors of exclusion, where a significant section of the most vulnerable population could not pass the means testing to access care, exacerbating inequities in care during the 1990s.
3. BIA studies have also been instrumental in recent times in measuring the progress of UHC reforms, tracking equity in access and measuring financial protection.
4. BIA studies have been instrumental in finding out the distributional impact of health insurance programs. It is crucial that policymakers engage with the research community to conduct context-specific BIAs. In this context, greater collaboration is needed among various agencies involved in the implementation of insurance schemes, social health insurance agencies and those involved in the production of national health accounts need to collaborate. Regular production of robust, independent and large household surveys is the backbone of such analysis.

References

1. Asante A, Man N, Wiseman V. Evaluating equity in health financing using benefit incidence analysis: a framework for accounting for quality of care. Appl Health Econ Health Policy. 2020;18:759–66. https://doi.org/10.1007/s40258-020-00597-2.
2. Mahal A, Yazbeck AS, Peters DH, Ramana GNV. The poor and health service use in India. Health, nutrition and population discussion paper. Washington, DC: The World Bank; 2001.
3. Davoodi HR, Tiongson ER, Asawanuchit SS. How useful are benefit incidence analyses of public education and health spending? IMF Working Paper Fiscal Affairs Department and Middle Eastern Department. How useful are benefit incidence analyses of public education and health spending? 2003.
4. Gilson L, McIntyre D. Removing user fees for primary care in Africa: the need for careful action. Br Med J. 2005;331:762. https://doi.org/10.1136/BMJ.331.7519.762.
5. Mills A, Ataguba JE, Akazili J, Borghi J, Garshong B, Makawia S, et al. Equity in financing and use of health care in Ghana, South Africa, and Tanzania: implications for paths to universal coverage. Lancet. 2012;380:126–33. https://doi.org/10.1016/S0140-6736(12)60357-2.

6. Thum C, Weichenrieder AJ. The distributional impact of public goods provision: a veil of ignorance approach. Scand J Econ. 2000;102(4):737–46.
7. Chakraborty LS, Singh Y, Jacob JF. Analyzing public expenditure benefit incidence in health care: evidence from India. SSRN Electron J. 2013. https://doi.org/10.2139/SSRN.2202817.
8. Chuma J, Maina T, Ataguba J. Does the distribution of health care benefits in Kenya meet the principles of universal coverage? BMC Public Health. 2012;12:1–9. https://doi.org/10.1186/1471-2458-12-20/FIGURES/4.
9. O'Donnell O, van Doorslaer E, Rannan-Eliya RP, Somanathan A, Adhikari SR, Harbianto D, et al. The incidence of public spending on healthcare: comparative evidence from Asia. World Bank Econ Rev. 2007;21:93–123. https://doi.org/10.1093/WBER/LHL009.
10. Singh RR, Mishra S, Mohanty SK. Are cesarean deliveries equitable in India: assessment using benefit incidence analysis. BMC Health Serv Res. 2022;22. https://doi.org/10.1186/s12913-022-07984-6.
11. Selvaraj S, Karan AK, Mao W, Hasan H, Bharali I, Kumar P, et al. Did the poor gain from India's health policy interventions? Evidence from benefit-incidence analysis, 2004–2018. Int J Equity Health. 2021;20. https://doi.org/10.1186/s12939-021-01489-0.
12. Hu M, Mao W, Xu R, Chen W, Yip W. Have lower-income groups benefited more from increased government health insurance subsidies? Benefit incidence analysis in Ningxia, China. Health Policy Plan. 2022;37:1295–306. https://doi.org/10.1093/HEAPOL/CZAC054.
13. McLure Jr CE. The theory of expenditure incidence on JSTOR. J Store 1972:432–53 (22 pages). https://www.jstor.org/stable/40910904. Accessed 22 Dec 2024.
14. Bowser D, Patenaude B, Bhawalkar M, Duran D, Berman P. Benefit incidence analysis in public health facilities in India: utilization and benefits at the national and state levels. Int J Equity Health. 2019;18. https://doi.org/10.1186/s12939-019-0921-6.
15. Lim L. Public Expenditure in Malaysia: Who Benefits and Why. By Jacob Meerman. New York: Oxford University Press (for the World Bank), 1979. xx, 383 pp. Figures, Tables, Appendixes, References, Index. 6.95. J Asian Stud. 1980;40(1):199–201.
16. Mathiasen Selden T, Wasylenko MJ, Mathiasen T. Benefit incidence analysis in developing countries, vol. 1015. The World Bank; 1992.
17. Aaron H, McGuire M. Public goods and income distribution. Econometrica. 1970;38:907. https://doi.org/10.2307/1909699.
18. Reynolds M, Smolensky E. Public expenditures, taxes, and the distribution of income: The United States, 1950, 1961, 1970. Academic Press; 2013. https://doi.org/10.1016/C2013-0-11360-8.
19. Meerman J. Public expenditure in Malaysia; who benefits and why. 1979; https://doi.org/10.2307/2055104.
20. Selowsky M. Who benefits from government expenditure? A case study of Colombia (English). A World Bank research publication Washington, D.C. : The World Bank. http://documents.worldbank.org/curated/en/991921468746775025.
21. Marshall DR. Who benefits from government expenditures? A case study of Colombia, by Marcelo Selowsky. Polit Sci Q. 1980;95:541–2. https://doi.org/10.2307/2150096.
22. Gertle P, Glewwe P. The willingness to pay for education in developing countries: Evidence from rural Peru. J Public Econ. 1990;42(3);251–75.
23. Gertler P, Gaag JVD. Measuring the willingness to pay for social services in developing countries, 1988. http://wwwwds.worldbank.org/external/default/main?pagePK=64193027&piPK=64187937&theSitePK=523679&menuPK=64187510&searchMenuPK=64187283&theSitePK=523679&entityID=000178830_98101902171753&searchMenuPK=64187283&theSitePK=523679.
24. Gertler P, Locay L, Sanderson W. Are user fees regressive?: The welfare implications of health care financing proposals in Peru. J Econometr. 1987;36(1-2):67–88. https://doi.org/10.1016/0304-4076(87)90044-3.
25. Lanjouw P, Ravallion M. Benefit incidence, public spending reforms, and the timing of program capture. World Bank Econ Rev. 1999;13:257–73. https://doi.org/10.1093/WBER/13.2.257.

26. Marginal benefit incidence analysis using a single cross-section of data. n.d. https://documents.worldbank.org/en/publication/documents-reports/documentdetail/558051468141262174/marginal-benefit-incidence-analysis-using-a-single-cross-section-of-data. Accessed 24 Dec 2024.
27. De Allegri M, Rudasingwa M, Yeboah E, Bonnet E, Somé PA, Ridde V. Does the implementation of UHC reforms foster greater equality in health spending? Evidence from a benefit incidence analysis in Burkina Faso. BMJ Glob Health. 2021;6:5810. https://doi.org/10.1136/BMJGH-2021-005810.
28. Sheikh N, Sultana M, Sarker AR, Morton A. Equity assessment of maternal and child healthcare benefits utilization and distribution in public healthcare facilities in Bangladesh: a benefit incidence analysis. Popul Health Metrics. 2023;21:1–14. https://doi.org/10.1186/S12963-023-00312-Y/FIGURES/4.
29. Asante A, Price J, Hayen A, Jan S, Wiseman V. Equity in health care financing in low- and middle-income countries: a systematic review of evidence from studies using benefit and financing incidence analyses. PLoS One. 2016;11(4). https://doi.org/10.1371/journal.pone.0152866.
30. McIntyre D, Ataguba JE. How to do (or not to do)…a benefit incidence analysis. Health Policy Plan. 2011;26:174–82. https://doi.org/10.1093/HEAPOL/CZQ031.
31. Koolman X, van Doorslaer E. On the interpretation of a concentration index of inequality. Health Econ. 2004;13:649–56. https://doi.org/10.1002/HEC.884.
32. Nundoochan A. Improving equity in the distribution and financing of health services in Mauritius, a small island state with deeply rooted welfare state standards. BMJ Glob Health. 2021;6:6757. https://doi.org/10.1136/BMJGH-2021-006757.
33. Wagstaff RAS. Benefit incidence analysis are government health expenditures: more pro-rich than we think? 2011. https://documents.worldbank.org/en/publication/documents-reports/documentdetail/213341467987908141/benefit-incidence-analysis-are-government-health-expenditures-more-pro-rich-than-we-think. Accessed 24 Dec 2024.
34. Mahal A, Singh J, Afridi BAF, Lamba MAV, Gumber BAA, Selvaraju V. Who benefits from public health spending in India? Study Team. 2000.
35. Chakraborty L, Singh Y, Jacob JF. Public expenditure benefit incidence on health: selective evidence from India. New Delhi: National Institute of Public Finance and Policy; 2011.
36. Acharya D, Vaidyanathan G, Muraleedharan V, Dheenadayalan D, Dash U. Do the poor benefit from public spending on healthcare in India? Results from benefit (utilization) incidence analysis in Tamil Nadu and Orissa. 2011.
37. Ngangbam S. Burden of disease and benefit incidence of public health expenditure in Northeast India. J Healthc Manag. 2015;17(3):328–338. https://doi.org/10.1177/0972063415589226.
38. Bose M, Banerjee S. Equity in distribution of public subsidy for noncommunicable diseases among the elderly in India: an application of benefit incidence analysis. BMC Public Health. 2019;19. https://doi.org/10.1186/s12889-019-8089-y.
39. Ministry of Health and Medical Services. The Minister for Health and Medical Services. Ministry of Health and Medical Services Suva. n.d.
40. Asante AD, Irava W, Limwattananon S, Hayen A, Martins J, Guinness L, et al. Financing for universal health coverage in small island states: evidence from the Fiji Islands. BMJ Glob Health. 2017;2(2):e000200. https://doi.org/10.1136/bmjgh-2016-000200.
41. Mensah J, Oppong JR, Bobi-Barimah K, Frempong G, Sabi W. An evaluation of the Ghana national health insurance scheme in the context of the health MDGs, Working Paper No. 40. 2010.
42. Schneider P, Diop F. Synopsis of results on the impact of community-based health insurance on financial access to health care in Rwanda. Washington, DC; 2001. Report No.: 28903. [Google Scholar].
43. Jimenez E. The public subsidization of education and health in developing countries: a review of equity and efficiency. World Bank Res Observ. 1986;1(1):111–29. https://doi.org/10.1093/wbro/1.1.111.

44. Robert E, Ridde V. Global health actors no longer in favor of user fees: a documentary study. 2013. https://reference.medscape.com/medline/abstract/23889807?form=MG0AV3. Accessed 24 Dec 2024.
45. Yates R. Universal health care and the removal of user fees. Lancet. 2009;373:2078–81. https://doi.org/10.1016/S0140-6736(09)60258-0.
46. Brian N, Vincent T. Cost recovery in public health services in Sub-Saharan Africa. The World Bank (EDI); 1995. p. 106.

MIX
Papier aus verantwortungsvollen Quellen
Paper from responsible sources
FSC® C105338

If you have any concerns about our products,
you can contact us on
ProductSafety@springernature.com

In case Publisher is established outside the EU,
the EU authorized representative is:
Springer Nature Customer Service Center GmbH
Europaplatz 3, 69115 Heidelberg, Germany

Printed by Libri Plureos GmbH
in Hamburg, Germany